782.1

D0937030

There isn't a one of us who wouldn't have

gone out and died for him.

Francis Robinson
ASSISTANT MANAGER,
METROPOLITAN OPERA

# THE TENOR OF HIS TIME

## Edward Johnson of the Met

Ruby Mercer

with Discography by J. B. McPherson and W. R. Moran

Clarke, Irwin & Company Limited/Toronto/Vancouver

Canadian Cataloguing in Publication Data

Mercer, Ruby, date
    The tenor of his time

Includes index.
ISBN 0-7720-0736-5

1. Johnson, Edward, 1878-1959. I. Title.

ML420.J64M47      782.1'092'4      C76-017105-X

ISBN   0-7720-07365

Published simultaneously in the United States by
Books Canada Inc., 33 East Tupper Street, Buffalo, New York 14203, and in the United Kingdom by Books Canada Limited, 1 Bedford Road,
London N2.

1 2 3 4 5   JD   80 79 78 77 76

Printed in Canada.

*To Edward Johnson's grandchildren,*

*Alexandra Drew Scholey and Edward Drew,*

*and great-grandchildren,*

*Fiorenza and Christopher Scholey.*

# Foreword

In 1971, when I was asked by Dr. Floyd Chalmers, then a director of Clarke Irwin, whether I would be interested in writing a book on the life of Edward Johnson, I immediately said Yes. The prospect was intriguing. Although I had not known Dr. Johnson well, he had exerted a great influence on my life.

The first and last times I met him will always be as vivid in my memory as though they had happened only yesterday. Both were unexpected, and both were unusual.

I had heard Edward Johnson as a tenor at the Metropolitan Opera, and I knew that after Herbert Witherspoon's sudden death he had become the Met's general manager. So it was a great surprise to me to see him standing at my dressing room door after the Juilliard School production of Richard Strauss's *Ariadne auf Naxos* on the evening of May 19, 1936. He introduced himself, and with a beaming smile complimented me on my performance as Zerbinetta. He told me that my trill on the high D in the opera was the most thrilling thing he had heard since Lily Pons interpolated a high G in her début in *Lucia* at the Metropolitan. Then he asked whether I knew the role of Nedda in *Pagliacci*. When I said I did, he invited me for an audition at the Opera House that coming Thursday— two days later.

I could hardly wait to get home to look over the score. I had never coached the opera with anyone, but had learned it quite thoroughly by myself a few years previously while at the Conservatory of Music in Cincinnati. When I looked at the music that night, however, I was dismayed: not only had I completely forgotten it, but I couldn't even sight-read it. I worked most of that night and all day Wednesday to make sure I could sing the "Ballatella" and the two duet scenes from memory. That was probably as much as they'd want to hear anyway, I reasoned.

The audition took place at ten o'clock Thursday morning in one of the rehearsal rooms at the Metropolitan with Johnson, an accompanist and several maestri present. I sang the "Ballatella" and it went well. There was a brief whispered conference after which Dr. Johnson said they would like to hear me in the House. Standing in the middle of the big Metropolitan Opera House stage, facing the huge dark auditorium, I repeated the aria. A voice from the cavernous blackness asked to hear the Nedda-Silvio duet. After that, the Nedda-Tonio scene. The pianist rasped out the cues and I was feeling quite pleased with myself until they asked to hear the other bits from the score! I tried, but even when I was allowed to stand by the piano and look at the score it didn't help. Obviously I didn't know it.

Mortified, and with tears running down my cheeks, I called out, "I knew it. Really I did!" Suddenly Edward Johnson materialized from the darkness and stood at the orchestra rail.

"That's all right," he consoled me. "There was a chance for a performance coming up, but there will be other times."

"But I *do* know it," I insisted. "Really I do, Mr. Johnson. I can sing it for you tomorrow."

He smiled indulgently and told me I could come the next day to go over the score with Maestro Dellera. I did. That was Friday. And when I returned to Dellera on Monday, I knew the music so thoroughly that all of his attempts to trick me failed. He seemed pleased, but was noncommittal. I had barely reached home, however, when I was called to the phone. It was Johnson's secretary at the Opera House informing me that I was to make my début at the Metropolitan as Nedda in *I Pagliacci* a week from the following Saturday evening.

When the big night came, Edward Johnson was not there. He had left for Europe unexpectedly on May 26. But Edward Ziegler came to my dressing room with some flattering comments after the performance.

Many years later in the winter of 1958-59, soon after I had moved to Canada, I happened to be on a streetcar in Toronto one day. At an uptown stop an elderly white-haired gentleman seemed to have great difficulty getting up the steps. "Poor old man," I thought as I saw him pay his fare. Then, as he turned around, I saw it was Edward Johnson! The same moment, he spotted me sitting near the back of the car. Instantly his face lighted up with a big smile. His infirmities were forgotten as he walked down the aisle and sat beside me.

Where was I singing? What was I doing in Toronto? He was living in Guelph, he said, not far from Toronto. I told him about my CBC radio program, "Opera Time." He was immediately interested and asked whether it was anything like the "Mr. and Mrs. Opera" program I had had in New York. As I was explaining that the format was similar, an idea came to me. "Why don't *you* be my Mr. Opera?" I asked him. He surprised me by quickly agreeing that he would enjoy that. He even began to speak of what operas we might present and some of the details we might include in our programs. We were both excited over the prospect of working together.

Then he hesitated a moment and, rather sadly I thought, said he was afraid he couldn't guarantee to be in the studio every week. I assured him that wouldn't be necessary, that the programs had to be taped ahead of time anyway in order to be broadcast simultaneously across Canada. He was reassured and happy again as he gave me his address and phone number. I promised to call him in May, in plenty of time to make final plans for the series that in those days was scheduled for only two months, July and **August.**

It would have been a most interesting experience and have meant a lot to both of us, I'm sure, had that collaboration materialized. But on April 20 he was gone.

R. Mercer

# Acknowledgments

It would be impossible to mention all of the many people whose helpful interest was a source of encouragement to me from the beginning of this project. It was as though everybody felt such a book was long overdue and wanted to contribute what they could towards it. I owe them a great debt of gratitude for their time, honesty and frankness.

First, I should like to thank Dr. Floyd S. Chalmers for suggesting that I write the book, and Edward Johnson's two grandchildren, Alexandra Drew Scholey and Edward Drew, for their personal devotion and cooperation. Not only did they make all existing material available, but Mrs. Scholey spent many days with me, going through the trunks and boxes of papers, pictures, clippings and letters stored in her home in London, England, and Edward Drew, then living in Toronto, made office space and family files available to me and was always ready to lend a sympathetic hand. I only hope, as partial payment of my debt to them, and to the many others who have been so kind, that I have done some justice to the subject and that a personality will be found in the pages of this book, rather than a mere recording of dry facts.

I am also indebted to Dr. Chalmers, the late Dr. Arnold Walter and the late Sir Ernest MacMillan for providing documented accounts of the important events in the history of the Royal Conservatory of Music of Toronto, and to Max Rudolf for the invaluable assistance of his careful, straightforward and sympathetic review of the period of his association with Edward Johnson as conductor and musical secretary at the Met. Then, within the Metropolitan Opera House itself, everyone seemed to take a genuine pleasure in recalling the man who had spent so much of his life there: assistant manager Francis Robinson and the members of the publicity department, especially Anne Gordon; Sir Rudolf Bing, and his successor as general manager Schuyler Chapin and his wife Betty; Mrs. John DeWitt Peltz and her assistants in the Metropolitan Opera Archives; Ozie Hawkins, Charles Riecker, Herman Krawitz, Reginald

Allen, Paul Jaretzki and others of the administrative staff; also Frank Merkling, Ann M. Lingg, Gerald Fitzgerald and their associates at *Opera News*.

There were long interviews with countless numbers of people, most of whom are quoted in the book and many of whom were personal friends and colleagues of mine. Their very names, I find, provoke a flood of memories, including those of our discussions about Edward Johnson and the settings in which they occurred: Maestro Fausto Cleva, in the friendly big family apartment in the old Ansonia Hotel in New York City; Nino Martini and his wife in their lovely home in Verona, Italy; Maestro Vittorio Gui, in his large studio overlooking Florence; Baroness Renata Rapisardi, in her picturesque palazzo that was visited so often by Edward Johnson whenever he was in Florence; Richard and Mildred Crooks, in their California mountain retreat, where we were joined at lunch by Frederick Jagel; Florence Eaton McEachren and Evlyn Eaton Payton; Ruth Chamlee and Mrs. Frank Forrest; Lauritz Melchior; Eleanor Robson Belmont; Richard Bonelli; the Honourable George Drew; Dr. Herbert Graf in Geneva, where he was general director of the Grand Théâtre at the time; Maestro Wilfrid Pelletier and Rose Bampton; Risë Stevens and her husband, Walter Surovy; Jean Tory; Quaintance Eaton, offering helpful information and suggestions in her crowded, manuscript-filled apartment on New York's West Fifty-seventh Street; lunch hours with Magdalene 'Hammie' Hammesfahr and her sister in New York, and visits with Margaret 'Madge' Day and her sister in Toronto; an unforgettable afternoon with Lotte Lehmann at her home in Santa Barbara; an afternoon and evening with Martial Singher in Santa Barbara; talks with AGMA lawyer Albert Gins; Milton Cross; Gina Cigna Ferrari; Nicholas Goldschmidt; Lauder Greenway; Lowell Wadmond; Arthur Judson, so long associated with Columbia Artists Management Inc.; John Majesky, former owner and publisher of *Musical America*; Richard Tucker; Suzanne Ziegler Gleaves; Edouard Albion-Meek, a former tenor and impresario of Johnson's era, in his memento-crowded home near St. Thomas, Ontario; helpful discussions with Eva Howlett in her apartment, and at work in the Public Library in Guelph; Stella Johnson; Irving Kolodin, who generously put more material at my disposal than I was ultimately able to use; Edwin McArthur; a weekend with Rosa Ponselle in her home outside Baltimore; Isaac Van Grove; Leone Paci, at the Casa di Riposo per Musicisti in Milan; Boyd Neel; Assunta Leita, Josephine Casali's companion for over thirty years, first in her apartment, in Florence, and the next day on a visit to the Cimiterio degli Inglese outside the city; Maria and Rudi Russi, who had been with Edward Johnson more than anyone else during his years of retirement in Guelph.

Additional important information came to me, frequently over breakfast, lunch or dinner, from people in all walks of life and all parts of the world. Most of them are quoted and identified in the book: Pierrette Alarie, Licia Albanese, Josephine Antoine, Hyde Auld, Louis Biancolli, Edith Binnie, E. J. 'Manny' Birnbaum, Margaret Carson, Winifred Cecil, Amy Dunbar, Margaret Eaton Dunn, Herman Geiger-Torel, Joseph Gimma, Eleanor Grundy, Clifford Hall, Dr. and Mrs. Norman Higinbotham, Jerome Hines, Helen Jepson, Irene Jessner, Theodate Johnson, Ralph and Edith Kidd, Dorothy Kirsten, Mabel Krug, Horace Lapp, Estelle Liebling, George London, Carol Longone, Mrs. Ettore Mazzoleni, Robert Merrill, Zinka Milanov, David Ouchterlony, Vida H. Peene, Jan Peerce, Edith Piper, Lily Pons, Gilles Potvin, Regina Resnik, Elisabeth Rethberg, Stella Roman, Bidú Sayao, Ezra Schabas, Greta Shutt, Eleanor Steber, John Steinway, Howard Taubman, Virgil Thomson, Kerstin Thorborg, Astrid Varnay, John Vickers, Henry Wrong, Dino Yannapoulos, Bruno Zirato and many, many more.

I found everyone in the theatres, archives, libraries, museums and newspaper offices in Italy most friendly and helpful. First of all, in the Museo and Biblioteca at La Scala, Milan, where I discovered a tremendous amount of useful material, I was grateful for the cooperation of the director, Dr. Giampiero Tintori, and for the patient and friendly assistance of Signora Adreana Corbella and Lorenzo Siliotto. Also in Milan, at the Biblioteca Comunale, the files of the *Corriere della Sera* proved rewarding; at the Biblioteca del Conservatorio, Signora Azzali was most cooperative; at the Casa di Riposo per Musicisti, Signor Gualiani provided some worthwhile information; and I spent hours in the great Museo di Brera, the Biblioteca del Risorgimento and the Castello di Milano. In Rome, my thanks go to Signora Tognelli at the Teatro del Opera, and to Giuliano Bocchino in the *Messagero* Archives. In Florence, I found the officials of the Maggio Musicale Fiorentino and the Biblioteca more than cooperative. In Padova, there was Commendatore Bertinelli and his staff at the Teatro (Comunale) Verdi; also Foto Lux; the attendants at the Museo Civico; and those in charge of the files of *La Gazzettina*, *Il Veneto* and *La Provincia di Padova*. In Torino, Dr. Giulio Galerzi and the Sipra Publishing House were most helpful. At the Teatro La Fenice in Venice, Dottore Giuseppe Pugliese provided all possible assistance. In London, the Archives of the *Times*, through the cooperation of Bruce Coward, provided valuable information; as did the Victoria and Albert Museum, with the guidance of G. W. Nash of the Theatre Section; and the Covent Garden Archives and Library files were useful, thanks to the cooperation of Ken Davison. In New York, the Music Library at Lincoln Center was a gold mine; the Public Library useful; also newspaper files, particularly those of the *New York Times*. In Toronto, the Edward Johnson Music Library, with the help of Jean Lavendar as guide, was of great value; as were the files of the Royal Conservatory of Music and the Faculty of Music, University of Toronto, which Mrs. Binnie kindly made available to me. Then there was the Metropolitan Toronto Music Library, the Theatre Section of the Central Library, and the files of the *Globe and Mail*, the *Star* and the *Telegram*, all of which were important. My thanks also to the registrar of the University of Western Ontario, London, Ontario, for his research into old records. In Guelph, the Public Library, the Archives of the University of Guelph, the files of the Guelph *Mercury* and the Court House records were most useful. Furthermore, I greatly appreciated the assistance of Dr. M. H. M. MacKinnon and Dr. Eugene Benson of the Edward Johnson Music Foundation.

I should like to acknowledge the cooperation of *Chatelaine* magazine in granting permission to reproduce excerpts from "My Life in Two Worlds" by Fiorenza Drew, as told to Eva-Lis Wuorio, in the April, 1963, issue.

My thanks to CBC's Tom Prentice who made available to me the interviews he had taped at one time in connection with a broadcast about Dr. Johnson, and to Holly Middleton for the use of the interviews she had recorded about Edward Johnson in preparation for a Guelph Spring Festival opening.

Special appreciation must be given to Jim McPherson of Toronto, an operatic historian, whose careful and meticulous criticism of the manuscript for factual accuracy was invaluable. Together with W. R. Moran, he also provided the discography which completes the book and should prove to be of particular interest to the students of Johnson's career.

In conclusion, I should like to express my deep appreciation to the Canada Council and the Ontario Arts Council. Their faith and financial assistance were a source of great encouragement and inspiration to me from the time my research began until this book materialized.

Toronto

April, 1976

# Contents

EDWARD JOHNSON made his début before an adult audience on a hot Sunday afternoon in August, 1885. Everyone who could travel had come to Exhibition Park in Guelph for the weekly band concert. His mother and his brother Fred were there to watch father Jimmie Johnson play the clarinet, and maybe conduct Professor Phillips' band as he sometimes did.

The park benches were filled; people were sitting around on the grass; children were running about while their elders listened to the music or visited among themselves. Eddie, just past his seventh birthday, was in his favourite spot next to the bandstand.

All at once the music stopped, everyone was applauding and he was being lifted up onto the platform. Professor Phillips himself put merchant Shaw's high silk hat on Eddie's head. It went right down over his eyes, but as he started to lift it up with one hand, someone put a cane in the other, and there he stood, looking like a miniature vaudevillian.

"Sing us a song, Eddie," people were calling.

He shot a surprised and half-frightened glance at his father. " 'Little Annie Rooney,' " Jimmie said, and the band struck up the tune. In no time at all, the boy's high clear tones could be heard ringing through the park. He put his whole heart into the music and was rewarded by a rousing reception. To the applause of the crowd he bowed grandly, as he had seen visiting stars do, to the right, to the left and to the centre.

"Someday," he thought excitedly, "there will be thousands of people out there in a great big auditorium, clapping their hands just for me." And he bowed again.

"You're going to be a big star someday, Eddie," people told him. He grinned, but said little. Deep down inside, he was sure he was destined to become famous; but he knew it was best to keep such ideas to himself. People would only laugh.

1

They were laughing now. "You've got a real little ham there, Jimmie," one man said, as he lifted the boy down from the platform.

"You've got an uncommonly sweet tone, young lad," others commented, as they patted him encouragingly on the head. He took it all in, but was too shy to speak.

"What's the matter, son, cat got your tongue?" Jimmie teased him good-naturedly.

A few weeks after that triumphant Exhibition Park début, Eddie decided he should be allowed to wear a belt with a buckle, like the big boys. "It only costs twenty-five cents," he told his father confidently.

But Jimmie laughed. "You're too little and skinny for that. It'd fall right off." Annoyed when Eddie stubbornly insisted, he told him bluntly, "If you want one, you'll have to buy it yourself."

It sounded impossible, but far from being discouraged, Eddie was more determined than ever. The only question was where could a seven-year-old boy make twenty-five cents in 1885.

His mother didn't dare give him the money, but she did come to his rescue. "Jimmie, you're always grumbling because you don't want to take the cows out to pasture in the morning and bring them back at night. Why don't you let Eddie try it? Pay him a nickel a week," she suggested.

"All right, if you think he can do it," Jimmie reluctantly agreed.

It took Eddie six weeks instead of five to get the coveted belt, because he'd broken into a nickel one day to buy two cents worth of chocolate drops. Tears of disappointment hadn't helped him at home. "It isn't the nickel," Jimmie told him. "You might as well learn here and now what happens when you throw your money away."

The belt Eddie bought was worn out in a few months, but the lesson he learned lasted him a lifetime.

The next year, when he was eight years old, Eddie set his heart on playing a fife in the Fife and Drum Corps at school. "All the instruments have been given out," he was told. "Besides, you're too small for anything but a piccolo." A piccolo? Eddie hadn't thought of that. But why not? With typical determination he looked around until he found a secondhand piccolo he could buy for a dollar. No use to mention it at home. He knew what the answer would be! Earn the money yourself. He canvassed the neighbourhood and picked up a number of odd jobs earning a nickel here and a nickel there. He worked and he saved. Two months later he appeared triumphantly at a rehearsal, piccolo in hand. He was so happy and proud that the Corps leader, who had no use whatever for a piccolo player, didn't have the heart to turn him away.

Eddie set about learning to play the piccolo with all the enthusiasm of which he was capable, and by the end of a year considered himself to be quite an accomplished musician. He approached his father about playing in the Guelph band.

"You're too little yet," Jimmie told him. "And besides, we don't need a piccolo player."

"What could I play then?" Eddie persisted. "Could I play a clarinet, like you?"

"A flute's more your size," his father said. "But dinner's ready now, so we won't talk about it anymore."

Eddie was bursting to continue the subject, but there was a strict rule in the Johnson household forbidding the boys to speak at the table unless spoken to first. Besides, that evening Jimmie monopolized the conversation with one after another of his favourite stories. Even so, Eddie was undaunted. Remembering his experience at school with the piccolo, he was sure that if he had a flute they'd let him play in the band. So he made up his mind to get one.

The cheapest secondhand flute Eddie was able to find cost thirty dollars. His heart sank. Once again, instead of keeping his own counsel, he told his mother about the problem. She thought for a while, then frightened him by saying, "I'm going to speak to your father."

"Now I'll be in for it," Eddie thought.

That evening Margaret Johnson suggested to her husband, "Let the boy have what he wants."

Jimmie was impatient. "Aw! Eddie this and Eddie that! Why is he always wanting something different?"

The next day, however, he surprised Eddie by saying, "Son, we're going to start you on piano lessons. If you practice hard and learn to read music real well, maybe in a year or two we can talk about that flute."

Eddie didn't want to learn to play the piano, but if it was his only way of getting a flute he knew he'd have to try it. Playing the piano, as it turned out, wasn't as bad as he had expected. He worked hard and made so much progress that before the first year was up Jimmie had relented. "You'll have to continue your piano lessons, but we'll start you on the flute next week and see how you make out."

Almost from the time he was born, August 22, 1878, in a rough-cast cottage in Guelph, Ontario, Edward Johnson had commanded attention, and as he grew up he always liked to be out in front of people, showing off. Before he was ten, he had appeared in *Snow White and the Seven Dwarfs*, an operetta produced by Mr. and Mrs. Charles R. Crowe in the Guelph City Hall (1888) with a mixed chorus of 125. Eddie was listed as "First Dwarf" in the semi-chorus, but there is nothing to indicate that he had either a solo passage or spoken line. The following year, July 4, 1889, his name appeared in the *Guelph Mercury* for the first time as having participated in the closing concert given by pupils of Miss McLean's Private School, in the basement of a house on Kent Street, where Eddie had been attending classes. According to the newspaper, "Willie Liphardt and Eddie Johnson played very beautifully together and won prizes in vocal and instrumental music."

Secretly, Jimmie was proud of his older son's talent and interest in music. "Of course, he gets it from the Johnson side of the family," he would brag. "We're all musical."

He liked to tell people how, in 1838, a Welshman by the name of Coningsby William Evans had settled in the village that John Galt founded. Evans was a real Welshman, according to Jimmie, with a tune on the tip of his tongue. His wife and his three girls all sang and played the organ. "One of the girls, Helen, was my mother," Jimmie would say. "She married John Johnson when he came over from Yorkshire, England, and they had three boys: me, Robert and William. People used to call us 'The Johnson Band' because we all played instruments and made music in the evenings. My mother had been married before, you know," he invariably added, as a kind of afterthought, "and one of her daughters married John Verney, the one they named Verney Street for—the street where my two boys were born."

"But wasn't your wife's family musical, too?" someone would ask.

Whereupon Jimmie would become somewhat less enthusiastic, not wanting to take any credit away from the Johnsons. "Oh, yes, they liked music, but they didn't do much about it. Margaret's father, John Brown, came over from Ireland in 1847. He learned the shoemaker's trade in Canada, and married a McConnell from Montreal; he finally opened up a shoe store here in Guelph.

"Everyone was self-made in the old days," Jimmie said. "Why, I used to deliver bread to the Wells family at the Edinborough Road house, and the future mayor and tax collector and city manager George Hastings used to deliver the groceries there. We didn't mind. If it was honest work and made us a penny or two, we'd do anything."

Just as he said, Jimmie had run errands, helped in one of the stores, worked on neighbouring farms, in the local hotels and at the mill. He played baseball and hockey and dabbled in horse racing and boxing. On the other hand, he loved music. He and his brothers played several instruments and were mainstays in the town band. The surprising and irrepressible James Johnson started as the bouncer and eventually became the proprietor of the European Hotel, was a director of the Guelph

4

Riding and Driving Association and an alderman of the City of Guelph. In addition, he had gained some renown as a breeder of animals on his Elora Road farm, particularly for his new strain of purebred sheep.

Jimmie, a real town character, always had a hearty greeting for everyone. He would stop to chat with people as he drove by in his little donkey-drawn cart, and with or without encouragement would regale them with some of his favourite stories and tell them about Eddie's latest successes. "He's a chip off the old block," he invariably concluded, "the Johnson block."

By the time Edward Johnson was in his teens, Jimmie was already the owner of the hotel, later renamed the King Edward after Edward VII's ascension to the throne of England. The Johnson family lived in the hotel, and Eddie's private castle for most of his early life was his third-floor room there, overlooking Market Square.

One of Jimmie's brothers, William, owned the profitable boat and canoe business "on the River Speed at the bridge en route to the Ontario Agricultural College." There it was that Eddie Johnson worked every summer from the time he was big enough to handle the ropes. Boating was popular, and Uncle Bill's dock always busy, so the gregarious young Eddie found it his favourite place to be.

"You're kind of small to be tying up these big boats all by yourself," one of the customers remarked one day. "How old are you?"

"Almost eleven, sir," came the reply. The man was surprised, having judged the boy to be no more than seven or eight.

Eddie might be small for his age, but after what had happened at school that winter he knew he could take care of himself. He had always been kidded about being small, but being a scrappy little fellow he had usually held his own in a fight. When a big bully showed up at school, however, and began terrorizing the smaller boys, even Eddie was outclassed. But whereas most of the boys went out of their way to avoid an encounter with the newcomer, little Eddie Johnson stood his ground. Day after day his younger brother Fred would beg him to stay away from the boy. But Eddie insisted on taking his accustomed route home even though it meant arriving bruised and scratched and with torn clothes. His mother was able to keep the news of what was happening from Jimmie until one day when Eddie came home unusually late, unusually dishevelled and with a black eye.

"What's going on? What happened? Who gave you that black eye?" Jimmie was fuming.

When he finally heard the story, more from Fred than Eddie, he burst into a colourful verbal torrent, then laid down the law. "You keep away from that boy, no matter what anybody says. No son of mine is going to be beaten up by any bully. You're going to learn how to take care of yourself—you and Fred both. I'll be waiting for you in the woodshed right after school tomorrow."

The boys didn't know what to expect, but they hurried home the next day. And there was Jimmie, waiting for them in the woodshed, holding out two pairs of new boxing gloves! For the next two months they worked out every afternoon, boxing and wrestling. Fred didn't have too much heart for it, but Eddie was enthusiastic: "Hey! This is swell. Maybe I'll decide to be a boxer some day."

"Humph!" was Jimmie's eloquent reply.

Eddie's first test came unexpectedly. The boy he had been avoiding blocked the path he and several of his friends were taking as they left school. The others ran, but Eddie hesitated. And in that moment the older boy attacked him, expecting an easy victory. At first Eddie was paralyzed with fear and got the worst of things. Then he remembered some of the lessons he had been learning in the woodshed and suddenly his confidence returned. The thought of what his father would do to him if he came home beaten up again gave him a special kind of courage.

"Run, Eddie, run," his friends shouted from a safe distance.

But that never occurred to Eddie. Right then and there he had done some fast growing up. He stood his ground and remembered his father's repeated warning: "Keep your head down and your mitts up."

As the fight continued, the younger boys drew closer and Eddie proceeded to give the dreaded bully a real beating. "And I'll do it again if you don't stay away from me and my friends," he shouted as the boy limped away.

Then Eddie hurried home to tell his father all about it, blow by blow. "I knew you could do it; you're a chip off the old block. This calls for a celebration." And Jimmie, who never needed much excuse for a celebration, was soon on his way to spread the good news. By the next day everyone in Guelph had heard Jimmie's colourful account of how his son had beaten the tar out of a boy twice his size.

Whether his success as a pugilist had anything to do with it or not, Eddie was never quite sure, but soon after the big fight his father told him he could bring his flute and play with the Guelph Band on practice nights. That summer he was allowed to sing a few solos in the concerts.

By the time he was twelve years old "Jimmie Johnson's little boy Eddie" was a seasoned performer; a regular soloist with the band, a special attraction at school concerts, luncheons, parties and dinners of all kinds, and soprano soloist in church choirs—first at the Norfolk

6

Street Methodist Church, then at the Dublin Street Methodist where he was paid fifty cents a Sunday. He was saving every penny he earned, and spending hours daydreaming about all the wonderful things he was going to buy someday.

One Saturday morning, when he was thirteen, Eddie awakened with a strange cracked voice he couldn't control. "Hey, what's wrong? Could it be . . .?" He didn't have a sore throat, but he couldn't trust himself to speak. "Must be a cold," he concluded. "Maybe it'll be all right when I sing." And off he went to choir practice.

Things didn't go too badly at first, but in the middle of a solo his voice seemed to go to pieces. He struggled against it but finally had to give up, and his eyes filled with angry tears of frustration. Oddly enough, no one laughed. They all knew what had happened and that sooner or later the same would happen to them. To Eddie it seemed like a catastrophe. He would lose his job as soloist and, with it, his handsome weekly income. "Now what'll I do?" he wondered.

But not for long. Being both optimistic and resourceful, the frustrated singer decided to go in for sports. He was small for his age, he knew, but maybe if he put enough determination and fighting spirit into it he could win. He tried out for the football team and was accepted, on probation. Next, he joined the cadet corps and, in his spare time, took boxing lessons. He loved sports and gave them everything he had. "Of course music pays better," he kept remembering.

And, although he couldn't sing at the moment, he kept his hand in music by playing the flute in the band and by conducting the Norfolk Street Sunday School choir. Naturally, as soon as his voice settled down, Eddie began singing again. Two years almost to the day after that embarrassing morning, he was offered a job as tenor soloist at St. George's Anglican Church. He could hardly believe his good fortune, particularly when the director told him he would be paid a dollar a week. Obviously it was more profitable to be a tenor than a boy soprano.

Although Eddie sang with the Guelph Collegiate Society and the Guelph Choir, and for social gatherings in neighbouring communities, it was his church work that made the deepest impression on him. He wrote lengthy tracts and often gave talks about religion and his own strong convictions about the importance of leading "a good clean religious life." From 1894-96, in addition to his choir work, Eddie attended Sunday School regularly and was choir leader for the Saturday evening meetings of the Epworth League at the Norfolk Methodist. In 1896, he joined the many others who pledged two cents a week toward the cost of "supporting a missionary to represent the members of the Guelph

7

District who cannot go to the foreign fields themselves." From 1897–99, he was the tenor in Professor Charles Kelly's popular concert group, The Scotch Quartette.

Otherwise, Eddie's life, at least on the surface, was about the same as that of any of the other young boys in Guelph. He did chores around the hotel, and on summer evenings went swimming down at Pipe's Mill. In the wintertime he shovelled snow before going to school in the mornings and risked his neck on homemade toboggans after school, in spite of warnings from his parents. "Little Eddie" had a mind of his own and could be very stubborn. "Plain bullheaded," were his father's words for it.

The only thing that really bothered Eddie was that girls were beginning to follow him around. Whenever he sang, they would crowd up to the platform and embarrass him with their noisy expressions of admiration. They were silly, he thought. Besides, he had more serious things on his mind; he had to decide what he was going to be when he grew up. He was always getting a new idea. After a particularly painful series of toothaches, for example, that were relieved by the healing ministrations of the family dentist, he was convinced that dentistry was the greatest of all callings. So he announced at home that he was going to become a dentist.

"I need a lawyer in the family," his father grunted, "and that's what you're going to be." A lawyer, however, was the one thing Eddie was determined not to be.

Eddie's indifference to girls ended suddenly when he was sixteen and fell in love. He never knew when or how it happened, but he was sure she was the only girl in the world for him. She was a couple of years ahead of him in school, which made it all the more exciting and flattering when she told him she loved him too. "Jo Dowler!" What magic there was in the name, he thought, as he mumbled it to himself during the day and went to sleep whispering it to himself at night.

Unfortunately, the name of Johnson did not seem to hold the same magic for Jo's parents. Considering themselves to be of Guelph's socially elite, they deemed the son of the local pubkeeper unworthy of their daughter, and unacceptable in their home. So Eddie and Jo began seeing each other secretly for Sunday evening suppers at the home of their Sunday School teacher, James M. Kenny.

When Miss Dowler's parents learned that a romance was in the making, they promptly sent Jo off to boarding school. Their love never blossomed again, even though Eddie and Jo became lifelong friends.

The experience made a lasting impression on Edward Johnson. Being kidded about being small was something he had learned to handle, but social discrimination was different. He couldn't understand it. Fighting was the only way he knew of settling an argument, but he couldn't very well pick a fight with Mr. Dowler. For the first time in his life he was deeply hurt. Eddie was proud—proud of himself and proud of his father and mother. There was nobody any better. He gritted his teeth. "I'll show them," he muttered, over and over again. "I'll show them. They'll see." Fortunately time was on his side.

BEFORE HE COULD show the Dowlers or anyone else anything, Eddie Johnson had to decide what he was going to do with his life. The trouble was, he seemed to be equally gifted in a number of different directions.

"He has a great future ahead of him," his teachers predicted, and made every effort to turn him into a scholar.

"They made me study Latin and Greek and calculus," Johnson recalled in later years. "I would have been a lot better off spending all that time studying music instead."

Even as a young boy, Edward Johnson was considered to be musically talented. Miss McLean, director of the private school he attended on Kent Street, featured him in her annual closing concert of June 28, 1889. It was from the conductors of the choirs in the churches that he received his first bits of vocal training, but he also took some lessons from Mrs. John Crowe, grandmother of Guelph teacher and writer Mrs. Greta M. Shutt. After he became a tenor, he studied off and on with Charles Kelly, well-known teacher and musical director in Guelph. His lessons with Mr. Kelly, and the concert experience he gained in The Scotch Quartette, stood him in good stead in his early years in New York.

Sportsmen, after watching Eddie play hockey, baseball or basketball, also spoke highly of his talent, but they invariably concluded by saying, "Too bad that kid's not a little bigger; Captain Clark could send him right to the top."

Certainly, if anyone could have made a professional athlete out of Eddie, it would have been Walter Clark, who had come to Canada from England after long years of military service.

As drill sergeant for the Guelph Militia and gym teacher at Eddie's high school, the Captain had a profound influence on the lives of Guelph's young men. He emphasized good posture, good carriage and good stance so successfully that Johnson once remarked, "I can still recognize a fellow Guelphite anywhere by his walk."

The Captain so firmly implanted the idea of keeping fit into Eddie's mind that it eventually became a fetish. After he became general manager of the Metropolitan Opera, his pet advice to tenors was, "Keep in trim. You'll look better, sing better and move better." He once said, "I wouldn't give much for a tenor who couldn't run a hundred yards in eleven seconds. An hour a day in the gymnasium was always just as important to me as the three or four hours I spent on music."

All things considered, it wasn't an easy decision that Eddie had to make. During his final year in high school he was in a quandary whether to go in for sports, enter an academic or business profession, or make music his career.

The one thing he was sure of was that he didn't want to become a lawyer. So when his father came home one night and announced quite matter-of-factly that they were going to sit down together and fill out an application for law school, Eddie balked.

"I don't want to be a lawyer," he told Jimmie in the argument that followed. "I'm eighteen now and making good money singing in churches, and at concerts and parties. So why should I go to school any more? I'm going to quit."

And with that, over his father's strenuous objections, Eddie did leave school. He got a job in his uncle's shoe store, worked there for several months, then clerked in the local drug store for a few weeks. Finally he settled on a job as a bookkeeper's apprentice.

At first it was exciting to be independent, but gradually he began to feel trapped. Working all day left him no time for sports and no heart for music. By spring, the feeling had become so strong that he couldn't stand it any longer. So he quit and went back to his Uncle Bill's dock for the summer. In July, when he told his father that he had decided to go back to school, Jimmie's curt comment was, "I thought you'd come to your senses." But it was obvious that he was pleased.

Eddie enjoyed the rest of his time in high school. He said in later years, "I did pretty well. What's more, I was popular with the girls, I was playing the flute in the local band, and I was captain of the Collegiate soccer and hockey teams. I was having a good time, but I knew the moment of truth was bound to come eventually." And come it did. One day, at his father's insistence, Eddie found himself signing an application for enrollment as a pre-law student at the University of Western Ontario. Everything within him rebelled at the idea, but there didn't seem to be any alternative.

While he was waiting to hear from the university, Eddie became involved in some activities which made him realize that the only thing he had any real heart for was music.

He had always enjoyed sitting in the Town Hall on Saturday nights watching whatever show was on, but he didn't know what fun it could be behind the scenes until he organized a minstrel show to raise money

10

for new band instruments. It was so successful that the proceeds more than paid for the instruments.

Then one night at a party when he was playing the piano while his friend D'Arcy Gilpin whistled "The Mocking Bird," Eddie had a bright idea. "Hey! Why don't we get up a vaudeville show?"

Soon after that the team of Gilpin and Johnson came into being, and proved so popular the boys could hardly keep up with their many engagements.

During the summer the manager of the Town Hall invited D'Arcy and Eddie to come to his office. Without preamble he said, "I think you boys are ready for the vaudeville circuit."

Eddie was enthusiastic and did most of the talking. "We're made!" he said to D'Arcy afterward. "Now I won't have to go to law school—for a while, anyway."

Gilpin was silent.

"Hey! What's the matter with you, D'Arc? You hardly said anything in there."

"I couldn't, Eddie. You see . . . I'm sorry . . . but I'm going to Toronto this fall to study advertising."

Eddie was stunned. "How can you throw everything away after we've worked so hard?"

"I'm sorry," D'Arcy said, "I only found out about it today. I didn't want to say anything in there in case you could get someone else to go in with you."

"I don't know who I'd get. And besides, it was the two of us he wanted, as a team. I guess I'll have to give up the idea." Eddie was as downcast as he had been jubilant a few minutes before. He could see his dreams vanishing over the horizon.

Not long after that, however, luck played into Eddie's hands. A popular tenor who had been engaged to sing in a church organ recital in London had to cancel at the last minute. The minister had heard there was a good young tenor in Guelph, only sixty-five miles away. "The lad is still in high school," he told the organist, "but this is a crisis."

So Edward P. Johnson was called in to share the program with a Winnipeg contralto, Edith Miller, soloist at the famed St. Bartholomew's Church in New York.

"What's the P for?" Jimmie wanted to know.

Eddie explained that he had added it on the spur of the moment because he thought it made him sound more important. "Everyone who's anyone has a middle name," he asserted.

After the concert, in spite of the fact that Miss Miller sang well, the comments were mainly about "the fine voice of the young man from Guelph." Miss Miller herself complimented Eddie on his singing of "The Lost Chord" and "The Holy City," and asked him what he planned to do. He surprised himself by blurting out that all he liked to do was sing, but his father wanted him to be a lawyer.

"If you want to sing," Miss Miller said, "why don't you come to New York? Try it. I've had good luck and I'm sure you will too. You might even get to be an opera singer someday."

"I hadn't thought of that," he said. "Maybe I will."

He could hardly wait to get home to talk over the idea with his friend and accompanist, Jessie Hill.

He had known she would understand and be sympathetic, but he was surprised that her immediate reaction was so positive. "Forget about the law," she said. "Go to New York and study voice. Singing's what you're cut out for."

He wasn't so sure. "I don't know," he replied. "The best review I ever got was in the Guelph newspaper, after a Town Hall concert last year. And the girl who wrote the article was a friend of mine. As a matter of fact, I once had a big crush on her. Do you really think I'd be able to get along in New York?"

"Give yourself a chance. Go down and try it."

Eddie thought it over. It was a big step. His father would be against it. Besides, he had no money.

The idea was taking root, however. All that was required for Eddie to make up his mind were the encouraging words of Dr. Augustus Stephen Vogt, founder of Toronto's Mendelssohn Choir. After hearing Johnson sing a performance of *Elijah*, Vogt told him, "I predict a big future for you, young man."

From that moment Eddie began to notice a ringing in his head. "It's a bell," he told Jessie, "and it keeps saying, 'New York, New York, New York, New York.' "

When he broached the subject at home the reaction was just what he had expected. "Quit school again and go to New York to study music?" Jimmie exploded. "You'll go to school as long as I can send you, and you're going to be a lawyer!" And that ended it, for the time being.

Several months went by. Then one Sunday, while Eddie was performing his usual duties as tenor soloist, at St. George's Anglican Church, the choir sang "Throw Out the Life-line." That had been his first solo when he was five. "I'm twenty now," he reasoned, "and in another fifteen years, if I become a lawyer and settle in Guelph, I'll still be singing that hymn here in the choir on Sundays!"

12

When he got home he told his father, "I'm going to chuck the whole thing and go to New York to sing."

Jimmie was silent for a long time. He could see it was useless to argue. "All right, Eddie," he said at last, "you go, if you think that's what you want. I won't say a word. But if you find you want something else, don't be proud—don't stay there and struggle. Come home and I'll send you to the university."

All Guelph turned out for the "Farewell Complimentary Concert to E. P. Johnson," presented at the Guelph City Hall on Tuesday evening, March 28, 1899. Admission was twenty-five cents. The next day the local paper reported: "The success of the complimentary concert . . . was a glowing tribute to the esteem in which Mr. E. P. Johnson is held in this city. The hall was filled with a fashionable audience . . . [for an] excellent program provided by local talent entirely. . . . At the conclusion Mr. Johnson was called [upon] and made a great speech thanking the audience for their kindness in honouring him by their presence."

Eddie had one hundred dollars that he had managed to save from his singing engagements, and after a long argument his father reluctantly agreed to lend him another hundred. So, on April 4, 1899, Mr. E. P. Johnson packed his tin-bound trunk and, with his two hundred dollars and a letter of introduction to former Guelph resident Arthur Higinbotham in his pocket, boarded the train for New York, to start on his great adventure.

2

NEW YORK, that spring of 1899, was heady stuff for the young man from Guelph. The driver of the hack was friendly and chatty, and obviously took great delight in telling his fare some of the things he ought to know about the big city.

"See that big building over there?" he suddenly asked, pointing to a large, forbidding-looking structure on the left. "That's the famous Metropolitan Opera House."

Eddie was dismayed. "It looks more like a warehouse," he muttered.

"I know," the driver agreed. "It's not much to look at from the outside, but inside there's plenty of plush they tell me."

Eddie couldn't resist mentioning that he had come to New York to study singing.

"Well, now, maybe you'll be singing there someday yourself, young fella. And that Mrs. Jacob Astor'll be sitting there wearing her rocks, listening to you."

"She's a great supporter of the opera, I hear."

"Yep. And she's real society. Takes a lot of work and a lot of money to be a society lady these days, they say.

"Well, here we are, young fella—the YMCA. Corner of Eighth Avenue and 57th Street. Fine new building; just been opened a year. Kinda far uptown, but I hear they've got everything in there."

Eddie and the driver lugged the trunk over to the entrance. Before they had time to ring the bell, however, a man had opened the door and was welcoming Eddie with a big smile.

"This here young fella's a singer," the hackie said, before Eddie or the "Y" man could say anything. "You'll be hearing him at the Metropolitan someday."

Eddie was embarrassed, but pleased all the same. He gave the driver the ten-cent fare and thanked him for his help. Then he was given a hearty welcome by three of the Y's directors, Mr. Hoppin, Dr. Welz-

14

miller and Mr. McCastline—all men whom Eddie later came to know well. They showed him to his quarters—a large student dormitory.

"We have two floors of dorms," one of his guides said. "They're well furnished, and you'll find we have efficient service. There's an elevator, incandescent light, steam heat, and baths on each floor. Come on; you can unpack later. Let us show you around."

It was days before Eddie was able to check back on all the rooms and facilities he saw that evening, and some of the men he met in the reception room and parlour he never did see again. By the time he got back up to the dormitory, he was tired. But three young men were up there, talking among themselves, and he couldn't very well just go to bed and not join in.

They told him a bit about the athletic field they could see from the window. It had just about everything—running track, a fifty-yard straightaway, complete facilities for pole-vaulting, jumping, running, hammer-throwing and shot-putting—not to mention a handball court that was lighted by electricity every weekday evening!

How long they talked Eddie never knew, and he could only vaguely recall having opened his trunk, but when he woke up it was nine o'clock the next morning. His toothbrush was on the table beside his bed, his clothes were hung up, the dormitory was deserted, and he was hungry. If he hurried he might just get into the dining room for breakfast before it closed. The prospectus had listed the prices: "Breakfast 25¢; luncheon 25¢; dinner 50¢; full week's board $5.00." Members of the Association could get full board for $4.00. After breakfast, first thing, he'd present his letter to Arthur Higinbotham. Then maybe he'd try to get in touch with Edith Miller.

But the lure of New York was too much for Eddie. There was so much to be seen, and so much to do! It was a whole new world, and he couldn't resist the temptation to explore. It was six days after his arrival in the city before he finally went to see Arthur Higinbotham, who turned out to be just a few years older than Eddie—a slender, fairly tall, neatly dressed young man with a small moustache that made him appear almost forbiddingly serious. He was busy arranging things in his new drug store. "I'm still getting settled here. Just moved in," he explained.

Eddie produced Alice Higinbotham's letter. Her brother read it quickly, gave Eddie a warm smile, and said, "Be glad to help you all I can. One of the first things you'll have to bear in mind is that you'll have to watch your money in New York or it'll go right through your fingers. Two hundred dollars you have?"

"That's right."

15

"Better put it in a bank and hold on to it. We ought to be able to get you a church job to pay your expenses, and I know several good singing teachers in town. You might start out with Frank Dossert and see how you like him. Then we'll find you a room. . . ."

"But I'm in the dorm at the YMCA and there's a good gym there. . . ."

"Yes, yes. But you need a room of your own. We'll find you a place for half the money and you can go over and use the gym at the Y every day. I'll tell you what. You come up to the house for supper tonight and we'll work things out."

It so happened that it was Arthur's birthday and his aunt and cousin were having a few friends in that evening to celebrate. Among the guests was a Mrs. Davidson, who agreed to take Eddie to her own voice teacher, Dr. Dossert, the next day.

That was the first step. In a friendly and efficient fashion Arthur continued to take charge of Eddie's affairs. And before the week ended, Edward Johnson had not only started studying with Dr. Dossert but he had landed his first church job in New York City: tenor soloist at the Church of the Transfiguration on 29th Street, east of Fifth Avenue.

After the beautiful churches he had been used to in Guelph, Eddie was disappointed in the building. It was nice enough, but small and very simple. When he was handed a five dollar bill after the service however, he was impressed. It was all he could do to keep from exclaiming, "Wow! I didn't expect that much!" (Although he didn't realize it, that particular church had already been dubbed "The Little Church Around the Corner," a name by which it was to become famous all over North America.)

Eddie had thought several times of trying to see Miss Miller, but there didn't seem to be much point in it. Dr. Dossert had already found an agent to manage his church engagements. It would be better to make a go of things on his own before contacting her.

The engagements took him to a different church almost every Sunday —usually Protestant, but occasionally Catholic. He liked the pageantry and the incense in the Catholic churches, and he liked the music too, once he got the hang of the Mass. Then one Saturday he was sent over to Brooklyn to sing in a Jewish synagogue. That was certainly different, but he liked it—and they evidently liked him, for they had him back almost every week.

Meanwhile, Arthur had found Eddie a room in a house on 40th Street owned by a Mrs. Bousch. He moved there the first of May. It was so nice that he figured he'd probably stay there for a long time.

Before the year was out, however, Arthur's aunt died and his cousin

16

went to live with relatives out west. Young Higinbotham was left alone in the big house they had all shared.

"How would you like to move into the house with me?" he said to Eddie one day.

"Only if you'll let me pay my share of the expenses."

It was agreed, and Eddie moved up to 68 West 107th Street—a place he was to call home for many years.

One morning after he had been living in the house for some weeks, he decided to lend a hand with breakfast. He could boil water and put the porridge on as well as Arthur. That turned out to be almost his first and last appearance as a cook; he made the porridge from a package of Gold Dust Twins scouring powder!

"Why didn't you read what it said on the box?"

"I didn't think it was necessary. It looked like porridge."

"Well, you stick to washing dishes after this. I'll do the cooking."

Eddie made friends everywhere he went and was soon invited to all kinds of fancy parties in Manhattan and Brooklyn.

"Arthur," he confessed one day, "I feel like an ignoramus. They're always talking about books and plays and people I never heard of, and places I've never been. I don't know what to do."

"Don't worry about it," Arthur told him. "Society clamours for invitations to such parties. They are given only to produce a friction of ideas, you know. It's a kind of game—a play of minds. It's not important."

The next day, however, Eddie discovered a little book about New York in his pocket, and from then on, every time he left the house, he found that Arthur had slipped a little booklet of some kind into one of his pockets. He read them on subways and trains, travelling back and forth to churches and synagogues in New York, Brooklyn and New Jersey. Reading as he rode became a habit.

His first official New York engagement aside from church jobs was as soloist at the Reception and Musicale of the Minerva Club, June 5, 1899. "Not much maybe," he wrote his mother, "but it was a beginning and it went well."

His next public concert appearance in New York was on February 11, 1900, in the Carnegie Hall Studio. A review of the program by Frank Dossert's students included this line: "Mr. E. P. Johnson, the only newcomer in the class, turned out to be the star of the occasion."

Things were going well and by the end of Eddie's first year in New York he was already fairly well known. He liked Dr. Dossert, who was very kind and helpful, and who seemed to know all the organists and managers in town. Also, he was obviously interested in the progress and success of all his pupils. But Eddie was not satisfied.

"What am I going to do, Arthur?" he asked one evening. "I've got to change voice teachers and I don't know how. Dr. Dossert's a good musician and a good friend but he's not teaching me anything. Everybody seems to think that because I can sing higher than most other tenors I have no problems. But I need help. I watch some of the big artists sing and they seem to do it a lot easier than I do. This 'clear voice' they talk about isn't going to be clear very long if I go on pushing it like I'm doing now."

Arthur, usually so helpful, was taken by surprise. He said that he'd have to think it over.

That evening he told Eddie he agreed he *should* make a change if he was not satisfied. As a matter of fact, he had gone ahead and made arrangements for Eddie to go to see J. Armour Galloway, another well-known teacher in New York.

At first Mr. Galloway seemed to have all the answers. But not for long. Like Dr. Dossert, he was a good man, a good musician, had a fine personality, knew a lot about singing, and liked and believed in his new pupil. But Eddie was a young man in a hurry to get to the top, and he had vocal problems which neither teacher seemed to be able to solve for him.

"You're singing perfectly as it is. Don't be in such a hurry," they both told him. And they pointed out, just as Charles Kelly had done in Guelph, that anyone who could take a high E with such remarkable ease had nothing to worry about.

But Eddie was worried. What about the rest of his voice? He often ran out of breath, and he couldn't control the tones and the volume at will. That year he had become a member of the Amphion Male Quartet Concert Company, and he was expanding further into the concert and oratorio fields. He knew he was on his way, and he couldn't afford to ignore any vocal problems.

On March 6, 1902, Eddie sang the lead in Sarah Hadley's *Hiawatha's Wooing* in a concert that included Estelle Liebling in a group of songs. He and Miss Liebling had a long talk afterwards. He admired her voice, the way she presented her songs, her attitude toward her career, and was interested to discover that she, too, was in a hurry. "Don't let anything get you down," she advised. "You've got a beautiful voice and you're good-looking. Don't be afraid to smile when you're on the stage. That smile of yours can make you a lot of money." She even suggested they might team up for some concerts and he felt that was a good idea, but nothing ever came of it.

18

Instead, he digressed into the field of popular music. Two of his best friends in the musical profession, Margaret and Tom Mason, knew the leader of The Bostonians, a light opera troupe in Boston, who was looking for a tenor to understudy the hero in De Koven's *Maid Marian.* "Why don't you sing for him? We'll arrange it."

Eddie did sing and was immediately given a contract "to understudy the role of Robin Hood and sing chorus when necessary." Then, almost before he knew the music, and with practically no rehearsal, he found himself singing the lead; the tenor Vernon Stiles had become ill. Eddie sang only one performance, however, before Mr. Stiles recovered and returned to the role. After that, Stiles remained in such good health that at the end of five weeks Eddie became discouraged and quit. Nevertheless, it was Edward Johnson who took over the role of Robin Hood when The Bostonians went on tour in April and May, 1902, to Elmira and Syracuse, New York, and Meadville and Pittsburgh, Pennsylvania. And when De Koven's *Robin Hood,* to which *Maid Marian* was a sequel, was presented at the Boston Theatre, May 12, 1902, it was Edward Johnson who sang the title role. Two weeks later, he sang the role of Lopez in the company's production of Victor Herbert's *The Serenade.*

Meanwhile, Eddie's many appearances in oratorio had not gone unnoticed, and one day he found himself sitting in the office of Henry Wolfsohn, head of New York's leading concert bureau.

"Eddie," Mr. Wolfsohn began, "I've been watching you for some time now. You've been making excellent progress and doing good things. I think you're ready to step into more important engagements and I'd like to help you. Do you know 'The Holy City'?"

"Sure," Eddie replied. "I ought to; I've sung it enough times in Guelph. Why?"

"How would you like to sing it for me in Carnegie Hall on the seventeenth of January? It won't pay much, but it will be a good break for you. After that, if it goes well, I think we can do some business together."

It sounded exciting and easy. But when the time came to walk out on the stage of Carnegie Hall, the young Guelph tenor experienced a few moments of real stage fright. In spite of it, he sang well, and one reviewer spoke of him as "today's most promising oratorio tenor."

The following week Wolfsohn offered Edward Johnson an exclusive contract which, needless to say, he accepted.

"How lucky can I be?" Eddie thought. "In New York less than four years and already with the Wolfsohn Bureau, billed as 'church, concert, oratorio and opera tenor' for the season of 1903-4!"

Eddie had no illusions, however, and even at that early date he realized there was much more to a successful musical career than voice alone. For example, he had agreed to sing a concert for the New York Chapter of the American Institute of Bank Clerks (January 8, 1903) even though he knew it wouldn't mean much money. But he had told himself, "There'll be money all around me; some of it may rub off. Besides, a few of those clerks may be bank presidents one day."

Wolfsohn offered Eddie more engagements for the next season than he could possibly fill, which was good news. No more getting behind in paying his share of the household expenses nor in paying for voice lessons. Nevertheless, he would have to live frugally that spring if he was going to save enough money to go to Naples with his friends the Masons in the summer. "It'll be good for you," Arthur had urged him. "You *must* go; it will give you a glimpse of some of those places you've been hearing people talk about but have never seen."

It made sense, and when the Masons sailed for Europe a few months later, Eddie was with them.

He loved shipboard life, was "Eddie" to everyone by the second day, and proved to be an excellent sailor. All in all, it was such a good crossing he was sorry when they docked in Naples.

Even though they were in Naples less than two weeks, there were few streets or places of interest that escaped Eddie's inquisitive eye. He darted here and there as avidly as a thirsty plant absorbs water, certain that everything he saw and did would be etched indelibly on his mind. By the time he was back in New York, however, he discovered that his memories of the streets, churches, restaurants, museums, statues, famous monuments and even some of his favourite spots around the harbour, had already become confused in his mind. "I should have kept a diary. Well, I didn't, but I'll never make a mistake like that again."

With a heavy schedule of concert bookings for the year ahead, at higher fees than ever before, Eddie should have been on top of the world. But his vocal problems were still with him. He complained to Arthur that neither of the two voice teachers he was working with— Mr. Galloway and William G. Hammond—was helping him. "I've heard the best teacher in town is a Mme von Feilitsch. Ever heard of her?"

Arthur had not, but his inquiries next day confirmed the good reports.

So Eddie went off to sing for Mme von Feilitsch and was overjoyed when she not only agreed to take him as a pupil but was sure she knew exactly what his problems were and how to solve them. Her words were music to his ears: "You're wasting your time in concerts and oratorios. With a voice like that, you should sing opera. All you need is to learn

20

to use your breath and to work with someone who knows opera and languages." Mme von Feilitsch knew both. Eddie began studying with her and was certain he had made the right choice at last.

With his fees going up, and reviewers writing about his voice as being "in the nature of a revelation" and "of a quality seldom found," he went home for Christmas that year feeling quite proud of himself. "My managers are talking about me singing at the Metropolitan some day," he told his parents.

His mother, always sympathetic and trusting, thought that would be wonderful.

Jimmie, always tough and skeptical, asked, "How much money are you going to get out of it? How much do these managers keep for themselves? They're getting rich, not you."

His father was more impressed when Eddie was asked to sing at Carnegie Hall with Walter Damrosch and the New York Symphony in Elgar's *The Apostles,* with Madame Caroline Mihr Hardy and David Bispham on January 17 and February 9, 1904; in the *Messiah* with the People's Choral Union, February 22; and in symphony concerts in New York, Chicago, St. Louis, Salem, Richmond, Halifax and Toronto, for which his earnings would be more than $1,500.

Jimmie was still more impressed when he learned that his son was the highest-paid church singer in New York, as regular tenor soloist at the Brick Church on Fifth Avenue. "That's something you can depend on," he said. "That's steady. That's the way to get ahead."

When a reviewer wrote only that "Edward Johnson sang the part of Siegfried in a pleasing manner," after Eddie's first Wagner program, Jimmie pressed his point. "Humph! What did I tell you? Better stick to your church work. Forget about that opera stuff; you're wasting your time."

Eddie refused to worry about it. He had adopted a bit of his father's philosophy: "If it's honest work, I'll do it." He turned nothing down. That spring he sang excerpts from *Parsifal* with the New York Symphony and *Elijah* for the Philharmonic Club in Minneapolis; "Samson" to Louise Homer's "Delilah" in the Worcester, Massachusetts, festival; the Verdi *Requiem,* and *Faust,* in Portland, Oregon; and had contracts in his pocket for as high as $200 a performance for engagements in Boston, Pittsburgh and Baltimore. He was also committed, for the fourth consecutive year, to sing during the fall festival in Maine.

Feeling secure and confident, he decided to make another trip to Europe. The Guelph *Mercury* of June 22, 1904, told the story: "Edward Johnson was visiting his parents before sailing for Europe on July 2nd

21

to spend two weeks in London, England, two weeks in Paris, then go on to the Wagner Festival at Munich. He will fill some few engagements in the Old Land, but his visit is largely for instruction."

The engagements were mythical. Edward Johnson was in Europe to expand his knowledge and horizons. He worked on oratorios in London, where the coaches were impressed by the "unusually strong but remarkably sweet" quality of his voice and by the "dramatic intensity, range and the ease" with which he could sing the highest notes. Eddie was pleased and flattered but he had set his mind on opera.

In Paris he coached every day with Richard Barthélemy, famed as Caruso's *répétiteur,* who advised him to go to Italy to study opera. "I am going to write to Maestro Lombardi in Florence. He's the best," Barthélemy told him. "He usually insists on hearing anyone before he will accept him in his studio, but if I tell him about you, I'm sure he'll take you. When could you go?"

"How much money would it take?"

"Enough to live on and pay for lessons—and you would have to agree not to sing publicly for two or three years, most probably."

"Then I can't do it. I haven't got the money. I'll have to go back to New York until I can save enough."

Barthélemy nodded his head understandingly. "Let me know when you decide, I would like to help you. I believe you have a big career ahead of you but you must not waste time. You are old enough now."

From Paris Eddie went to Munich. "I feel lost," he wrote to his mother. "I wish I had studied German before I came. I don't know what anyone is talking about. But the music is the most beautiful I've ever heard. Wagner sounds different over here. By the way, don't be shocked when I get home. I've put on some weight now and look rather plump."

Eddie returned to New York for the 1904/5 season, and promptly set about the business of making enough money to get back to Europe.

"Look at this," he said to Arthur Higinbotham one evening toward the end of June, 1905. "Would you believe it? I made $1,050 in May and look at this month so far: Spartanburg, $250; Stewart, $300; Syracuse, $100; Philadelphia, $100; Brooklyn, $75; Scranton, $115; New Haven, $75; Newark, $200; Lynn, Gloucester, Boston, Guelph, Terre Haute, Chicago, Orange—and four more to go. And Mr. Wolfsohn says he thinks he can get me from $150 to $400 next year. Let's go out and celebrate!"

"We'll eat in." Arthur was practical. "You've got to get to Italy. Remember?"

"Then let's give a party and invite everybody."

"Good idea," Arthur agreed. "I'll give the party—next Sunday; and invite a few of our best friends and some of the people who are most important to your career. That's the way to get ahead."

Eddie didn't like to admit it, but he knew Arthur was right. So the party was given and Eddie went on singing, and saving his money. Between concerts, oratorios, summer festivals, symphony appearances and his church engagements, he kept busy learning new music and working on operatic roles.

During the season of 1905/6 his scheduled appearances took him to forty-eight different cities in the United States. In addition, he made an extended Canadian tour that was followed by festivals in Syracuse, Brockton (Massachusetts) and Ithaca (New York) between June 13 and October 1, 1905. He sang opera with some of the most famous artists of the day: Johanna Gadski, Schumann-Heink, David Bispham, the young bass Herbert Witherspoon, and others. Invariably the reviewers singled out Edward Johnson for special praise: "The gifted young tenor gave some of the best singing of the evening" (Chicago); Edward Johnson "won a triumph with his first number" (Toronto). In April 1906, he made a triumphant return to his hometown to sing with soprano Mary Hissem de Moss in the first concert in the new Guelph Opera House, with an ensemble conducted by Ernest Shildrick.

He sang oratorios, recitals, and opera and symphony concerts in constant succession—in New York, Chicago, Scranton, Salem, Spartanburg, Springfield; in Calgary, Guelph and Toronto. The Spartanburg *Herald* report was typical of the reviews: "The eminent tenor, who is always full of smiles and good music, was at his best last night. His voice was sweet and silvery and his enunciation is most perfect. All other sounds were hushed as his marvellous voice, with its resonant tones, reverberated."

*Musical America,* one of Eddie's early supporters, wrote: "Mr. Johnson has established a reputation as one of the leading tenors of the country. His success is due to a voice of decided beauty, a refined personality and an artistic temperament."

Eddie was supremely sure of himself, convinced that he was on the threshold of a big career. So it was in a mood of almost belligerent self-confidence that he set sail for Europe on June 13, 1906. He was bent on adding the finishing touches to some of the operatic roles he had been studying. He stopped in London long enough to polish some of his oratorios, but he was impatient to get to Paris and start working again with Barthélemy. After that, he planned to go to Germany for some auditions. Wolfsohn had told him, "You're ready now, Eddie, but a year or two with an opera company in Europe might be a good idea before we put you in the Met. I'll arrange some auditions for you in Germany, but only because you insist; Italy's the place for you."

Eddie thought that while he was in Italy he might as well take a few lessons with Caruso's teacher, Maestro Vincenzo Lombardi, as Barthélemy had suggested. He was certain, however, that in the end he would probably wind up in Germany.

"I've been singing *Siegfried* and *Lohengrin* and *Tannhäuser* over here and I like them," he told Wolfsohn, stubbornly.

"Take my advice, Eddie. Forget Wagner for the time being. A concert is one thing, but to be on the stage and have to sing in German over a Wagner orchestra is another. And in Germany you'd have to sing in German. Besides, you have a lyric tenor voice. You should concentrate on Verdi and Puccini and some of the French operas. *Faust,* for instance."

"And *Samson*," Eddie interjected.

"I know you like to sing Samson, but your voice is too lyric and most Delilahs are big, tall, heavy women. Believe me, Eddie, your stock-in-trade lies in the lilting quality of your voice, your easy high tones, your personality, your charm and your figure. With lyric, or even coloratura sopranos, you present a romantic figure, but as Samson or Siegfried . . . well . . ."

His young client got the point, but he wasn't sure Mr. Wolfsohn was right. Perhaps he'd have to show him, too, just as he had to show Jo Dowler's parents back in Guelph, what he could do.

WHEN EDDIE ARRIVED in Paris he was given a hearty welcome by Harry Higinbotham, Arthur's brother, who had taken a couple of days off to show him around the city. Harry had also arranged a tea party for the following Sunday so that a few influential people could meet Johnson and hear him sing.

Eddie was just as impressed and awed by Paris this time as he had been on his first visit. At tea on Sunday he was especially taken by the elegance of the young women. In a letter to his mother, he mentioned their "tight-waisted dresses with swishing skirts," and their "high bouffant hair with little hats perched on top." He also reported that the men wore frock coats, cravats and jewelled pins. "They left their gloves, canes and tall hats in the hall."

Although some French was spoken, conversations were primarily in English. Eddie found the knowledge and sophistication of the guests he met, and the variety of subjects they discussed, almost as far removed from what he had come to know in New York as he had found the ways of New York different from what he was used to in Guelph. Now, as then, he found himself feeling like an ignoramus. But when it came time for him to sing, his confidence returned. "I've conquered them all over the United States and Canada," he thought, "and this is just another audience."

A titled young Portuguese woman, Beatrice d'Arneiro, was his accompanist. Harry had informed him that she played the piano well, had a pretty good voice herself and spoke six languages fluently. "So don't worry about a thing," Harry said. "She'll follow you all right."

Eddie gave Beatrice a quick once-over. Not bad looking—small and slender, a rather large nose but luxuriant auburn hair and quite beautiful hands. She was smiling at him. He was used to that; most young women did. But Miss d'Arneiro's eyes seemed to betray an almost mocking amusement. Suddenly he was nervous. He couldn't understand why, but he thought he had never been as nervous before in his life. It was suddenly terribly important to him that he make a good impression on this strange young woman.

He sang an aria and an Irish ballad, giving them all he had. Everyone immediately crowded around, showering him with compliments. Miss d'Arneiro said nothing, but at Harry's suggestion she remained behind after the other guests had gone.

"Well, what is your opinion?" Harry asked. He obviously valued her judgment and was expecting to hear her confirm his own feeling that all Eddie needed was a little European experience to provide polish.

Miss d'Arneiro was silent for a long moment. Then, very seriously, and looking Eddie straight in the eyes, she said, "You're not bad. You can go far, if you will really work."

Both Harry and Eddie were taken aback. But actually she had confirmed Eddie's own inner convictions. In spite of all his successes, he still had certain questions about his vocal technique that none of his teachers had been able to answer. He knew better than anyone else that he had been getting by on natural talent, hard work, a ready smile and a winning personality. This young woman obviously knew what she was talking about and she was honest—someone a man could trust. He surprised himself by asking her if she were free for dinner that evening.

"Yes, I am free," she replied simply.

Harry was invited to join them, but gallantly pleaded a previous engagement.

During the course of the evening Eddie learned that Miss d'Arneiro did indeed have a background that qualified her to judge his musical ability. Her father, a prominent lawyer, politician and composer, had been largely responsible—with his brother—for making the Lisbon

Opera one of the leading houses in Europe. She had been brought up in an atmosphere in which music was a matter of prime importance and a subject of constant discussion.

Eddie stayed on in Paris for the rest of the summer. He and Beatrice worked together for hours every day, their relationship all business. He was convinced that she was interested more in his voice and career than she was in him. She played and he sang. They discussed his problems and tried to work them out. It was uncanny how she seemed to know exactly what things were bothering him. He came to have such confidence in her ideas and judgment that he couldn't imagine getting along without her. How good it was, after working hard, to walk with her through the enchanted streets of Paris, stopping at a special little bistro they came to call their own. She began calling him "Gounod," a word that came to have a special meaning for them both later on, and to him she was "Bebe." Under her guidance, he gave up his ideas about Wagner and Germany. He would return to New York and save his money until he could afford to go to Italy to study with Lombardi. When they discussed this proposal with Barthélemy, with whom Eddie had been coaching again, he was delighted; he would be able to send the Maestro a letter about Edward Johnson at last. Bebe was to follow through on the financial arrangements.

The evening before Eddie set sail for New York, he and Bebe were walking along the banks of the Seine. They were in love. The words had never been spoken but they both knew it. Finally, the realization that it was their last evening together overwhelmed them.

"Bebe, I don't know what I'm going to do without you. I want to ask you to marry me now, but I'm not in a position to do it. Would you be willing to wait for me? As soon as I can make enough money I'll come back and marry you and we can go to Florence together. I need you. I love you."

Without realizing it, Bebe lapsed into French, "*Oh, mon cher Gounod, tu dois savoir que je t'adore, que tu es la lumière de mes yeux et que sans toi la vie ne me vaudrait pas.*"

He kissed her ardently, oblivious of passers-by. Then they walked on together, hand in hand, reminiscing about the glorious times they had had together.

Eddie said, "That first day in the Louvre. Wasn't it wonderful? How hungry for knowledge I was, and how well you satisfied my hunger! Your philosophy, 'To build, not to destroy; to enjoy, not condemn,' is part of me now. I am convinced that our meeting in life was not simple chance. Promise that you will wait for me."

"I will wait," she said, "and I will be with you always, in spirit."

As Eddie set sail the next day, Bebe handed him a little package. When he opened it, tears welled up in his eyes. She had given him a tiny locket containing a lock of her hair, and with it a note: "My love: The Divinity that disposes of our existence certainly prepared the encounter between us so that it should bear fruit in our souls. May God bless you ever. This is the earnest and single-hearted wish of your Bebe."

During the voyage Eddie kept thinking back on his stay in Paris—the happiest time of his life. Every day he wrote a long letter to Bebe. He saved them all up and mailed them when he landed in New York.

Her first letter to him assured him that it hadn't been a dream:

> I met in you the incarnation of an acknowledged ideal, and you— you met in me what you needed at this precise moment in your life, someone to open new vistas for the future, to spur you on to success, to fame, to all your mind craves for. . . . Let me thank you for all the good you did for me, for the help you were to me, for all the happy, happy hours we spent together, for your appreciation of the little I did for you. On my part it was no work, no effort, it was pleasure and joy unminded. I shall school myself into believing that our good-bye was only *au revoir.* I shall look forward to Florence, Fiesole, Rome and all they mean to us if we ever see them together. My heart will always be with you. . . .
>
> A few instructions: do not forget to accentuate your *Ah* in Latin and French; keep your pianissimos high in the mask; keep your voice in the same position all through the middle register, place it high and search where to get more resonance, then open carefully, but never let it come breathy through the mouth. Keep it *douce,* a little *sombre* even.
>
> May God bless you.
>
> Your Bebe

That winter Bebe and Edward often wrote to each other twice a day. He told her about his work, sent her lists of his engagements. He spoke of his three church services every Sunday—"a lot of hard singing"—and of how, after the last service, he usually dropped into the Metropolitan Opera to hear the last part of the regular Sunday evening concert there. As a rule his reports of those programs were enthusiastic, but one time he wrote her, "It was a mighty poor concert and the director of the Metropolitan ought to be ashamed of such a performance."

In preparing his own concerts, Edward was always wishing Bebe were with him. "I need you very, very badly," he wrote again and again.

He deplored the fact that touring kept him on the jump almost continually: "I hate to live my life in bunches this way. Still, I don't mind so much in this instance, for every day that goes by brings me closer to

Paris and you. There's so much in store for me, and I only pray that it will bring something to you. I can never realize I give you anything. I wish I could, then I wouldn't feel so selfish. Are friendships meant to be so much more than that usually, an amalgamation of strength and affection rolled into one? It's a rare combination, but where do you come in, that's all I keep asking myself. I'm a blockhead where your brain is concerned. You're always pouring blessings upon me, and what have I to give you?"

One of Eddie's problems in those days was interviews. "Whenever they ask me to talk about myself, I find it very difficult," he wrote Bebe. "I know what is expected, but I feel such a fool trying to tell people what a great artist I am. It may fool some people, but it doesn't fool me a bit."

It was an attitude that would always make it hard for him to be tough with other people. One time when a woman concert manager in Terre Haute was in financial trouble, for example, "up against New York managers," and ran out of money, Johnson's manager, Mr. Wilson of the Wolfsohn Bureau, wired him not to sing until he was paid. But the concert manager cried, and Eddie felt sorry for her. "Of course I'll sing in spite of Wilson's telegram, for I wouldn't leave anybody in the lurch," he wrote Bebe. "I have four days' hotel board to pay and my last day of railroad fare, besides the expense of putting in a substitute this Sunday, and now get no money for my date. But I'd rather sing for nothing than do the poor woman any injury."

The next day he reported: "If I judge the lady right, she will be my friend for life for having helped her out of such a hole. If not, I'm not much worse off and have the inner satisfaction of having done a kind thing. *C'est tout.* And now, my Bebe, I must rest. Concert time will be here before I know it. I'm leaving here at five o'clock in the morning, and that means up at four, and travelling all day and all night Tuesday, reaching Guelph at 5:45 Wednesday morning. But there is nothing else for it and I must face the music."

Later (February 12, 1907), he wrote that he had been forced to take a day-coach to Detroit and roll up in a corner all night. "I fell asleep and awakened cold and cross, with my back almost broken and my neck so stiff I couldn't move my head. The breakfast car was put on at Indianapolis and after that I felt some better. At noon I had to change cars and from then on I had a parlour car. That was better."

He arrived in Detroit at five in the morning and couldn't get a connection out until nine o'clock. By the time he finally reached Guelph, at five-thirty that evening, he was exhausted. He wrote Bebe immediately, nevertheless: "I will take a walk in the air and get to bed as soon as possible. *Je suis très fatigué ce soir. La vie d'un musicien est très difficile, n'est-ce pas? Bon soir ma cherie. Songez rêves beaux."*

The concert in Guelph went comparatively well, he thought. Jessie Hill played for him. "She was coaching in Paris last summer, do you remember?" he asked Bebe. "She did a good job; some parts were ragged, but it passed off all right. Today I went out to my old school and sang four songs for the pupils. They gave me a great send-off, and my old schoolmaster delivered a regular funeral oration."

One of Edward Johnson's most impressive engagements during the winter of 1907 was as a soloist with the New York Oratorio Society in Elgar's *The Apostles,* with Sir Edward Elgar himself over from England to conduct. In rehearsals, the composer told Eddie something he would never forget: "Remember, the real substance of the music is the meaning of the word."

Johnson's fame as an oratorio singer was by now widespread. To be an opera singer, however, he knew he would have to go abroad and stay for an extended period of time. His plan now was to marry Bebe, live in Florence and study with Maestro Lombardi. But first, he had to have more money. His fees were around $300 an engagement as a rule, and he was saving every penny possible, but it was going to take time. He would have to start out with enough to support himself and a wife for two or three years, and pay for lessons. It looked almost hopeless.

"Bebe, what am I going to do?" he wrote. "You say you will wait for me, no matter how long. But sometimes I get so discouraged I think I'll never make it."

From working and singing almost every waking moment, he was so tired he began to wonder whether he could keep up the pace. But he had a goal, and Bebe gave him courage. Her inner strength, as it happened, had been developed perforce over the years. For all the affluence and prestige of her prominent family, her own life had never been easy. She had been torn between her duty to her mother, a most difficult woman, and her love for her father, for whose mistress she had a great affection. Though her father had been dead for three years she still kept in touch with "Mother Margaret," as she called his mistress, and said once, in a letter to Eddie: "Compare her with my mother, then uphold the conventional virtues, if you can, and condemn those who have slipped out of the social formalities. Rot. Rot."

Edward closed his 1906/7 season "in a blaze," as he put it, with an operatic concert in New York. "It was a splendid climax to my season. It was a knockout. How happy I felt. I was in good voice, good company, and good *pay*. An excellent combination, isn't it? Eames, Homer, de Gogorza, Witherspoon, and the Metropolitan Opera Orchestra, and

I had a room to myself. Not like last fall in Ann Arbor, when I was sharing a room with Witherspoon and found it impossible, because he and Campanari, whose room was near ours, were talking all the time."

From April 1 to June 1, 1907, Edward Johnson sang thirty-six performances—recitals, miscellaneous concerts, and such works as *Samson and Delilah, Faust, The Damnation of Faust,* the Verdi *Requiem, Elijah,* the *Messiah, Hiawatha, The Dream of Gerontius,* and *The Redemption.* In addition, he made fifteen appearances with the Theodore Thomas Orchestra, sang seven performances with the Boston Orchestra, two with the New York Symphony and one with the Metropolitan Opera House Orchestra.

On May 28, he wrote Bebe: "The time can't go too fast. Joy! Oh joy! In two weeks I will be in Paris with you. It is too good to be true. I am tickled pink over your finding Marroni's apartment for me. Great Scott! That is luck. My! I can see myself already installed. Lovely, lovely, lovely. Better than hotels and pensions."

Eddie had been getting such increasingly enthusiastic reviews everywhere that his head was swimming with success. The sound of applause was ringing in his ears as he finally set sail for Europe, on June 13, 1907.

THAT SUMMER, studying and working with Bebe and Barthélemy in Paris, was the most wonderful time Edward Johnson had ever had in his life. In the hours that he and his "Bee" were together, their love blossomed. The most difficult thing he had ever had to do was to leave her that year. But they had agreed that they would marry, and she philosophically said they must be patient.

By the first of October, he was back in the United States, and the next week he told Bee: "I lost my locket with your beautiful curl in it. I am heartbroken. I will advertise but I doubt if I'll ever have it again. I feel all upset over it. . . . How I'd love to have you. Would you like to come to me tonight—put your head on my shoulder and let me read you poetry till you fall asleep? Do you remember long ago?"

On November 16, after one of Johnson's concerts in Minneapolis, he wrote: "Witherspoon gave me a long talking-to after we came home, and begs me to go abroad to study. He was delighted with my performance and thinks I have grown tremendously in the past two seasons. I couldn't tell him very well how hard you worked with me those two summers, but in my heart I gave you the compliment and all the credit. You did so much for me, my dearest, you are my rock and tower for our future plans. Never in my life have I leaned on anyone as I do on you. I am ashamed when I think of it, for you have already more than you can bear. . . . There is no hesitancy now! I am going to 'chuck' it all

30

and leave. . . . Just be patient, my dear, and we will carry the day."

In spite of the brave tone of his words, he wondered how he would be able to marry and study and live, if he stopped singing for two years or more. He plunged into each engagement with a desperate determination to make good, and he took everything that came his way, singing night and day, often at three church services on Sunday as well as at synagogues on Saturday.

The ovations he received everywhere made him happy, but there was always another side to touring: travelling night and day, bad hotels, poor food, anything but comfort. He was often tired and cross. Sometimes he was so lonesome that he thought he would cry out. At moments his heart ached to be near Bebe once more.

She too was finding the separation difficult. "I won't feel peace until you are near. Your presence gives me a sense of safety and security and seems to dispel the tense atmosphere that often oppresses me into stifling."

Travelling 9,000 miles to fulfill engagements that fall, Eddie said he felt like a drudge. It was only Bee's letters and the thought of their future plans that kept him going. He did his best to hold up his end of housekeeping responsibilities with Arthur, but he had to admit he wasn't good at it, considered it time wasted. "What a bore!" he complained in a letter to Bebe. "But it made me think of you and the time we bought things together. A.H. has just come in and discovered I left the gas under the oatmeal and the water has boiled dry and the stuff all burned! What a cook!"

Although it was a demanding life, Eddie's fortunes were slowly but surely improving. Wolfsohn wanted him to sign a five-year contract, giving the Wolfsohn Bureau 10 per cent of everything he made, whether in Europe or America. He also offered Eddie the leading tenor role in *Les Contes d'Hoffmann*, which was to be translated into English, and presented by a new group in New York. It sounded good, but for some inexplicable reason Eddie said No.

Then his big break came. In the winter of 1907-8 the producers of a new Broadway show, Oscar Straus's *A Waltz Dream,* were auditioning tenor after tenor for the role of the hero, Niki. Eventually they decided it was impossible to find, among the popular singers of the day, a voice capable of singing seven high B's in each performance. They went to the Metropolitan to hear Caruso, Bonci and others, not one of whom could pass on the operetta stage as a slender young naval officer, however. The Metropolitan then referred them to the Henry Wolfsohn Bureau which had among its artists both the noted basso Herbert Witherspoon and the new young tenor Edward Johnson.

Witherspoon happened to be in Wolfsohn's office when the call for the tenor came in. He immediately spoke up. "Why don't you send young Johnson down? He would be perfect for the part. I've sung with him and he's good."

Wolfsohn considered the suggestion. Johnson had been a success as a member of the New York Artists Quartet that season, singing with Janet Spencer, Corinne Rider-Kelsey and Herbert Witherspoon. What was more, he had been a success as a tenor soloist for the entire spring tour of the Theodore Thomas Orchestra, had sung with Walter Damrosch and the New York Symphony Orchestra in the south, and in the east with the Boston Festival Orchestra under Emil Mollenhauer. And the press notices had been glowing. In all his solo appearances Johnson had been greeted with a tumult of applause.

Without further hesitation Wolfsohn made an appointment for Eddie to sing for the producers Klaus and Erlanger, the biggest theatrical men in America. Afterward, Eddie wrote to Bebe: "I sang, and they offered me flat, then and there, the title role in the new Broadway production on practically my own terms. The role is not very difficult—light and medium, with a few high B's—no travelling and $500 a week for seven performances. I have considered it from all angles. I know you will say it is risky, but I can't see where it will hurt me and I do need the stage experience and I need the money. So now I can see that I will have a few dollars to come to Europe. I agreed to sign a contract for only three months, because of my concert and oratorio commitments for next season."

After the rehearsals for *A Waltz Dream* began in December, Eddie's letters to Bebe gradually became more and more impersonal. They mirrored the atmosphere of the theatrical life—what it was like backstage, audience reactions, what happened after the opening, personal relationships. He was caught up in the excitement and glamour of it all. In spite of his long hours in the theatre and the rigorous demands of the role he was playing and singing, he found himself being tempted by social invitations. He accepted certain ones that seemed a safe distance away when he'd have plenty of time, only to discover later on that he was trapped and had to push himself to honour these obligations. For all that, he enjoyed the life—he liked people and liked to be with people. Eddie was essentially a "social" being. Also, like most people of the theatre, he was somewhat of a chameleon, reflecting the colours inspired by his associates and surroundings. He was romantic and "intellectual" when with Bebe; fun-loving and carefree when with his Broadway friends; and touched by religious fervour in church on Sundays.

Bebe tried to reach Eddie, but he kept on writing about backstage bickerings and problems. There was jealousy among the seasoned members of the company; they were annoyed that an unseasoned oratorio and church singer should come into the show and steal the limelight. Later, as his solo number, the theme song of the show, had to be repeated each night by popular demand, there were those in the company who tried to insist that encores be outlawed. The soprano, although fine to work with, had gone to the management to insist that her spotlight be the stronger one when the two of them were on the stage together; one of the older members of the company insisted that she couldn't climb the stairs and must have a dressing room on stage, just as Eddie had (it was necessary in his case because of quick changes); his messages were sometimes deliberately not delivered. All of which had nothing to do with the fact that everyone succumbed to the charm of Eddie's smile, wit and disarming personality offstage. It was all a sort of sickness of the ego. He wrote more and more of such petty things; his head was full of them; and he thought less and less of his ambitions for the future.

Bebe was worried, and finally decided to tell Eddie how she felt. If that didn't draw a different response, then all their hopes and dreams would never be realized. Their idyll would have come to an end. Eddie, instead of being a hero in shining armour, would be settling for the big money, spotlights and adulation of the musical comedy field. His glorious voice would become metallic and edgy; the finer elements of his nature would be relegated to the background; his soul would lose its gleaming purity; his heart and life, instead of being filled with art, beauty and poetry, would become superficial and meaningless. Bebe had to let him know what she was thinking—she had to save him, if possible. But still she hesitated.

It was difficult for Eddie to keep his feet on the ground after the big January 27 Broadway opening. Headlines proclaimed: "The Man of the Hour!" "The Latest Matinée Hero"; "Concert Tenor's Success in Light Opera Encourages Colleagues"; "Edward Johnson and Sophie Brandt Share Smash Records in *A Waltz Dream*"; "Concert Tenor, in Opera, Makes Hit: Johnson's High B's Surprise New York." Reviewers searched for superlatives. The *New York Times*, for example:

> It is hard to conceive of a better Niki than Edward Johnson made. He has an exceedingly good voice of the sort which is seldom heard in light opera. His high notes are true and powerful, and last night, the opening, his singing fairly lifted the audience. He is extremely good-looking, has a good stage presence, and made a success of the evening.

Johnson was especially pleased with the references to his acting; he had been concerned about that. "Of course, I'm a quick study as you know," he wrote Bee. "Actually, I learned my part in five days so that when the rehearsals began in earnest I could devote all my attention to the study of what I was to do on the stage. That part of it was absolutely new to me, and I must say that I was nervous when the first performances came. But my singing has seemed to please the audiences and I am getting more accustomed to the stage part by now."

The *Evening Herald* spoke of Edward Johnson as the man who could "coo like a dove or hit the top of the ceiling with his high notes." Stage Director Herbert Gresham introduced a kiss that was so long drawn out that "commuters will lose their trains if they try it."

Little wonder that the producers offered Edward Johnson $800 a week to tour with the show at the end of the Broadway run (January 27 to April 6), and a return engagement at the same price for the following year. But Eddie turned it down in order to honour his concert tour with the Chicago Orchestra for the month of May and his appearance with the Metropolitan Opera House Orchestra in Norfolk, Connecticut, the first three days in June. Moreover, he had other plans. His goal was grand opera.

The papers, meanwhile, were reporting all sorts of things for the new Broadway discovery: that he would return to *A Waltz Dream* on Broadway the next season, and that he would sing *A Waltz Dream* in London. Bebe was disturbed, but Eddie reassured her: "Don't pay any attention to what the papers say. I've told no one my plans. Everyone is planning for me and since they seem to enjoy it, I just let them go ahead."

Blaming Wolfsohn for the rumours, he assured Bee: "He can make more mistakes to the square inch than anyone I have dealt with. That's why he gets 10 per cent! Besides, I accepted the role in *A Waltz Dream* with mixed emotions. I am elated, naturally, by the success, applause, and the fact that there is sudden recognition. But I admit I am cynical about the reason for people's sudden discoveries. I have worked hard and sung better and received no acclaim. Also, I'm dead tired."

Eddie *was* tired, but he was having great fun. He liked the life, if he could just hold out. Bebe was disappointed. She could hesitate no longer. So, February 7, 1908, she wrote:

> As you write me again, I am disappointed, terribly so. I have watched and waited patiently for the excitement to tone down, to find you again. I am losing hope, not only that one but many others! I am sorry, very sorry, that you take things so much to heart, so that even physically you begin to feel the results. You complain of being tired, worn out, thin, and weary. I am sorry, very sorry. I repeat it, but I can not help but think that you make

34

much ado about nothing, or near to it. I fear also for your future. I can hardly see how you will stand, if all through your life your nervous system is going to be overpowered, even by things that prove a success, and would and should in consequence be a source of relaxation. I've lived too much in the intimacy of art not to see that your taking matters to heart to such an extent is abnormal. You absolutely lose grip of yourself, and all that constitutes life is displaced. Your soul seems to be absent from you and only one part of your mind exists, the one that is centred in your role in *A Waltz Dream*. You may not understand it now, but this state of things is, to me, a source of anxiety and extreme sorrow. . . . I fear you will grow warped, and cramped mentally. I fear a stoppage in your mental development. . . . My interest in your art is because of you, because I see in you the elements and mind capable of all that forms the total of a high mental status. Your love of knowledge, your comprehension of the beautiful. . . . But those are things to be cultivated assiduously. They must hold the first place, they must form the basis of our existence, or else they dwindle into nothing—and remain only as a memory of a thing of which we had a passing glimpse but only half understood. . . .

He hadn't thought she would take him so seriously. She felt better when, in reply, he quoted William Blake to her. "To see a world in a grain of sand/ And a heaven in a wild flower/ Hold infinity in the palm of your hand/ And eternity in an hour." That sounded more like her "Boysey"; he was committed to her and to the future they had dreamed of together.

Then came a letter so filled with himself that Bebe was aghast. He had had a character reading by a palmist, and wrote proudly of it, as though he were speaking of absolute fact:

His rather square palms show an understanding of the practical side of life, while the firmness indicates the ability to "take the slings and arrows of outrageous fortune" and come up smiling. A victor in the end because of the unflagging determination and willpower shown in that long first phalange of his thumb directed by the logic and reason of the second phalange. . . . The length of his fingers reveals a carefulness in detail. They are smooth to the second joint, disclosing the inspiration which he brings to the rendition of his roles. . . .

"Funny how they can tell such things just by looking at your hand, isn't it?" Eddie commented. He must be taking it seriously! Bebe was sick at heart.

"So what do you think of your Boysey now?" he added. "I am bound to do this show for only three months. But already I have some tempting offers for next year—to go on with this show at $800 a week, to

have the lead in Lehar's *The Merry Widow* starting at $700 a week—
and I think they might go as high as a thousand. Think of it! How would
you like to start life together in New York instead of Florence?"

Bebe was stunned. She must be careful, but she *must* speak out. Her
reply went right to the heart of things: "I want to establish you in your
circle where you will find all that answers to the claims of your mind,
heart and soul. I want to feel you have something to replace me in case
I am called away."

Eddie sailed for Europe on the *Kaiserin Auguste Victoria* on June
18. He was riding high, with the Broadway success behind him, applause
for his concert appearances and the words of both Enrico Caruso and
Luisa Tetrazzini ringing in his ears: "We expect to hear you soon in
grand opera productions in New York."

That summer Bee and Edward went to Normandy with friends for
July and August, renting a house for 500 francs a month. Eddie was
exhausted after *A Waltz Dream* and his subsequent concerts. It was the
third time that Bebe had arranged such a vacation for Eddie, and this
time he really needed it. He had lost twenty pounds.

Bee didn't allow him to relax completely and do nothing, however.
She found many flaws in his singing, including a certain edginess of tone,
that she knew had to be eliminated. So she insisted that they work a
little each day. His Broadway career was over and his future lay in
opera. He was committed to it. Bee believed he could reach "the top,"
and he had confidence in her judgment. They worked and planned, took
long walks, talked, and, during long romantic evenings, felt their very
souls being bathed in the bliss and joy of their love. They read many
things together, discussed their future, Eddie's career, and the fact that
Maestro Lombardi was waiting to hear when Edward Johnson could
begin studying with him. Letters came from Harry Higinbotham and his
fiancée, Agnes Elizabeth Hatton, who were planning to be married on
December 23, 1908, in All Saints Church, West Dulwich, London. "We
do hope you will decide to make it a double wedding," they wrote.

Eddie and Bee would have been happy to do so, but there were certain problems that would have to be solved first, and certain religious
obstacles to be overcome. Bebe was a Catholic and, whereas Eddie had
often said that "all roads lead to Heaven," when he was faced with the
idea of becoming a Catholic himself in order to marry Bee, he balked.
He was used to talking directly to God, he said. "I just can't bring
myself to start going through any other human being." Bee patiently
explained the significance of the bishop and the priest, but Eddie was
adamant. "I can't do it, dearest. I'm sorry." As Bee herself didn't want

36

him to do anything against his inner convictions, the only solution was to obtain a Papal dispensation.

With the assistance of Bebe's priest in Paris, the necessary application was made and the waiting began. It was a new experience for both of them and the old Chinese proverb that the compass has five points, north, south, east, west, and where-you-stand, came to have a special meaning, for they felt they were standing in a completely new spot, trembling as their fate hung in the balance. They waited in vain for word from Rome, and Eddie finally had to sail for New York with nothing settled. There was no possibility, therefore, of a double wedding with Harry and Agnes, although they hoped to be married by the same minister and in the same church in London later on. Tentatively, they set the date for August 2, 1909, which would allow Eddie to honour his concert commitments in America during the winter. "After we're married," he wrote from the boat, "we can go directly to Florence and I can start working with Maestro Lombardi. Joy! Oh joy! I can't wait. Grand opera. That's my goal—the top."

"Don't worry," Bebe wrote back, "you'll make it to the *very* top."

Because of his sensational success in *A Waltz Dream* on Broadway the previous season, Johnson's fees for all new engagements had more than doubled. His earnings that winter, for four or five concerts a week, were going to be at least four times what he would have received singing seven shows a week on Broadway, and he could still take church jobs on Sundays and sing in a temple on Saturdays without killing himself. Life looked very bright. He was vocally refreshed, physically rested and in high spirits.

That year was an exciting one for both Eddie and Bebe, but a difficult one too, as their longing for each other became all but unbearable. Bee would have no peace, she wrote him, until she held him in her arms again; while he repeatedly felt "like chucking it all and taking the first boat to Paris." They were sustained by their daily letters, by their love and by the knowledge that the money he was earning as the months dragged by was necessary for his studies and for starting their life together. But they would never be separated again, ever, they agreed.

The Papal dispensation was granted on November 16, 1908, and they immediately began completing plans for the wedding. It would take place in London, with Harry Higinbotham and Agnes, who planned to live in Brussels, as the only guests. Eddie had thought of arranging for his parents to attend, but he and Bebe agreed the expense would be too great. Bebe wished that her father had lived to be there, but as for her mother, she wrote: "The monstrosity of that woman's character is a ghastly revelation, and to be in a way subject to it and involved with it makes me shiver with horror, and makes life a hideous problem to me! The idea of her being with us at our wedding is out of the question."

Eddie sailed for Paris that spring, immediately following his last singing engagement. He met Bebe and the Higinbothams there, and they all attended to some last-minute shopping before going together to London.

Mr. Edward Johnson, aged thirty-one, and Mademoiselle Beatriz Maria Ferrura da Veiga d'Arneiro, aged thirty-six, were married on August 2, 1909, in All Saints Church, West Dulwich, London. A wedding reception was held at the home of Harry's friends, Charles and Ella Stryker-Lloyd, and the wedding supper at the Carlton Hotel. It was a small, intimate supper, with only Harry and Agnes Higinbotham and the Lloyds present. Arthur Higinbotham, unable to be in London at the time, had written, "I shall be present in spirit. . . ."

*3*

THE NEWLYWEDS left immediately for Italy, to honeymoon in Florence. They went first to a little *pensione* that was owned and operated by a young couple named Casali. Mrs. Casali, the former Josephine O'Dell, had originally come to Italy from the southern part of the United States to study singing, but she had met and married a handsome young Italian instead. Later, her husband had inherited the family hostel, Kirsch-Casali.

Eddie and Bebe took an immediate liking to the Casalis. Edward found Josephine particularly charming, almost too charming for Bee's liking; she soon decided it was important for them to have a home of their own. "Eddie must be able to study and practise freely at any hour he chooses," she rationalized. "He must not be distracted with concern about disturbing guests. Also, we can control his diet more easily. He must never become plump again." Within a very short time they were established in a small apartment.

In the meantime—the day after their arrival, in fact—Eddie had gone to sing for Maestro Lombardi. After the first aria the Maestro had said *Basta!* and immediately got up and embraced the young tenor. He didn't need to hear any more; this was the voice he had been waiting for ever since his last sessions with Enrico Caruso. *Bella voce! Bravissimo! Son felice, molto coontento. Si, si!*

Immediately he began to plan. "We will work hard, every day. You will have a great career. With Caruso the problem was to build the top part of the voice, to add a couple of notes and make them all secure so he would no longer crack on A's, B's and C's. But with you, it is only a matter of breath and of strengthening the middle voice."

He was obviously enthusiastic. Here was a young man of personality and charm who could toss off high C's, D's and even E's with the greatest of ease.

"The only problem," Lombardi went on, "will be to make the scale even, the support constant, and to teach you the nuances of the Italian language and the musical traditions of opera."

It was agreed that Bebe would sit in on all the lessons, inasmuch as she would be coaching her husband at home in both music and languages.

"I was only the clay; she was the artist," Johnson always said in later life. "It was her faith and determination that gave me the confidence and courage to dream of fame which she was sure would come one day if we worked hard enough together."

The first few weeks in the Lombardi studio were exhilarating, even fun. But Eddie soon began to see that he had never known the kind of discipline Bebe proved capable of imposing. In his way, he was as much of a perfectionist as she, but was inclined to suggest they stop work sometimes, in the middle of a coaching session, to take a walk through the romantic streets of Florence.

Bebe could see she was going to have to be diplomatic and proceed slowly. So she frequently agreed to his suggestion, and they would have a wonderful afternoon or evening marvelling at the glories of the Duomo and the beauty of Giotto's Tower as they wandered through the city. Often they would stop at one of the tiny restaurants for a cappuccino or, on rare occasions, treat themselves to dinner, and afterward wander along the banks of the Arno hand in hand. At times, from sheer exuberance of spirit, Eddie would dash ahead, kick up his heels, throw back his head and send a few high C's floating out into the sympathetic Italian air, while Bebe, who was always preaching self-control, would find herself laughing too, happy and carefree. Passersby, used to such natural expression of spirits, would smile and add some good-natured bravos.

The young couple spent many happy hours in the Ufizzi and Pitti Palace galleries where Bebe would talk at length about the paintings and the sculpture. One of Eddie's favourite spots, however, was Michelangelo's Piazza, where he liked to pretend that he had already arrived on the operatic scene. There, as he looked out over Florence, or up and down the winding Arno River, he let his soul expand as he contemplated the wonder and beauty of everything he saw. "If my old friends could see me now," he thought. "Me, Eddie Johnson, from Guelph, Ontario, here in Italy to become an opera singer!" He had the greatest maestro of them all—Lombardi, who had taught Caruso, and who already treated him with the affection and proprietary interest of a father. Furthermore, Eddie had the most wonderful girl in the world beside him as his wife. The world was his.

40

Months passed. There were times when Eddie and Bebe were both impatient for him to begin working on opera roles, but Maestro Lombardi was very firm. *"Pazienza,"* he said on one occasion, putting his arm affectionately around the shoulders of his pupil. "We have much to do. We have to work on language, repertoire and breath. You must remember that there are three kinds of breathing techniques for singers: the *clavicolare,* in which one lifts the clavicals high—a very high, almost shoulder breathing; the *costale,* a wide expansion of the rib cage and dependency on that for the support needed for singing; and the *addominale.* It is the *addominale* that is the only true way. When you can fill your whole body with air you are ready for anything. But it is not easy to master, so you must be patient!"

In the spring, after nine months of work, Maestro Lombardi finally gave Eddie a few easy arias. Then one day he handed him the score of *Andrea Chénier.* That evening the Johnsons went to the Casalis' *pensione* to celebrate with their friends.

It was only a month or so later, in that same spring of 1910, that Bebe discovered she was pregnant, and with characteristic decisiveness she began to look for another apartment. They would have to have a place for a nanny, as well as regular help in the house.

It was about this time that the Higinbothams visited them in Florence. Eddie and Bebe cajoled Maestro Lombardi into breaking another rule; he allowed the Higinbothams to attend one of Eddie's lessons. Eddie sang the entire first act of *Andrea Chénier.* Harry and Agnes were deeply moved, but when the Maestro turned around from the piano, they were surprised to see tears rolling down his cheeks—tears of sheer pride and joy.

That evening, when the two young couples were alone together, Eddie could contain himself no longer. Exuberantly he blurted out the big news: "We're going to have a baby!" It was a fitting climax to an exciting day, and Harry insisted they all go out to a good restaurant to top things off.

Some weeks later, it was Edward, not Bebe, who was in a hospital. A sudden attack of appendicitis had necessitated an operation, but in a couple of weeks he was back working and feeling like himself again.

That summer, although they had budgeted themselves to live on 500 lire ($100) a month, they decided it would be wise to add a nurse to their little household. That was when Tata joined them. She was the sister of their cleaning woman, and was introduced as Maria del Moro Tazzi. Immediately, they began calling her Tata (Nanny). A young Italian girl, under five feet tall, with black curly hair, brown twinkling eyes and gold-looped earrings, Tata proved to be intelligent, quick and efficient, and within days had taken over the household. She remained with the family for the rest of her life.

The Johnsons had made a number of good friends, but they seldom went out during the next few months, unless it was to honour invitations from people who could be helpful to Eddie. They were working long hours together on opera scores. Bebe was also teaching Edward French and Italian, and exposing him to long sessions on art appreciation of all kinds. The strenuous schedule seemed to sap her strength at this crucial time, and her physical resources were low when the baby finally came on December 21, 1910.

Years later, the doctor's daughter, Baroness Rapisardi, remembered the birth: "They had been expecting the baby any time and finally Eddie called my father, Dr. Alessandro Rostear. It was in the middle of the night, but he went right over. He said it was a long and very difficult birth—he had had to operate—and he told them that Bebe should not take a chance on having another baby. Edward always insisted that it was my father who had saved Bee's life that night."

The baby, a girl, was christened Fiorenza Margherita d'Arneiro Johnson. Bebe thought she was beautiful, but Eddie, when he first saw her, blurted out, "She looks more like a tomato than anything."

Life in the Johnson household was like that of any other young couple with their first baby. Bebe wrote in her diary: "[At night] after mother has nursed her, she hasn't enough milk, so dear father gets up and warms the bottle. Poor father, who does love to have a good night's sleep, has to get up every night in the small hours when the room is cold. Sometimes he takes the baby in his arms and holds her against him in bed while mother rearranges the cradle." Another time she wrote: "Baby sometimes frets a little and refuses to stay in her cot, but the first day she heard father sing, she instantly quieted down, and listened in deep silence with her little blue eyes wide open. Father's voice is so beautiful!"

In Bebe's diary there are also accounts of Baby's first outings to visit friends, on February 6 and 8; Baby's first smile, February 15; Baby's first cooing in answer to their chatting to her; Baby's first photograph, February 27; Baby's first drive, April 15, in a cab with Uncle Harry Higinbotham, Dad and Mother; and a happy time when Baby, at four months "laughed aloud when Daddy tickled her feet."

THE DAY FINALLY came for Eddie's big chance—his operatic début. The director of the Teatro Verdi in Padova had offered him the title role in *Andrea Chénier,* but then the question of his name came up. "Edward

Johnson" would never do, the impresario said; it would have to be Edoardo di Giovanni. Maestro Lombardi agreed.

"Why should I change my name?" Eddie asked.

"Because the Italians are very chauvinistic about their opera. They resent foreigners. Because of your perfect Italian accent they will accept you as one of their own, but only if you have an Italian name. Anyway, why *not* Edoardo di Giovanni? It's a direct translation of Edward Johnson."

Eddie still wasn't sure. But Bebe liked the idea, so he agreed. It took him a while to get used to the name, however, and on the night of his début he couldn't help feeling that he was being a bit of a phoney.

Moreover, on that opening night of January 10, 1912, he was suddenly struck by a tremendous attack of stage fright. "The romance and poetry of *Andrea Chénier* appealed to me," Eddie said later, "and I felt at home in the broad melodic phrases and declamatory style. But, nevertheless, fear was in my heart. The Italian language was new to me, and though I had translated my name from Edward Johnson to Edoardo di Giovanni, a certain self-consciousness was upon me. The change of name might fool some of the public, but it couldn't fool me."

Then there was the matter of the claque. Word reached Eddie just after he had entered the theatre, that the tenor originally engaged to sing the title role that evening, a protegé of the manager of the Teatro Verdi, had hired a claque to hiss and boo Edward Johnson off the stage and put an end to his career then and there. Eddie's temper flared out of control, and without stopping in the dressing room to tell Bebe about it, he dashed outside. There, on the corner of the street, stood the leader of the claque. Eddie recognized him from having seen him around the theatre many times. He went straight up to the man, grabbed him by the lapels, and told him in fluent Italian he knew what was being planned. "I'm warning you," Eddie said, in a menacing tone, "you *listen* tonight and applaud what you *hear*—and keep your hands in your pockets and your mouth shut the rest of the time! I've worked hard for three years and this is my big chance, and you're not going to ruin it for me. So you listen! And if you know what's good for you, do what you feel like doing, not what you're paid to do!"

Eddie was still shaking with rage when he returned to his dressing room where Bebe was waiting to put on his make-up and help him with his costume. "Forget it, dear," she said. "Rise above it. They'll applaud, you'll see."

That was true. When Edward Johnson stepped on the stage he forgot the claque—even forgot his nerves. The delightful little opera house was like a miniature of the Costanzi in Rome, like a tiny La Scala—four tiers of boxes, deep stage and auditorium, everything all red and gold and cream. The whole place resounded to the great applause that greeted Edoardo di Giovanni's first aria.

Later Edward described his feelings during that performance: "As my great moment in the last act arrived, there arose within me the profound emotion which brings sincerity and conviction, and through which one acquires assurance and authority. It was an emotion which by its force not only released me from myself but gave me power to translate the true feeling and meaning of the librettist and the composer."

According to the number one newspaper *Gazzettino,* Di Giovanni had stopped the show with his first aria, but also everyone had shared in the applause for the overall excellent performance: soprano Teresina Bruchi; the director, Cavalliere Zuccani; the conductor, Vittorio Orefice; the baritone, Formichi; and the bass, Montico.

*Il Veneto* of Thursday, January 11, 1912, carried a two-and-a-half column story about *Chénier* and its impact:

> The tenor Di Giovanni so marvellously captured the public with the vigour of his perfect *bel canto* singing and with his acting that few spectators could believe he was making his début. . . . *Evviva la Bruchi! Bravo Di Giovanni! Auguri Zuccani! Bravo Orefice!* came from the audience throughout the performance. It was an evening, all in all, that will never be forgotten.

Eddie knew he had passed the ultimate test of a real artist. As he said once later in life: "To have conquered the preconceived notion of his auditors, and impressed his own interpretation and mood upon the listener is for the artist to have become master of the situation."

Lest anyone think that singing opera in Italy in those days was a breeze, let them consider the test of endurance that was part of Edoardo di Giovanni's baptism. He had been called upon to sing a general rehearsal of *Andrea Chénier* on January 9. The opening night, January 10, was followed by performances on January 11, 13, 14, 18, 20, 21, 24, 27, 28, and February 6! Eleven performances in three and a half weeks, with the twelfth, thirteenth and fourteenth performances on February 15, 18 and 22. The theatre's total repertoire during that portion of the season consisted of just three operas—*Chénier, Die Walküre* and *Mefistofele.*

Next came an engagement in Ancona—the first production there of Mascagni's *Isabeau,* April 27, 1912, which had had its world première in Buenos Aires the previous year. Edoardo di Giovanni as Folco, reviewers agreed, "was the ideal embodiment of the ingenuous hero."

Bebe and Eddie were working hard every day, but they had some fun, too. They cultivated a group of friends who shared their appreciation of great masterpieces of both art and music, as well as their love of life and in some cases, a homey sense of humour. Their menu at one dinner at the Casa di Edoardo di Giovanni, 12 Via Solferino, for example, was typical:

*Hors d'oeuvres*: Cold hoarseness, sciatica, boils, and nettle rash
*Potage*: Si naturale
*Rôti*: Roast Beef à la Marshall
*Légumes*: Potatoes à la Metropolitan
        Sweet Potatoes à la Geraldine (Farrar)
        Broccoli à la (Antonio) Scotti
*Salade*: Veri rigo-letto
*Dessert*: Poire à la Germaine Leonore
*Fruits*: Witherspoon nuts and Spencer figs . . .
*Vin*: Nihil . . .         *Liqueur*: Salvation Army
*Cigares*: Tuscan Stinkers . . .
*Café*: Insomnia . . .

Amen!

Some of Bebe's notes of the time included one on June 12, 1912, in which she recorded the fact that Eddie had signed a contract to sing Puccini's *La fanciulla del West* at Bergamo. Edward made the note: "Contract for Bergamo ordered me to be there on August 14th to stay up to September 21st, 1912—number of performances not specified— pay 2,000 francs." Tullio Serafin was to conduct.

When Edward and Bebe went to Bergamo, they left Fiorenza in Lugano with Mother Margaret and her daughter Mary. (Mary d'Arneiro, a singer, was the adopted daughter of Bebe's father, Visconde d'Arneiro, and had been his pupil.) They arrived in Bergamo on August 12, and by the time rehearsals began on the fourteenth, they were settled in a new inn, the Albergo Reale Italia.

Serafin seemed pleased from the very first hearing of the part, and found nothing to disapprove of or correct. By the time the season opened, on August 24, 1912, Edward was in complete favour.

Bebe told the story of the first night: "While I was making Edward up, Serafin opened the dressing room door and ushered in Tito Ricordi [a prominent music publisher]! For a second we didn't know who it was . . . but he introduced himself, and stayed awhile, chatting pleasantly, and told Edward he had heard much good of him. The theatre was full—and all the powers of Milan were there to judge: Mingardi, Puccini's son, Lusardi, Eugenia Burzio—and so many others I forget. The first act over, Tito Ricordi came to compliment Edward on his success—and after him came Lusardi, Gino Rosetti, Emma Carelli and others. The second act went even better and signalled the evening as a thorough success. Ricordi told Edward he had sung his *racconto* magnificently."

Now, all at once, Edoardo di Giovanni was in wide demand. What's more, he was represented by two of the leading Italian managers, Lusardi and Buldrini, a duplication which later caused certain conflicts. "Do not take any engagements with anybody," advised Giuseppe Lusardi, a friend of Maestro Lombardi. Buldrini, feeling Di Giovanni should capitalize on his recent acclaim, was mystified that Eddie turned offers down.

A New York manager, Charles Wagner, strongly urged Johnson to return to America as First Tenor with the Boston Opera Company. La Scala director Mingardi asked that he be prepared to sing *Tannhäuser*, *Isabeau* and *Fanciulla,* and not to accept South American contracts without speaking to him. More offers were coming Eddie's way than he could possibly accept.

It was as though Italy had been waiting for Edward Johnson. Not only was his Italian impeccable and his voice magnificent, but he was a singer who could act as well as he sang and who, being slender, looked the part of the romantic heroes he portrayed. Nor did it take long for the world beyond Italy to learn that a tenor who was an excellent musician and a quick study had appeared upon the scene.

Italian composers were all seeking the services of the sensational Di Giovanni for their latest works, and he soon signed up to sing the leading role in *Isabeau* again, this time at the Costanzi in Rome on February 8, 1913. He would appear there in several other operas as well during a four-month engagement beginning with *Don Carlo*.

It was all very well to be a star, but it wasn't going to be easy to accomplish so much work in so short a time. Years before, when he had said he could sing *Aida* much more easily than his Broadway show, he had spoken theoretically. At this point in his career, he wasn't quite so sure that it was true. Every waking moment was spent in learning new music, rehearsing, staging, costume fittings and coachings. He and Bebe had very little chance to relax together, and practically no time to spend with friends.

Edoardo di Giovanni was serious about his career, but there were times when he felt like kicking up his heels and celebrating. On such occasions it took all the persuasion of both his wife and Maestro Lombardi to convince him that there was still a long road ahead before he could be said to have arrived.

"Opera is not Broadway," Bebe would remind him.

The venerable Maestro would add, "Learning the words and notes of an opera score are only the first steps toward creating a role. The music must be in your throat, then you must polish the musical phrases."

One time, when Bebe and Eddie were working, as they did every day, he started to walk away after singing a scene from memory.

"Let's do it again," said Bebe patiently.

"Why?" Eddie was impatient. "I know it perfectly. Why should we go through it again? Let's chuck it for the day, and take a walk. Look outside, it's . . ."

"Let's do it again, just to be sure," Bebe insisted. That time Eddie missed a note.

"You see?" Bebe was triumphant. "Now we'll do it *two* more times for good measure. Then we'll begin to polish it."

"We never have any fun," Eddie grumbled. "Work, work, work, that's all I ever do. Sing a score 'one more time'; repeat a phrase 'one more time'; read a book, study a language—I'm sick of it all. Drive, drive, drive. You can sit there and play all day, if you want to, but I'm fed up. I quit! I'm going out!"

The door slammed behind him as Eddie left the house. Bebe sat for a long time, stunned. She had known such a scene was inevitable—it had been coming for a long time, but Eddie had never spoken that way before. Tears filled her eyes. Was all they had worked for going to be thrown away so easily? Had she and Maestro Lombardi really pushed too hard? But she mustn't give in; there was so much to be done and so little time in which to do it. A successful début in Padova was only the first step. Rome, Milan, Paris, London, Buenos Aires and New York lay ahead. What should she do? Should she try to share his carefree mood at such a time?

She had to admit, in retrospect, that they hadn't had much fun recently, nor would they have much during the coming weeks and months if he was to master the lead in *Isabeau*. No! It could not be. She wiped the tears from her cheeks and her eyes shone with greater determination than ever. She would explain things to him when he came back, and sympathize with him. She would make him see that he was tired, that they were both tired, but that they could not afford to relax their schedule, even a little bit, at the moment. Their whole future was at stake.

Just then the door opened and Eddie came in. He rushed over to her and took her in his arms.

"My darling! Forgive me, my darling. I'm a stupid blockhead. How could I behave like that? You were right, as always."

The work began again. After a few moments, however, it was Bebe who stopped and said, "No, no more music today. We'll work twice as hard tomorrow."

Eddie added, "And the next day, and the next. Bebe, I owe everything to you. How can you be so sweet and patient with me? You'll never see me lose control of myself again." And she never did.

In May Edward had signed a contract to sing at the Teatro Comunale, Bologna. He had agreed to open the season in *Isabeau* and to sing Verdi's *Don Carlo* at 4,000 francs. The engagement was an important milestone in his career; it was vital that he gain the wholehearted approval of the Bologna public.

Rehearsals for *Isabeau* were to start on October 26, under Maestro Gino Marinuzzi, so the Johnsons left for Bologna on October 21. They took an apartment at 4 Via del Suzzo, and as soon as they were settled went to visit the noted Italian tenor Giuseppe Borgatti. Bebe asked Signora Borgatti to beg her husband to coach Edward, but it wasn't necessary for her to do so; he immediately and enthusiastically agreed. From that day, Edward went every morning to discuss the score and go over the part with Borgatti, who came to be almost like a brother to him.

On the opening night of *Isabeau,* November 12, 1912, the theatre was packed to the top. Edoardo had the public with him from the moment of Folco's aria in the first act. Later Bebe recorded: "The ice has broken and Bologna has accepted him. Borgatti and his daughter gave the signal for bravos during the performance, after having prepared Bologna to accept Edoardo as out-of-the-ordinary. Crowds of theatrical people had come from Milan for the performance. . . . After the first act, our dressing room was crowded to the door. At the end of the second act Edward received an imposing ovation. Enthusiasm kept up until the end of the performance. Bologna is won. Next morning there were the most wonderful press notices. The critic of *Avvenire,* known as the most difficult and hard to please, proclaimed it was 'a revelation.' "

Two days later, on November 14, rehearsals began for *Don Carlo.* Edward was worried about the tessitura of the duet in the fourth act, so Marinuzzi transposed it half a tone lower. Borgatti attended nearly all the rehearsals, and many of the artists were annoyed, but for Eddie it was reassuring.

The evening of November 22 was one of immense triumph for Di Giovanni. Many important people from the opera world were on hand that night, but the tenor's success in that performance was only the first of ten. All successive nine performances drew crowded houses, and Edoardo di Giovanni received enthusiastic approval from one and all. Bologna was his.

On December 7 he took part in an all-Verdi concert, a benefit to raise funds for a Verdi monument. He sang the trio from *Lombardi* with his colleagues Cappella and Benazzo, and the committee presented him with a porcelain group of "Love and Psyche." The next day he received a letter of thanks from the Music Academy of Bologna.

During successive performances of *Don Carlo*, Edoardo had visits from composers Franco Alfano and Giacomo Puccini, and from other greats of the music world. He made the acquaintance of baritone Mariano Stabile, and formed a close friendship with the baritone Luigi Montesanto and his wife.

Eddie could hardly believe the success he had had. Everyone was congratulating him and every manager wanted Edoardo di Giovanni in his company. Buldrini and the impresario of Bologna were profuse in their thanks and admiration. After performances, Bebe and Edoardo often went out for supper with the Marinuzzis. The Borgattis gave an afternoon in Johnson's honour. Famous personalities from all over Italy visited the couple, and several people who had formerly been Johnson's detractors became enthusiastic supporters.

EXCEPT FOR ONE performance of *La fanciulla del West* in Messina, Edoardo was in Bologna until after the last performance of *Don Carlo* on December 10. The only jarring note in the entire engagement was when he learned that Trentini, the tenor who sang the performances of *Isabeau* when Edoardo was otherwise engaged, went around speaking badly about him. And this after Johnson had spent many hours helping Trentini with the stage business and had been the first to applaud him in the role! Edoardo had the satisfaction, however, of hearing that Trentini had a limited success and was tolerated only because the public knew Di Giovanni could not possibly sing all of the performances.

Bebe wrote the family in Guelph that Edward was terribly tired but that they were both very happy. "We had eight performances of *Isabeau*, ten of *Don Carlo* and the Verdi concert here. Every performance a big success. The papers praised Edward's Don Carlo to the skies. May God be thanked for all graces received."

After that, the Johnsons went to Florence for a week, then left for Rome to fulfil the engagement at the Costanzi from December 15 to April 15. Edoardo was to sing *Don Carlo, Isabeau, Uguale Fortuna, Melenis* and *La fanciulla del West*.

When they arrived in Rome on December 18, Edward and Bebe went to the theatre and found themselves engaged immediately in a violent scene with Walter Mocchi, the director, and Madame Carelli, his wife, who acted as his assistant. They wanted Edward to agree to go to South America with some members of the company. Mocchi raved, discussed, argued and tore his hair, but to no avail. The Johnsons were adamant. The time was not ripe. Edward had already refused to go to the Teatro Colón in Buenos Aires, even though the director, Mancinelli, wrote him a private letter begging him to accept. After the argument subsided, they all went out to a restaurant and then attended a rehearsal of *La Walkiria*. Edward was by then accustomed to such Italian storms that came up and blew over with equal suddenness.

Rehearsals for *Don Carlo* began on December 27, with an impressive cast: Juanita Cappella as Elisabetta; Mattia Battistini as the Marquese di Posa; Nazzareno De Angelis as Filippo II; Luisa Garibaldi as Eboli. The conductor, Edoardo Vitale, was most cooperative, but the Johnsons were particularly impressed because the famous singer Battistini was kindness itself and predicted a great future for Di Giovanni.

After the opening night of *Don Carlo*, on January 4, 1913, Eddie wrote to his mother telling her who was in the cast and what his own reactions had been. "The rehearsals went magnificently, but a bad throat and nerves made the première unsteady. The public was disposed only toward the old favourites, and I was most coldly received. Battistini and Cappella had the theatre beautifully prepared and there was no chance for me. . . . The second and third performances went somewhat better, but I could not seem to make any ground. Then came a bad cold —almost pneumonia—and I went to bed for ten days. But don't worry, I'm alright now. Cappella was taken ill and so was Battistini. De Angelis and Garibaldi were called to La Scala, so *Don Carlo* ended a *vero disastro*."

The well-known critic Edoardo Pompei wrote in *Il Messagero,* however: "The tenor Edoardo di Giovanni—new for Rome, but noted for his recent successes—conquered in spite of the evident panic caused by the artistic problems."

Then, on February 8, 1913, came *Isabeau*, the first presentation of the Mascagni opera in Rome, and expectations ran high. After the opening, the critics were divided, but the public came for nineteen nights. Pompei spoke of the beautiful timbre of Di Giovanni's voice and the perfection of his vocal technique.

Eddie's next adventure was the creation of the tenor role in *Uguale Fortuna* by Maestro Vincenzo Tommasini opposite Gilda Dalla Rizza, with whom he was to sing often in succeeding years. Unfortunately that particular opera turned out to be a work in which he felt out of place and one he said he preferred to forget after its première, February 21.

Nevertheless, when Pompei reviewed the opening performance of *Uguale Fortuna* in *Il Messagero,* he was extravagant in his praise, especially of the tenor, Di Giovanni, and the baritone, Corradetti. The opera

50

itself was not an outstanding success, but the composer wrote Eddie a gracious letter: "We both know now how it is that you didn't sing my opera more than once. Let me tell you, nevertheless, how thankful I am to you for having sung my opera so well. I hope you will keep a little souvenir of my deep admiration and sincere sympathy. . . ." A copy of the score accompanied the note.

It was essential that every engagement be successful in those days, because Di Giovanni had been offered a contract at La Scala for the period September 15, 1913, to April 15, 1914, at 42,000 lire in all, with three months off during which he could sing wherever he chose.

He had asked for several considerations in the La Scala contract, and after his successes in Bologna the director, Mingardi, brought the contract around with all the modifications demanded. Mocchi, hearing of the contract, sent a furious telegram to Madame Carelli saying that Edoardo had failed in his duty as a friend; he had wanted him for the Costanzi for the 1913/14 season.

Meanwhile, there was still a portion of the current engagement to run. Edward's next role was in *Melenis* by Zandonai, an opera which had already been done at the Dal Verme theatre in Milan, though without success. It was hoped that the Costanzi production would improve the fortunes of the work. That was March 22, 1913.

Di Giovanni sang well, as did Pasini-Vitale opposite him, but though Edward found his own role of Marzio interesting, he said he felt the opera was "just not effective." The composer was delighted with his interpretation, however, and thanked him profusely. He also presented him with a copy of the score, together with the score of his previous work *Conchita*.

The reviews of *Melenis* added to Edoardo's rapidly growing reputation. The critics spoke of his vocal resilience and consummate artistry.

But his greatest success in Rome was yet to come—in an opera he had sung the previous year in Bergamo. It was Puccini's *La fanciulla del West*, which had its first production of the season on April 7, 1913. The role of Minnie was sung by Poli-Randaccio, who had just appeared in the opera at La Scala and who had also sung the part in Paris and Monte Carlo. All in all, it was an excellent production and received plaudits from both the press and the public.

Writing home, Edward remarked, "My newspaper criticisms were the best, and everybody conceded that it was the best thing I've done. We sang fourteen performances, the protagonista being Dalla Rizza, when Poli-Randaccio finished her contract. Again Dalla Rizza made an excellent impression. . . . Bebe used to help her [with her costume] so she looked like a young American girl."

The management of the theatre was delighted with the new tenor, and gave him quite a send-off at the last performance. There were large posters outside announcing the last performance of *Fanciulla* with tenor Di Giovanni. At the end of the second act there were many calls and bravos, and Edoardo was presented with a large laurel wreath and three huge baskets of flowers. Mme Emma Carelli also bestowed on him, in the name of the director, a magnificent pair of cuff links set with sapphires. And so ended the season in Rome—on a resounding note of triumph.

THE YEAR HAD BEEN gruelling and exacting. Eddie needed a rest and a change, and decided on a vacation in Canada. He and Bebe, with Fiorenza and Tata, arrived in New York, June 24, where they spent two days. While Eddie visited with his manager and attended to business, the others engaged in sightseeing. After that, they went to Niagara Falls for a day and, finally, to Guelph. The hometown paper reported: "Eddie Johnson home for a rest from Italy. Guelph boy, now one of the world's most famous tenors, has pleased the greatest Italian critics." The writer commented that because of Edward Johnson's natural modesty, "it was like pulling teeth to get an interview."

Replies to questions were evidently straightforward and brief. When asked what his intentions were, for example, Eddie said, "First to rest. I, and my voice, have worked hard, and we both need a rest. I do not wish, though my friends may think it is hard, to sing at all while I am here. I am here to rest and my friends will do me the greatest favour, if they just remember that I am Eddie Johnson, as of old, and let them meet me, but not make me sing. My maestro has ordered a rest—a complete rest—and I must obey."

Eddie and Bebe spent most of their vacation with family and friends in Guelph, but they also visited Eddie's brother Fred and his family in Bay City, Michigan, and called on an aunt in Detroit. They told everyone how impressed they were by the low price of seats in Italy that made it possible for Italians to hear an opera every time it was presented. What a difference there was, Eddie remarked, between his own background and that of the average Italian boy who at twelve, just starting to appreciate opera, was thoroughly familiar with five or more operas during his first year. He told them how excited Bebe and he had been one night, after the third performance of *Isabeau* in Rome, when they heard someone passing their house, near the theatre, whistling note for note the principal melody from the opera. It was especially surprising, Bebe interjected, inasmuch as Mascagni had gone into the modern field of composition and the music was more fragmentary and disjointed than usual. But the Italians were quick to absorb the melody of any opera.

Someone asked Eddie whether he thought his popular and financial success as Niki in *A Waltz Dream* in New York had given him the inspiration to study for grand opera. "It didn't give me the inspiration," Eddie replied, "but it did give me the cash."

An interview Eddie had given in New York, on his way to Canada that summer, appeared in the July 3, 1913, edition of *Musical America* under the heading: "Don't blame foreign prejudice for your failure in European opera, counsels Edward Johnson, latest operatic idol of Italy." The sub-heading was: "Be man enough to admit that you couldn't make good, urges young tenor to singers whose ventures turn out unhappily. Opposition to Americans not observed abroad by this artist. Repeated hearing of same operas makes Italians well informed and intolerant of bad singing, declares Edoardo di Giovanni." The article quoted Eddie at length about Maestro Lombardi, who had meant so much to him in his studies and on whom he depended greatly in his career. Yes, Maestro Lombardi had been ill, as reported, but he was now hale and hearty. The comment was made at the request of Lombardi who wished to nullify reports that he was no longer able to teach. Actually, the determined maestro had taken several cures but was still in much pain and was convinced he would find relief "only in Paradise." Meanwhile, he didn't want anyone to think of him as ill. Dedicated musician that he was, he forgot his pain while teaching, he said. So, with tears in his eyes, he had begged Eddie to dispel the rumours that he was closing his studio and giving up teaching.

Bebe and Eddie were enthusiastic as they described Maestro Lombardi to the family that summer: "He has a nature that can hardly be described by any other word than adorable, and he is like a father to all of us. With his white hair and beard, he is quite fatherly and venerable in appearance. . . . Each of his lessons is for three-quarters of an hour and the remaining fifteen minutes he devotes to rest. That is, he may wander around the house, read a paper, or do anything else that will rest his brain. With this sort of schedule, he is unable to teach more than twenty-five pupils or so in a week. There are over fifty applying, so many are disappointed. His chief aim is naturalness. He believes that if we put into our singing the full meaning of the lines, we can scarcely help portraying the character with dramatic force. He has a little stage in his studio, where he puts a singer through his roles. Edoardo, for instance, was ready for *Andrea Chénier* because the maestro had rehearsed him there in the entire part."

At the end of their vacation, in August, the Johnsons stopped off in

Toronto for a couple of days en route to New York and the boat back to Italy. On shipboard, Eddie and Bee talked about the signing of the La Scala contract that had been done in their house in Rome. He had been offered a début in *Un ballo in maschera,* but had refused it. There had been much soul-searching and worrying as to whether or not he had done right. What would replace it? Perhaps he would be asked to do something of much less importance, or perhaps he would be allowed to create the role of Parsifal, as he hoped. In the end, it had been decided that he would make his début in the title role in Wagner's *Parsifal.* It was to be the first Italian production of the opera.

So it was with great expectations that Edward and Bebe looked forward to Europe again and to the important début at La Scala. They had been living frugally but comfortably through the years, wasting neither time nor energy as they worked toward the goal of La Scala. Their home that fall was Pensione Lelli, 3 Via Collestro, in Florence. But the La Scala contract would mean moving to Milan.

What concerned Eddie now, however, was that word had come that La Scala would not need him for rehearsals until November 22. This meant his pay would not start until December 15. He talked it over with Bee and after much figuring they came to the conclusion that they could not only manage, but, if they were very careful, they would be able to spend the month of September on the Riviera! Eddie didn't question the decision; it was such a delightful prospect. He hated to admit it, but the time in Guelph had not been much of a vacation. Too much to do, too many places to go, too many people to see.

The Riviera was relaxing and wonderful. The Di Giovannis spent their time bathing, eating, and rambling in the woods and mountains, then they went to Florence for "two glorious months." They took long walks around Florence, up to Fiesole and into the countryside. The air was warm, caressing and balmy. Bebe spoke of "a thin veil of Indian gold, that gently caressed the trees, blending in various shades of russet and copper." In such a setting, it was easy to lose track of the realities of life.

Arthur Higinbotham, who visited Edward and Bebe on their return to Florence, wrote to his brother Harry: "I was especially surprised to note the tremendous progress Eddie Johnson has made, not only in his voice culture, but generally. He speaks Italian with a marked fluency and correctness that is quite unusual, and the same applies to his French. Of course, he has had an unusual advantage in having such an intellectual wife whose knowledge of the language is phenomenal, and permits of no laxity on Eddie's part in the speaking. She just holds him up and makes him say it correctly at the time, and wherever an error is made. This applies to their work at the piano as well. My visit to Florence and Pisa was made particularly agreeable; their knowledge of things Florentine being by no means superficial, and there is much to know of its prodigious wealth and treasures."

On November 5, 1913, Bebe went off to Milan to look for an apartment. She wrote enthusiastically to Edoardo: "Saw a flat, more central, but also small—two bedrooms, three beds in all, and a salon and dining room all in one—a lovely bathroom and kitchen, but I thought we would be too crowded with the maid and nurse [Tata] and Baby sharing the same room, and one room for us. And in case of company, such as Fifi or anyone else, we would all go crazy huddled up in such a small place! I found another apartment, not too far away from La Scala, and grabbed it for 350 a month—but in the end I changed my mind in favour of another one for 250, on the top floor (the fourth). There's no lift!" And that seemed to be that, but Eddie was not sure what the final decision would be, knowing Bebe as he did. She had to be careful of money, they both knew, because the trip back to America had drained them financially. He was not surprised, nevertheless, when another letter, the next day, informed him: "I liked the 350 one so much better that I decided it was worth it."

After several final and blissful days in Florence, Bebe and Edward took Fiorenza and Tata and moved to Milan on November 22, 1913. But they knew that wherever they were they could always count on the fatherly interest and attention of Maestro Lombardi. One of his letters tore their hearts, for he told them that he had been taking the cure, but that he was in as much pain as ever, repeating that he expected relief "only in Paradise." Of course, there was little chance he would be able to attend Eddie's La Scala début toward which he had worked so hard. Early in the previous February, the maestro had become seriously ill, although he had continued his teaching, refusing to talk about himself and, in fact, actually forgetting his pain in his enthusiasm for his pupils. He had not seen his Edoardo as often as he would have liked, inasmuch as his pupil's rehearsals and engagements kept him moving all over Italy. When Eddie did return to Florence, between engagements, he was always shocked by the change in his beloved maestro. What was it? The doctors did not seem to be able to give a definite diagnosis, nor to do anything to give him much relief. In pain as he was, nevertheless, his thoughts were always with Edoardo and singing. He was constantly sending letters, giving suggestions as to what operas Eddie should or should not accept, the people he should or should not depend on, and invariably closing his letters with "eternal embraces and deep affection."

Eddie and Bebe kept hoping that he would be able to join them in

Milan for *Parsifal*. But at the end of November the Di Giovannis received a letter from the ailing maestro that completely dashed all their hopes of having him there. He was in Naples, Lombardi explained, where he had been subjected to three operations and to "atrocious" suffering from the effects of the medicine the doctors were giving him. He said he felt "they are only experimenting, with no result except to completely destroy me." He was heartbroken that he would not be able to attend Eddie's début in *Parsifal*, and even more unhappy that he could not work with him daily on the role.

Nevertheless, the Johnsons continued to receive letters from the maestro advising Eddie how he should work on *Parsifal*: "You must study it in depth—everything that is written about the poem, the mysticism, philosophy and the music. If I can return to Florence I will send you several books to read which treat these important arguments . . . but it would be so much better to have the opportunity of working with you in the creation of the character . . . you must be scrupulous in your study and know this great part thoroughly and intimately."

EDDIE'S DÉBUT at La Scala was a signal occasion—the first time that *Parsifal* had been staged in Italy. In the distinguished audience were composers Boito, Mascagni, Puccini, Montemezzi, Zandonai among others; leading conductors, headed by Mancinelli; many of the great artists, past and present; correspondents from all over Italy and critics from abroad. These, in addition to the regular Milanese public—subscribers whose boxes were passed down from generation to generation, as Canadians pass down hockey tickets—packed the house.

As was understandable on such a special occasion, everyone backstage was nervous. Oddly enough, Edward Johnson was probably the least nervous of all, inasmuch as he was so new to the opera game and had known nothing but a long series of successes since his début barely two years previously. Besides, he was somewhat like a race horse before a race—filled with so much excitement that fear had little place in his emotions. "Aren't you nervous?" Bee asked him. "I'm frozen stiff, for the first time in my life."

Eddie could not understand her. Nor could he understand why the older members of the cast were so surprised that he had a smile on his face, when they were all petrified with fright over the momentousness of the occasion.

"Aren't you nervous?" they asked him, one after another, incredulously.

*Si, certo!* was his reply. *Ma farò il meglio ch'è possibile; non posso fare di più.*

56

The evening of January 9, 1914, proved to be one of those historic occasions in the distinguished annals of La Scala. As Bebe wrote a friend, Professor Stark Young, in New York: "After the first act, the public rose en masse and gave the artists nine curtain calls. Everything was perfect—orchestra, show, staging, and the single parts entrusted to first-class artists, produced an ensemble which has been proclaimed unique among the different editions of *Parsifal* given even at Bayreuth. Edward was the only newcomer to Milano, and his was a hard battle for the artist is a giant in his line. Do you fear? Don't! He won his battle with the highest honours and is now placed as one of the leading tenors, and according to many of the judges, the *first!*"

With their heads together, Bebe and Edoardo avidly read the reviews and headlines. *Il grande successo del* Parsifal *alla Scala* headed one review which included a glowing report of the tenor: ". . . Parsifal made a sudden entrance on the scene, after the death of the swan, and truly he was a Parsifal one had read about in the poem—tall, young, handsome, innocent, covered only with a brief tunic. The tenor Di Giovanni had understood the character . . . every detail was studied and digested and presented with the greatest dignity. . . . There was an excellent blend of voices in the scene between Parsifal and Kundry . . . an acute and lively interpretation of the theme." That review went on to say that during the scene with Kundry, Parsifal and Klingsor, "the public interrupted in a furious applause four different times. It was an exceptional *Parsifal*. Also, Di Giovanni appeared worthy of the highest praise. His voice is a warm timbre and he has a fine appearance, his manner of phrasing is very clean. The diction is good and clear, and, above all, Di Giovanni met every exterior detail of the role, with his interpretative gestures, the *truccatura*, the costumes, with taste and intelligence."

The Johnsons were on what they called "giddy heights" after that, and found it difficult to keep their feet on the ground.

"But we're doing it," Eddie wrote home. "Our heads are just as steady as before." To which Bee added, "God be praised, we can face all this happiness in a humble and peaceful state of mind, just as though we were still in old Via Solferino in Florence. I would kick myself if I could detect the slightest symptoms of change."

By this time, Edward had found out that his pay was reduced from 42,000 lire to 27,000 lire because the three months of the season during which he had been inactive had been deducted from his salary. The contract was faulty: a lawsuit would have settled matters to Edward's advantage, but he didn't even contemplate such a proceeding, as a suit against La Scala would have ruined his prospects.

Lucy Weidt left *Parsifal* for engagements in Berlin, and was replaced as Kundry by Margot Kaftal, a Polish soprano already known at La Scala. "She only made the public appreciate Weidt, to whom full justice has not been done," Bee reported. Galeffi was replaced as Amfortas by Angelo Scandiana—"a sad change." In order to free Eddie for his new role in *L'Ombra di Don Giovanni*, the great Italian Wagnerian tenor Borgatti, who had been such a good friend when the Johnsons first arrived in Italy, was called in to sing *Parsifal,* and responded with alacrity. Bebe told in her diary of the public's reaction: "He was going to show Milan a Parsifal—yes—so he did. We went to the first night—it was pathetic; in some points it became grotesque—in others he was great. It showed what mere instinct can do, without a basis on which to work. He was Siegfried, Tristan—but *not* Parsifal. The press was cruel to its favourite of one time. His downfall was Edward's final victory over the Milanese public who had, up until then, been doubtful about the 'new tenor.' Next day he was 'great.' *Sic transit gloria mundi.* I can't complain. The box holders demanded that Edward should take up Parsifal again.

"Meanwhile," Bee noted, "the rehearsals of *L'Ombra* proceeded among a million incidents. Alfano [the composer] had everyone against him, from the Duke of Modrone to the last chorus man. The difficulty of the work excited them all against him. Fights, rows, discussions—nothing lacked to make things lively. Tito Ricordi's behaviour to him was unfair and insincere. Serafin was equally so. Marinuzzi tried his best to preserve a calm face, but he saw how everything was."

It was a great honour creating the part of Don Miguel Manara (Don Giovanni), but it was quite difficult to be working on both *L'Ombra* and *Parsifal* at the same time. The Alfano work aroused a great deal of speculation and talk, not only for its subject, but for the fact that the composer was well-known in Italy for his symphonic works. What would his opera be like?

Looking at the score, and going over it with Bebe as well as with the composer, Edward was enthusiastic. It gave him a marvellous opportunity to show everything he had learned, both as an actor and as a singer. In addition he felt a heavy responsibility for the success of the work, since Alfano was a close personal friend. As he said to the composer one day, "I feel this opera is going to be a great success. Of course, no one knows how the mass of the public will take to it, but I don't see how it can fail."

Alfano was the type of man who knew the public taste, at least in symphonic music. He had high artistic ideals and his previous scores had achieved sensational success as seen by box-office sales. He and his wife, and Edward and Bebe were inseparable during those days, and all four of them were filled with great expectations. Later, when the Johnsons looked back on the whole experience, they found that the first performance of *L'Ombra di Don Giovanni,* April 2, 1914, was an unforgettable night, although not an altogether happy one.

Bebe sat in the director's box with Marta Alfano (wife of the composer). "Poor little Marta. She saw what was coming halfway through the first act, but she was very brave," she told Eddie later. "She was a brick and steered steadily through the storm. After the first act, which was really the best and most effective, you remember the applause was weak and controlled? Remember how I told you I went down and found Franco all alone at the end of the performance—the ship deserted by rats when wreckage is near? He was as pale as death itself. I brought him into our *camerino* and tried to disguise the fact, but he laughed in my face and in Marta's too. I'm not at all sure you knew any of this was going on. For you, the very difficulty of the work and the height of the tessitura signified a triumph. Those who doubted the extension of your voice gave in. As a creation, I think your impersonation of Don Giovanni was your best. I think you never appeared to better advantage as a singer or as an actor, and you really looked as if you had stepped out of a Van Dyck picture. You saved the opera from a clamorous fall, of course."

Ricordi, Serafin, Clausetti (of the review *Symphonia*), all called Di Giovanni the "saviour of the evening." But *L'Ombra* just didn't work. All of Alfano's dreams and ambitions were shattered. The day after the opening, he was treated as a failure. Such is the fickleness of the public that Alfano's symphonic successes were forgotten. As an opera composer, he was a failure. Therefore, to the Italians, he was a failure. Only his wife fought and believed.

Eddie had the good fortune to have many close friends in Milan that season. He and Bebe spent as much time as possible, for example, with the Marronis, from Florence, who were most sympathetic about the *L'Ombra* fiasco.

"Just a moment," Bebe said calmly one evening when they were talking about the opera. "It certainly was not all bad for Edoardo. Of course, the critics did say that his Parsifal was truly a revelation, but they said that in *L'Ombra di Don Giovanni* he made a great impression on the public for the power of his voice, his clean style and phrasing, and the intensity and variety of his dramatic portrayal. They said it was wonderful."

"It *was* wonderful," the Marronis agreed.

"I wish they had said a few kind words at least about Franco," was Eddie's comment. "Not a single word!"

Meanwhile, papers and magazines in Italy and in the United States featured headlines bearing the name of Edoardo di Giovanni and telling the story of "Italy's sensational new tenor," who had made the giant leap in four short years from Broadway to La Scala.

It may have been the responsibility of family life that helped Bebe and Edward keep their heads in those days. Or it may have been Edward's need to stay in condition for his performances, or perhaps it was the pleasure they derived from a few minutes with Fiorenza, something that the applause of five thousand people could not touch. Then, again, it may have been the intense cold of Milan "clothed in snow for two weeks." Whatever the reason, the fact is that somehow they managed to hold steady despite Eddie's sudden acclaim.

If they were at a party all Eddie had to say to Bee was, "Let's go home." It was part of the formula they had developed for keeping out of trouble when he had reached the limit of his endurance and patience. He had learned to control his temper, and Bee was proud of that accomplishment. She had worked very hard to help him see that he could win much more, even among the volatile Italians, by smiles than by angry outbursts. "Save your energies for more constructive use," had been her maxim.

Fiorenza was a constant joy with her smiles, imagination, trust and confidence, and always full of surprises—like the day she amazed some friends who had dropped in by actually singing bits from *Parsifal*. Everyone said it was amazing for a child of three to retain such music and words. Eddie and Bee beamed with pride.

It was a glamorous life, even though they were too busy to appreciate it—a successful life, but a hectically busy one. Oftentimes both Bebe and Edward were too tired to enjoy anything. The baby was always a source of relaxation, but they were even forced to be away from her all too often.

"It was not for nothing that they have spoken of you, my darling, my Gounod," Bee told him, "as *una vera rivelazione* after *Parsifal*–they are only discovering what I have known from the first. It has all been worth it—La Scala now; next Paris, Buenos Aires and the Metropolitan in New York."

"I know all too well what can happen at the Metropolitan," he responded wearily.

"What about Berlin, darling?"

"Yes, you were right," he admitted. "It would be foolish for me to go to Berlin. I am not a heldentenor. I can sing some of the Wagner roles, but to try to live with them all the time would be—what did you call it?—a colossal mistake. That is not my *Fach* as the Germans say."

Bebe was a demanding helpmate, but she also kept in personal touch with people and cultivated everyone who could possibly be of use in Edward's career. Carlo Giametti in Paris, for example, who wrote that he "hoped to have something about the season in Paris for you in a few days," ended his letter with "many kisses to your dear little girl."

It was early in 1914 that the impresario of the Costanzi, Signora Carelli, had come forward with a most exciting idea: an international operatic syndicate. The proposal called for a permanent annual company, dividing its time among the Teatro Costanzi in Rome, from December 25 to April 25 each season, the Paris Opéra for the month of May, Covent Garden in London for June and July, the municipal theatres of Rio de Janeiro and Sao Paulo in Brazil from September 1 to October 10, the Urquisa at Montevideo and the Coliseo at Buenos Aires from October 15 to November 15. The time from November 15 to December 15 would be taken up by the return boat trip to Italy. The entire proposal had special merit inasmuch as it was a joint idea between Signora Carelli and her husband, Walter Mocchi, who had directed the Costanzi since 1910. He had entrusted the affairs of the opera house to Emma Carelli after she retired from the stage as a singer. Signor Mocchi was also the impresario for STIN (La Società Teatrale Internazionale e Nazionale).

Plans were drawn up and details carefully worked out. Edoardo di Giovanni had been one of the first artists approached with the idea. He and Bebe thought it sounded "very, very interesting," but wanted to think it over and wait until the financial basis was more secure before committing themselves. It looked good, however, and would guarantee year-round employment for the artists. For the companies, it meant a great variety of repertoire and the amortizing of production expenses among all the theatres involved. What time would he have left for the big theatres—La Scala, Berlin, the Metropolitan, and the Teatro Colón— Eddie wondered. Many of the other artists, as well as the conductors and directors, were asking the same question. Nor did the scheme receive unanimous approval insofar as the theatres themselves were concerned. In the final analysis, it was a brave and brilliant plan, but it failed to materialize.

Perhaps it was just as well, Edward and Bebe agreed, as they sat in their modest apartment in Milan one evening in April before leaving the next day for Florence. They were both tired to the point of exhaustion from the long hours of hard work and from the tension of performances —Edward was desperately nervous before every appearance now, something he was never able to overcome throughout his long career. The backstage fights, rows, discussions, the ordeal of *L'Ombra di Don Giovanni,* coupled with the unhappiness for their friend, Alfano, and the

*Parsifal* début had all taken their toll. But, suddenly, the Johnsons both burst out laughing, from the sheer relief of having nothing to do. It was the first relaxed moment they had had for months. Then Eddie jumped up. "Oh, I almost forgot!" He took a paper from his pocket and waved it exuberantly before Bee's eyes. "Look at this!"

"Edward, do be serious! What is it?"

"My contract for La Scala for next season."

It was just cause for celebration—a contract from December, 1914, to April, 1915: fourteen performances in a new type of role for Eddie, Loge, in the La Scala production of Wagner's *L'Oro del Reno (Das Rheingold)* in Italian; sixteen performances of Catalani's opera *Loreley*; and four performances of the new work by Pizzetti *Fedra*.

The next day, April 22, they left for Florence. There was renewed peace and joy in their hearts. They loved Florence and felt at home there as in no other spot. There were tears of happiness in Maestro Lombardi's eyes as he embraced them both. *Bacioni infiniti*, he murmured. *Auguri e saluti, carissimo Edoardo, di successo trionfale.* He had many words of advice about *Don Carlo*—and wanted to review the score with his pupil the next day, before rehearsals began, in spite of Edoardo's great success in the opera in Bologna in 1912. The maestro was elated over the new La Scala contract and the offers from the Colón, but advised that nothing be said about either until the new Costanzi contract came through. In his opinion, the manager Lusardi could best arrange Edoardo's affairs: "He knows the situations well, and you can have complete confidence in his counsel, which is wise and honest."

May of that year (1914) proved to be a month of decisions as well as added successes for Eddie. It began on the third of the month with Verdi's *Don Carlo* at the Politeamo in Florence. He considered the role of Don Carlo an unattractive one for him, even though he had a great personal triumph in it. Only one reviewer was even slightly negative. "Perhaps you should have paid him, as he wanted," Bebe suggested.

"How can you say that to me?" Eddie was momentarily furious. "I won't give in to bribing at any time, you know that."

He had a contract for twelve performances of *Don Carlo* at 800 francs each. Most of the artists were those with whom he had sung the opera previously: Juanita Cappella, Carlo Walter, Luigi Montesanto, Ria Berlalucci, a newcomer, as Eboli, and Sebastiano Cirotta, the Inquisitor. The conductor was Carmago Guarnieri.

As Edoardo's star kept rising, he and Bee were sought after socially, but kept very much to themselves. Things had gone well, but they were still very ambitious, and they knew they had to continue to "deliver" in order to reach their goal. That meant work. They risked turning their backs on most overtures for favour from society figures. The Marchese Orazio Capello, for example, turned against them when they refused to be drawn into his social circle. "We kept our ground and our peace," Bebe recorded. "God be praised."

In a letter dated May 20, 1914, Lusardi finally advised Edoardo that he felt the time had come for the tenor to consider the Metropolitan. Gatti-Casazza would be coming to Italy that summer, he told him, to sign contracts with various artists for the 1915/16 season at the Metropolitan. Eddie was tempted, in spite of the fact that he still felt his repertoire was insufficient for entering such a big house. Then his anger flared. Lusardi was only thinking of the money!

"Dear Mr. Blood," Eddie began a letter to him. Bee, who had come in just then and was looking over his shoulder, exclaimed. Eddie laughed, and changed the salutation.

"It was only a first draft anyway," he explained, as he went on to thank Lusardi, politely, for his letter.

"It's contents were rather a surprise, I must confess," he wrote. "However, if you think the moment has come to consider a contract with the Metropolitan of New York, I must certainly let myself be guided by your advice. The place I have reached in my career under your direction is the best proof of your wise and able judgment. Still, I beg of you to think well on the fact that I have absolutely no repertoire which coincides with that of the New York theatre, with the exception of *Fanciulla del West*. The other operas, *Isabeau, Chénier, Don Carlo,* are never done, nor is *Loreley,* and the Wagner operas are always sung in German. Under no circumstances will I accept to go as utility, and, in fact, unless Mr. Gatti can offer something really extraordinary, I prefer to remain in Italy."

When Wolfsohn, in New York, also began pushing him, just for the sake of the money Eddie felt, he was even more furious, and made up his mind to wait. A second letter from Wolfsohn specifically urged him to accept a contract with the Metropolitan. He put Wolfsohn's letter aside rather impatiently. "If they would just show me the contract they're talking about, I could tell them better what to do. I've already said I would not accept to go as utility, and I've already given them my terms." Eddie didn't answer the letter.

Words from Tissot's *La Russie et les Russes* flashed through Edward's mind: *En fait, d'ancêtres, un homme doit être satisfait, s'il a su pour père un honnête homme.* Nevertheless, he was confused. He planned to take the problem to Maestro Lombardi, his "father in heart."

Meanwhile a letter came from Lusardi that left him in an even greater quandary. He was in perfect accord, it said, that Edward should *not* go to the Metropolitan unless the management offered the right conditions. "Nevertheless," Lusardi added, "one must not forget the fact that it is not every day that one has an offer from a theatre such as the Metropolitan, and sometimes it is necessary to take an opportunity when it presents itself." He wanted to know what Edward's ideas were about the Met so that he could go over the situation with Gatti-Casazza when he saw him in Milan in the middle of June.

On June 17, 1914, Edward Johnson received word from the Wolfsohn Bureau that they had written to Otto Kahn of the Met's Board about him. Mr. Adams, the Wolfsohn representative, stated: "Beneath the surface I know positively that Gatti-Casazza is not favourable to Americans. On the other hand, Mr. Kahn is one of the most broadminded, clever businessmen, in addition to which he has a wonderful musical intelligence, etc." Adams felt sure, he said, that Kahn would mention Edward's name at the Paris Opéra that summer and also look him up at La Scala.

There were constant decisions to be made, but the world seemed to belong to Edoardo di Giovanni in 1914. Italy officially recognized the young tenor's achievements by making him a Cavaliere della Corona d'Italia, an honour bestowed by King Victor Emmanuel III.

JUST AS EVERYTHING seemed to be progressing so smoothly for Edoardo, several tragic elements intruded. The rest of Europe was torn by political and territorial rivalries that came to a head with the assassination, by a Serbian nationalist, of Archduke Francis Ferdinand of Austria-Hungary on June 28, 1914. Even though Italy was not directly involved, war in Europe seemed imminent.

Edoardo di Giovanni knew that a great chapter in his life had ended. New times and new problems for him and his Beatrice lay ahead. They would go to Maestro Lombardi and talk things over. They would have a long and understanding visit; he would put everything in perspective and give them a feeling of security again. When they arrived in Florence, looking forward to that meeting, they learned that their beloved maestro was too weak and in too much pain to rise from his bed. They looked at each other in dismay. Would they ever again see the elegant tall figure coming to embrace them?

When they entered the maestro's room, they almost gasped at the ravages his illness had wrought in just a few short days. The handsome head on the pillows was the same, but the face, behind the neatly trimmed and characteristically elegant moustache, was pale and drawn, and his eyes, usually so direct and full of enthusiasm, seemed like pale dots at the end of unfathomable tunnels. Only at one point did he seem

64

to be his old self for a few moments, as he spoke warm and affectionate words of praise and good wishes for his pupil. Then in the beloved accent they knew so well, he admonished Edoardo, as he had done so many hundreds of times, not to neglect his breathing exercises and not to forget to be true to his own talent. "Keep your head high, your jaw loose and stand straight."

The old man smiled as he said that, for the lessons of posture Edward had learned from Captain Clark in Guelph had pleased Lombardi immensely from the start. "Have confidence in yourself; you have a great gift and a great heart and a great helpmate in your loving Bebe. A big career and life lie before you. Be true to the wish of your old maestro who thinks of you always as a beloved son. You have made me very proud and happy."

As his voice began to fade, they heard him saying, almost to himself, *Bacioni infiniti alla angelica Fiorenza.* He murmured affectionate thanks for their prayers, and spoke of paternal embraces to them both. Then, faintly, he repeated Beethoven's words, that he had adopted as the motto for his studio—they felt he was repeating them for himself in that hour of sorrow and pain: *Pazienza, perseveranza, costanza, fiducia in se stesso, saper sperare ed attendere.*

They slipped out of the room and took leave of Signora Lombardi. A few days later, Vincenzo Lombardi was taken to Germany where the new miraculous cures were supposed to relieve his suffering. But on July 21, 1914, Edward received the sombre black-bordered note from Signora Lombardi. The maestro was gone.

Edward and Bebe had always felt there were three of them facing the world as long as Lombardi lived. Now they were alone; they would have to make their decisions without his wise counsel. In that moment they felt closer together than ever before, and Bebe uttered a special prayer: "God be thanked for all the goodness we have received—for Edward's success, for our dear sweet Fiorenza, for dear, faithful Tata, for our health, for our good friends, for our love for each other."

It was hard for Eddie to think of singing without Lombardi. Besides, he was tired. His first season at La Scala had been hard, but now he was on the top, mentioned beside such artists as Claudia Muzio, Zenatello, Scotti, Lucrezia Bori and others. He had sung twenty-seven performances of *Parsifal* and four of Alfano's *L'Ombra di Don Giovanni* at La Scala, and twelve performances of *Don Carlo* in Florence, and ahead of him was *Loreley,* under Toscanini's direction. But on July 28, 1914, Austria-Hungary declared war on Serbia and the *Loreley* production was cancelled.

With Serbia backed by Russia, the latter's mobilization precipitated

Germany's declaration of war on Russia (August 1). Two days later, convinced that France was about to attack her western frontier, Germany declared war on France and marched across Luxembourg and Belgium. The violation of the Belgian neutrality caused Great Britain to enter the war. Italy still was not involved, but she was affected and everyone feared that the time was short before she would be forced into the war.

That winter Edoardo di Giovanni sang four performances of the role of Loge in *L'Oro del Reno* at La Scala to Giuseppe de Luca's Alberich. After the première, on December 20, 1914, *La Sera* reported that Di Giovanni "was a most intelligent Loge, being able to conjure all the grotesque efforts of that character and still give even more importance to his fickle character. As a singer, we found in him the exquisite, impeccable diction that we have already admired last year."

The Milan première of Catalani's *Loreley* finally took place at La Scala on February 5, 1915, conducted by Gino Marinuzzi. Carlo Monticelli commented in *La Sera*: "The most highly valued tenor gave shining proof of his magnificent vocal interpretative gifts."

Next came the world première of Pizzetti's *Fedra* (March 20), again under the baton of Marinuzzi. Reviewers spoke of Di Giovanni as "an Ippolito of bold, fearless bearing," although the opera itself did not meet with much favour. The libretto, based on D'Annunzio's tragedy, was criticized as being dry and verbose. Pizzetti agreed, but he had been too young and inexperienced to insist on the cuts he said were necessary, and he was still too young as a composer to capture the hearts of the characters in his music. Knowing the limitations of his work, he was profusely grateful to Edoardo di Giovanni for his contribution to the presentation.

Opening night of the new opera had brought a record crowd to the theatre. Notables included the Conte di Torino and the Duca di Bergamo, Alberto di Savoia. At the end of the first act of the opera, according to the *Corriere della Sera,* "there were four calls for the author, the artists and Maestro Marinuzzi. There were also four after the second and four after the third and tremendous applause after the threnody. The tenor Di Giovanni was ideally suited to the role of the young hunter, making a strong and convincing impact and singing in bold phrases." It went on to say he "exhibited a rare vocal and interpretive talent. The ardour and warmth of his characterization of the hero manifested itself from the time of his first entrance. His physical appearance and the vibrant tone of his voice immediately conquered the public . . . *e quando egli ebbe trionfato dell'aggressiva cupidigia carnale di* Fedra . . . he triumphed in the opinion of everyone. It was, for us, *un completo successo.*"

During rehearsals and performances, a close friendship grew up between the Pizzettis, Ildebrando and Maria, and the Di Giovannis. They were all near the same age, and all were beginning to experience the joys as well as the disappointments attendant to a musical career. Among Edward and Bebe's other friends in those days were Marinuzzi, Borgatti, Mariano Stabile, Tullio Serafin, the then-young Arturo Toscanini, Pertile, Franco Alfano, Gigli, Montesanto, the La Scala impresario Buldrini, leading artists, directors and conductors, and members of the nobility. Edoardo di Giovanni was a star.

Although Italy entered the war on May 23, 1915, the Italians continued to take opera as a part of everyday living. To the Italian public, opera was as widely popular as bull-fighting in Spain and baseball in the United States. As one writer put it, "An Italian goes to the theatre to be amused, to be thrilled, to get, in short, his money's worth. Of course he is intolerant, because he is finely critical; he does not like to be cheated. He can be as ardent in his praise as he can be bitter in his condemnation."

Like New York in 1899, all of Italy, in 1915, was exciting to the young tenor from Guelph. When he entered any Italian theatre or restaurant, no matter how large or how small, he was immediately recognized and treated as a celebrity. Nevertheless, with ninety-six opera houses in Italy closed that summer, Eddie signed up with Chautauqua circuit concerts in Canada and the United States and returned to America in spite of warnings about wartime danger in trans-Atlantic crossings. Eddie had certain lucrative concert and festival commitments he wanted to fulfill in addition to the Chautauqua appearances. Besides, with Europe about to be plunged even deeper into a general war, he and Bee both thought it wise to visit his parents, with Fiorenzina, before the situation became worse.

It turned out to be a good and remarkably peaceful summer for them after the wartime tensions in Italy. Singing in the Chautauqua tents, after the glamour of Italy's finest opera houses, was quite an experience, but to Eddie's surprise he found he liked it. He liked being close to people; liked to relax and be himself; liked to joke and tell a story now and then. For him, the summer was over all too soon, and he was on his way back to Italy.

Bee and Eddie had come to rely more and more on Tata, whose devotion to Fiorenza could not have been more complete had the child been her own. No worries when "baby" was left with her, and Tata was as much a part of Fiorenza's life as her father and mother. It was Tata, with her ready sense of humour, who often kept the Johnsons from losing theirs. When things got rough and they were overtired, it was she, with her wholesomely earthy philosophy, who helped them regain their own perspective and outlook.

Fiorenza supplied her share of diversion in those days also. Having been given a diet of bedtime stories of the operas, instead of children's fairy tales, her favourite indoor sport was to wrap herself in an old leopard rug and pretend she was Siegfried, or dress up in one of her mother's negligées and, still with Siegfried's helmet on her head, pretend she was Brünnhilde. There were also embarrassing moments. In cases when her father's role in an opera called for him to be hit by another character, audiences in Rome, Milan or Bologna might hear her childish voice pipe up with a warning cry: "Stop it! That's my Daddy!"

The year 1915 brought a shower of offers from Italy, South America and the United States. When Eddie insisted he still was not ready, Buldrini remonstrated, "If other artists are going to America, why not you?"

Eddie was engaged to sing *Manon Lescaut, Andrea Chénier* and *Isabeau* at the Costanzi between December 28, 1915, and February 14, 1916, billed as the *primo tenore*. He received 6,000 lire, with 5 per cent commission to be deducted, and the contract, signed by Emma Carelli, stipulated that Edoardo di Giovanni was not to sing more than four times in any one week, and not more than two performances in succession, particularly not a matinée on the afternoon following a performance the night before.

In spite of the fact that most of Italy's important theatres were closed due to wartime conditions, the season's first production of *Manon Lescaut* in Rome, January 9, 1916, was a gala affair, and a glittering list of royalty and other notables attended. The *Cronache Teatrale* gave a long and glowing report of the performance as a whole, noting that the great applause that began for Di Giovanni after the first act aria grew in intensity during the evening.

After ten performances of *Manon Lescaut* at the Costanzi, and eight performances each of *Andrea Chénier* and *Isabeau*, there was unfailing praise for the tenor. In the case of *Manon Lescaut*, for example, one reviewer wrote: *Canto l'intera parte senzo risparmiarsi smoggiando i suoi robusti mezzi e ottendo applausi convinci e calorosi.*

All over Italy there was a lack of personnel, artists and money, because of the war, and theatres were operating on spasmodic and curtailed schedules. Even La Scala was threatened. Limited wartime finances there brought about a shortened season and austerity measures until the "Victory Celebration" performance of *Mefistofele* on November 19,

1918, conducted by Arturo Toscanini. (Later, the house was closed for extensive renovations. It reopened December 26, 1921.)

With the country in the midst of war, tensions mounting and the future insecure, many La Scala artists took kindly to the suggestion of a South American tour. As for Eddie, he would have preferred to go to the United States and Canada, but had not arranged any bookings. Then, too, with the North Atlantic submarine-infested, it was not a particularly safe place to be. A crossing to South America sounded less dangerous.

Many of the La Scala artists refused to take the risk of leaving the country, but the majority were in favour of it. It meant being away for five months, but they would all be travelling with their families. So arrangements were made, a repertoire of twenty-two operas chosen and performances agreed upon for Buenos Aires, Rio de Janeiro and Montevideo.

Perhaps young Edoardo di Giovanni and his wife had less time to ponder the dangers of the trip than many of the older artists who were not involved in learning and rehearsing new roles. Each time that Bebe found herself worrying about the possibility of the ship's being sunk by torpedoes, she was consoled, as all the other wives were, by the knowledge that everything she valued in the world would be with her: Edward, Fiorenza and Tata. Edward, for his part, said he would worry when he was on the boat!

All precautions were taken, and everyone hoped that they would escape a German submarine attack in the crossing. Edward and Bebe sent Tata ahead to Genoa with their luggage and to get things settled in their stateroom. When they arrived for the midnight sailing, the ship was all dark. There were no lights. Even the waters looked ominously black. In a moment of misgiving for the venture ahead, Bebe squeezed Fiorenza's hand, even as she clutched Edoardo's arm for reassurance. Finally, the big *Tomaso di Savoia* sailed silently out of the Genoa harbour at the end of April, 1916, and headed toward the southern end of Italy on the first lap of the long voyage. The ship had been chartered for the La Scala artists, their costumes, sets, props and personal luggage.

Even though Edoardo was looking forward to singing *Andrea Chénier, Meistersinger, Loreley* and *Isabeau,* and most of the artists in the company were excited at the prospect of visiting a new continent, everyone was subconsciously apprehensive about the crossing as they departed on the big adventure.

THE SHIP BEGAN to pull away from the Naples dock which was shrouded in a dense dank fog. Everyone on board was in a state of tension. Children were racing around all over the deck. Fiorenza Johnson, dancing up and down for joy, startled everyone by singing into the night air, at the top of her piping soprano voice, the phrase from *Andrea Chénier*: *Vive la morte! Vive la morte!* ("Long live death!").

There was a sudden hush. The child had voiced what they all feared—the danger ahead. She had innocently chosen music with which she was familiar—the final duet between Chénier and Madeleine as they are led away to the guillotine.

Bebe grabbed Fiorenza and quickly rushed her into their cabin below, before panic had a chance to spread among the superstitious artists.

The first few days at sea were unpleasant, with everyone carrying life-belts around with them all the time and being constantly drilled on how to find the lifeboats in case of attack. At night, it was pitch black; no lights must be seen from the cabin windows.

Among the passengers on that memorable tour were sopranos Rosa Raïsa and Maria Barrientos; the great Italian baritone Titta Ruffo; the composer Saint-Saëns; the French actor Lucien Guitry and his wife Jeanne and son Sacha, who became close friends of the Johnsons.

The trip, on the whole, was more like an outing for a huge family than a business venture. Fiorenza and some of the other children were taught the opera ballets and were royally pampered. Every cabin and stateroom was occupied. In addition to the leading artists, directors and conductors, there were utility artists, a chorus master, a teacher for the children, a choreographer, a *maestro de banda,* two prima ballerinas, a corps de ballet of sixty-four ballerinas and twenty-four male dancers, nineteen *mimos genericos,* twenty-eight *coriseos,* forty-four *niños de baile,* eighty orchestral musicians, eighty choristers of both sexes, twenty-three *músicos de banda,* and twenty-four *niños cantores,* along with an electrician, a *maquinista, atrecista, apuntador,* an archivist and a wig-man.

Although the children seemed to enjoy every minute, the grownups were looking forward to the end of the three-week voyage. The ship stopped briefly at Gibraltar, and briefly in Dakar where they saw French men-of-war standing in the port and Dakar natives in their canoes. From there, it was straight across the ocean. Aside from the usual scattered cases of seasickness, the trip in general was a delightful experience. By May they were off the South American shore in the Bay of Santos where German and Austrian boats were being held. But more interesting for the passengers of the Italian liner was the sight of huge bags of coffee being loaded onto ships from the backs of muscular South American workers at the Buenos Aires dock.

On May 25, 1916, Argentina celebrated its first century as a Republic, and members of the visiting opera company saw an impressive review of troops in front of Government House. The families of the singers had time on their hands, and Bee especially enjoyed a visit to the famed Gardens of Palermo. She hoped Edward could go with her to the Gardens another time. But the members of the Company were in rehearsal, getting used to the new House and to their revamped casts; their schedule was a busy one, requiring some trips for appearances outside Buenos Aires as well as at Teatro Colón. They were in Buenos Aires for the better part of two months.

*Boris Godunov,* with Titta Ruffo in the title role, opened the program given under the following heading: "Teatro Colón de Buenos Aires Official Season of 1916, in Artistic Collaboration with La Scala of Milan /General Manager: Faustino da Rosa and Walter Mocchi/Artistic Director: Vittorio Mingardi."

The opening production was successful, but the big event was to be the South American début of the sensational new Italian tenor. Beneath the headline *Edoardo di Giovanni del* Andrea Chénier *al Teatro Colón de Buenos Aires,* the prestigious *Gazetta* reported: "The début of this celebrated tenor was made in *Andrea Chénier* which was marked with great success, meeting full favour with the public and being a cause of great celebration."

June and July meant work for Edoardo, even though there were a few times he could join Bee and some of their friends on the lovely Roof Garden of the Grand Hotel where most of the company were staying. And once, during July, he had enough time off so they could take a boat trip down the Las Conchas, through the jungle to Tigre, seeing natives in their primitive huts along the banks of the river.

In August, they all left their Buenos Aires headquarters and sailed to Montevideo. They had hoped to be able to discard the heavy coats they had been obliged to wear in Buenos Aires, but it was even colder in Montevideo. The singers were free to join their families on only a few of their excursions to the beaches and to Montevideo's famed Prado Park, but in general it was too cold—it was "bad for the voice." "Besides," Eddie grumbled, "what fun is it to go to the beach in an overcoat and muffler?"

The Company boarded the *S.S. Frisie* in Montevideo and sailed through Santos again on their way to Rio de Janeiro, in and around which they were to spend September and October.

Bebe usually went everywhere with Edoardo. But on the boat to Rio Fiorenza caught the whooping cough, so her mother and Tata had to miss Sao Paulo completely. To keep the child amused, the Guitrys gave her a little monkey, thus increasing the Johnson household by a mischievous one. It was pleasant, though, to spend the time in their palm-shaded chalet at the Hotel International on the side of the mountain overlooking the famed harbour. From their windows they had a breath-taking panorama of the most magical of all South American cities, of the sparkling waters of the great bay and of the islands off the coast. Also, wonder of wonders, the weather was almost balmy, although the Brazilian summer was still a couple of months away.

There were few mishaps or unexpected disturbances on the long tour. It proved to be both interesting and gratifying, and the South Americans were delighted to have the opportunity of seeing and hearing one of the world's greatest opera companies in some of its famous productions, and showed their approval in vociferous acclaim.

The Canadian-born tenor's conquest was complete. *Epoca, Patria degli Italiana, Mañana, Prensa, Nación, Nacional, Diario Espagñol, Critica Razón, Diario, Argentina* and *Ultima Hora* all carried unqualified raves for the quality and range of the voice, and for his exemplary integration of the art of singing with the art of acting. They spoke of him as a great interpreter. Eddie had conquered in South America. Buenos Aires reported his success as "full, complete and of utmost brilliance." São Paulo praised him as a "true and consummate artist." In Montevideo he "made a complete conquest of the public with his superior qualities and extraordinary voice." Rio called him "a singer incomparable." For them he was "ideal" whether in *Chénier, Meistersinger* (*Cantores de Nuremberg*, as they called it) or *Loreley.*

In spite of Edward Johnson's personal triumph everywhere, both he and Bebe found themselves homesick for their little house in Florence. So they were not altogether reluctant to board the *S.S. Hollandia,* on October 25, 1916, for the long voyage back. Again, Fiorenza was the centre of attention on the ship, with the Guitrys constantly giving beautiful presents to their *querida.* Later, they sent her a long-cherished blue velvet bag, with a cock embroidered on it in gold, that Guitry had used in the first performance of *Chantecler* in Paris.

WHILE EDDIE had been away from Italy, Lusardi had arranged some prestigious appearances for him in Europe. Consequently, when they reached Lisbon, on November 11, the Di Giovannis parted from their friends and fellow passengers and the ship's crew who had been part of their big opera family for the past six months. Eddie's two concerts in Lisbon seemed anticlimactic after the big opera performances in which he had recently been starring, in spite of his being given the same enthusiastic reception to which he had become accustomed.

After Lisbon, they made their way across Portugal and Spain, which was no mean task inasmuch as they were carrying their trunks and cases from the South American tour. Tata had gone ahead with the trunks when they were leaving Italy, but going back they all stayed together. Bee was determined, however, to introduce Edward to some of her relatives and friends, including the Duchess of Dalmella whose seaside villa and palace they visited.

When they went to Barcelona (November 19, 1916) Bee had hoped for a happier reception than she received. Her mother was ill, she knew, and had become very eccentric, but she was unprepared for the surprise encounter: they chanced to meet on the street and her mother pretended not to recognize her.

"But I am Bebe, Mother. Your daughter."

Brushing her aside, austerely, her mother said, "I have no daughter." Her attitude had never changed since the day she was told that her Bebe was marrying a man "who was an artist and a Protestant."

Time flew by and more and more Eddie was longing for the peace of Florence, but first he was scheduled to sing in Paris. It was an engagement he would have accepted in any case, for it was a benefit appearance for the war effort, and singing was his means of doing his bit. Deeply moved by the cause of the war when it first broke out, he had tried to enlist, much against Bee's will. He had come home depressed, however, after he had been rejected. "I couldn't pass the eyesight test without my glasses," he said unhappily. Bee had been greatly relieved, but consoled him by reminding him that he could serve by entertaining the troops.

The occasion in Paris was a matinée, under the patronage of M. le Président de la République and of the Princess Eulalie of Spain, in the famed Opéra, on January 22, 1917. The program, presented solely for the purpose of raising money, was attended by members of the government, representatives of the diplomatic corps, and some of the top personalities of Paris society and proved to be a tremendous success both artistically and financially. Edward Johnson's appearance, the only one he ever made in the Paris Opéra, as it happened, was in the final act of Mascagni's *Isabeau,* under the composer's direction.

After South America and the deference shown them amid the formal elegance of Paris, the Johnsons' final trip, to Florence, was in sharp contrast. They boarded a train, with their assortment of countless trunks and cases, full of Edward's costumes and musical scores, and their personal effects, all in the luggage van of their compartment. Everything went well until the officials at the frontier of Modane looked at their passports. There was a Canadian artist with a Portuguese wife, a child, an Italian nanny—and an attractive young woman travelling on a Spanish diplomatic passport. (The latter was a cousin of Bee's, Fiorenza's *belle cousine Isabelle,* who had joined them in Paris for the trip to Italy.) The whole menage looked suspicious to the wartime customs officers, who took them all off the train and held up the train while they escorted them into the customs shed, where the officers proceeded to open every piece of luggage. What they found only confirmed their suspicions. "They'll think I'm a super spy," Edward uttered wryly. "Wigs, costumes, cases of make-up. What else?"

"At least," Bee commented, "they'll realize we are harmless when they come to your scores." But not so. For the scores, with all Edoardo's singing parts underlined in red, could be cleverly coded messages, particularly when they were accompanied by a collection of dictionaries in various languages, bearing myriad dots under the words he had looked up from time to time!

No amount of talking would allay the officers' suspicions, and Bebe had difficulty keeping Edward from giving each of them a punch in the nose. Finally, however, in a fury as violent as the wintry blizzards swirling about them, he demanded that they contact the British Ambassador in Rome. They did—hours later. All was well, of course, and they were then allowed to continue on their journey. But the little group was avoided as though they were lepers by the other passengers on the train, who had been delayed all day because of them.

FLORENCE. HOME AT LAST. They breathed a sigh of happy relief. Their house at the time—they had lived in several since 1909—was the ground floor of an old fifteenth-century palace, with big rooms and a luxurious walled garden. Tata's sister had taken good care of everything in their absence, including Fiorenza's menagerie—a little dog, two pigeons, two rabbits, two ducks and a turtle—with all of whom the child was quickly and happily reunited. A marvellous scallopini, a pasta, a glass of their favourite *vino,* and a salad as only the Italians could prepare it made the homecoming celebration complete.

Fiorenza never forgot that first evening back in Florence. After supper they all went for a walk along their beloved narrow cobble-stoned streets, past the familiar statues and the squares, and along the Arno. They all felt their hearts expand with joy. They had forgotten how wonderful it was, and how much they loved the trees and the buildings, silhouetted against the golden glow from the rays of the setting sun. In a holiday mood they decided on a carriage ride up to the magically beautiful Etruscan village, Fiesole, from whence they could look down on the Cupola of the Duomo, the slender towers of the Campanile and the Palazzo Vecchio and across the blue ribbon of the winding Arno

River to Michelangelo's Piazza. On the way back down to Florence, they stopped by the monastery to say hello to their old friend Padre Caramelli, *il frate bello*, and received a hearty welcome. Before they left, Edoardo had promised the padre to return the next week to sing in his lovely little thirteenth-century church with the padre playing the organ, as they had sometimes done before.

The next day the great loss in not being able to visit that other dear friend Maestro Lombardi came over Bee and Eddie like a cloud. How they needed his counsel. There were renewed offers from the Metropolitan Opera, and Lusardi had sent Gatti-Casazza a detailed list of Edoardo's repertoire. If word came, and their conditions were met, should they accept? Perhaps, as Lusardi suggested, the time *had* come for the Metropolitan. Certainly Edward's repertoire was no longer insufficient, for he could sing any one of more than a dozen operas on an hour's notice: *Aida, Il Trovatore, Un ballo in maschera, Madama Butterfly, Tosca, Manon Lescaut, I Pagliacci, La Gioconda, Cavalleria Rusticana, La Bohème, L'Amore dei tre re, Andrea Chénier*, and lesser known ones such as *Gli Ugonotti, Francesca da Rimini* and *Loreley*. On the other hand, there was also a question as to whether he should sign for the Metropolitan through Lusardi in Italy, or through the Wolfsohn Bureau in New York. Wolfsohn wrote that he had spent a time with Otto Kahn (the financier who backed Gatti's régime with millions of dollars) and had "got him quite interested."

Gatti wanted to know "on what terms you would agree to sing with the Metropolitan, and, at the same time, your entire repertoire." Wolfsohn himself frankly admitted he wanted to get Edward Johnson over to the Met so he could capitalize on the connection in order to make more money in concerts. Fees would be doubled, at least. Eddie's mind was in a turmoil of indecision, and for once even Bee wasn't certain as to what was best.

The war had made a big difference in Italy during the short months they had been in South America: the rigours of the wartime had made it impossible to have heat in the houses, and food was both rationed and scarce. Eddie had little time to worry, however. Besides, he knew Bebe would take care of everything. His job was to study, rehearse and sing. He had finally accepted Mingardi's insistent invitation that he appear with the La Scala Company at the Reale in Madrid (February to April, 1917). Once that decision had been made, Bebe received a cable from André Messager, from the Palace Hotel in Madrid: *Je suis ravi que votre mari aura l'occasion de faire une saison à Madrid, et j'espère qu'il aura beaucoup de succès. Mille très affectueuses amitiés.*

Following a successful *Fanciulla* production at the Costanzi, conducted by Vitale, Eddie went to Madrid on February 19. He sang *Tann-häuser, Fedora* and *Meistersinger,* with Serafin conducting. When the heavy schedule was over, Eddie was tired—he was always tired, it seemed to him.

His Madrid reviews were enthusiastic. *Meistersinger:* "Fresh voice, of sympathetic quality . . . well suited art and perfect declamation"— *Globo;* "Good voice; excellent style"—*Epoca;* "beautiful voice and exquisite art"—*La Tribuna.* All agreed that Di Giovanni's voice was of "memorable quality" and that he sang with "great artistry at all times."

Still, Edoardo was thinking of the war. It was not enough for him that he, Gigli, Pertile and others of the La Scala group for the Madrid engagement had appeared in a concert, March 22, 1917, presented by the Association of Artists and Writers, for the benefit of the Cervantes Institute. Papers had given public thanks and profuse praise to all involved for their services. But such performances didn't satisfy Eddie. He felt he should be contributing more directly to the war effort.

On the first of April Eddie returned to Florence. The whole operatic world was beginning to open up for him, insofar as the war economy and travel would allow. A cable from Charles Wagner in New York advised: "Can arrange Metropolitan sure." That was June 8, 1917.

Prior to that, a cable from John Frothingham in May asked: "Would you consider concert tour, States and Canada next season, our management. Cable Frothmus, New York. Answer and terms."

On April 2 Lusardi had offered: "If you wish to go to Colón, they offer you 30,000 lire monthly for three months, guaranteed, leaving Barcelona May 10th. Telegram. *Saluti.*"

Honest and loyal that he was, Eddie sent a copy of Frothingham's cable to Charles Wagner, and on August 7, 1917, he received the following reply: "They have done nothing to set the world on fire that I know of, and I know nothing against them."

Eddie asked Wagner for more particulars about the Metropolitan Opera offer:

> I presume it is for the season of 1918/19, and would therefore fall in nicely with your proposition, but let me inform you of some already existing conditions. When I sailed for South America last year I left Italy fully prepared that a contract with the Chicago Opera Company would follow me to Buenos Aires. However, on my arrival in that city, I learned that the tenor Giulio Crimi was to accompany Signor Campanini to Chicago and that for me was reserved a contract with the Metropolitan in New York. My agent here, Lusardi, arranged a conditional contract with Mr. Gatti for three years, to be ratified or cancelled before June 30th, 1917. But

Mr. Gatti, who evidently had more artists than he knew what to do with, allowed the offer to expire, much to my satisfaction, as my agent had persuaded me to accept very inferior terms. It was at this moment that a cable reached me from Frothingham, and I had the idea to try my luck once more in the United States. You will understand readily, however, that I cannot throw down what I have so patiently built up over here unless I have a reasonable guarantee awaiting me on that side, and it is for that reason that a contract with one of the opera companies interests me. But as my agent has already interested himself on my behalf with Gatti and Campanini, and as I have also been approached by persons connected with Rabinoff and Russell, my position becomes very delicate, and a treaty or trading with you must be maintained with the utmost care.

My present contract can be liquidated on six months' notice, but in the meantime all my business is subject to it. Therefore, our dealings must be, for the moment, more-or-less secret. When I have in my hand a genuine offer from the Metropolitan Opera Company, I can easily fix my situation here with a small percentage on the contract. But since Lusardi is an intimate friend of Gatti, learning of your efforts on my behalf, he may try to forestall you by making the same or even better offers in order to obtain the entire commission. Consequently, I don't want to bind you to any set conditions. You must simply get all you can out of Gatti for each performance, and a sufficient number guaranteed to make it worthwhile. I shall also naturally expect conditions allowed to all artists residing in Europe. Certainly without some real assurance of this kind I could not possibly undertake this trip. Gatti is too well informed of the theatrical doings in Europe not to know that I was engaged for four consecutive seasons at La Scala.

A second cable arrived from Wagner, August 8, 1917: "I have just had a telephone message from Mr. Gatti-Casazza. He assured me there would be no trouble to arrange for your appearance over here when I bring you over."

That same day Mr. Adams, of the Wolfsohn Bureau, cabled: "I am very much of the opinion that right now is a psychological moment for you to come to this country. As you can imagine, with this war situation, Americans for the first time are at a premium, and we all consider you an American. . . . Campanini is giving a season in Chicago and one in New York. I might be able to make arrangements with him for a New York appearance in January."

Adams, it seems, had written previously wanting to know when Edward Johnson would be arriving from Buenos Aires and saying that no stone would be left unturned to make his career the biggest one since Caruso. "We are announcing you," he cabled, "as Edward Johnson, and will continue to do so unless we hear from you to the contrary immediately."

Edward's letter to Adams, of August 17, explained: "Had I received your letter of last November 3rd, the whole course of events of these last months might have been changed for me, and I would not have found myself in my present complications. To be honest and frank with you, I have a contract on my hands here in Italy, and I have a proposition by cable from New York to which I replied, and I am now awaiting events. What will happen I don't know. I turned down the Lyman-Frothingham combination, and am happy to have had your cooperation and am exceedingly sorry that I am not able to give you carte blanche for my affairs in America. When something definite is settled I will write you immediately."

On November 5, 1917, Charles L. Wagner wrote, in reply to Edward's concern over the investment of $5,000 toward his career in America: "Don't worry about the $5,000—I would not be investing it if I didn't see something like $25,000 to $35,000 in sight for you." He explained that his office had spent $10,000 on Galli-Curci's publicity, and realized nearly $100,000 net to her. "I wish I could persuade you," he cabled, "to simply turn your business over to me, just as Galli-Curci and McCormack did, and await results. I think Gatti's idea is about $500 a performance at the Metropolitan the first season. I think it should be $750 or $1,000."

While this managerial controversy was raging, Eddie was busy (May to November, 1917) singing for soldiers in the hospitals throughout Italy, and in France and Belgium. "I remember him well," one soldier recalled many, many years later. "He was like a breath of life to all of us. . . . We had never heard of him before, but 'Edward Johnson,' that's what he called himself in France, was a name that sounded like home to us. He bounded on the platform stage and told stories and sang . . . and had us all singing with him . . . Irish songs and things like 'Pack up your troubles in your old kit bag and smile, smile, smile.' . . . Oh, I tell you, I'll never forget that smile of his. I never saw him again and never heard him again, but I've never forgotten him."

There was a happy reunion when Edward Johnson arrived back in Florence from the hospitals in France and Belgium. Bee was "happy and proud" of him, but had not known a moment's peace, she said, while he was gone, because her heart had been so filled every moment with anxiety and fear for his safety.

She handed him the new contracts for the Costanzi, February to April, 1918, and the Teatro Argentina in Rome for May, followed by a special concert for the Prince of Wales in Rome in June. It all sounded good, but there were times when he felt so tired of touring and moving around that he thought he couldn't stand it. "I know I can't chuck it all," he said to Bee, "but I'd sure like to sometimes." Then he smiled somewhat sheepishly as he showed her his contract for the Politeamo in Genoa for eight performances of *Andrea Chénier*, from December 12, 1917, to January 15, 1918, at 1,250 francs per performance. "Less only 2½ per cent to Agenzia dell'Impresa, of course," he enthused. "Joy, oh joy! That's not bad."

In spite of all the restrictions, opera continued to be given in Italy. Early in 1918, Eddie appeared as scheduled at the Costanzi, where he sang Puccini's *Fanciulla del West*, conducted by Ettore Panizza. During that engagement, he and Bee developed a close friendship with Puccini and his wife. Being anxious to please the composer, Eddie was more nervous than usual. He was even impatient with Bee when she was putting on his make-up and helping him with his costumes. She had never seen him so nervous and agitated, she said. Why? Puccini was only part of it, he told her.

The idea that he was not being part of the war effort constantly upset him; he couldn't get it out of his mind. Besides, he was perturbed because word had reached him that day that it might not be possible for him to accept a Monte Carlo engagement. The passport office in Rome had recognized his request for a permit for his wife and himself, but noted that an exemption certificate was required.

On February 27, 1918, the Distretto Militare di Firenze (Military District of Florence) notified Edward Johnson, aged thirty-nine, living at Via San Nicolo, 95, Florence, to appear on May 24, 1918, for a hearing before the Comandante del Distretto. In no time at all, the pathway was cleared, but such things were annoying.

Between engagements, Edward and Bebe made another of their quick trips to their beloved Florence, to be with Fiorenza. At that time she had a governess, as well as Tata, because of her parents' unsettled life, and could always be released from her studies for an outing with Mother and Babbino. On such occasions they would take long walks, and she would see, through their eyes, the treasures of Florence, and hear how her father copied many of the costumes, even the attitudes and postures, of the figures they saw in paintings of different periods. Also, when her parents were home, the house was suddenly and miraculously full of interesting people—artists, writers, composers, and officers and soldiers of all nationalities on leave. The Johnsons' was a favourite meeting place for one and all in wartime even though there was no heat in their living-room—only a tiny stove which they called "the pig," with four legs and a pipe up the chimney. No luxuries, such as tea or sugar—guests brought their own rations and everyone shared.

Fiorenza was seven years old by then and, as is often the case with only children, was treated very much as an adult. When Eddie went to Rome, he wrote her (March, 1918) that he had signed with Signora Carelli to stay at the Costanzi until April for performances of *Fanciulla* and *Fedora*. In another letter in March he wrote: "This evening is the general rehearsal for the new opera and your poor Babbino doesn't feel well—but for me it is not possible to stay at home. I am tired of hotel life."

The new work was *Maria di Magdala,* by Vincenzo Micchetti, in which Edoardo di Giovanni was creating the role of John the Baptist. The opera itself showed the sincerity and daring of the young composer, and the management of the Costanzi exhibited courage in putting the visible characters of Jesus, Mary Magdalene, Judas, John the Baptist and others before a public that was loathe to accept any sacred figure, or religious theme, even *Parsifal.* Furthermore, the people preferred melody to the Wagner-like declamatory music drama, which was Micchetti's style.

After gruelling weeks of musical and stage rehearsals, the première took place on March 8, 1918. The *Cronache Teatrale* had praise for the opera, and for Di Giovanni as the "very embodiment of the character of John the Baptist," and it spoke of his sharing the great applause for the soprano, Elena Rakowska, for the baritone, Giuseppe Danise, and for Maestro Panizza. Nevertheless, the work lasted for only four performances.

As in the case of Zandonai's *Melenis* five years before in Rome, Alfano's *L'Ombra di Don Giovanni*, Catalani's *Loreley* and Pizzetti's *Fedra* in Milan, Edoardo di Giovanni again emerged as a favourite. But that didn't alter his feeling that his life was nothing but constant work; learning new operas, learning new roles, rehearsing, performing, studying. And all the time the war was still raging.

On the night of April 3, 1918, Edward and Bebe had just gone to sleep when Tata awakened them and insisted on dragging them and Fiorenza to the cellar. It was an April Fool's Day game, Fiorenza was told, but she was disdainful—she knew April Fool's Day had passed. A German plane had dropped a bomb on the city; the alarm had been sounded by a cannon shot, warning everyone to go to their cellars. At first Eddie refused to move: "I'm tired; I'd rather be blown to pieces than get out of my comfortable bed," he said. Bebe finally got him out, but the moment she wasn't looking, he slipped away and went back to his room. No sooner were they all in their rooms again than there was another shot. That time Eddie flatly refused to budge. So Bebe, Fiorenza and Tata went back to what Fiorenza called "the hole in the ground," and stayed there until 7 A.M.

Eddie's next engagement was supposed to have been the world pre-mière of Montemezzi's *La Nave*, but that opera became a casualty of the familiar wartime production problems at La Scala and was post-poned until November.

In May, Eddie went to Rome to sing the première of Pietro Canoni-ca's *La Sposa di Corinto* in the big Teatro Argentina. He had memorized his music, and had "passed" his part, as he mentioned in his diary on May 14, with the composer and with Tullio Serafin. But there were other problems in connection with the production, which Edward pointed out to Bee one evening: "The Costanzi has decided to continue the season and is preparing *Aida* and *Chénier*. That leaves Serafin without a chorus for the *Sposa* rehearsals. The orchestra begins tomorrow, and he says the parts aren't even corrected yet. And how do you like this? The première is booked for the 27th, and the baritone doesn't arrive until the 20th!"

Eddie was worried, but Bee told him: "You've done your part! You're prepared. What are you worrying about? We must be calm and strong, and adapt ourselves to whatever the future holds. They called you 'ideal in every way' in *Maria di Magdala* and I am sure they will say the same thing when you sing Pietro's *La Sposa*."

True to her prediction, after the première of *La Sposa di Corinto* on May 27, Edward won ecstatic acclaim from the press.

On June 16, 1918, Eddie wrote his parents that he had sung for the Prince of Wales on three different occasions during His Highness' visit and that he felt very happy about the entire encounter.

> The first time was at the English Embassy, where the Ambassador, Sir Rennell Rodd, gave a dinner and a party afterwards, and I ended the program by singing "Rule Britannia" with the orchestra, and everybody standing and cheering lustily after. . . . The Mayor of Rome wrote me a charming letter, thanking me for my assist-ance, and gave me a beautiful gold medal with the arms of Rome on one side and my name on the other, to commemorate the his-torical event. The second was at a reception given by the City of Rome to the Prince in the historical capital to which all the nota-bles, political and social, were invited. . . . The third time I sang for His Highness was at the performance of a new opera, *La Sposa di Corinto,* sung for the first time in any theatre. At the end of the second act I was greeted with a special round of applause, and requested by the Prince to come to his box. . . . We chatted for a

quarter of an hour or so and I reminded His Highness that his grandfather, the late King Edward, had visited our city [Guelph] while he was Prince of Wales, and I said that I hoped that he himself would confer the honour a second time. . . . He told me that it was his intention to visit Canada as soon as the war was over and most assuredly he would look in on the City of Guelph. You may imagine how happy I felt.

That summer Bebe drilled Edward mercilessly on *La Nave*. When the time came for him to go to Milan for rehearsals, however, Bebe was feeling tired, which was unusual for her, and decided it would be wiser to stay behind to rest awhile. So Eddie went ahead alone.

From Milan, on September 11, Eddie reported having received 2,370 lire, "the first fifth, less five per cent" of his salary there. Then he confessed to worries other than vocal ones! "I think I'm getting bald! Bring that stuff I put on my hair—I've rubbed my head two or three times with vaseline. Hope it helps. Also be sure to bring some Petrolax and thirdly, the drops for my eyes, and the new white shirts with the soft cuffs." He confidently reported that he had sung two acts of *La Nave* from memory, with the répétiteur Molaioli, at 9:30 that morning. "By tomorrow or the day after I'll be ready for the rehearsal of *Don Pasquale,* too."

He was lost without Bebe, he wrote (September 21, 1918), and was waiting for her to come to clear up lots of rough points for him. He asked that she bring a lemon, but no sugar. "We can get that here, a little at a time; we can take some back with us."

His letter of September 25 was full of a different concern: "I had a letter this morning from Titta Ruffo. He has been transferred to Rome. He said he had sent his conditions to Bonnetti but doubts if Bonnetti will accept them. I suppose he doesn't care to go and asked an exaggerated amount. I've heard nothing further about the Colón, and my demand for 50,000 lire remains. In fact, I doubt if I will lower it. In proportion to what the others are asking it isn't exaggerated. At any rate, I will wait and see. Destiny has guided me more or less to date and I suppose things must take their course. 'We do what we have to do,' as Maeterlinck says. I worried myself to a frazzle over the pros and cons, but what worries me more than anything else is the responsibility of subjecting you and the baby to any risk. But we must live, and there is nothing to do but struggle on. . . . Love and happiness, duty and suffering, go with your highly developed instinct and extraordinary intelligence. And I am sure that somehow, with your firmness of character, we ought not to go far astray."

There were the usual backstage bickerings, quarrels and jealousies that bothered Eddie, at La Scala as in most theatres. On September 27,

82

he complained in a letter: "I have tried to show goodness all my life, and it seems to me like a very great waste." Later in that same letter, he wrote: "Good Lord, what prices. Roses—18 to 25 lire per dozen! I paid 18 lire for a cyclamen of not very large proportions for the Baroness Rapisardi and felt cheap in the modesty of my offering."

When Bebe finally arrived in Milan, she saw how desperately Edward really did need her and how, having gone through so many of the early rehearsals without her help and criticism, he had become apprehensive and nervous about the new opera. She dared not upset him further by telling him how badly she felt, physically. After all, it was just a few pains. They could wait. The trouble would be cleared up when she returned to her doctor in Florence, she thought, as she plunged into the work at hand.

The première of Montemezzi's *La Nave* took place at La Scala on November 3, 1918. In the role of Marco Polo, Edoardo di Giovanni had one of his most outstanding successes and personal triumphs.

There were words of praise for his voice, for his bearing and for his dramatic interpretation. He wrote to Fiorenza: "*La Nave* was a great success for Babbino and for Signora Rakowska. It was a memorable evening, and there was not a vacant seat in all of La Scala! Your poor Babbino had a cold, but he sang as though there was nothing wrong."

When Titta Ruffo wrote Edward Johnson with "infinite congratulations" on the success of *La Nave,* he also told of receiving offers from American theatres. He said nothing had come of them, but that actually he wasn't anxious to go over. Eddie couldn't quite understand why Ruffo wouldn't jump at the chance, particularly with things so unsettled in Europe, and Florence itself "overrun with soldiers."

Puccini insisted that Edoardo di Giovanni create the tenor roles in two of the operas of his *Trittico—Gianni Schicchi* and *Il Tabarro*—the third, *Suor Angelica,* being for an all-female cast. Leaving Bee in Florence for a few days, Eddie went on ahead to Rome. He wrote her that the train from Florence to Rome had been "full of soldiers and officers on leave from the front. The atmosphere was sad." Rooms in Rome were hard to come by, he said, but he had finally found one at the Quirinale.

He found Puccini impatiently awaiting his arrival in Rome to start rehearsals on the first Italian production of his *Trittico*. It was to have its world première at the Metropolitan in New York on December 14, 1918, less than a month before the scheduled European première (January 11, 1919) at the Costanzi. The composer hadn't really worried about the New York production, but everything had to be right for Italy. It was one thing to be fêted in New York; quite another to be acclaimed at home.

On December 17, after having rehearsed until eleven o'clock at night, Edward, Puccini and soprano Gilda Dalla Rizza went to the Bar Americano and drank orangeade until midnight. Eddie was up at ten o'clock the next morning, and in the theatre at 2 P.M. to go through *Il Tabarro*. Puccini was full of praise and, Eddie thought, a most sympathetic person. He and Bebe and Gilda and the Puccinis had dinner together fairly often in Via de Pretino, mainly because they found they could eat well and cheaply there. During those days Puccini's melodies were in everyone's head—even Fiorenza had learned *O mio Babbino caro* and sang it around the house. She thought it had been written especially for her to sing to her *own* beloved Babbino!

Puccini had been right in his choice of a tenor it seemed, for Di Giovanni was highly praised after the opening. Puccini himself reached a new peak in popularity and was fêted everywhere, notably at a big Grand Hotel dinner presided over by Prince Prospero Colonna. The Prince even suggested that evening that a new national hymn be written by Puccini, who should draw his inspiration from the hymn written by Horace for Emperor Augustus. Puccini was willing, even though his talent would be fettered by the majestic type of music called for. The work was finally completed and the Prince arranged for the first performance to take place in one of the great Roman squares in the presence of the Royal Family. The chorus and orchestra assembled, but the concert was rained out by a veritable deluge on the three attempts made to present the work. "An unfortunate beginning and a worse ending for my hymn," was Puccini's only comment as he left Rome for his home at Torre del Lago.

IT HAD WORRIED Eddie when Bee seemed so tired and had had to take time out to rest before joining him in Rome. But she had been on hand for all the performances as usual, and for the première of *Trittico* as well as for the rehearsals and the general rehearsal. Her eyes were bright and she seemed to have more colour than in recent weeks. Eddie was reassured. Bee knew that the colour was due to fever. She had an infection, the doctor had discovered, for which she was quietly taking medicine. She wrote Fiorenza that she felt ill and thought she had a fever, but didn't want to worry Babbo. In the same envelope, a letter from Eddie to Fiorenza reported that "this is a terrible day, in two ways. First, Mother doesn't feel well, and it's cold, and inside I'm preoccupied with tonight's première. The only thing that gave me courage and put a bit of sun into things was your little letter. In a little while I go to the theatre, and in the *O mio Babbino caro* I'll be thinking of you."

Two days after the première, Bee wrote Fiorenza: "Babbo had a great success in the operas by Puccini and was complimented by everyone. I know these words will make you happy." She enclosed a review that had praised the vigour of Eddie's portrayals, the security of his singing and his highly intelligent and dramatic conceptions.

In the midst of all the excitement, the daily rehearsals continued at home with Bebe making sure that Eddie's diction should be perfect, that he didn't allow his voice to slip out of the mask, that his vowels should all be properly placed and that his breath was solid. There were also daily rehearsals at the theatre for the new work by Gino Marinuzzi, *Jacquerie*. At the same time, Edoardo was studying the role of Pelléas. Little wonder that there didn't seem to be much sun in his life. Little wonder, too, that he failed to notice how much effort Bee was putting into their daily life at the moment.

On February 20 they received a long letter from the Wolfsohn Bureau in New York with an offer of a guaranteed minimum of thirty performances for the next season, beginning the middle of November, with $700 per performance, whether concert or opera, "all expenses to be paid by us, except railroad, hotel and musical paper." And they asked for 15 per cent of any talking machine (phonograph) contract. After unfruitful negotiations with the Met, they had finally signed a contract for Edoardo di Giovanni with Campanini in Chicago, they reported.

Neither Eddie nor Bee wanted to leave Europe, but the contract at Chicago was good and they concurred that it was time for Edward to return to America.

The first *Jacquerie* performance at the Costanzi, on March 6, 1919, brought praise for the composer/conductor and for the two "marvellous stars," Dalla Rizza and Di Giovanni—the tenor "whose interpretation of the role made the performance especially memorable."

In contrast to his usual repertoire, Edward Johnson was tackling in *Pelléas et Mélisande* the music of Debussy for the first time. He found the rehearsals taxing and the role of Pelléas the most exacting he had ever sung, not because it was difficult vocally but because of the elusive quality of the character. "Pelléas is a mere lad," he remarked, "but he is also a man."

Opening night was April 11. Reviewers devoted columns to the work itself, spoke of its being based on Maeterlinck's "static drama," but praised the "impeccable Mélisande" of Bianca Bellincioni Stagno, the "excellent Pelléas" of Di Giovanni and the "very effective Golaud" of Eugenio Giraldoni. All three artists were said to have "contributed miraculously to the inestimable success of this exceptional opera." Marinuzzi, the conductor, was applauded at the end of each act.

Bee and Edward had expected to go to Covent Garden the first of

May, but a rather cryptic letter from the manager, Harry Higgins, negated previous overtures: "I trust that another year we may have the pleasure of seeing you here."

It was a disappointment insofar as the Johnsons were concerned. And neither did it seem quite ethical, even though no contract had been signed, Eddie wrote Higgins. The reply came in May: Mr. Higgins regretted that Mr. Johnson felt he was not wanted there. Besides, Higgins had had the impression that Eddie was American, rather than Canadian, and Covent Garden gave preference to Commonwealth artists. Having already vented his disappointment and ire in his own letter, Eddie gave a shrug. His mind was concentrated just then on other matters—in particular the second Italian production of Puccini's *Trittico*, scheduled for Teatro della Pergola in Florence on May 24, 1919. He would be singing again the roles of Rinuccio in *Gianni Schicchi* and Luigi in *Il Tabarro*, which he had created at the Italian première in Rome.

With Puccini a national figure now, it was a great honour for Florence to have the second Italian production of the *Trittico,* with Puccini himself attending. It was also cause for special elation for the Johnsons that Edoardo was to be a star in his hometown at last.

They returned from Rome in a mood of such excitement and jubilation that, even though the skies were overcast and Florence gave them a cold and damp welcome, they hardly noticed. They were busy unpacking and telling stories to Fiorenza who wanted to know all about everything. It was a happy homecoming.

The weather in Florence continued to be miserable and everyone caught cold. On Monday morning, Bee awakened with a severe "stitch" in her side. Edward's first thought was of pneumonia, so he immediately called the doctor, then insisted that Bee go back to bed. Later in the week, he happily told friends that her lungs and heart were sound, and that after two days' rubbing with Eliman's Imbrocation she was already better. The next day, however, she had a fever again. Even so, she intended to go to the theatre. It was Edward who insisted that she stay in bed; again he called the doctor. The necessary things to reduce fever were prescribed, but the doctor told Edward he feared Bee was seriously ill. To make things easier at home, it was arranged for Fiorenza to stay with the Casalis for a few days.

The fever was down again the next day, and Bee, though weak, seemed like herself. Seeing no cause for alarm, Edward left for his *Trittico* rehearsal with a light heart, particularly inasmuch as their friend, Fifi Moulton, had arrived to visit them for a few days and Bee would not be alone.

The evening after the general rehearsal, Bee wanted to hear how everything had gone. Had Eddie had any difficulty? Had his voice stayed in line? How was the orchestra, and the conductor? They talked and talked and finally Bebe became drowsy and they said good-night. Her last words were: *In bocca al lupo domani* ("Good luck tomorrow").

The next morning they found Bee unconscious. Edward sent frantically for the doctor, then rushed to the hospital for the analysis of some tests and for a second doctor. But it was no use. On his return she was all but gone! "We gave her puncture," he wrote his parents later, "but to no avail. I took her hands—those beautiful hands that for ten years had loved and cared for me as a mother for her child. I spoke to her, but she heard nothing. She seemed to sleep quietly away, and at 1:30 P.M. she had left me forever."

At first Edward couldn't believe what had happened, but when the doctor put his hand on his shoulder, he suddenly burst into uncontrollable sobs.

News was sent to the theatre that Di Giovanni would not be singing that evening. There was complete consternation—and a deputation of directors and friends immediately came from the theatre to talk to him. The house was sold out. Money had been spent. There wasn't enough to refund. Many of the singers and musicians had been depending on the performances for their very bread. He *must* sing. Their hearts were wrung for him in his terrible loss—most of them had known and loved Bee also—but the situation was desperate. Through his tears Edoardo said he understood but that it was impossible. "I *can't* sing, don't you see? I *can't!"*

To go through a romantic comedy (*Gianni Schicchi*) and a tragic melodrama involving love, jealousy and murder (*Il Tabarro*) was more than Eddie felt he could face. But someone reminded him that Bee would have wanted him to carry on, and that the greatest tribute to her memory would be to sing—that *she,* of all people, would not have wanted hundreds of people thrown out of work because of her—that he should sing "in memory of her." Finally, less than two hours before curtain time, he agreed to try—but he said the only way he could possibly get through was to have his close friends there in the theatre in front of him.

"It was the greatest impression of my life," the Baroness Rapisardi related years later. "I was a young girl at the time, but my parents took me, and I have never seen such sorrow nor such courage. There were twelve of us sitting together in the centre of the house, near the stage. We all kept thinking: 'That poor young man.' We could see his agony, and the struggle he was making to fight back the tears. But he sang as he had never sung before, and the public went wild—not knowing that his emotion and his tears were real. Afterwards, he told us that he was sure Bee had been watching over him and had pulled him through."

Not having been told of the tragedy in the personal life of Di Giovanni, the press next day carried supreme words of praise for his interpretations: "Edoardo di Giovanni sang with consummate artistry and greater feeling than ever before." He himself never knew quite how he got through that evening, with his eyes so filled with tears at times that it was impossible to see the conductor, Guy Bavagnoli.

Friends helped with the funeral, after which Fifi Moulton went home, and Edward left 95 Via San Nicolo and moved into the Casali *pensione* with Fiorenza. Fiorenza felt at home with her "Auntie Jo." Tata and her sister were left behind to take care of the house.

Letters of condolence poured in from friends and colleagues. A letter from Puccini, May 25, read: *Con molto condoglio ho preso parte al tuo grande dolore. Povera Signora, così buona e cara! . . .*

Eddie continued singing every performance until the end of the season in Florence (June 1). Then he had to leave immediately for Turin for rehearsals with Toscanini of Beethoven's *Ninth Symphony*. He thought of cancelling, but the doctor and his friends all told him what he knew to be true, that he must go on, and that Bee would have wanted him to honour the engagements that meant so much in the career for which they had both worked so hard. Also, there was the future; he had Fiorenza to think of and care for. As he carried on, Bee's eyes were always before him, her voice always in his ears.

Fifi Moulton deluged him with letters during the weeks that followed. She said she thought they might help a bit. Edward confided to her that with Bee just gone, he was already being pursued. He wasn't interested, but he found himself making comparisons. Fifi's wise words were: "The more you draw comparisons, the more you'll be miserable. If you could only forget for one minute the 'What would Bee say,' you would make a great step towards recovery." Meanwhile, Eddie had his own share of sympathy to give to Fifi who had lost a dear one, and to Josephine Casali, whose husband was suffering from tuberculosis.

After his second Beethoven *Ninth* performance in Milan, Eddie was invited to sing in Trieste, but he returned to Florence instead. Fiorenza threw herself into his arms and clung to him with a desperation that wrung his heart. She was too young to realize fully what had happened, but she and her mother had been very close, and now she was lost and bewildered.

It wasn't until several weeks after Bee's death that Edward could bear to write any letters. His singing had been a blessing; it had kept him going and made it impossible for him to let down as he felt like doing. What would Bee think? This was the question he kept asking himself, as he used to ask her, before making every decision. He was due to go to America and make his début at the Chicago Opera—they had decided that together. She would have wanted him to carry on. But what about Fiorenza? Time and time again Edward felt himself reaching out. "Oh, Bebe, my beloved, tell me what do do." Then he would hear her words and take courage: "Believe in yourself . . . trust yourself . . . have confidence."

On June 16, he wrote home:

> Dear Mother and Father:
>
> Where and how to begin! Never has a letter been so difficult to write! Three weeks have passed since I laid my poor Bebe to rest, and each day that passes only serves to accentuate the terrible loss that has come to me. . . . Hardly had I the time to realize that she was ill, than she had gone. Oh! The pain! The pain! And I had to sing that night. And the next day! And the next day! And all the successive performances. . . . The doctor and my friends advised me to go on with my work, so I did. . . . I must be brave for Fiorenza's sake. Life must go on and the future lies with her. Excuse me for not writing sooner. I didn't have the courage. I know how you both loved my dear Bee, and I am sure you are broken-hearted. . . .
>
> With the best love and affection of your sadly-afflicted son,
>
> Edward
>
> P.S. The doctor said that Bebe died of "uremia"—the kidneys refused to function and poisoned the blood.

Then from Florence on June 24, 1919, Edward sent a letter to Bebe's cousin, Mme Alfred Bensaude, in Lisbon:

> *Très chère Tante Jane:*
>
> Already a month has passed since I lost my dear Bebe and it seems still impossible—a horrible dream. Life drags on, I know not how. A week after I laid my poor Bebe in her last resting place I left for Turin and Milan to finish the contracts I had assumed. It was awful! Alone—without her! My God! What I suffered! For ten years we never left each other. Ten years of work, sacrifice, communion and happiness. In a moment broken forever. Oh! ! ! I came back two days ago to our little home—the home that she had prepared and loved—the baby was waiting with outstretched arms to receive a lonely and bowed father. I tried to be strong for her sake, but the tears filled my eyes in spite of myself. Poor little Fiorenza! So young and so affectionate! She needed her mother so much in her life. She is still too young to realize the intensity of her loss. . . .
>
> Won't you please advise me what ought to be done. In my telegram to you I begged you to inform the persons you thought best.

I did *not* inform Bebe's mother. Should it be done? Nor did I tell anyone in Lisbon, but yourself. . . . I am depending on you to help me. You were to Bee what a family ought to have been and I know you will continue to extend to her little baby the love and affection you so generously bestowed on her. Perhaps you will inform the lawyer, and he will suggest if any important documents are necessary. Shall I put the lawyer in Lisbon in touch with my lawyer here in Florence, so that in case we were absent things would not drag? I am leaving for Canada in August or early September, and am engaged for next season in Chicago, so I will be absent for a year or more.

I want to ask you also to give me some information about Bee's family in connection with her effects. I have never insisted with her on this point and you know better than I do that she never wanted it for herself. It is only for Fiorenza, in the future. Time passes and the little one so easily forgets. I want to construct for my baby a tangible memory such as she will carry with her all her days. Few children have the good fortune to be born of such mothers, and since she had the ill-fortune to lose her mother so soon, it will be my duty to keep the noble example ever before her mind. . . . I hope you will see Miss Moulton when you go to Paris. She also loved Bee dearly and assisted her to the last. Oh! What a shame! How sad life is! We were so happy, and the future seemed so bright —I might say brilliant. But it was not to be. Life can never be the same. There was only one Bee in the world.

Write us here in Florence at the same address. And believe me, with all love and affection, your sad and broken-hearted friend,

Edward Johnson

Fifi's attitude seemed to change slightly as the weeks went by and Edward diplomatically reminded her that for the moment Fiorenza came first in his life. "Good for her," was Fifi's prompt reply. "But for God's sake get the situation in order for her. It's true that in case anything happened to you, your mother would have the rights over the child, but she is far away and when I think of Bee's mother, I just grind my teeth. Please give a big hug to the baby and to you."

Another time she wrote: "Bee was wise to make such good friends as the Mellinis, the Casalis, the Prezzis—the whole bunch, but you have always had some too. . . . But what a time you are having there now— first earthquakes, then machine guns on the Ponte Vecchio. Do the papers exaggerate?" And still another time: "Poor Bee and her hatred of disease—and the arguments about her age! What did it matter? And you, poor honey. You keep touching the bottom of the pit of despair!" Actually, she and Edward kept showering encouragement on each other by letter until it was time for him to leave Florence.

90

Johnson's voice had often been spoken of in Italy as "robust" although it was never really that kind of voice, and he knew it. His constant problem was to be sure he was singing in such a way as to make the most telling impression. Many years later, baritone Leone Paci was reminiscing about Edward Johnson. Signor Paci, who had made his début in *The Barber of Seville* in Rome in 1910, and his final appearance in Venice in the 1950's, was living at the time in the Casa di Riposo per Musicisti ("Rest Home for Musicians") in Milan.

> Johnson was the most fantastic Loge [*L'Oro del Reno*] I ever saw. He and Marinuzzi and I were the closest friends in the company at La Scala. . . . Artists in those days got whatever they were able to negotiate for—young ones might get only 10 lire a day, while 1,000 lire a concert was just about tops. . . . I remember that Edward Johnson always had a respiratory weakness—his lungs bothered him sometimes if he wasn't feeling at his best—but he was determined not to give in. "I'll sing lightly tonight—not forced," he would say. He was seldom sick enough not to sing at all. I don't know whether it was Maestro Lombardi who taught Edoardo that "breath is a second maestro," but he believed it, and often said so.

In the *Dizionario dei Cantanti con Discografia* in Milan's Biblioteca del Conservatorio, under the heading *Le Grandi Voci* ("The Great Voices"), it is erroneously recorded (as in many biographical sketches) that Edoardo di Giovanni was born on August 22, 1881. Nevertheless, the same dictionary does give an excellent and detailed account of Di Giovanni's voice during his days in Italy: "His voice was judged to be among the most beautiful of the day, possessing, in addition to a notable volume, a bright polish and a homogeneity of colour almost Mediterranean, and completely devoid of the nasal and gutteral inflections so often found in Anglo-Saxon tenors."

Eddie's final few days in Florence before leaving for America were painful. He was saying good-bye to all that he had held so dear. Also, he dreaded going to the States and making his début at a new opera house without Bee. Then there was Fiorenza—it was reassuring to know that he had been able to arrange for Tata and a governess to come with them to America.

"I do pity you," wrote Fifi Moulton from Paris (August 15, 1919), "but nothing else can be done!"

"And right she is," Eddie thought, "nothing else can be done. Life must go on. My responsibility now is to my little daughter—mine and Bee's."

# 4

EDOARDO DI GIOVANNI and his little family—Fiorenza, Tata and a governess—left for America. The Atlantic crossing was uneventful; the little group kept mostly to themselves. Once they had arrived safely in New York, they immediately took a train for Guelph.

In later years, Mrs. Angus Dunbar recalled meeting Fiorenza for the first time: "We were both eight or nine years old, and we were friends right away, even though she spoke no English. She learned to ride my little two-wheel bike. . . . She was here off and on for several years. She went to Bishop Strachan School in Toronto, then to Switzerland for awhile, then she studied in Germany. Her father saw her whenever he could, but he was very busy. Fiorenza used to say to me, 'You're lucky to have your mother and father.' We always felt very close. And poor Tata! I can still see her wading after us through water one cold, stormy Sunday when we had thought it fun to run away!"

From Guelph, Eddie took Fiorenza, Tata and the governess to his brother Fred's in Michigan while he went apartment hunting. Once having found what he thought was a suitable place, he brought them there to live with him in Chicago.

Fiorenza's Italian name, her Italian habit of curtseying to her teacher and her way of wearing an apron to keep her dress clean, caused the children in the Chicago private school to dub her "the Wop." That hurt; Eddie resented it, too. He couldn't take his daughter out to the wood-shed, as his father had him and his brother, and teach her to box to defend herself, but he could offer his advice: "You'll have to reason things out for yourself. Make some friends, and develop your own defenses." It was partially because of this situation, however, that he didn't argue too strongly when the Chicago Opera insisted that he officially return to his own name of Johnson and drop Di Giovanni. Chicago headlines, as it happened, had already proclaimed: "Edward Johnson,

Considered First Dramatic Tenor in Italy, Returns This Fall After Ten Years' Absence—Story of His Remarkable Career."

Meanwhile, Fiorenza, once she was used to the setting, soon wanted to become part of her new environment. So it wasn't long until she and the governess, who spoke no English and insisted that Fiorenza speak only Italian at home, came to the parting of the ways. To the delight of both Fiorenza and Tata, who had developed a very proprietary attitude toward her young charge, the governess was sent back to Italy.

Eddie's first appearance with the Chicago Opera was as Loris in *Fedora,* on November 20, 1919. As Edward Johnson, he received the same kind of critical acclaim to which Edoardo di Giovanni had become accustomed. *Musical America* carried the headline, "Johnson, in *Fedora,* Wins Rare Triumph; Halts Opera"; *The American* proclaimed, "Johnson Sensation in *Fedora*"; and *The Evening Post,* "New Opera Idol Appears: Johnson, American Tenor, Hits the Bell."

He had conquered Chicago on his own, instead of riding on the laurels of Edoardo di Giovanni. He still wondered, however, whether the management had been right in assuring him there was more publicity value in his own name, as a former Broadway star and the most popular oratorio tenor in the country, than in the name he had made famous in Italy. "You may be right," he told them, "but I can't help feeling it will cost me at least two years of my career to win the prestige here that the name Di Giovanni automatically carried with it." As it happened he proved to be right. Meanwhile, he had other problems: when he found himself billed as an "American Tenor," his blood boiled. He told the management, quite calmly but definitely, that he was not American, but "Canadian, and proud of it."

As had been the case with the Chicago Opera début, Eddie's first appearance with the Chicago Symphony (December 20, 1919) was an outstanding success. "He received an ovation from the audience," according to the *Chicago Tribune,* but the reviewer found a "lack of repose and freedom [in his concert manner] that marred the effect of some beautiful singing. And the English of the *Meistersinger* excerpts proved somewhat of a stumbling block, too. Learning to sing his own language as well as he does foreign tongues is still something for Mr. Johnson to add to his repertoire."

Eddie wondered, time and time again, how long he was going to be able to go on without Bebe. He felt like a ship without a captain, for it was she who had steered the course of their lives, and watched over his singing. He thought wistfully of Edoardo di Giovanni, the hard-working yet carefree and happy young man, who had lived such a full life. He had not yet quite come to terms with the new Edward Johnson, acclaimed a star again in the United States, with all the glamour and glitter that went with it. "He was young and handsome," Eddie smiled ruefully to himself as he read the concert review, "a still slender man, built on clean-cut American lines, who can wear a dress suit as though he were accustomed to it and he had one that was a triumph of the tailor's skill." Tears suddenly filled Eddie's eyes. He had brought that suit with him from Italy. Bee had insisted he buy it, and had been so proud of him at the fitting.

Edward Johnson was entertained, fêted, lionized; the pattern of his future life was becoming clear. "Do you plan to marry again?" He always winced when anyone asked that question. Then one evening, when he was being interrogated by a most charming young woman, he looked into her eyes and found himself wondering whether he might not marry again some day. This particular young woman was to feature prominently in his personal life for many years. In any case, it was obvious at the time that there was not going to be any lack of opportunity if and when he did decide to marry. His dinner partner the previous evening, for instance, had made it clear that she was his for the asking. Suddenly he had felt very much alone.

As the weeks went by, he, who was accustomed to singing several times a week in Italy, found himself singing only once every two or three weeks in Chicago. Used to being the "star" and coming in for special productions and plenty of rehearsals, he found himself sharing the tenor repertoire with Tito Schipa, Bonci, Dolci, Forrest Lamont and others and walking into performances with little or no rehearsal. In addition, he and Mary Garden, the reigning diva, did not exactly hit it off. Their two egos had met head on, and Mary was not about to be upstaged by "that young Canadian upstart from Italy." Soon after Johnson's début, Miss Garden made it clear both to him and to the management that she would not sing *Pelléas et Mélisande* with him in Chicago.

"In that opera," she said, "*I* am the star."

"But after all," he reminded her, "the opera is called *Pelléas et Mélisande*."

"When I sing the opera," was Mary's acid rejoinder, "Mélisande is the star of the show."

They looked steadily at each other for a few seconds, but in that brief moment, war was declared.

Between his début in Chicago, and his final opera that season on January 17, 1920, Johnson was scheduled for only seven performances: *Fedora* (two), *Il Trittico* (three) and *L'Amore dei tre re* (two). He was only one of many in a company that was discontented, performing in an atmosphere of rivalry and petty bickerings. The sudden death of Cleofonte Campanini on December 19 was a great blow. As head of the company as well as principal conductor, he was respected and beloved. He was a tiny man who could be both temperamental and difficult, but the artists always knew they could depend on him to cast them in the roles that were best for them, and the management knew it could depend on his wisdom both in casting and choice of repertoire. With his sense of the dramatic, Campanini would have appreciated the scene in the opera house, in his honour, Eddie always thought, for it was full of drama in the best operatic tradition. There he was, lying in state in the centre of the great open flower-filled stage of the opera house. The orchestra played, the members of the company sang and wept as they filed past the coffin, and when the last mourner had passed, the curtain slowly lowered.

It was a relief to Eddie that his friend Gino Marinuzzi, with whom he had sung so often in Italy, was appointed to succeed Campanini as artistic director. Marinuzzi was a great conductor, and Eddie was sure he could do great things for the Chicago Opera. But he stepped into an impossible situation: Mary Garden insisted upon stating openly that "nobody can touch Campanini, nobody in the world."

Between opera performances, Johnson filled in with concert engagements. Once, he hopped over to Toledo for a joint concert with the American contralto Sophie Braslau. They hit it off so well that she didn't even seem to resent it when he was given the lion's share of the reviews, being compared to Jean de Reszke and praised for his "towering expression and tonal beauty." She even suggested that it might be profitable for both of them if they teamed up for some joint concerts the next year.

The season closed in Chicago on January 24, 1920, with *The Barber of Seville,* and opened two days later at the Lexington Opera House in New York, January 26, with *L'Amore dei tre re.* Edward Johnson, as Avito, was not only the hero of the opera, but of the occasion. Hundreds of telegrams and good wishes came in, but one that pleased him especially was from an old voice teacher in New York: "Heartfelt wishes for brilliant success of the star. I shall hear him from the fourth row tonight." It was signed "L. von Feilitsch."

Although Eddie sang opposite Mary Garden that night, there was no doubt of his conquest of New York. The *New York Tribune* reported that he "was all that he had been heralded, a fine figure of a man, tall, lithe, graceful—a romantic figure if ever there was one. His voice, too, was a fine one, and beautifully used, a dramatic tenor of rather light quality, but capable of expressing deep emotion. The curtain fell with Mr. Johnson a great success."

IT HAD BEEN good for Eddie to have Fiorenza and Tata in Chicago with him that first winter, but he wanted Fiorenza to develop a feeling for Canada. Besides, there was that most charming young woman he had met when he first arrived in Chicago and in whom he had become interested. He would like to be free to see more of her. So, before he started on his round of summer concerts, he took his daughter and Tata to his parents in Guelph and made arrangements for Fiorenza to attend public school there in the fall. "I want you to lead a fine, healthy, normal Canadian life," he told her. "It will be good for you."

Actually, Eddie's summer engagements might be said to have started with the recital he had agreed to give in the Opera House in Guelph, March 29, 1920. The old house had never been as crowded nor resounded to louder applause for anything or anybody. It was a real triumph for Eddie to have conquered his hometown in such a way. His mother was flushed with pride and happiness, and his father, true to form, had a bit of celebrating to do, and for days after Eddie had left town was telling tales of Eddie's boyhood, how the boy had inherited his talent from the Johnsons and how he, Jimmie, had been the one who had encouraged him from the beginning to go into singing.

On March 30, Eddie received an official letter from the town's Mayor Westaby:

> Our own dear gifted Son:
> Your fellow citizens, one and all, unite in bidding you welcome, a thousand welcomes, back to the home of your boyhood days, and we do so with a rare pleasure, because of the fact that from this City you went forth into the great world without, to conquer it with your gift of song. . . . It is a pleasure to know that your pre-eminent success has not in any way robbed you of the joyous hand clasp, the friendly grace, and congenial charm of your boyhood days. You are still one of us, our own dear gifted son with surpassing talent and fame, but with the same glad, home-loving heart, as of yore. . . . The Mayor and Aldermen, the Chamber of Commerce, the Canadian Club, as well as the men, women and children of Guelph rejoice together in the pleasure of having you with us again, and will ever wish and pray for your welfare and continued success in contributing to the happiness and enjoyment of your fellow countrymen, and of all music lovers throughout the world.
> W. Westaby, in behalf of all the citizens of Guelph.

Fiorenza had been allowed to stay up late that night and had been intensely proud of her Babbo. Her heart was broken next day, however, when he told her that he would be away most of the summer. At first her only consolation was that her beloved Tata was with her, but she soon came to love her grandparents—her sweet warm-hearted grandmother and her funny grandfather, who was always either blustering or making jokes. Later, after she had started school in Guelph, and become friends with some other girls and boys, she discovered that her language gave her a kind of importance. Her letters to Eddie bubbled with such enthusiastic accounts of her new friends and activities that his mind was at ease. He had done the right thing; his little girl was going to be fine.

One of his singing engagements that summer of 1920 had been as a soloist in the Syracuse Music Festival in May, where he met two fellow Canadians, Lady Eaton and Mrs. William Dobie. Lady Eaton saw and heard Edward Johnson that evening from the box of the president of the Festival and his wife, and many years later, in her autobiography, *Memory's Wall*, told an amusing anecdote about the singer's entrance: "A young, handsome, slight man walked onto the stage and smiled at his audience. There was an 'A-ah!' over the house and my hostess turned to me and said, 'That man can make love to me whenever he likes!'" At a supper party in his honour afterward, Eddie was sitting with Flora Eaton, discussing music and her own vocal studies and personal ambitions. They hummed along together on some of their favourite songs, and Edward found himself impulsively offering to sing a concert in Toronto with her, as a benefit for any one of her favourite charities. When Lady Eaton and Mrs. Dobie were accused by their husbands of being "just two women bowled over by a charming man," Flora suggested they could see for themselves, inasmuch as she had invited Mr. Johnson to be their guest the next time he came to Toronto, which he promised would be soon.

"He came, he saw, and he conquered all," Lady Eaton recorded. "Our men are so mad about Edward that we don't even get a chance to speak to him." And true it was that Sir John had invited Eddie to be their guest aboard their private railway car, the *Eatonia*, during Eddie's projected recital tour of western Ontario cities the following year.

Eventually, the subject of the Toronto concert for charity came up, "with both Edward and Jack," as Flora Eaton put it, "prodding me into action." She secured the enthusiastic support of Mrs. Lionel Clarke, wife of the Lieutenant Governor of Ontario, and her Women's Committee for the work of the blind. Suddenly Lady Eaton realized she was being forced into taking her own singing seriously. "It was a case of putting up or shutting up," she admitted. So she worked five hours a day with a coach all summer, then with a pianist, Arthur Blight, for several weeks, prior to trying out her own part of the program in a studio soirée which Edward Johnson attended. Heartened by his suggestions and comments, she worked some more and did another try-out. This time it was for students at the Toronto Conservatory Concert Hall. Soon after that, it was decided that she was ready to appear before an audience in Massey Hall, and a date (October 29, 1920) was set for what turned out to be a gala event.

The Hall was sold out, to an audience in full evening dress, with the Lieutenant Governor himself and other dignitaries occupying the loge seats at the right of the stage. The concert was a great success for the cause it sponsored, the proceeds being the highest ever realized for a single event in Toronto. As a singer, Lady Eaton was not up to the demands of being a partner to the famous Edward Johnson on a concert platform, but then she herself had said beforehand, "He is a famous artist; I am an amateur." Nevertheless, Edward Johnson complimented her on her "triumph," and told everyone how good it was to be back home, singing for Canadians again.

The 1920/21 season at the Chicago Opera promised much for Edward Johnson. It opened on November 17, as advertised, with Marinuzzi's *Jacquerie*, based on a story of the fourteenth-century peasant revolt in France, with Yvonne Gall and Edward Johnson heading the cast. The sets and costumes alone cost $50,000—an extravagance that did not pay off at the box office, although the stars, particularly Johnson, fared well in the reviews. Eddie had felt secure about his appearance in that, having first sung the opera at the Costanzi in March, 1919. He also liked the prospect of singing several *Pagliacci*'s, a *Trittico,* two performances of *L'Amore dei tre re*, and two *Lohengrin*'s. (The thought crossed his mind that Bee would have been pleased about that.) All in all, it was more interesting than the first season.

But after Maestro Marinuzzi's sudden resignation in January, 1921, the big boss of opera, Harold McCormick, whose wife was a daughter of John D. Rockefeller, appointed Mary Garden the new director. He wanted the season to go out with a flourish, and said he felt that she, experienced or not, could supply that flourish. She accepted that challenge and immediately planned to culminate the 1920/21 season with a grand national tour.

Miss Garden, unfortunately, proved to be more capricious than efficient as a general manager, and there was dissension and unrest everywhere in the opera house, from stagehands to stars and from secretaries to directors. The season finished more or less on schedule, however, even though the company was operating under an annual deficit of approximately $350,000. Miss Garden's idea of making an

American opera company of it, existing primarily so that young Americans would be welcome and feel at home when applying for auditions, struck home for Edward Johnson. It was an idea that he was to nurture until he was able to put it into effect as general manager of the Metropolitan Opera in New York fifteen years later.

Johnson and Mary Garden avoided each other whenever possible, but were carefully polite when they met. She made no bones about the fact that she would not have him in a performance with her if she could help it. She had to recognize his popularity at the box office, however, and therefore condescended to appear in *L'Amore dei tre re* with him. "You get a lot of applause," she would say. "Why, I'll never know. You must have a good claque." Then she would sweep off before he could reply. Had she been a man, he knew what he would have done.

Meanwhile, he was engaged in a struggle to build up the name of Johnson to the heights he had attained as Edoardo di Giovanni. Feeling very much alone without Bebe at his side, he found himself subconsciously wondering what she would have advised in certain situations. How would she have reacted to the rumours and comments on all sides? From what he could see, he agreed with the New York critic who had written that the Chicago Opera performances had deteriorated since the death of Campanini.

Following the Spring Tour of 1921 (March 9 to April 20) that took them from Pennsylvania to Texas and California, Eddie made his first trip back to Italy since Bee's death. He left Fiorenza and Tata in Guelph with his parents. Drawn as by a magnet to Florence, he first visited Bee's grave, then went to see old friends. He was saddened to find the Casalis in trouble, with Giuseppe's health having deteriorated dramatically and Jo being too worried to be her usual spritely self. She clung to Eddie as though he had the power to restore her husband to health. But he was as helpless as she had been at the time of Bee's fatal illness. They visited Bee's grave together and both cried as they talked of the happy days of such a short time ago. He tried to be as cheerful as possible, but when he said good-bye to the Casalis, he was convinced that he would never see them both together again.

Edward Johnson stopped in Paris, from where he wrote Fiorenza, in a mixture of English and Italian as usual, that he would be home soon, that he had seen "Sir John and Lady Eaton . . . on their way to Switzerland . . . dined with them yesterday and expect to again today. Have not seen Mme Guitry as yet, but hope to very soon . . . *Parto a Parigi 16 Settembre sulla* Finland . . . *Sarò a New York il 25.*"

What a joyous reunion they had in Guelph. Fiorenza was beaming with happiness until she learned that her father's schedule of concerts and festival appearances would keep him on the go most of the time. The month of October flew by; the only personal invitations he accepted were those from the Eatons. Otherwise, he spent most of his weekends in Guelph. When it came time for him to leave for Chicago and another season of opera there, he had to face a tearful good-bye from Fiorenza.

Things did not go as well for him as he had been led to believe they would. First of all, the unrest in the company was serious. Worrying about that, and being occupied hours a day learning new concert repertoire, he found himself seeing fewer and fewer people and spending more and more time with his "charming friend." She had been on his mind much of the time since he had left Chicago in the spring. Of course they talked about the Chicago Opera, inasmuch as she was connected with one phase of the organization. The season had offered some great performances, they agreed: Charles Marshall's Otello, Rosa Raïsa's Desdemona, Mary Garden's Fiora and, of course, Edward Johnson's Avito. Then there was Titta Ruffo's performance in the title role of Leoncavallo's ill-starred *Edipo Re.*

Actually Miss Garden had gone to Europe during the summer and returned with contracts, it was reported, for the largest number of artists in the Chicago Opera's entire history, promising them fees that were more than generous. The trouble was that "La Directa," as she was known, had contracts for almost twice as many singers in each category as were actually needed or that she could possibly use! The morale went from bad to worse and there was a notable lowering of the artistic standards, generally. Every time Mary Garden appeared in an opera, critics continued to speak of her beauty and the fascination she held for her audiences. But the company was getting deeper and deeper into debt: $100,000 was lavished on the world première of Prokofiev's *The Love for Three Oranges,* on December 30, 1921, which was termed by many a disaster.

Artists who were given no opportunity to sing were being paid; Johanna Gadski, hired to sing Isolde at $1,500 per performance, had arrived for rehearsals, waited for two weeks, heard nothing, was never able to get the management to set the date for her performances and, eventually, was given a cheque for $7,500 and told her services would not be required. Another singer, the noted tenor Lucien Muratore, signed to sing as Samson at $2,800 a performance, refused to sing at all when he learned that some of his performances were being given to Charles Marshall. In actual fact Mr. Marshall, like Edward Johnson, sang only one role that season. For Eddie it was six performances as Lieutenant Pinkerton!

He went back to Guelph for Christmas (1921) with the intention of leaving the family early and spending New Year's Eve in Chicago. Fiorenza was furious and hurt when she heard about it. "Why, why, why?" she stormed. "Why are you always leaving me?" Momentarily off guard, he tried to calm her by suggesting he might have a new "mother" for her soon—then they could all be together all the time. It was a mistake. Fiorenza burst into uncontrollable tears and was so hysterically unhappy that Eddie found himself promising her that no one would ever come between them—that he would "not marry anybody ever." It had been in the back of his mind, he realized, to propose to his Chicago friend on New Year's Eve, but he abandoned the thought and, oddly enough, had to confess to himself that he was relieved! In which case, he must have been deluding himself, he thought. If Fiorenza's tears could turn him aside from his intentions so easily, he could not have been in love. He resolved to be more careful in the future. Much as he disliked living alone, it had its advantages.

It was about this time that he received word of the death of Giuseppe Casali, Jo's husband. She was lost without him and needed Eddie's counsel and sympathy. So he turned his thoughts toward her and planned to go to Italy again as soon as possible.

In the meantime, the friendship established in Syracuse between Edward Johnson and the John Eatons continued to grow. He was often a guest at *Ardwold*, their home in Toronto on the hill above Davenport Road. A daughter, Florence Eaton McEachren, recalled that some of her earliest memories were of Edward Johnson at the piano in their living room: "Mother would be singing and he would be playing for her."

The time he used to spend with them in the early months of the friendship were happy and carefree days, for all of them were still young, healthy and venturesome. Flora Eaton found Edward Johnson handsome, charming and always full of fun; he found her unpredictable, charming, and interested in all things—travel, sports, music—and, at the same time, a realist. He and Sir John both enjoyed boating, golf and tennis, whereas he and Flora spoke of music and far-away places. In the evenings, there would be animated conversations in which the Eatons were always amazed at their guest's sound business sense and his grasp of the political developments in Canada and the world.

In January, 1922, Edward Johnson received word that Sir John had been stricken with pneumonia and, in spite of all efforts of leading doctors in the ensuing weeks, he died on March 30. It was at that time that Edward Johnson, with his own bereavement so vivid, was able to offer sympathetic words and friendship to Flora Eaton that helped give her courage as she faced the future and her responsibilities both in business

101

and as mother of three young children. A deep affection and bond of understanding developed that was to set tongues wagging repeatedly through the years about a romance.

In view of the Chicago Opera situation, it was fortunate that the negotiations of Eddie's managers with the Metropolitan Opera were proceeding favourably. He assured Mary Garden, however, that he would stay with the Company for the ambitious national tour that would take them from New York to San Francisco, with a guarantee of a sufficient number of performances to make the trip worthwhile. Actually, Eddie needed every penny at the moment, because he had bought some property in Guelph during the year. A friend there, Tom Hannigan, advised it as a good investment.

With the Chicago tour little more than started, Eddie received an encouraging wire from Wolfsohn (March 24, 1922): "Met contract to start November 14, end February 14, then concerts start in spring, leaving no time for Chicago. In addition, their contracts do not allow singing for any other company. Curci [Galli-Curci] an isolated case. Will be glad to do anything for Shaw [C. A. Shaw, business manager and tour director of Chicago Opera under Mary Garden], but you owe company and directors nothing. Make decision for the future of your career only."

Eddie's reply was immediate: "Loyalty demands that Shaw be given an option on at least one month since I can't be among his possibilities for next season. Give him chance before signing. Price seems low, prestige may warrant sacrifice and increased concerts compensate financial loss. Leave detailed repertoire until my return. Otherwise go ahead."

To which Wolfsohn rejoined that, in the three seasons Edward Johnson had sung with the Chicago Opera Company, they had given him very meagre returns for all he'd done and was willing to do for them. Then he added: "Now that you have left them, you have become a Caruso, and the whole organization is disrupted because you left. I explained to them that under no circumstances whatever would we make a contract while Mary Garden was head of the company, and that we had every reason to believe that she was going to remain in charge up to April 24."

The 1922 Spring Tour of the Chicago Opera had opened in February with a month-long engagement at the Manhattan Opera House in New York. During that visit, everyone said, the company had done themselves no special good. One New York critic spoke of them as the "Lake Michigan Minnesingers." Another wrote: "Not even the Chicago Opera Company, which has apparently thrown to the winds most of its earlier pretensions to fine art, can continue to live by noise alone." Mary

Garden had retorted: "New York critics are dried up old men, with no modern sap in their veins." She didn't like to admit it, but she found herself trying to fill a position for which she had not only no training and no experience, but very few qualifications.

At the same time, a feeling of insecurity and apprehension existed within the company itself. Over and over again, throughout the tour, Miss Garden was asked whether she planned to continue as the company's director, and over and over again she was non-committal. But at the end of the tour she did resign her post as general director and was succeeded by Samuel Insull. "Yes," she admitted in her autobiography, when discussing her brief tenure as general director, "it cost a million dollars, but I'm sure it was worth it." Few Chicagoans disagreed with her—not even Harold McCormick, whose dollars had kept the company afloat.

When the tour was over, Eddie spent a couple of weeks in Guelph. Then, with Fiorenza happy to be left there with her grandparents and her new friends in Guelph for the summer, he headed for Italy. He went directly to Florence where he had little difficulty in persuading Jo Casali that a few weeks on Elba with him (the Mellinis had invited them both) would do her good. "The most delightful days of my summer," he wrote Fiorenza, "were spent on the island of Elba in a charming corner on the southern shore, under Monte Ceparne. Next time, we will come over together," he promised. "It was wonderfully silent and restful. From our bathing beach we enjoyed a splendid view of the other islands. To the south, only a few miles away, lies that island of mystery and adventure, Monte Cristo." His words fired Fiorenza's impressionable imagination. "Then there is the profile of Corsica, birthplace of Napoleon. Within driving distance San Martino, the villa where Napoleon passed his exile and which today is owned and maintained as a museum by Max Bondi, the Otto Kahn of Italy. On Elba everything moves slowly. There are no railroads, but there are big vincyards everywhere, providing the most delicious wine, and Elba's iron mines and her quarries of chocolate-coloured marble promise greatness for the future. The quarries, by the way, belong to our friend Count Mellini and his wife. They tell me these same quarries furnished the granite for the Pantheon in Rome, for the Cathedral in Cologne and even for St. Paul's in London."

*5*
EDDIE RETURNED to America earlier than he had intended. Because of a rheumatic infection that had been threatening him most of the season, he went back to Guelph on his doctor's orders, for a complete rest. The enforced vacation meant the cancellation of his early engagements that season, but it was a blessing in that he was mentally, physically and vocally rested for his Metropolitan Opera début, November 16, 1922, as Avito in *L'Amore dei tre re*. He found the cast cooperative during the rehearsals, especially the soprano, Lucrezia Bori, and the conductor, Roberto Moranzoni, most sympathetic and complimentary. Nevertheless, the night of the opening Eddie was sure he had never been as nervous before in his life. He was in the corridor outside his dressing room when the general manager, Giulio Gatti-Casazza, and the administrative director, Edward Ziegler, suddenly emerged from the tiny backstage elevator to wish him well.

Gatti's *In bocca al lupo*, and his quietly sad but friendly smile, restored Eddie's confidence.

"*Grazie, tante grazie*, Signor Gatti."

"What an odd couple they are," he thought, as Gatti's great sloping figure, with Ziegler's small trim one beside him, went down the broad stairway to the stage level. Edward Johnson had seen very little of the general manager since coming to the Met, but the inexplicable and instantaneous sense of rapport he felt for Gatti, from the time of their first meeting backstage, was to grow into a relationship that was unique for Gatti.

Gatti-Casazza's life was the opera house. He was always there, turning up quite unexpectedly if a decision had to be made or a dispute settled. Insofar as anyone knew, he spoke only Italian, yet nothing that was ever said in English seemed to escape him. He was respected and admired. Everybody knew that they could come to him at any time with their problems: they also knew better than to try to get information from him before he was ready to give it, or to influence him in any decisions. He confided in no one and his rule was absolute. It was often said he ran his office from scraps of paper in his pockets and the memory of his secretary, Luigi Villa! Gatti-Casazza also had a prodigious memory, as young Edward Ziegler had discovered soon after coming to work for him as "administrative secretary."

All these thoughts, racing through Edward Johnson's mind, left no room for the nervousness he had felt a few moments earlier. Long before his call to the stage, however, the familiar sinking feeling had returned to his stomach and the drinking glass trembled in his hand when he tried to wet his dry throat. Another tenor, Richard Crooks, grasped his hand and wished him luck just as he was about to set foot on the stage. "Nice of him," thought Eddie. Then he heard the familiar music of his cue.

And so it was that on the third night of the 1922/23 season at the Metropolitan Opera House, Edward Johnson strode onto the stage, exuding charm and confidence. Avito was not new to him—he had sung it all over Italy and had captivated the Chicago audiences with it.

Richard Aldrich, in the *New York Times*, told the story the next day: "Mr. Johnson as a singing actor is remembered as one of the finest members of the Chicago Opera in his recent visits to New York. He has a voice of warm tenor quality, which he uses with skill and with telling dramatic effect; a voice of power, but capable of reserves and subject to the discipline of musical understanding. He enacted the part with a chivalrous romantic ardor, with intelligence and feeling; for here is a tenor who is something more than a voice, who is an artistic personality. What he did last evening seems to assure the value of his membership in the company."

By the time his father and mother, and his brother Fred and his wife reached the dressing room after the performance, another successful appearance was behind him. For the first time his father, basking in the reflected glory of the moment, said, "I'm proud of you, Eddie," loud enough for everyone to hear him. They were words which would have meant much to his son during the long years of training and struggle, but they failed to stir much emotion in the heart of the Metropolitan Opera tenor Edward Johnson, who turned to respond to his mother's warm emotion-filled embrace, and the congratulations of his brother and other friends and colleagues who were crowding into the room. The dressing room wall was lined with telegrams and letters of good wishes from all over the world, but Eddie prized most highly the concisely-worded cable from composer Montemezzi himself, from Milan: *Vivissime congratulazioni. Auguri.*

Four nights later, on Monday evening, November 20, Edward Johnson was called upon to replace Orville Harrold, and to sing, for the first time in his life, the role of Dimitri to Feodor Chaliapin's Boris Godunov, with Margarete Matzenauer as Marina. *Godunov* was staged by von Wymetal and conducted by Gennaro Papi. In spite of good reviews, Edward looked on it as a waste of time, a role for which he had no affinity. He was more comfortable and on familiar ground five days later (November 25, 1922) in *Manon Lescaut,* and scored once again opposite Frances Alda's Manon, with Antonio Scotti as Lescaut.

*Tosca* (December 1) gave Eddie an opportunity to prove his skill against the glamorous Maria Jeritza; *Boris* (December 7), *Carmen* (December 16), *Tosca* (December 19), *Pagliacci* (January 3), *Butterfly* (January 19) and *Pagliacci* (January 20) were to follow. Then on February 2 came an opera in which he and his partner, Lucrezia Bori, completely captivated the public: *Roméo et Juliette.* There was a *Faust* on February 8, and a final *Roméo* on February 10, and Edward Johnson's stint for his first season at the Metropolitan Opera was over. He had been successful even when the roster included such other tenors as Gigli, Martinelli, Tokatyan, Harrold, Paul Althouse, Mario Chamlee, Rafaelo Diaz, Giacomo Lauri-Volpi, Manuel Salazar and Morgan Kingston.

Edward Johnson had made a good impression on everyone at the Metropolitan, particularly on the coaches, conductors and management, in more ways than one. For example, Maestro Wilfrid Pelletier says in his book *Une Symphonie Inachevée*: "It was reassuring to see Johnson arrive for rehearsal. He already knew, by memory, the role we were studying. He was also very talented. I do not recall seeing him make the smallest mistake in any roles he sang. His greatest success was as Romeo of which he was the very incarnation, and Pelléas, which he created at the Met in March, 1925. His success was such that Gatti kept that opera in the repertoire, with Johnson in the title role, until the end of his administration."

Eddie was preoccupied with family affairs in Guelph, for his father was causing his mother concern because he was spending too much time with his drinking companions in the hotel bar. Then there was Fiorenza, whom he had decided to send to a private school, the Bishop Strachan School in Toronto, that fall.

At the end of his Metropolitan contract for the 1922/23 season, Eddie embarked immediately on a heavy concert schedule. Following that, on May 24, he sailed on the *Olympic* for England to make his début at the Royal Opera House, Covent Garden, with Nellie Melba and the British National Opera Company in *Faust* (June 21, 1923). Fiorenza would like to have gone with him, but it was the sensible thing to do to leave her in Guelph with his parents, and under the watchful eye of Tata.

Rehearsals went well in England, and Edward Johnson found Nellie Melba not at all as temperamental as he had been led to expect, although she was inclined to be strangely uncommunicative. Then, too, she was capricious as far as rehearsals were concerned—she might or might not appear, and she might or might not stay until the end. This was both baffling and frustrating.

During this period, Johnson met Melba's accompanist, Frank St. Leger, for the first time, and the two men promptly formed a friendship and professional relationship which would continue throughout their lives.

After the first performance of *Faust* on June 21, 1923, the Harry Higinbothams and Edward were among the party of sixteen entertained by Melba at her beautiful house on Mansfield Avenue. "Our party," Harry recorded in his diary, "consisted of Bobby and Lilly Waldi, Mona and Norman Morrison, Colonel Somerville, Mary Waldon and the Earles and Frank St. Leger."

The *Times* of June 22, 1923, reported that in the performance of the evening before Melba had introduced the new tenor Edward Johnson, "of whom great things were expected," and had naturally made the occasion "something like a full dress parade of old days. But it is the 'something like' that is disturbing and leaves a sense of dissatisfaction. . . . The fact that Faust and Marguerite sang in French and the rest in English left the disturbing sense of something like, but not quite. . . . *Faust* is essentially an opera for young voices. Dame Nellie Melba, with all her finished style, which made itself felt constantly (the 'Jewel Song' was exquisite in its way) has no longer the sparkle in her voice which the garden scene needs. Mr. Edward Johnson's singing seemed marked more by ease than by refinement and fervour of force. He rarely let himself go, and though we recognized the merits of his singing and the fine quality of the voice, especially the upper part, his performance had not the glow and thrill of the great tenor . . . the fact is that it takes either very distinguished solo work or very vivid ensemble work if *Faust* is to be anything more than a suitable entertainment after a day at Ascot. His performance certainly reached that standard, but not much more."

On Sunday, the 28th, the second and final performance of *Faust* was given and, according to Harry Higinbotham, was "a great success." Fifi Moulton, over from Paris, and Mrs. Lesseur Simpson were in the box with the Higinbothams.

The following day Eddie left for a week in Paris to see the city again and renew old acquaintances and visit with Fifi, who seemed to need his advice and companionship. Then he left for Florence where he immediately called Jo Casali. He had been looking forward to seeing her again—no need for subterfuge or pretense; he found it very comfortable to be with her and their mutual friends there.

Everyone wanted to hear about his experiences at the Metropolitan during the season, and everyone wanted to know how he liked singing with Mme Melba. When he finally left Florence, Jo went with him as they were both to be guests again of the Mellinis on Elba. It was obvious that Jo had fallen in love with Eddie, and that he wasn't unmoved himself. "But Fiorenza is very possessive," he told her, thinking back to the incident with his Chicago friend two years previously, "and I wouldn't do anything in the world to hurt her."

"But you have your own life to lead and your own happiness to think of," Jo countered. "Do you think you are being fair to yourself? Or to Fiorenza? Tata can't possibly take the place of a mother."

Eddie was happier in those days than he had been in all the time since Bebe died. But would it work with Jo? Did he love her, or was it just that she, and Florence, gave him back a piece of the past? He must wait and see—think it over once he was back in New York.

They parted on Elba that year—a romantic parting. Then, after a short stop in Paris, Eddie took the boat for New York. He was looking forward to another good workout at the "Y" in New York—he hadn't had one for months and he missed it. He spent several days there before going to Guelph to make final arrangements for the winter. Fiorenza was to be transferred to the Bishop Strachan School in Toronto, and Tata would go back to Florence for the winter.

By the time all the decisions were made, Edward Johnson was feeling tired. Nevertheless, he had a heavily-booked schedule of concert and oratorio engagements that would precede his first appearance at the Met. He got through them all, he never knew how, by calling upon every bit of vocal technique and every trick he could command. His final concert was in Canada, as it happened, for the Women's Musical Club in Edmonton, on January 8, 1924. He had a cold, and considered cancelling the concert. But he feared there might be those who would think he hadn't considered the engagement important. Also, he didn't want to let them down. So he gave the full program, even several encores. He sang with restraint until the printed program was finished, in order to last through to the end. "But in the *Pagliacci* number," Wilfrid Horner reported in the *Calgary Albertan,* "he threw off all restraint and gave of his best. It was a moment long to be remembered . . . and a thoroughly aroused, delighted audience gave him their unstinted adoration. [They]

108

all left with a feeling of intense gratification at having heard the world's greatest tenor, direct from the Metropolitan Opera House—a Canadian who is proud of his homeland and who has brought much honour to it."

Edward Johnson's contract with the Metropolitan that season (1923/ 24) started on January 30 with a Roméo to Queena Mario's Juliette. He didn't feel well, but he sang the performance; also a *Pagliacci* on February 1, and *Roméo,* February 11, with Galli-Curci. But he was forced to cancel the rest of his Metropolitan Opera engagements for the season, on doctor's advice. His agent tried to console him by saying: "Your concert fees have gone up so much that it costs you money every time you sing at the Metropolitan, anyway." But it wasn't the money that was worrying Eddie. He was ill and he knew it. It was a new experience. Except for minor aches and pains, an occasional cold and the chronic problem that a "bedtime cocktail" (castor oil) always solved, he had enjoyed good health. Seldom in his life had he ever had to give up. This time, it was his back. The doctor advised him to wear a support.

"It's nothing but a corset, that's what it is," was Eddie's reaction. But after he had consulted two other doctors, the verdict was the same. "Wear a support and take a couple of months of complete rest . . . it will make a new man of you." So he went home to Guelph where his friend Jessie Hill told him it was a blessing in disguise, for it would give him time to work on new roles and learn new concert repertoire. She promised to stop in two or three times a week to play for him. Actually, that enforced holiday proved to be one of the most relaxed and heart-warming periods he had had for many a year. The climax came at Easter time when the family was all together—his parents, Fiorenza and Tata, with relatives and friends. When the time came to begin his spring concerts, he was ready .

Edward Johnson was popular wherever he went. He had a way, in his concerts, of making an audience feel that each person there mattered to him. Any woman meeting him for the first time got the impression that she was the most important person in his life. He had to develop a technique whereby he could extricate himself successfully before becoming involved in any serious entanglements. But Edward Johnson was also a man's man. He could hold his own when it came to telling stories, and was the envy of many for his speechmaking ability. His prowess was not limited to the drawing room nor the platform, however, for he could "wield a wicked niblick," as one of his friends put it, "and loved a good game of baseball, too."

His accompanist that year was Alexander Smallens who would later conduct many a grand opera. Mr. Smallens, who shared honours in the reviews that season, had the highest praise for Edward Johnson: "He was a first-rate colleague and an excellent musician. It was Edward Johnson who made possible the triumph of song, on legitimate lines of great interpretation, with quality of tone, legato line, polished phrasing, clear enunciation and a true regard for the intentions of the composer. And he sang his opera arias, particularly *Vesti la giubba* with which he often closed his programs, with a passion and intensity that carried all before it."

Edward found himself writing to Fiorenza almost as though she were Bebe—and after a time she began to feel, too, that there was only a fine line of distinction in her father's mind between her and her mother. "You must keep up your languages," he wrote, "and read constantly, and learn to absorb what you read; and learn to play the piano well and, above all, learn to laugh—a laugh will take you smoothly over many a hurdle." Little by little Bebe had assumed superhuman proportions in Fiorenza's mind, as Edward and Tata filled her head with stories about how wonderful her mother had been. She was torn—to be what her father wanted her to be was to be different from her new Canadian friends. "At some point," she later commented, "the Canadian influence won."

Meanwhile, she was a constant problem insofar as her father was concerned: by her own admission, she had never applied herself in school and that year, at Bishop Strachan School, it was the same thing. Eddie was disturbed also that she seemed to be losing all traces of her European heritage. So he decided that the time had come to send her to a European school. Money being no longer any obstacle—his income and investments were substantial—he made a thorough inquiry of possible places, and finally settled on Les Fougères, in Lausanne, Switzerland. "Then next year," he told her, "I think you should study in Dresden. That way you will perfect your French and German, to add to your Italian and English." He said that the two of them would take a holiday together in Italy first, and that he would go with her to see her safely installed in the new school.

There was a delay, because Eddie had been invited to sing at Ravinia Park outside Chicago. The conditions and the pay were so good that he could hardly refuse, even if he had wanted to. In addition, it would bring him back to the area of his first success after his return to America. Some of his associates at the Metropolitan, including Maestro Wilfrid Pelletier and the young American tenor Mario Chamlee, formed the nucleus for a group of friends at Ravinia that summer of 1924. Fiorenza begged to be allowed to go with her father, but he thought it best for her to spend the time in Guelph. Besides, the entire operation at Ravinia would be

110

comparatively new and challenging for him. "You don't love me," was Fiorenza's petulant accusation.

Ravinia, an estate of thirty-seven acres, had opened as an amusement park in 1904 under the aegis of the Chicago and Milwaukee Railway Company. Later, the ownership and operation of the park passed into the hands of a group of local citizens headed by Louis Eckstein, a prominent Chicago businessman. At first their musical offerings were limited to band concerts, but in 1906 a symphony orchestra was introduced, conducted by Walter Damrosch. Before long, the bandstand was replaced by a pavilion seating eighteen hundred, with space, according to one report, "for thousands more to sit on blankets or stools while they listened to the music."

Eckstein's musical evenings were offered every night of the week, except Mondays, in that beautiful and spacious setting. By 1912, the programs had expanded from duos and various ensembles to include scenes from operas. Finally, in 1915, full opera productions were inaugurated, and were given each summer thereafter until 1932 for five of the ten weeks of the season. Claudia Muzio sang at Ravinia in 1918; Antonio Scotti, in 1919 (*L'Oracolo*), and in 1920 (*La Tosca*); and Charles Hackett, in 1921. Tito Schipa appeared there for the first time in 1923, and Edward Johnson, over the years, was heard in many of the operas in his repertoire, including *L'Amore dei tre re* with Lucrezia Bori, and with Louis Hasselmans, Papi and young Wilfrid Pelletier on the conducting staff. Two other prominent artists at Ravinia in those days were soprano Rosa Raïsa and her husband, baritone Giacomo Rimini.

The opera ended at ten o'clock so the public could get back to Chicago at a reasonable hour. The members of the company, free so early in the evening, would congregate at the home of first one and then the other for some libation and a sample of the host's or hostess's special Italian pasta and scallopini, French soup, American roast, or whatever. When it was Edward Johnson's turn to play host, he supplied the wine, but someone else had to bring the food. He had never trusted himself in a kitchen since the disastrous experiences during his student days back in New York. "It was in the time of prohibition," he related. "We had to content ourselves with a red wine made by a local Italian family, but it was pretty good, and it had a way of putting us all in a good mood for the next day's rehearsals."

By the time the Ravinia engagement was over, there was only a month left of the summer. Eddie returned to Guelph for Fiorenza and they left immediately for Europe. They stopped briefly in Florence, where all their old friends were amazed that the little girl they remembered was

111

now a young woman of fifteen—albeit somewhat pudgy. Eddie still maintained a small apartment in Florence as a sort of *pied-à-terre* for himself and, during the winter, Tata kept it in order so Fiorenza could spend her school holidays there.

Eddie and Jo Casali had little time to be alone together that summer, but Fiorenza sensed the danger of the situation. Again it was a case of hysterical sobbing: "You promised, you promised!"

"You are nothing but a spoiled child," he said, accusing her of not wanting him to be happy. Nevertheless, he found himself assuring her that he would never bring anyone else in to take her mother's place. Again Edward and Jo parted romantically, but with a certain sadness.

Once Fiorenza was safely deposited in the school in Lausanne, Eddie ignored Fifi's pleas to stop in Paris and went directly back to America. On his arrival there he was met by newspaper reporters who plied him with questions about life in Italy under Mussolini. Believing, as did many others at the time, even astute politicians, that the Italians stood to benefit under Fascism, Edward Johnson told them: "Fascism is a force that is necessary for the development of the political and social unity of all Italians, and without which no such unity could ever have been reached. They have protected private property against socialistic tendencies and have done much that has been good for the country. People say there was no revolution in Italy, but the Fascist revolution was a real one. There was no shedding of blood because Mussolini, as soon as he became master of the field, controlled the outcome. This is the most beautiful side of his mind and the best proof of his Fascisti. He has introduced economy into the government; he has increased the political standing of Italy abroad; and he has brought about the formation of a true national conscience, the germ of which was formed by the war and which the socialist party tried to suffocate. He has established religious liberty and he has reorganized the army while, on the artistic side, everybody knows the fine place Italy holds in the world of art."

The 1924/25 season at the Metropolitan would not begin for Edward Johnson until February 6, 1925, when he would sing *Carmen*. The most important thing was that he was scheduled to appear at the end of March in the first Metropolitan production of *Pelléas et Mélisande,* with Bori as Mélisande.

Again Fiorenza was becoming a bit of a nuisance. She was not serious. Eddie was disappointed in her; he told her so. Her letter of December 12, 1924, from Switzerland, began, "Daddy, mon cher," and continued in French for a page, after which she switched to English. She hoped the next year would bring them together oftener than in the past. "I want you, Daddy, darling. I need you. I need your love and your

# Edward Johnson

## Stardom on Broadway, in Italy and at the Met

As Niki, in the première, January 27, 1908,
of Oscar Straus's *A Waltz Dream*, Edward Johnson
became a Broadway star overnight.

# Italy, 1912-1919

As Ippolito, in the world première of Pizzetti's *Fedra*, La Scala, Milan, March 20, 1915

Teatro Verdi, Padova, at the time of Johnson's operatic début, 1912

In leading tenor role of *Mascagni's Isabeau*, Ancona, 1912

In operatic début, as Andrea Chénier, Padova, January 10, 1912

As the hero in the world première, November 3, 1918, of Montemezzi's *La Nave* at La Scala

Edoardo di Giovanni in the La Scala première of *Parsifal,* January 9, 1914

As Rinuccio in Puccini's *Gianni Schicchi,* in the Italian première at the Costanzi, Rome, January 11, 1919

# Chicago, 1919-1922

As Avito in *L'Amore dei tre re*, 1919/20 season in Chicago. This was also the role in which Edward Johnson made his Metropolitan Opera début, November 16, 1922.

As Canio in *I Pagliacci*, 1920/21 season in Chicago

As Don José in *Carmen* at the Metropolitan, 1922

As Radames in *Aida*, 1925

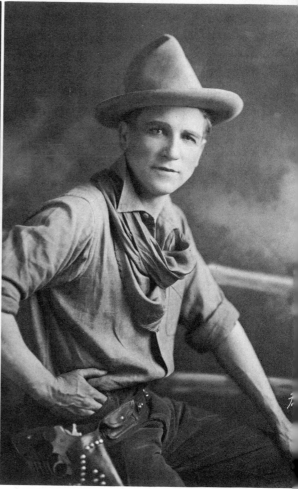

Cavaradossi in *Tosca* was one of
Edward Johnson's favourite roles.

As Dick Johnson in Puccini's
*La fanciulla del West*

As Aethelwold in the world première of Deems Taylor's opera *The King's Henchman*, February 17, 1927

...ward Johnson was Rodolfo when ...ace Moore made her Metropolitan ...era début as Mimi in *La Bohème*, ...bruary 7, 1928.

...son sang his first Roméo at the ...opolitan on February 2, 1923.

*Left, and below*   In the title role of Deems Taylor's opera *Peter Ibbetson* that had its world première at the Metropolitan, February 7, 1931

direction. Otherwise I will be like a ship that has no rudder. Will you forgive the hasty words that I have said and written? Will you not try to forget my wickedness and see the little bit of good that I have in me? Daddy, please forgive my egoism; forgive my faults and love me for my virtues—I want to make you happy. I wish to see you happy. If you are not, nobody will be. So now we are all working for your happiness. Please Daddy, be glad—not for me but for yourself. My happiness will never be complete until I hear you say: I am at last happy. That is my greatest wish and if it comes true, I shall be the happiest person on earth. When I say my virtues, I mean my virtue. It is not big, but it is there, and that is my love and affection. Please never more say to me: you don't love me. You know that is not true. I do love you, Daddy— I give you all the love that a daughter has for her father. You have everything that I can give you because I have not the right to give it to anyone else yet. A Merry Christmas, my Babbo. Please love and forgive me as I love you."

In Eddie's reply, January 1, he told Fiorenza: "I am so ambitious for you and I want you to succeed in whatever you do. Don't disappoint me! I see so many flighty, light-headed little flappers around that the thought of being the father of one drives me almost to suicide. Be serious, concentrate, and show the world the stuff you are made of. Think of your father once in a while and write oftener. This has not been a happy year for me; I hope 1925 will be better."

On February 6, after commiserating with her because she was lonely back at school, after the fun of the holidays, he closed his letter: "I can't write any more today. I am so nervous about the opera tonight. I make my début tonight in *Carmen* and this letter must be posted today. *Butterfly* on Monday. *Pagliacci* next Saturday. *Roméo* the following Tuesday. Lots of work! I'd like to run away, too, but I don't. And I don't have anyone to whom to carry my troubles, and I can't cry at night. I just stick to it! *Tanti baci dal tuo Babbo chi t'adora.*"

Shortly after that he wrote that his schedule was nervously, physically and vocally exhausting: "I have to sing *Carmen,* then *Bohème, Butterfly, Aida* and *Fedora,* with rehearsals all the time for *Pelléas. Roméo* last night in Philadelphia wore me out and I am tired today. Besides, we didn't get back to New York this morning till 5 A.M.! *Boris* on Saturday will make five operas I have sung in two weeks! I wish I could run away but I can not. Besides, if I don't work, who will pay the bills? You see, the same difficulties exist for everybody."

While Eddie was working on *Pelléas,* he wrote: "My! It is a very difficult role. Sometimes I think I will never be able to relearn it in French. But each time a new scene comes along, and sticks, I feel a little more encouraged. I don't know how it sticks, but there it is. So no doubt, when the time comes, I'll have it all by memory. But oh! it takes so much concentration! . . . Miss Lucrezia Bori is the Mélisande, and she is charming. . . . *Pelléas* is an extremely difficult opera to sing and we are having our troubles. However, it will soon be over now. Monday, Tuesday and Wednesday will see the end of the rehearsals, and the première is set for the Saturday matinée, March 21. Here's hoping."

It was rumoured that Edward Johnson and Lucrezia Bori were sweethearts, and it wasn't the first time his name had been linked with that of a prima donna. It had even happened with Mary Garden. In the case of Bori, there was more basis for the story: for more than a month of *Pelléas et Mélisande* rehearsals, and long before the première, they had been seen going in and out of the opera house morning, noon and night. Conductor Wilfrid Pelletier, who worked with them on the score, explained it this way when interviewed in 1972:

> They would often meet for breakfast someplace before coming to rehearsal, in order to talk over the various points that had come up the day before. This way, they would usually arrive at the opera house together. Often the three of us would go out for a bite of lunch. Then at dinner time Bori and Johnson usually left the House together. The fact that they went their separate ways for dinner was something no one necessarily knew. People saw them going in and coming out in each other's company every day. Then late at night—most of our rehearsals lasted until late—they would be seen going out together again.
>
> Of course, people thought it was a romance. But it was just a great friendship. That was all. Actually, Bori was very pure in mind. We were always telling naughty stories. She would laugh, but only once did she tell a story that was a bit off colour, and of course we just winked at one another and said, "You, woman, go out of this house. It is terrible to hear you talk that way." At first she thought we were serious! Then she understood. She was a wonderful person. The two of them had great fun doing *Pelléas*. Sometimes, jokingly, after having done a scene that would break your heart because it was so beautiful, they would do it again and, by way of relief, they would make all the traditional and exaggeratedly wide grand opera gestures. Then we would all laugh.

Rehearsals and performances at the Metropolitan, and preoccupation with Fiorenza's teenage lack of seriousness kept Eddie busy. In another letter at the time he appealed to Fiorenza again: "Your dear mother had character like few people in the world, and when I see you fall below the standards set by her, my heart bleeds. No! No! You must not disappoint me. I could not bear it." He was emphatic in saying that when

114

their ideas for her education clashed, she should "make no mistake about it, it will have to be *my* way, whether you see the error of your way or not. I'm sorry to be so hard, but I am only thinking of your good."

The *Pelléas et Mélisande* première came and went, and the optimistic predictions which were made for it were borne out by the reviews. The *New York Herald Tribune*'s Lawrence Gilman reported: "Bori brought Mélisande to life . . . an incarnation that had unity of plan and line, sensitiveness of feeling, delicacy and vividness of denotement . . . and Mr. Johnson's Pelléas is a memorable performance. In no other of his roles has he made more telling use of his rare intelligence, his insight, his art as a singer and actor. He struck the right balance between the gravity, the simplicity, the aloofness and reserve that are essential to the character, and the sense of passion under difficult restraint. This passion shows itself in the curious tension and sudden vehemence which Debussy conveys in his marvellously subtle declamation—as in that piercing lift of the voice part in Pelléas's first speech about his dying friend, Marcellus, at the words *avant elle si je veux*, or as in that most perturbing of all the passages that Pelléas has to sing: his soliloquy as he awaits his last interview with Mélisande in the park. It was a delight to hear the beautiful voice part, with its infinite varieties of nuance, so beautifully and so eloquently delivered as they were by Mr. Johnson . . . both *Pelléas* and its public have at last come into their own."

After it was all over and the reviews were universally so good, Eddie was happy, even apologetic, to Fiorenza: "It is really terrible to get so absorbed by one's work that one is out of touch with everything else. That is what happens with us. We really have no time for other things. It takes all one's time and all one's thoughts to learn and remember all the roles. One has to concentrate to such a point that there is little room for anything else. However, as long as I keep fit (and I have been oh so careful this season!), I don't mind. In fact, I'm glad to escape a lot of the invitations. I have grown thin again, but I feel O.K. so it doesn't matter. Besides, they think a thin tenor is quite a novelty!"

What Mario Chamlee's wife Ruth, herself a singer, always remembered best about Edward Johnson during the twenties was his "perfection of style." She recalled:

> His Pelléas was one of the most appealing performances that one could see. There was a delicacy, an impeccable diction; he had grace, and his whole feeling for the role was unique. And I remember him as being such a charming, polished man. Always immaculately groomed. Even when he took off his hat it was with a flourish; he had that—what you call—panache. His French was good

115

too. I suppose that's why I remember his Pelléas the best. As Ziegler remarked to Mario and me, "Just listen to that man's French! Just listen to that Pelléas!"

Actually, we all admired him and were pulling for him—that was the feeling he inspired. He was always conscientious, trying to do what was right, whether as a performer or, later, as general director. I think we all admired him too, the way he had come into opera. How he had turned his back on Broadway at the time that he was the toast of the town in *A Waltz Dream* and had gone to Italy, taking every cent he had to invest in operatic study. He had had a tremendous success in *L'Amore dei tre re*, and he was still the best Avito in the business. He also originated *La Nave* and, out of thirty performances of *Meistersinger* at La Scala, had sung the part of Walther twenty-seven times. Then, of course, he had been one of the Chicago company's most admirable artists and, well, we just liked him, and during the summers at Ravinia we became very close.

That's where we first met Eddie. I had made my own début there at a concert in 1917—then I gave up singing in favour of marriage later, one big career in the family was enough. But it was when we were all there during the summer that we became like one big family. Ravinia was a marvellous place, because Eckstein secured the finest artists available at the time, and there was the great discipline of the conductors, I mean Papi was a master. But in that theatre where the sound was so wonderful, there was an intimate feeling. It was a great thing, but it was in the summertime and the theatre was different. There was a lack of tension, such as one felt at the Metropolitan. I mean there was no formality at Ravinia, and the performances were perfectly beautiful. People, I think, sang their best there because of this lack of tension. And after the performances at night we would all go to each others' houses for spaghetti or whatever it was, so we had a companionship there that was among the richest of our memory. I remember that Johnson was always telling stories and laughing about things. Mario was a good raconteur too, and the two of them were always vying with each other as to which could tell more and better stories. I can remember a lot of them, but most of them I wouldn't dare tell! Of course they didn't always invite us to hear those stories—we had to imagine what was going on, by the laughter.

Very few people ever saw him when he wasn't in a good mood. One time after a *Peter Ibbetson* performance at the Met a New York critic wrote about "the Peter of Edward Johnson." Eddie thought that was a great joke and cut out the clipping and carried it around with him! And I'll never forget his telling me about the time when he was on a concert tour and the audience was so small that he invited the people to come right up near the stage and he said to them, "It is the quality that counts, not the quantity."

Johnson also told us that when he first went to the Met and had his first meeting with Gatti, the impresario looked over his long list of roles, then asked him if he knew Samson. Eddie assured him he did. Then Gatti looked him over and asked,"How much do you weigh?" When Eddie told him "one hundred and forty pounds," Gatti didn't say anything, but he drew a line through the word Samson.

With the 1924/25 season at the Met an outstanding success, it began to look as though Edward Johnson's fame was about to equal that of Edoardo di Giovanni at last. His fees had gone up again, and his concert bookings were as heavy as he could accept. So many offers came in from China, Hong Kong, Japan, however, and other places in the East, that his managers asked him how he would feel about taking time out for a tour to the Orient. He found the idea fascinating, as long as such a tour could be arranged during a comparatively slack period insofar as opera, oratorio and concert engagements in the United States were concerned. He was especially agreeable when he discovered that the fees would be very high. So such a tour was arranged for the summer of 1925.

Edward's final engagement before leaving was to be the Cincinnati May Festival. He wrote Fiorenza, April 27, 1925: "I'm off Friday for Cincinnati and won't be back in New York until next October. Gee! This trip to the Orient is making me sweat. But I hope to make some money for our nest egg—so we are off. It sounds to me as though you are very fat—138 pounds—and I only weigh 145! . . . I have rented my studio for the five months I will be away and must arrange my things accordingly. Gee! But I will be busy for the next few days. *Addio, amor' mio. E tanti baci dal tuo Babbo, chi t'adora più di tutto al mondo.*"

He had already written her on April 24 that "the cheque for my tour in the Orient came yesterday and I am sailing from Seattle May 15 on the *President Jackson*. I sing in Tokyo, Kobe, Hong Kong, Tientsin, Manila and other places I don't remember . . . and sail from Manila June 28 for Naples by way of India and the Red Sea. It will be a wonderful trip but I hope to make some money."

WHEN THE *President Jackson* docked in Yokohama on Wednesday, May 27, 1925, Edward Johnson, travelling as Edoardo di Giovanni, was besieged by reporters and photographers. He was also met by a Mr. and Mrs. Chapman and Paul Messer, friends of the Higinbothams. The Rolls Royce of Canadian Ambassador and Mrs. Carew was awaiting him and his accompanist, Elmer Zoller. Eddie's entry in his diary referred to Japan's great disaster of 1925: "Drove to the Carew home, formerly Higinbothams', past devastated regions . . . train to Tokyo . . . more reporters and pictures. Imperial Hotel—older building not damaged during the quake. Unfortunately we missed seeing the great Daibutsu, the world's greatest statue of Buddha."

On May 28 he recorded: "Concert at Theatre Kabuki at 7 P.M. . . . The native Japanese groaned mournfully when I sang the *Chénier* aria. I couldn't imagine what it meant, and was rather put out until the local managers told me that it was their way of expressing approval. They also yelled, *Banzai!* and the Italian, *Bravo!* so the concert was pretty exciting for me. The Japanese listened to our music with curiosity, like we do to theirs."

By train and by boat, Eddie made his way through the Orient. On arriving in Korea, he jotted down many points of interest: "Fusan [Pusan] a busy little harbour—Koreans all in white—sign of mourning —passports—polite Japanese official asked to open trunk—most obliging—first railway carriage with observation car. Noted the thatched and clayed low huts and the fact that men and women wore white; little girls contrasted with long black skirts and magenta waists, like bodices." He received a warm welcome for his performance in Seoul, Korea, where they had an audience of "about a thousand, of which at least seven hundred were white."

"Sorry not to see more of the capital of Korea," he wrote home. "Korea boasts rice, beets, excellent honey, tigers, leopards, boars, bears, wolves, foxes, deer, sables, otters. People wear light colours of gauze during the summer; mourning hemp clothes, with big round sleeves; everyone with an umbrella, hats bamboo. Houses have two apartments —the inner for females and the outer for males. No stove. Heated from under floor, made of clay on flat thick stone covered with thick oil paper. Cushions are for sitting and sleeping. All stations have three names—Korean, Chinese and Japanese—everywhere the same mud villages, clay huts."

In Mukden, the Manchurian capital, the travellers were fascinated by the narrow streets in the Chinese section and by the very modern buildings and the wide streets in the new Japanese part. The men here were large, the women small. "No shoes," Eddie recorded. "Town all walled —houses long, straight middle door and no windows. Clay bridge. Country always the same: plain rice fields, horses and donkeys, coffee, spitting—enough to drive one crazy."

When they left Mukden for Peking, Eddie thought they had escaped the surging revolution that had begun with a riot in Shanghai, but he soon discovered that Peking was also in a turmoil. The theatre where the concert was given, "a rickety movie house," was policed to keep the natives out, in order to avoid any demonstrations against foreigners! There were heated discussions over the Shanghai riot. A general strike was feared; students from all over the country were taking part in protests, marching up and down the streets with banners. All foreigners were uneasy. Troops landed at Shanghai and warships assembled in demonstration. Hopes for quiet were expressed, along with fear that the Bolsheviki would fan the flame of unrest.

"By the time we got to Tientsin," Eddie wrote his mother, "the revolution was bubbling, and our concert was attended by only the foreign population. Our journey to Shanghai, a matter of about six hundred miles, was by no means a primrose path. The trains were all crammed full of soldiers and we had to sit around and wait. Crossing the Yangtze-Kyang River at Nanking we ran into trouble. It was pouring rain and we had missed the regular ferry. When we got to the other side, pretty well wet through, Mr. Zoller started ahead in one rickshaw and I followed.

"Suddenly a man leaped out from the side of the road and stopped my coolie. 'You go to Shanghai Station?' I said we were. 'Fi'dollars!' he said. Naturally I had to do some quick thinking. I was good and mad, as you can imagine, so I said, 'Nothing doing!' 'All-lightee,' he said, 'you no give me fi'dollars, you no go to station!' And at that he dumped the coolie out of the shafts, tilted the rickshaw forward, sending me out with a bang. I hated to give in, but there I was in a foreign land, darkness coming on, outside the city walls, and above all, not knowing whether or not my friend was merely the outrider of a large gang. So I decided to compromise, and without much conviction, I'm afraid, though being as gruff as I could, I said, 'I give you two dollars!' To my amazement, he broke into a cheerful smile and said, 'All-lightee!' So I paid our tribute money and we were allowed to pass on our way."

When they finally reached Shanghai, Eddie was told it was impossible to give a concert there that night inasmuch as all public gatherings had been forbidden. Nothing to do but sit around for a week. There were soldiers stationed everywhere, and warships in the harbour. Finally, Eddie said impulsively, "If I can't give a concert for the civilians, how about giving one for the soldiers?" And it was arranged.

"We performed in the grandstand of the race course, of all places!" Eddie recorded. "We made such a hit, though, that the mayor of the foreign section of the town gave us permission to give a concert in the theatre! They had soldiers stationed for blocks each way, and plain-clothesmen in the theatre, so there would be no unpleasant incidents."

The concert had been scheduled for Tuesday, was postponed until

Thursday, but finally, in view of the overall situation, took place on Wednesday. "Received with great enthusiasm," Eddie noted. "After the concert, went to Cabaret Plaza and danced, then on to the Hotel Majestic, formerly a very fine and beautiful private home, and danced until about two o'clock."

One of the most interesting experiences of the entire trip for Eddie was meeting the well-known foreign correspondent George Sokolsky during their week in Shanghai. "He is a Russian Jew," Eddie wrote in his diary, "a most intelligent man, married to a Chinese woman who was born in Jamaica and educated in London. They are a brilliant and charming couple. He was the one who told us about the trouble in Starkert, in a Japanese mill in a British concession where a strike was on. A Japanese was killed by a Chinese; the latter was arrested; students demanded his release and stormed the British jail. Police were attacked and threatened by several thousand. They fired and several were killed. During this time the rioters returned, tearing up streets and sniping. Some of the results were the anti-foreign demonstrations, a general strike proclaimed, business being paralyzed, ships tied up, Chinese shops and banks closed, and volunteer service corps mustered to guard the city. Armoured cars are seen at all dangerous points—motor cars go about with machine guns. The society ladies take over the duties of telephone operators and canteen workers. Soldiers are encamped every place, at the race course and cricket clubs. British, American, French, Japs, Italian, Portuguese—it is the general opinion that the Soviet is supplying the funds, also that the opium trade is the source of the trouble. The situation is really very grave."

After the report of several attacks—one of them on a soldier, who was severely wounded with a meat axe—Eddie decided the time had come to get out of Shanghai. Sokolsky agreed. It had been an exciting and interesting week, but once aboard the *President Adams* Eddie had to admit that he was glad to be safely on the boat, where everyone was friendly and everything was quiet. The next morning he slept late, and that night he danced late.

Hong Kong was a beautiful sight as they came into the fairyland-like harbour the following morning. It was a world of fascination as they walked through Kowloon and ferried across to Victoria City, with all its lovely shops. After the turbulent days in China, Hong Kong seemed to be a place of peace and sunshine. But when they began to make inquiries, they were soon to learn of unrest there also. Eddie's concert was cancelled; there was a general strike in the town; the hotel's servants were all out. Again Eddie was glad to be going back to the *President Adams*. But since he had been gone, the entire crew of stewards, cooks and boys had left the ship. It was mainly with the officers and members of the band serving as cooks and stewards that they lifted anchor on time, at 2 P.M. Twelve Filipino boys were hardly adequate replacement for the seventy employees who had gone on strike.

They passed through a small typhoon as they neared Manila, but to Eddie it was all part of a great big adventure. His concert in Manila drew a most enthusiastic crowd, and afterward, when he and Zoller returned to their hotel, they were greeted by a round of applause as they passed through the dining room. "Just like old times," Eddie said. They enjoyed their little supper party so much that time stood still. It was a shock to hear the boat whistle and to have to get up hurriedly and "make a run for it," arriving just as the gangplank was being lifted up. Once on board, Eddie shared a bottle of champagne with three friends —all of them women, as it happened—and watched the lights of Manila fade in the distance as the ship pulled out of the harbour.

After two days in Singapore, the *President Adams* made a "wonderful passage through the Archipelago." There was a new crew of Chinese this time, and the passengers had "nice clean food, clean boys, good service again"—and dancing. Eddie had always liked dancing, and on this trip he had all but danced his way through the Orient.

That evening, while sitting on deck, Eddie suddenly laughed aloud. "Remember that girl in Manila," he asked Zoller, "who screamed out during one of my arias and then jumped up on her chair because a large rat had invaded her box? I can still see her describing the size of that rat! I couldn't help it, but I sang the *Bohème* encore especially for her."

"Yes," said Zoller, "and you managed to break up the house when you came out and bowed to her and asked her, 'Did you get it?' "

Typhoons, a mutinous ship's crew and fights with coolies had all been part of Eddie's Oriental tour. He was now on his way back: Penang, Colombo, Cairo and Alexandria. From Penang he wrote that he was very much impressed by the primitive roads, beautiful views, rubber plantations, coconut groves, palm gardens, the Snake Temple with live snakes, the native huts and the villages.

When they reached the coast of the Italian Somaliland in East Africa, Zoller, Eddie, another man and one of the lady passengers, a Miss Magdalene Hammesfahr, motored to Cairo. "Our chauffeur was mad," Eddie related. "I never experienced such a trip—one hundred miles over desert, two punctures. We reached the Hotel Continental at 1:30 A.M., half dead, having driven since 7:30 in the evening. We were covered with sand, and our eyes were almost burned out. To me, a bath and bed felt good."

The next day was filled with new wonders—seeing the most recent discoveries from Tutankhamen's tomb, visiting the "dreadfully cheap" bazaars, motoring out to the pyramids, riding a camel. Eddie never forgot the wonderful thrill of watching the sunset on the pyramids: "a most impressive sight and a marvellous effect."

The next day they took the train for Alexandria and picked up the *President Adams* at 6:30 P.M. After dinner that night, Eddie admitted in his diary to being "even too tired to dance."

It took them three days to reach Naples. The final night, they saw Mount Etna in the distance, the Straits of Messina and the island of Stromboli. As Eddie stood by himself on the deck at one point, looking out over the moonlit waters, he thought, somewhat wistfully, "Such a moon, and me all alone."

In Naples, the little group broke up and all went in different directions. As they were saying good-bye, Eddie impulsively asked Miss Hammesfahr whether she really liked working for a bank or whether she would rather be his secretary? She didn't know what to say, but there was a light of excitement in her eyes as she murmured that she would "think it over." He quickly told her that he would have to do some thinking about it also, and that he would call her when he was back in New York.

6

REPORTERS MET Eddie as he stepped off the boat in Naples and asked him about his tour and how he liked it. "All in all," he told them, "the tour was something I wouldn't have missed for anything. As to the musical significance of the tour, I found that the Orientals, as I have said before, are much interested in our music and understand it much better than we do theirs. Many of them have studied in Europe and America, but we had our programs translated into the native languages. Of course, it was something of a shock to have the Chinese discuss my singing across the theatre, while it was going on, but it was explained to me afterwards that this was no sign of disapproval. An outburst after one of my high notes, I was told, was merely that they were amazed at hearing high tones from a chest voice, as the Chinese sing them in falsetto. They just couldn't wait, it appeared, until after the number was over to say what they had to say. One man called out to a friend at the other side of the theatre, in Chinese, 'He must have a throat of iron.' The emotional element of the operatic arias always got across, but the people did not get the narrative of songs, and the rhythm seemed to mean nothing."

Happy to be back in Italy, Eddie went straight to Florence, where Tata had his little house ready for him. His first call was to Josephine Casali. They visited over dinner in her new apartment—the second floor and garden of a lovely palace on the banks of the Arno. She had sold the Pensione Casali she said, because it was too difficult for her to manage alone, and also because it brought back memories that made her feel lonely. Eddie confessed to being lonely himself. They spent much time together and took long drives over the Italian countryside during the following weeks. They felt a peace and happiness in being together— "so comfortable." Again they talked of making it a permanent relationship. But this time Jo said she feared it would not work. "Your life is in America now," she told him, "and mine is here."

123

"New York's not so bad, you know," Eddie argued. "We'd have a busy time and we'd be here every summer." She was silent. "Come with me to New York when I go back," he urged. "Stay a while; get the feel of it; and I promise I'll make you appreciate it, as I do, my darling."

She agreed to "think it over" while he was on Elba with Fiorenza and Tata and the Mellinis. But when the time came to give her answer, she was still undecided, and Eddie had to leave Italy without her.

By way of consolation he stopped off in Paris, saw Fifi, and visited Marie-Muelle Costumier-de-l'Opéra, on Rue de la Victoire. He ordered new costumes for his Metropolitan Opera performances: Pelléas, 1 *manteau pervenche en popline de soie pervenche*—750 francs; Rodolfo [*La Bohème*], 1 *manteau drap*, 1 *chapeau noir*, 1 *redingote gilet foncée*, 1 *gilet piqué fleurette*, 1 *pantalon drap gris rayé écossais gris camayeux col et cravat*—for a total of 1,590 francs; Andrea Chénier—2400 francs; Mario Cavaradossi [*Tosca*]—295 francs; Roméo, 1 *manteau faille vert*—800 francs, 1 *costume*—900 francs, 1 *costume*—400 francs; and various supplementary items for a total of 7,810 francs. After Paris, he stopped briefly in Lausanne to make sure Fiorenza was happily settled in her school for the year.

Edward Johnson made a fetish of health and keeping fit. His only weakness, which he often mentioned, was his back. He wrote Fiorenza from New York that it had been a cold and fairly rough crossing. "I wasn't seasick, but I did take ill the first day on land. It hit me in my weak spot as usual, my back, and I've not been able to move for three days. The doctor came, and a nurse, and I'm feeling much better. I should be able to leave for Chicago in a few days, but I'll have to miss my first date. Hard luck. But I'll surely be ready for the second date which is a week off."

His next letter, a week later, read: "You will see that I am still in town. As a matter of fact, I never left. My back got worse and the doctors advised complete rest. It was impossible, as my studio telephone rang and rang and there were cleaners and painters, so I just packed a bag and came to the Canadian Club in this hotel, but today I am off. Dr. Harris filled me with electricity and strapped my back with strong adhesive plaster, so I am feeling much better and moving without so much pain, but it cost me my concert this week."

He fulfilled engagements in London (Ontario) and in Ottawa, then went to the Metropolitan, October 23, to begin rehearsals for his performances there on November 3, as Rodolfo in *La Bohème*, and on November 5—the third night of the 1925/26 season—as Pelléas.

He had a surprise telephone call a week or so later from a Miss Magdalene Hammesfahr. At first the name didn't ring a bell, but he quickly remembered—of course, the Oriental tour. He had intended calling her. She had met Mr. Zoller the previous day and he had said: "Mr. Johnson still needs a private secretary. Why don't you call him?"

"Yes that's right," Eddie said. "Would you like to take on the job? Work at home—or at my house, as you like."

She thought she would, so they made an appointment. She didn't know quite what to expect when she went into the apartment, remembering, as she did, the first time she had met him, on the steamer, a man with a top hat! But when she arrived, he was all smiles and—no top hat! She herself told the story many years afterward:

> He offered me the job at $1.50 an hour and I accepted. I paid all his bills, wrote all his cheques. He dictated almost all his own letters, I didn't have to make them up.
>
> "Hammie," he used to say to me, "live for today, don't worry about tomorrow."
>
> I wasn't with him every day, at first it was just one day a week, but it gradually increased until in the end, years later, it took all my spare time. It's an amazing thing, but I never saw him upset. Even one time I had his apartment done over while he was away in Europe. He looked startled at first when he came in, then gave me his familiar smile and put his arm around my shoulder and said, "Hammie, you did a good job. It did need it, didn't it?"
>
> I was with him for over thirty years in all, until it finally became necessary for me to give up work. And he didn't really need me any more. But in 1935, after ten years, he gave me a $1,000 bond—as a present. He was a wonderful man.

Hammie was in her mid-eighties when she was talking about those early years and some of the experiences she had had as Edward Johnson's secretary.

> He used to go to the Metropolitan at 10:30 every morning, 10:30 or 11:00, and he would be back at 3:00 or 4:00 in the afternoon to rest. Then he would have a bite, and at 7:00 or 7:30 he would leave again and wouldn't be back until after the performance. . . . There's a picture of Edward Johnson backstage, watching the clock. That's typical of him. I was secretary to a vice-president of the Central Savings Bank in New York and I never gave that up, really. I worked for Edward Johnson weekends. As he needed me more and more, I would work for him in the evenings. It was almost like a vacation to come over to his place. . . . Sometimes he would come to my house—I lived with my sister and her husband up in Yonkers—Mr. and Mrs. Burkhardt. He liked my sister's cooking so much, and they liked him. They loved to have him around. He was always so kind and so jolly and so interested in

them and everything they were doing. . . . He had the same house-keeper, Marie Newsum, for fourteen or fifteen years. She finally had to retire because of asthma, but he sent her money regularly, every month, for many years, just the same. I know, because I made out the cheques. . . .

I remember he said it had always meant so much to him to have somebody coming backstage to see him before and after a performance, when he was singing. That's why, I think, that after he became general manager he was always there to welcome the singers before a performance and wish them luck—his cheery *In bocca al lupo* was familiar to them all. Then he was back afterward to console them if they hadn't done well or to congratulate them if they had. . . . As his own voice was going, he used to say that experience was worth its weight in gold. He couldn't have carried on otherwise.

He could be a bit rigid at times. He certainly got fed up with Fiorenza often, especially before her marriage. She was so immaculately groomed always, but she would leave her room in a complete mess. Eddie would be furious. "What kind of wife do you think you're going to make?" He ate and drank lightly—took care of that by keeping nothing in the refrigerator. He wouldn't let me bring in anything. It was full of yoghurt, mostly! His apartment was all covered with tapestries. Many people thought it was overcrowded with things, and maybe it was. But I liked it and he loved it. Everything in the apartment meant something special to him. . . . Some people said he was stingy. He wasn't. He was just careful with money. He couldn't understand people who threw it away for no reason. . . .

He always was careful to be sure his hair was dyed when he was a singer. The minute he became general manager he literally "went white overnight." He said to me once, "Hammie, now I can afford to be myself. How do I look?" He looked more handsome than ever. He was a fine figure of a man. He always took very good care of himself, exercise and proper eating habits. . . .

He was always sending flowers to Bori—immense flowers—enormous flowers. He insisted that I keep an expense account especially for that. His flowers to Bori usually made headlines in the paper. . . . He was always telling stories, and many people said he was a very humorous man. He wasn't humorous. But he was very what I would call "merry." He calculated his effects, particularly on the opera stage, as Avito, or Pelléas or Roméo or Ibbetson. He was proud of his beautiful legs—used to say they were the handsomest in the House. He was proud, too, of his beautiful costumes. There was a special allowance in his budget to see that they were properly cleaned and taken care of at all times. . . .

Unlike Witherspoon, Mr. Johnson wanted to keep the older

people on after he became general manager. He was too sensitive to the feelings of the artists to let anyone go. If it had to be done, however, he would get Mr. St. Leger to do it. Gatti had already begun looking for Americans to add to the roster, and Edward Johnson liked that idea. He used to say, "I'm going to make that an American opera company." He very seldom made a mistake when he was hiring people, but he did once. It concerned a coloratura soprano, and he said afterward, "Quite a bird, but not a coloratura."

He always liked to have his box at the opera filled. Miss Kimball was often there. I remember being in the box with her one time at *Norma* and Mr. Johnson was sitting with us during one of the acts. She leaned over to him and said of the singer, "I think she thinks her voice is bigger than it is." Mr. Johnson smiled one of his enigmatic smiles and said, "She's a good lieder singer."

Rudolf Bing arrived at the Met a year before he became general manager, and Mr. Johnson invited him to the box [Manager's Box, No. 23]. It seems that Bing took it over as if it were his box. That got Edward Johnson's goat.

He went to Italy every summer—it was a kind of compulsion, a nostalgia. When he came back in the fall, he was always full of new energy and new spirit. He was always punctual and courteous, always opening doors and leaping to his feet whenever a lady entered the room.

He was a very mild man and he had great charm in handling people. He couldn't bear to hurt anybody. He admitted that if he had anything unpleasant to say, he would rather have somebody else say it. He was a wonderful man.

As Hammie talked, even at that point in her life, her voice took on new life and her expression was that of a young woman. It was obvious that even though there had evidently been nothing in their relationship of a romantic nature, Hammie had idolized him, as most women did, and had enjoyed his confidence in a very special kind of way. He often said she was the only one he could let off steam to, when he was about to blow up.

Hammie was one of the few people, aside from a very small handful of his closest friends, who was ever inside Edward Johnson's 687 Madison Avenue apartment. That was his haven, his palace—his very private castle. He couldn't stand to have anybody there who was not in complete sympathy with him. For there he was himself, as he had been with only one other person in the world, Bebe. He liked his apartment, he liked the location of it—he could walk from there to the Metropolitan Opera House in half an hour, which helped him to "keep fit." Once in a while the rumour reached him that he walked to save carfare. He smiled and kept his counsel; such comments weren't worth a thought.

Eddie's schedule at the Metropolitan that season included another première: the first Metropolitan Opera performance of Spontini's *La Vestale* (November 12, 1925) with Rosa Ponselle in the title role and Serafin conducting. Used to the close rapport he had had with Lucrezia Bori in *Pelléas,* Eddie was looking forward to the same kind of relationship with Miss Ponselle. But it didn't work out that way. The "Italian wing" seemed to feel that Edward Johnson, in spite of his excellent Italian and the fact that he visited Italy every summer, was now a part of the French and American wings of the company.

Miss Ponselle recalled, many years after her retirement:

> Johnson was a love, and he was very modest. He was actually two kinds of people: there was one side of him that was very simple, good, liked fun and was very down to earth—an ordinary person. The other side was proud and formal—I think that's what bothered me. But I remember he was always on time for rehearsals, always well dressed and beautifully groomed. Maybe it's my background or my being a Neapolitan—they're awfully sensitive you know—we do things with our whole heart, but we're easily hurt. Maybe it was Johnson's cold and formal side that threw me off. It's strange, because he was very human, and he had a reputation for being democratic, and he always had that big smile.
>
> Later I came to know him better, particularly on the Met tours. He was a good sport then, nothing of the temperamental tenor. You would never suspect he was one—only his speaking voice; it was pitched very high. In *Vestale* I was so nervous about my own performance I didn't have much time to think about anything else. But I do remember that I admired Johnson, and the way he handled himself on stage. He seemed so much at ease. I always envied that, for I was scared all the time. I was kind of fat. Gatti wanted me to sing *Norma,* but I wasn't ready, so they gave me *Vestale.* I didn't know that they were using it as a forerunner for *Norma.* I don't see any resemblance other than the classic line—very classic —and the voice technique. But the range was much more comfortable than the *Norma* range. Well, anyway, we had good reviews for *Vestale,* and I was stamped the big star.

As for Edward Johnson, he found himself a hit in two offbeat operas: one of them *La Vestale,* due mainly to the growing popularity of Miss Ponselle; the other *Pelléas,* with Lucrezia Bori, that proved to be a real box office draw. At the beginning of December, Eddie was called upon to sing a performance of *Boris Godunov,* which he had previously sworn he would never sing again, after which came *Faust, Pagliacci, Roméo, Fedora* and *Tosca.* His contract for the season ended with a performance of *Roméo* on February 15 and his concerts, which had already begun in December, kept him busy for the rest of the season, travelling through the United States and Canada.

For the summer (1926), he was engaged again for Ravinia, and Fiorenza was so adamant that she was perfectly capable now of running a house that Eddie gave in. He rented a house in Winnetka, on the "north shore" of Chicago, and hired a Japanese couple as servants.

"Unfortunately," Fiorenza once wrote about this particular summer, ". . . I was not yet at all as my father had hoped, like my mother. I was tall. I was fat. I was self-conscious. I was also very stubborn. When I stood up, I stumbled against everything and dropped whatever I was holding. My housekeeping efforts were lamentable . . . I was petrified from the moment I laid eyes on them [the Japanese couple]. The man seemed to be sharpening a big knife whenever I ventured into the kitchen to discuss the day's meals. If I ordered chicken, we'd get chops. If I ordered fish, we'd still get chops. We had chops all the time. My father remarked on the monotony of this diet and made a few pointed remarks about his mother's, my mother's and Tata's housekeeping. I wept and persevered, but we still got chops. However, I was saved, because the Japanese houseman ran our car into the back of a truck, and father let them go. But my troubles were not over, for our next cook loved her little nips and was seldom sober. One night when we were giving a party to the artists after a performance, she mingled with the guests and began to sit on the laps of the men. . . . Every time I spoke to her, she'd simply shove me away and shout, 'Go 'way, little girl!' Finally I asked Father to intervene, but she merely slapped him on the shoulder and said, 'G'wan Mishter Johnson!' Thank goodness artists don't take such behaviour too seriously."

At the end of the Ravinia season, Tata came over from Florence to stay with Fiorenza until she went away to school in the fall. Eddie himself, however, went to Italy. Among other things, he planned to attend a Toscanini concert in Milan. His report (October 21) was enthusiastic: "Marvellous. He certainly is a wizard; saw my friend Panizza [conductor] and Max Smith [New York music critic]."

By the time Eddie was ready to come home, the Atlantic was ready for winter; the sea was rough and he was not the best of sailors. He missed his daily walks on deck and found it more comfortable to stay in his stateroom, resting and reading, and thinking longingly of his calm, peaceful little apartment on Madison Avenue.

After the taxi driver had helped Eddie carry his bags up the narrow flight of stairs to his modest apartment, he made some comment about everything being small. Eddie smiled. It wasn't a luxurious setup, he had to admit to himself as he looked around, but it wasn't so bad either

—just a little cluttered, maybe. He shuddered to think of the move from 55th Street to his present address. He had come across hundreds of notes, it seemed, tucked in books, nooks and old coat pockets. What had started when he was with Bebe in Italy—writing down new words, facts, and thoughts to be remembered—had become a habit. He was never without a notebook in his pocket, and there was always a note pad beside his bed, so he could jot down at any time of the day or night anything he didn't want to forget.

In the early part of the 1926/27 season, Eddie was busy with concert engagements. The beginning of the holidays disappeared in rehearsals for the first *Roméo et Juliette* performance set for January 20. Then, with the new year, came rehearsals for the world première of the new Deems Taylor opera, *The King's Henchman,* in which Edward Johnson was creating the role of Aethelwold, with Lawrence Tibbett as Eadgar, Florence Easton as Aelfrida, and Tullio Serafin conducting. It was a tremendous cast and the music was exacting. The rehearsals were long and strenuous, but there was an excellent feeling of rapport in the whole cast. Nevertheless, on February 13, Eddie wrote Fiorenza: "Two more rehearsals of *King's Henchman* and then the première on Thursday, the 17th. I'll be glad when that is over." And could he have foreseen the incident that occurred opening night, he would have been twice as glad to have it behind him.

The night of the première came and Edward Johnson had invited his parents and Fiorenza and the Higinbothams and several other friends from Guelph to be on hand. As usual, he was nervous to the point of desperation, even though he knew there was not just cause. Or was there? It seemed that whenever he had had anything to do with a horse in an opera there was always a chance of a mishap—like the near catastrophe involving a horse at La Scala at the time of his *Parsifal.* The horse had come charging downstage and vaulted the orchestra pit and landed in the auditorium during a rehearsal. Eddie never forgot it. So naturally, after that he had always been especially apprehensive. And there was a definite "horse challenge" in *The Henchman.*

As Eddie told it to a group of Rotarian friends in Guelph, years later: "You see, I was this young noble who was sent by the king to carry a proposal of marriage to a nearby principality. At the end of the first act, the king delivered a very ornate address and sent me on my way. Then they were to bring in a big white horse that I was supposed to get on and ride off. So, when we came to the dress rehearsal, the day before the première, they brought in this animal that was a regular mountain. 'I can't get on that thing,' I told them. 'There's no way I can make it. Have you got a mounting block or something?'

"They said No, but one of the chorus men standing there volunteered to help out. 'I'll make a kind of stirrup with my hands, and you can step on that, and I'll lift you up.'

"We tried it and it worked fine. So I said to the man, 'Can I depend on you to be here tomorrow night, because if you're not, it's going to be ridiculous—I won't be able to do it.'

" 'Oh, you can count on me, Mr. Johnson, I'll be here,' the man assured me. 'I won't fail you.'

"He was there all right, but he was very tense and nervous—and so was I—to be sure to make this mountainous back up above us. The result was that he threw me so hard—and I jumped so hard—I went right over the horse's back and came down on the other side! So I got up and led the animal off the stage."

As to the merits of the opera itself, it remained for the critics to have their say and the public to give its reaction. Olin Downes in the *New York Times* of February 18, 1927, assessed it this way: *"The King's Henchman* has its qualities and its defects, variously to be estimated, and better to be estimated in a conclusive tone after more than one performance. But it has undeniably a theatrical effect, conciseness, movement, youthful spirit and sincerity; its text is poetic and well adapted to the needs of the singers; its music has the impact, the expressiveness and colour appropriate to music drama. . . . It is clear that Mr. Taylor and Miss Millay [Edna St. Vincent Millay] have produced the most effectively and artistically wrought American opera that has reached the stage." Mr. Downes mentioned Edward Johnson's unfortunate incident with the horse in a rather oblique way: "Broad and curving phrases for the singers, phrases reinforced by the surge and impact of the instruments. (And high notes for tenors–vide Mr. Johnson departing on his horse at the end of the first act.)" The review was given over, in the main, to an evaluation of the opera: "The close is dignified and pathetic, and Mr. Tibbett's enunciation of some of the best of Miss Millay's lines materially heightened its effect."

That same year, the widow of Enrico Caruso sent Edward Johnson, as a personal gift, the costumes her famous husband had worn as Dick Johnson in the world première at the Metropolitan of Puccini's *Girl of the Golden West*. A bit of alteration was necessary to trim them to fit the slender, youthful figure of Edward Johnson, but the gesture itself was a great inspiration to Edward who had always enjoyed Caruso's voice so much. Then, too, it was Enrico Caruso who had encouraged him to go to Italy to study for opera in the first place, and had recommended his own teacher, Maestro Lombardi. Mrs. Caruso's gesture and personal tribute happened to coincide with a tribute paid Johnson by a

131

contemporary tenor, John McCormack, who deprecated his own billing for an appearance in London's Queen's Hall as "the greatest tenor in the world." He publicly proclaimed: "I am not the greatest tenor in the world. I object to that title. There is no 'greatest tenor' today. The greatest tenor is dead and the next one has not arrived. The Canadian singer Edward Johnson is the best all-round operatic tenor in the world and in addition he has a perfect figure, which so few tenors possess."

Eddie had been profoundly moved by Mrs. Caruso's gift, and when told of Mr. McCormack's statement he said: "Coming from one tenor to another, I should say it was the acme of generosity. Further, although startled by its kindly flattery, I must say that Mr. McCormack's expression is exactly my feeling for him. John is a great artist and a generous kindly friend."

Edward Johnson's schedule and way of life left very little time for purely social activities, but there were constant intimate evenings among various groups that had become friendly. One such, that usually met at Maestro Pelletier's—but might also meet at Mario Chamlee's or at Lawrence Tibbett's—was a fun-loving group that enjoyed a good laugh, good conversation and good food.

Pelletier himself always had warm remembrances of those days:

> Eddie was a very amiable singer. He had no pretensions whatsoever. He was a fine musician and with Florence Easton and Marion Telva we were a group. We were at that time preparing a work of Deems Taylor's, *The King's Henchman,* with Telva, Easton, Johnson and Tibbett. We rehearsed practically every day with Serafin. At that time I lived on Seventh Avenue between 53rd and 54th Streets, and whenever we had evening performances or rehearsals, we would come back to my little apartment.
>
> We were very close friends and we were having lots of fun, telling all kinds of stories. Easton was a wonderful colleague and of course Telva was—well she was a real monkey. It was sometimes difficult to say a word because she would turn it around and make it very amusing. Eddie was great fun always. He had been a matinée idol, you know, years before on Broadway. He was very handsome, a very brilliant man—very brilliant—and had a kind word for everyone. He was not what we call the "tenor type" that we had been used to at the Opera House. He was quite a gentleman. Not that the other tenors were not gentlemen, but he had something different. He had something different from anyone else.
>
> Johnson was a great inspiration to all the young artists around and everyone who worked with him. . . . He managed his career well and his work was planned. He listed an enormous repertoire, but I don't really think he knew it all. Remembering some of those

discussions at the time of *The Henchman,* the singers couldn't talk about why they didn't get enough work because of being Americans—they were busy all the time, and they were favourites both with the public and the management, not because they were Americans, but because they were great artists. It was a wonderful period of great artists.

Louis Eckstein invited Edward Johnson to take over as manager at Ravinia Park for the summer of 1927. But Eddie, having weathered the days of Mary Garden's management at the Chicago Opera, was convinced it was impossible to be a good singer and a good manager at the same time. So he had declined, preferring to enjoy Ravinia that year again as an artist.

Some of his most memorable moments took place in that open-air theatre, on stage and off. He never forgot the hot, sultry summer night when he sang *Lohengrin* there, with the temperature over 90 degrees. It was so hot, he felt as though he was swimming inside his heavy coat of mail. Then, to add insult to injury, when he opened his mouth at one point to sing, he choked—Lohengrin had swallowed a butterfly! The situation was tragic at the moment, but ludicrously funny in retrospect. At a party after that particular performance, Edward Johnson was the object of many a good-natured joke. But his hostess, the popular soprano Elisabeth Rethberg, a great favourite that summer, was immediately serious when asked about Edward Johnson. "His Lohengrin," she said, "was not only vocally brilliant, but he made the whole story credible. And in *Pagliacci,* his *'Venite, onorateci, a ventitrè ore!'* was sung with a surprising full-throated upper register . . . he was a very elegant Canio, you know."

Johnson's reviews during that spring and summer had begun with the headline for a performance at the Cincinnati May Festival: "Edward Johnson Electrifies Throng with Romantic Singing." From there, he went on to "strike fire" at Ravinia, as one reviewer put it, "with his impassioned declamation of the 'Flower Song' in *Carmen.*" He also sang *L'Amore dei tre re* and *La Bohème.* "He was in splendid voice," another report read," and gave a new touch to the role of Rodolfo." His nose was somewhat out of joint, nevertheless, inasmuch as the big news of the year was the return of Giovanni Martinelli to sing both dramatic and lyric roles. And Mario Chamlee, also a Metropolitan Opera tenor, was again being heard in a wide repertoire.

At the end of the Ravinia season of 1927, Chicago's *Musical News* of August 17 had this to say: "If anyone can give the impression of the ideal Des Grieux [*Manon Lescaut*], it is Edward Johnson, nor do the Puccini melodies need a more able interpreter." Eddie had sung *Louise* there earlier (July 24) and been besieged by the usual number of letters and calls from adoring females. He had eyes for only one woman at the time, however, his "anonymous friend" who, they both realized, would probably never be free to become Mrs. Edward Johnson. Then, too, he wondered about his own emotions. When he had suggested that they throw caution to the winds and that she go to Italy with him that summer, he knew, even as he spoke, that she could not do so. And when she regretfully reminded him that it was impossible, he was surprised to find a certain feeling of relief within himself. It really would be better for him to be going to Italy alone.

That Ravinia friend was only one of the innumerable women in the long life of Edward Johnson for, in spite of the fact that he tried to avoid female entanglements, he was pursued by women wherever he went. He could never say no and, because he was so charming and polite, he found himself in hot water continually. But there was nothing he could do about it. He couldn't hurt them and he couldn't be rude —he simply smiled and continued to be sympathetic and charming. "What else could a gentleman do?" he wondered.

His mail brought him reams of poetry and love letters. Some of them were very embarrassing; some very simple; some fairly formal. They came from all corners of Canada and the United States, and some came from Europe. "I am deluged by letters from adoring females," he complained to a close friend one time. "They all say one way or another that I brought sunshine into their lives for a week, a month, or however long I was in their town. And you know," he confessed, "I usually can't remember them by the time their letters reach me. And if I do, the intimacy they say they felt has long since disappeared!"

Fiorenza used to misunderstand her father and once, when he was going off to meet one of his special friends, she asked, "Are you considering marrying her, Daddy?" To which he replied, as always, "When and if I decide to marry again, I'll be the first one to tell you, don't worry. But always remember this, there will never be another Bee." Always the diplomat, Edward Johnson easily gave his daughter the impression that *she* came first. "I guess she does," he surprised himself by thinking.

FROM THE TIME of the death of his wife in 1919, Edward Johnson's main purpose in life had been to see to it that Fiorenza had the proper schooling and upbringing. He lavished most of his personal affection on her and his parents, especially his mother. There were times when he felt as though his own life was somewhat of a grind—he had to keep after his managers continually, and watch very carefully what engage-

134

ments were made and not made for him. He had little real heart in it. It was his "business," the only way he had of making a living. He and Bebe had built his career so carefully, and it had meant so much to both of them. Now he was merely keeping on in the same track. He couldn't explain why it was, but things could mean so much to him and, at the same time, mean nothing at all.

When Eddie was asked one time to address the graduating class of his old alma mater, the Collegiate Institute in Guelph, a new idea dawned on him as he prepared his speech for that youthful audience. Why should other Canadian youngsters go through what he had gone through? Train youth. Music in the schools. Make Canada a singing nation with Guelph as its heartbeat. Eddie was alive with enthusiasm as he visualized what could be done. Getting an idea and implementing it were two different things, though, as he well knew. How could he bring this about?

It was in the back of his mind all the time he was in Europe the summer of 1927, and when he returned in the fall he was ready to take the first step. He proposed to give $25,000 to the Guelph Board of Education, at the rate of $5,000 a year for five years, for the purpose of establishing a program of music in the schools. In addition, he talked with Guelph friends S. Craig-Evans, J.L. Yule, choral director Reginald G. Geen, and others, about the possibility of starting an orchestra, a choir and a music festival in Guelph to supplement the school program.

It was nearly a year later, on July 11, 1928, that the Guelph Board of Education wrote Edward Johnson stating that the conditions he had stipulated in connection with his $25,000 gift toward a music program in the schools would be met. "The Board wishes to have your assistance at any time in its deliberations on musical matters. For the first time in the history of the Board it has conferred an honorary life membership, the idea being not only to do what is in its power to honour a worthy native son, but also to enable you to attend a Board or School Management Committee meeting at any time you are in the city and feel so inclined."

It was a unique gift, a unique opportunity for the children of Guelph, and it was given with the unique affection of a great artist for the welfare of his hometown.

As his ninth consecutive season as a popular opera and concert tenor in America began in the fall of 1927, Eddie suddenly realized that the years had slipped by and that Fiorenza would be seventeen in December. He was delighted that she was already more poised, less pudgy and supersensitive than she had been, and that he could hold intelligent conversations with her on music and current events. They could even laugh

135

together over some of her attempts to be grown up. He had been able to impose his will on her, thus far, in the matter of her schooling, and he was determined she should go to university so she would have the well-rounded education that he had always lacked. He couldn't help wondering what would have happened if he had heeded his own father's wishes, insofar as he was concerned, and gone to the university and studied to be a lawyer.

He had written Fiorenza in the spring: "Your time is short now. Short in the term, short for the school, short for the future. My great preoccupation has always been that you lose no time while you are young. I missed so much by having no one to tell me that."

And, the same month: "Travel, education and contact make us un-biased, take away our prejudices—and a sense of understanding the other fellow's point of view makes us tolerant. One of the greatest ene-mies of progress is intolerance."

But Fiorenza proved to be as stubborn as her father, it turned out, and definitely refused to go to college. Edward Johnson was forced to give in. She wanted to be an actress.

It was while she was at the Bennett School in Millbrook, New York, that she startled her father with a letter telling him that she was desper-ately in love. The whole tone of the letter sounded so dangerously serious that Eddie feared she might elope before he could get a letter back to her. "If marriage is on your mind," he wrote, "better wait a while. I sing for a living and, as long as I have to sing Romeo, for heaven's sake don't get married and make me a grandfather."

He need not have worried, for by the time Fiorenza wrote her next letter, the great love of her life had been forgotten and she was com-pletely immersed in dreams of a great career as an actress. She had heard of another school, she told her father, which she would like to attend, as the next step up the ladder: a drama school in Detroit, run by a well-known actress by the name of Jessie Bonstelle. Eddie laughed aloud from relief when he read that letter. The big romance was over. So he promptly dismissed the entire subject.

Fiorenza's periods of instruction at the Bennett School and subse-quently at the drama school in Detroit lasted less than a year altogether. From what she called her "grim retreat" in the Detroit Women's City Club she often dreamed of her carefree days in Florence. Nevertheless, she finally decided that she should let New York have the benefit of her dramatic talent.

She could have capitalized on her father's name, of course, but pre-ferred, she said in her memoirs, to obtain success on her own. "So I swept into the great world under the name of Fiorenza da Veiga, using

136

part of my mother's name . . . dressed in the latest style, in a skirt above the knees, the waist down to my hips. I completed the effect with a long cigarette holder! I am sure I visited all the agents. A few saw me and said, 'Oh yes, you're an Italian Type. You might get a walk-on part in *See Naples and Die.*' " But Fiorenza refused to be typecast; she was confident she would make her mark as a straight actress, once she got the chance.

Edward Johnson's 1927/28 Metropolitan season began with *Carmen* on January 13, with Maria Jeritza and Lawrence Tibbett. That was the year they had the unfortunate mishap. After an embrace between Carmen and Don José, José came away with a beautiful long black beard—Carmen's wig had caught on his epaulet—and she had turned blonde instantly, as her own hair came tumbling down. "And you know," Eddie said afterward, "very few people in the audience ever noticed it. She quickly put a scarf over her head and I quickly got rid of my beard!"

Eddie received a note from John McCormack for that opening night. It read: "Lily and Ivan join me in wishing you the greatest success of your career this evening, and *in bocca al lupo, sempre.* We wish we were there to cheer you, but then tonight is a millionaire's opera night. Nuf sed. Always your friend, John M. McCormack." Eddie liked John and Lily, but even more than that, it was wonderful to have another tenor really wish him well, and mean it.

From 1926 on, Eddie developed a more or less regular summer pattern: finish the Met, go to the Cincinnati May Festival, then to Ravinia and, the day after that closed—the day after Labour Day—take off for Europe. A few weeks in Italy always gave him new energy and enthusiasm for the winter ahead.

Thus far, Edward Johnson had never had any really bad reviews. On the contrary, most of them had been glowing. He also enjoyed enthusiastic comments from people with whom he worked. Blair Neale's words were typical: "I am merely Edward Johnson's accompanist. It is through the kindness and interest he takes in me that I have been given a chance to do solo work. I am a Canadian and was born in Chatham, New Brunswick. My early training was obtained at McGill University." He had played for several artists, it seemed. "Among them were Florence Easton, known in Canada, Marguerite D'Alvarez, and Queena Mario of the Metropolitan Opera. For the last two years I have been with Edward Johnson, of whose kindness, helpfulness and consideration I cannot say too much. He is really to be thanked for 'putting me over.' "

Edward Johnson was in demand in the United States, just as Edoardo di Giovanni had been in Italy, as a tenor who was a "sure study," and one who would assure the success of any new work. Composers all wanted him for their new operas. Certainly Pizzetti (recalling Edward Johnson's personal triumph in his opera *Fedra* at La Scala in 1915) was ecstatic that Edward Johnson would be creating the title role in his *Fra Gherardo* for its American première on March 21, 1929, at the Metropolitan Opera, with Maestro Serafin as musical director.

By the 1928/29 season, Edward Johnson was riding the crest of the wave of success, whether for concerts, orchestral appearances or opera. He was at his peak interpretatively, and at his peak vocally and psychologically, exuding even greater charm and confidence than ever. San Francisco wanted him; Chicago wanted him; New Orleans insisted they had to have him. His managers had again convinced the Metropolitan to leave him free to accept other engagements until the first of the year. Inasmuch as he had Gigli, Martinelli, Frederick Jagel, Lauri-Volpi, Everett Marshall, Lauritz Melchior (for the German repertoire) and Tokatyan, Gatti could afford to be agreeable.

In 1928 the San Francisco Opera moved into Dreamland Auditorium, purportedly for a more intimate atmosphere, and it was in this "large neighbourhood arena" that Eddie made his San Francisco Opera début in *Aida*. The cast list read as though the Metropolitan had moved to San Francisco: Edward Johnson as Radames on opening night (September 15), with Rethberg as Aida and Lawrence Tibbett as Amonasro (he had stepped in at the last moment to replace Giuseppe Danise), and the young and promising Ezio Pinza as Ramfis. Johnson also sang *L'Amore dei tre re, Fedora* and *Pagliacci* in San Francisco that year. But after that he was never free when they wanted him. "Too bad they didn't include *La Bohème* in their repertoire," Eddie told a friend, "with that young girl Grace Moore."

He had often thought of Grace since he, as Rodolfo to her Mimi, had helped to introduce her to the stage of the Metropolitan on February 7 of that year. He had been so tremendously impressed that night, that scarcely had the great asbestos curtain descended than he had gone over to her and grabbed her hand and said, "God bless you, child. You have a great future before you." She had impulsively kissed him. A few years later, as it turned out, Edward Johnson's name was to be linked romantically with that of Grace Moore.

"There's nothing to it," Grace said.

"We're only good colleagues," said Eddie.

But the rumours continued.

On December 1, after his stint with the San Francisco Opera, Eddie went to Guelph. Within the next few days, he met what seemed to him all of Guelph's school children, as well as the members of the Board of Education and of the Edward Johnson Music Foundation, and was

138

Guest of Honour at a banquet in Ryan's Auditorium. The local paper had announced: "Two hundred and fifty citizens will gather to do him honour. During the banquet on December 5, 1928, the G. M. S. Band will play dinner music. Mayor R. B. Robson is Toastmaster, and there are to be only two toasts, 'The King' and 'Our Guest.' The latter will be proposed by Honourable Hugh Guthrie, K.C., M.P. 'Eddie' himself will respond. As an indication of the results of his generous gift, Miss Elizabeth Taylor's class from the Central School, under the direction of Mr. J.L. Yule, and St. George's Church Boys' Choir, under Mr. R.G. Geen, will sing several selections." There was a reception in the Armoury after the affair, and Edward Johnson received the "illuminated address" from the grateful citizens.

All in all, 1928 was "a Johnson year," with Fiorenza holding her own, it seemed. She was to be a leading actress in a stock company in Evanston, Illinois, and was looking at the future through rose-coloured glasses. But the company went bankrupt, before she was able to make the hit she anticipated, and folded before Christmas! Even her first pay cheque came back marked "No Funds." She was crushed, and looked for sympathy from her father. But he, busy with opera and concert engagements, told her that it was all part of her education—learning to live with disappointments as well as successes. "Take the laughter and the tears," he told her. "And, above all, never let anything get you down." But he gave in when she begged to return to Florence and spend the rest of the year studying singing there, with the ever-faithful Tata to look after her. Eddie settled a small income on her to take care of expenses. He felt he had "brought her along" and was glad she was returning to study in Italy. As for himself, he was billed as "Tenor of the Metropolitan Opera House and Ravinia" and his concert fees had risen to $1,250 and $1,500, and in some cases as high as $1,750, per performance. As there was only a nominal income tax in those days, he was able to save what began to look like "a comfortable nest egg." "Yes," he admitted to himself, "I'm a rich man."

In New York, at 687 Madison Avenue, he felt completely at home in what was a veritable museum, reflecting his travels, successes and interests: marvellous century-old paintings of Paganini, endless European and Oriental *objets d'art,* etchings, photographs; an old spinet, a harpsichord, an old Chinese chest, an original shoemaker's bench; Russian icons, Japanese and Chinese idols, masks, jades, lacquers, teakwoods, cinnabar jars and boxes, Buddhas that Eddie had carried back from the Orient "by hand," and the many citations and medals he had received over the years. What had looked like a spacious apartment to him originally seemed small already—but he loved it.

139

Once his 1928/29 season at the Met started, Johnson had a full schedule, beginning on January 19, 1929, with *L'Amore dei tre re* and ending April 12 with a performance of *Fra Gherardo*, the new opera that was not destined to bring him the same success he had enjoyed in *Fedra*. The obstacles proved too insurmountable. As the eminent critic Olin Downes put it in the *New York Times:* "The audience's reception of the work was enthusiastic, and the superb choral ensemble of the last act, for example, fully justified this enthusiasm . . . and yet it fails, or appeared to fail last night, to completely 'arrive' as a music drama." It was the story of a medieval zealot, "a man of powerful passions and revolutionary temper, torn between the world of the flesh and the spirit, and at last a martyr to the truth and the cause that he espoused. . . . But deception and insincerity dog his steps." Fra Gherardo is hanged at the end of the story.

"The opera is exceptionally difficult to perform for many reasons," Mr. Downes wrote, "associated particularly with the number of small parts which must be interpreted effectively, yet remain integral factors of an effective ensemble, and also by reason of Pizzetti's technical methods. . . . Mr. Johnson sang with his customary fine intelligence, but his stage appearance was far from the character of Pizzetti's libretto. *Fra Gherardo,* of the later acts certainly, was an older and more powerful man. . . . And last but not least, in fact foremost, [was] the masterly direction of Mr. Serafin."

On April 20, 1929, Eddie wrote home to Guelph:

> Dear Mother:
> Yesterday I had lunch with the President and Mrs. Hoover at the White House, and enclosed you will find the invitation which I send you for a souvenir. We sing *Faust* over in Baltimore tonight and leave after the performance for Atlanta. The following week we go to Cleveland, and the week of May 6 I'll be home. Thank the Lord! It will be good to get away from this drive. The weather is so beautiful—so warm and balmy and takes away all desire to stick on the greasepaint and funny velvet clothes. I am really fed up. I hope this will find you both well. Take care of yourself and let's have a good time "feeding" when I get back. Fred said he would try to get over, too. Love to Margaret and Caroline. Regards to Lloyd and all friends. Loads of love for you and Dad.
> Always your loving son,
> Ed

When the Met spring tour ended, Eddie made a brief stop in New York before going to Guelph to inaugurate the first music festival there. He argued with his managers about his new Metropolitan Opera contract and accused them of selling him down the river. He was somewhat mollified by the prospect of appearing in the first American production of Rimsky-Korsakov's *Sadko,* but with only eleven performances scheduled for him at the Met, what was he going to do with himself the rest of the time?

"Concertize," they told him.

"O.K.," Eddie said testily. "But just let me see the dates."

During the summer of 1928 Edward Johnson had talked often about the possibilities for Guelph's musical future, and specifically about a Guelph musical festival. Finally, early in 1929, a meeting had been called of local people interested in a festival along the lines he was suggesting. A committee "to take action for a musical festival to be held sometime about May 1st" met on Tuesday, February 5, and again on Monday, February 11. Its officers included representatives from the Board of Education and the Separate School Board. At a third meeting held in Wyndham Inn on February 25, 1929, the committee had agreed that the first musical festival in Guelph should be held on May 7 and 8 of that year.

Edward Johnson had sent a letter officially offering his services; the Toronto Symphony Orchestra was to receive $1,500 for appearing. Tickets were to be 35¢ for the first evening; 50¢ the next afternoon (free to children); and $1.00 to $1.50 the second evening when Edward Johnson was to sing.

The first concert, May 7, 1929, was given over to the demonstration of the work done in the schools—the public and separate school classes, the Collegiate Orchestra and the Glee Club. The thunderous applause and general excitement "showed beyond the shade of a doubt," according to the newspaper, "that the new musical education will have a far-reaching effect, not only in developing latent talent, but in giving each one coming under the instruction a new source of enjoyment. . . . Marjory Bates, Jack Brown and Murray Young, the prize-winning soloists from the public schools, sang again the selections which had won them recognition. Hundreds of pupils from primary to entrance grade took part in selections of various degrees of difficulty. It was a gala evening for all."

The following afternoon, senior public and separate school pupils, together with the Collegiate students, assembled in the Civic Auditorium to hear the Toronto Symphony, conducted by Luigi von Kunits, and child violinist Bettina Vegara.

The closing event, that evening, was the program by Edward Johnson. His singing brought thunderous applause and generated great excitement. The management reported that "Mr. Johnson too appeared content that his venture was proving such a success. For he, who has had so much honour paid him by princes, musical critics, high-born and low-born, wealthy and poor, seemed thrilled with the appreciation of his youthful audience."

From the beginning the budget was of prime concern but, when the receipts were tallied for that first festival, there was an overall profit of $1,105.71. Immediately $1,100 was invested in Government Bonds against future expenses. Such a financial report was possible, of course, only because much had been donated, and Edward Johnson had contributed his services and even paid for his accompanist.

The Guelph Collegiate and Vocational Institute's magazine showed a snapshot of Edward Johnson in the park as "the man who made Guelph musically famous," and a photo of a section of the overflow audience in the Collegiate Auditorium during the festival. One could see the Toronto Symphony Orchestra onstage and, behind them, the Collegiate Glee Club. There was a small headshot of "Mr. J.L. Yule, Director of Music," and one of the young violinist prodigy, Bettina Vegara.

Before the end of that year had passed, letters from Guelph assured Eddie that plans were well in hand for a second musical festival, set for May 20-21, 1930, and they needed his help in the matter of a soloist. So he called on his good friend and fellow artist, the popular Chicago Civic Opera baritone Richard Bonelli, for the second concert.

The festival was budgeted at $2,885 with hope for another surplus. The programs followed much the same pattern as in 1929, but the financial picture was different: they paid Mr. Bonelli $800, his accompanist $250, and the orchestra $1,050. Then there were expenses for choirs and platforms and incidentals, including a surprise $168 amusement tax! They managed to break even only by selling a $500 Government of Canada bond. Nevertheless, in view of the general response, Johnson pushed for a 1931 festival, even though he said his losses in the stock market crash of 1929 made it impossible for him to do little other than offer advice, and help in securing artists. At that point, they all had to face the fact that the Guelph Festival, however successful artistically, represented a dangerous financial investment. Without more outside support and a wider public rallying behind it, it was a heavy responsibility resting on the shoulders of the same people year after year.

So the third festival shrank to a single item: the Vogt Choir and the Symphony Orchestra of Guelph in a "splendid concert before a large crowd" on February 11, 1931. It was held as a benefit with tenor H. Conklin as soloist, R.G. Geen, leader of the Vogt Choir and Horace Gray, musical director of the Guelph Symphony Orchestra. Although it was heralded as a "triumph," to Edward Johnson it looked like the

142

end of his cherished dream for a solidly-established music festival in his hometown.

He had hoped that once he had started a festival in Guelph the citizenry, especially the Rotary Club, would take it over and make a go of it. But they lacked the necessary vision and enthusiasm, and Edward Johnson couldn't do it all by himself. Nevertheless, in private as well as in public, he continually stressed his interest in young people and the importance of their having an early musical education and early exposure to good music. Years later, when he was a key figure in the preparation and presentation of CBC's "Singing Stars of Tomorrow" program, his constant theme was: "Canada as a singing nation."

"Had he lived longer," the noted educator Arnold Walter wrote in his tribute to Dr. Johnson, "I am sure he would have presented us with the model plan for 'musical education in a small town.' We discussed it often; there was something touching in his worrying over the musical fortunes of tiny tots in a small Ontario town. And yet, how right he was. It is only by worrying about the children of Guelph and a thousand little towns that we will make this one day 'a singing nation.' "

"Edward Johnson built surer than he knew," wrote poet/author and Guelph University professor Dr. Eugene Benson at the time of the opening of the 1968 Guelph Spring Festival, "for now, almost forty years after that first May Music Festival which Edward Johnson created, a new one has been established. It is most fitting that the new Guelph Spring Festival of the Arts is presented by the Edward Johnson Music Foundation [headed by Dr. M. H. M. MacKinnon], with generous support from the city and the University of Guelph, the Guelph Chamber of Commerce, the CBC, many industries and hundreds of interested citizens."

The prominent Canadian musician Nicholas Goldschmidt, director of music at the University of Guelph, had been appointed as artistic director of the new Guelph Spring Festival. The festival program, presented May 1-15, 1968, was comprised of five concerts, for which the Festival Singers of Toronto, the University of Toronto Faculty of Music "Showcase," local musical groups and featured soloists were engaged. The Board of Directors set an objective that would have warmed Edward Johnson's heart. One can almost hear him repeating to himself the words of famed Chicago waterfront architect Daniel Burnham: "Make no little plans; they have no magic to stir men's blood." Those words had so inspired Eddie when he first heard them that he had virtually adopted them as his own personal motto.

The objective of 1968 was "to establish by 1976 a capital sum of $100,000 and to use the interest from this amount for substantial scholarships, and to sponsor every two or three years a major competition for Canadian musicians under thirty years of age." The board confidently stated: "The new program will be launched in 1977 with a celebration of the 150th anniversary of the founding of Guelph by John Galt, and also with the tenth Guelph Spring Festival." An endowment fund committee was appointed. The arm of Edward Johnson, extended over his city in 1928, had proved to be a long one, stretching into the future to help guide the musical destiny of Guelph and of Canada itself.

WHEN JOHNSON was asked to create the title role in the French version of Rimsky-Korsakov's *Sadko* at the Metropolitan in 1930, he plunged into the preparations in his customarily thorough way. He read everything available about the history and legends of Russia to get the background; he looked for books that might help him capture the spirit and character of the adventurous hero of the story. Inasmuch as Sadko had to show great bravado, Eddie wanted it to look authentic. So he talked with the Russian dancers in the Met company. "What is your idea of 'bravado'?" he asked one after another.

He went over and over the words of the libretto in order to immerse himself in the story. The music? He found it difficult. But he wasn't the only one. There came a day when the whole company was discouraged and talking of its difficulties. Eddie relieved the tension by telling the others of an anecdote he'd run across about rehearsals for the first production, at a private opera house in Moscow, December 26, 1897. The ensemble had been ready to give up in disgust, and the composer had come forward with what he termed a formula for the rhythm. "Just remember this," he had said, counting off syllables on his fingers, "Rimsky-Korsakov, who wrote this work, is mad."

Edward Johnson was often asked how he learned a role. Sometimes he would have found it difficult to describe exactly, but with Sadko it was different. "After reading the libretto," he said, "and going over and over the score at the piano to get the 'feel' of the music, I underlined my own words in the score in red, so my eye would catch them easily— the words and the notes at the same time; then, to be sure, I copied out the whole role in order to test my knowledge of it, wherever I happened to be. Then, finally, I memorized the score, words and music. There was still the character, and I wasn't quite sure about that. But it is surprising what the clothes do for you. It's like a game of 'Make Believe.' You look at yourself in the mirror and you don't see yourself, you see the person of the role. That's what happened to me. Suddenly everything I had been studying fit into place. That's what gives you authority in a role, knowing it that well."

144

"Would that be a rule that would apply to anyone?" he was asked.

"Absolutely. It's what I try to impress on young singers. They must pay close attention to their appearance and makeup. If they will come on the stage with good makeup, dashing costume, their hat tilted at just the right angle, they'll have their audience with them. And if they don't, they'll just have to sing twice as well in order to get their audience. . . . Do you know who the people are I admire the most? They're the vaudevillians. Imagine? They have ten minutes to put themselves over. Just ten minutes! That's hustle for you!"

The New York press was full of articles about the "new" Russian opera, *Sadko*. Tickets for the opening, January 25, 1930, proved difficult to get. Even the great operatic soprano Marcella Sembrich had to call on Edward Johnson to intercede for her. She thanked him profusely later, saying: "I particularly enjoyed hearing your fine interpretation of that difficult role, and your beautiful singing." In the *New York Sun* the following day, W. J. Henderson reported the opera as "one of those sumptuous spectacles for which Giulio Gatti-Casazza is famous." But the work itself did not find favour, due to "one slow tempo after another, melancholy moods, and absence of a climax." Henderson added: "The short phrase mercilessly reiterated, which is the melodic pattern of too many Russian folk songs, becomes tiresome before the opera is half over. . . . Naturally, there was a large cast. Mr. Johnson laboured manfully with the music of Sadko. He won much applause and deserved much sympathy. But the interest of the afternoon was centred in the pictures, the dances and the ensembles. Katisha had a left shoulder blade which people went miles to see."

Eddie didn't have much time to brood. The second *Sadko,* on February 5, was followed, as too often happened in the scheduling he thought, by a *Pelléas* the next evening. After that, his performances came in less hectic frequency, but to keep *Pelléas, Sadko,* and *Roméo* ready to sing, as well as *Pagliacci, Carmen, Bohème, Faust* and others in his sixty-opera repertoire, meant daily work with his pianist. Then his recital and concert repertoire also required constant review.

Keeping track of his own career and of things in Guelph was one thing; keeping up with Fiorenza and her changes of mood was something else. She had wanted to share her father's apartment that season. She was almost nineteen years old, and a mature young woman, she had reasoned. The idea of life in New York, as the daughter of her famous father, appealed to her. But she was finally convinced, after a little reflection, that the apartment was too small for them both, and that her father was working so hard that she would scarcely see him anyway, and had said, "Then I'd like to go to the Toronto Conservatory of Music to work with Germaine Sanderson. She's an excellent coach for French music."

Eddie had been delighted at this apparent awakening of an interest in music, and secretly pleased that she was determined to support herself in Toronto. She would look for a part-time job, she had told him. She found it, in the dress department of the T. Eaton Company, and was doing very well, she thought, living at the Alexandra Palace, although dipping unmercifully into her salary for taxis from work to her lessons. But she was managing, and she was proud of herself. It was when young John David Eaton (later to become President of Eaton's) came into the department one day and invited her to the St. Andrew's Ball, that her associates realized she was not a struggling salesgirl like themselves. It made her so self-conscious and uncomfortable with them that she decided to stop working.

In those days, the Depression was beginning to affect everything and everybody. The Metropolitan, in need of financial support, called on Edward Johnson to help in their public appeal for funds. Loving both music and the old Metropolitan as he did, and being one of the most popular artists in the company, he was a natural to make appeals on behalf of the Opera. His phrase "Save the Met" became a slogan, and his successful pleas from the stage were followed by Mrs. Belmont's "tin cup" collection. (Mrs. Belmont was the former actress Eleanor Robson before marrying August Belmont, famed banker and sportsman. At her suggestion, a tin cup was passed through the Metropolitan audience at intermission for donations to help the Met.)

It was a precarious period for opera everywhere. There were even rumours that Eckstein would not be able to keep the Ravinia festival running. It had been something Eddie could always look forward to from the last Saturday in June until the first Monday in September. Fortunately, the rumours proved false, and the summer of 1930 saw him and all the other old faithfuls there again: Gennaro Papi and Louis Hasselmans as regular conductors; Wilfrid Pelletier as the leading répétiteur.

It was good that Eddie's commitments at the Metropolitan began early that fall (1930), inasmuch as his concert bookings were not as heavy as usual, with the concert business also feeling the pinch of the Depression. His first performance at the Metropolitan was *Roméo* on November 12, followed by *Fanciulla* on November 22. And he was already hard at work on the new opera by Deems Taylor, *Peter Ibbetson,* that was to have it première in February. He and Lucrezia Bori often worked together, usually with Pelletier (as they had on *Pelléas*), occasionally with Serafin who would conduct the première. Gatti-

Casazza had commissioned *Peter Ibbetson* after being impressed by Deems Taylor's *The King's Henchman*. Both productions were prepared musically by Pelletier in collaboration with the composer, who attended all the rehearsals. "Taylor was precise," Maestro Pelletier recalled. "He knew what he wanted and insisted that the artists respond. The preparation of those two operas with Serafin and Taylor afforded very good experience." It also further cemented the close friendship of the two Canadians, conductor Wilfrid Pelletier and tenor Edward Johnson.

The music was not easy, nor was the characterization. But as Eddie rehearsed, he began to feel more and more at one with the character of Peter Ibbetson. Even Bori one day laughingly commented, "I do believe, dear Edward, that you have forgotten Edward Johnson and really 'become' Peter Ibbetson."

He laughed, too, but he couldn't deny it. His apartment was always full of props, reminders, music, and details of costumes, when he was working on a new role, but this time it was different. He felt a special empathy with the character.

The première took place on Saturday afternoon, February 7, 1931, with Edward Johnson and Lucrezia Bori in roles that proved almost as popular as their Roméo and Juliette. W. J. Henderson, of the *New York Sun*, wrote afterwards: "A large audience received the new opera with favour. There were several recalls after the first act and Mr. Taylor appeared on the stage to accept his share of the applause. There were more calls at the close of the opera. Mr. Gatti-Casazza has given the work as good a cast as possible. Miss Bori, beautifully costumed, looked adorable, acted with dignity and charm, and sang as well as the dialogue form of nearly all her music would let her. Mr. Johnson, as Peter Ibbetson, had the most important role in the drama and acted it earnestly. His clear-cut diction went far toward sustaining the interest of his scenes. Mr. Tibbett made a gallant figure of the old roué, Colonel Ibbetson, and his acting had genuine theatrical value. Mr. Serafin conducted with authority."

But the greatest compliment for Johnson came two days later when he received a lavender-scented envelope and opened it to discover a note, not from a new female admirer, but from the composer, Deems Taylor, himself. It was brief, but beautiful: "Thank God for dreaming up Edward Johnson when He was creating tenors."

Of the many other letters he received in connection with the première, one was from Mary Garden. Eddie had to smile as he saw the familiar flamboyant handwriting: "Dear Mr. Johnson: Your creation of Peter Ibbetson, which I had the real pleasure of hearing last night, was simply delightful. So slim, young, sad and dreamy! Lots of luck to you always. Greetings. Mary Garden."

Practical man that he was, Eddie later liked to point to the financial success of this opera: "*Peter Ibbetson* made more money than any other single opera during the past twenty years—more than $150,000. For an American opera this is either a miracle or else it indicates a renewed public interest in opera, and I prefer to think it's the latter."

Eddie had arranged with a friend to have his portrait as Peter Ibbetson exhibited in a prominent Fifth Avenue window, "in order to give myself some publicity." He sometimes passed by to listen in on the conversations of people who might stop to look at the portrait. One day the experience backfired when two gentlemen paused in front of the window. They looked at the title under the picture, "Peter Ibbetson, Metropolitan Opera Company," but ignored the words in finer print which read, "Edward Johnson—in the role of Peter Ibbetson."

One of them said, "Oh, yes, Peter Ibbetson. This is the new tenor at the Metropolitan."

"Well," commented the other, "I hope he's better than the ones they have there now."

*Peter Ibbetson* closed the Metropolitan season on April 11. Then, after a final concert (April 12), the company began its annual spring tour. Edward Johnson was committed for *Ibbetson* in Washington, D.C., on April 16, and in Cleveland on May 2.

By the end of the 1930/31 season, there was no doubt that Edward Johnson had made at least four roles at the Metropolitan his all-but-exclusive property: Peter Ibbetson, Sadko, Pelléas and Roméo. Those were the roles in which he was most popular with the public, although he was also well known as Canio and Faust, and he and Lucrezia Bori were a popular stage couple.

Again, in 1931, the Ravinia festival took place and Eddie was there as usual. After the final performance, he lost no time in getting off to Europe. Only a short stop, to visit his parents in Guelph, then straight to Paris to see Fiorenza. She had been living there since the spring, ostensibly to study music, but Eddie could see there was another reason.

When Fiorenza had been sixteen, and on one of her infrequent visits to Guelph, she had attended a Caledon Fishing Club dinner where the young lawyer Lt. Col. George Drew had made a tremendous impression on her. He was strikingly good-looking, she thought, and fascinating—the first person she had met in the United States or Canada who could talk with her about Gabriele d'Annunzio, her favourite Italian author and a friend of her father's. She had no way of knowing it, but George was equally impressed to meet someone, particularly such an attractive

148

young girl, who had not only read d'Annunzio, but had read him in the original Italian.

These two young people didn't meet again, as it happened, for several years. By that time George was in Toronto, Master of the Supreme Court of Ontario, very popular with the women and, if possible (Fiorenza thought), better looking than ever. She was flattered that he invited her out to lunch or dinner occasionally, and she knew that she had fallen madly in love with him. She was convinced, however, that he had no time for, nor interest in, a permanent romantic entanglement. So when her vocal coach, Germaine Sanderson, was returning to Paris in the spring of 1931, Fiorenza decided to go with her. She would continue her studies there—and forget all about George Drew.

At first she lived with a French family, then wrote her father that she had "moved into a most stupendous studio room, just off the Boulevard Raspail, above Boulevard Montparnasse." When Eddie arrived that summer he was not quite as enthusiastic as she had been about her quarters; for example, he found that only an enormous Spanish shawl, draped over a bannister, prevented delivery people and tradesmen from seeing her when she took a bath.

"You have no privacy!" he exclaimed.

It was also unacceptable to him that the leaky skylight made it necessary for her to scurry for pots and pans whenever it rained. The only good thing about the entire arrangement, so far as Eddie could see, was that Fiorenza had sent for Tata who enthusiastically explained how she enjoyed bargaining at the Seine market for supplies.

He wondered how Fiorenza was able to dress so expensively on the small amount of money she had and the minute sum he sent her each month "to help out." She quickly explained that the girl in the studio next to hers was the editor of *Vogue* magazine in Paris and always got the *dernier cri* in clothes from all the great couturiers very inexpensively. "She wears them once or twice and sells them to me for next to nothing."

After they'd been together for a couple of weeks, Fiorenza was very happy when her father told her one day: "You're learning your mother's secret, Fiorenza *mia*. She thought we should never let down for an instant. We should give of our best, most particularly to those we love. Why should we woo the stranger with all our charm and intelligence, and not those who are closest to us?"

Delightful as it was in Paris, Eddie couldn't wait to get to Italy. He sent Tata ahead to prepare his little apartment in Florence for their arrival. He and Fiorenza then spent an idyllic three weeks in Italy, seeing old friends and new ones, before Eddie felt he had to return to

New York. So they all went back to Paris, where Tata and Fiorenza would stay for the winter, and Eddie reluctantly set sail for home.

MANY CHANGES were taking place around the Metropolitan Opera meanwhile. The wealthy backers who had thought nothing of writing cheques for anything from a few hundred thousand dollars to several million, had suffered from the 1929 stock-market crash and the resultant depression. Gatti's impressive financial surplus had disappeared. The Metropolitan was in serious difficulties.

The amazing rumour around the House that fall was that Gatti-Casazza, constantly on the outlook for new sources of revenue, had made a deal with NBC for broadcasts of opera from the stage of the Metropolitan Opera House! It was unheard of! Opera would be going out over the airwaves for one and all to enjoy.

The first public Metropolitan Opera broadcast, December 25, 1931, was *Hansel and Gretel,* with Editha Fleischer and Queena Mario in the title roles, Dorothée Manski as the witch, and conducted by Karl Riedel.

As for his own career, Edward Johnson had begun to have a gnawing sense of insecurity, in spite of the reassuring publicity given premières such as *Sadko* and *Peter Ibbetson.* His other repertoire at the Metropolitan had diminished year by year. He was seldom cast in any of the operas in which he had made his name in Italy, the operas that win a popular following. There was some reassurance as long as others weren't brought in to replace him as Roméo, Pelléas and Sadko. But in 1931 even those roles were invaded by Beniamino Gigli, Armand Tokatyan, Georges Thill and Frederick Jagel. Eddie was left with only Peter Ibbetson as his "exclusive" property. His schedule for the 1931/32 season included all six performances of *Peter Ibbetson,* but only two of *Pelléas et Mélisande* and one of *Sadko*—not a single *Roméo et Juliette*!

Although his position in opera was of concern to him, Edward Johnson was in great demand as a concert artist by some of the most prestigious of musical concert organizations such as the Bagby Musicales at the Plaza Hotel in New York City and Mrs. Lawrence Townsend's Musical Mornings at the Mayflower Hotel in Washington, D.C. In addition, his speaking schedule on behalf of the Metropolitan Opera filled every available moment, and there was much relief work to be done. He gave unstintingly of his time and talent.

That winter he returned to Guelph and donated his services for a concert that netted $1,800 for the *Guelph Daily Mercury* Relief Fund. *Toronto Daily Star* critic Augustus Bridle began his review this way: "Edward Johnson sang better last night than he has ever done but once or twice in his twelve years of recitals here; his voice had more of a golden glow than it had had in his previous two visits. . . . There are always two voices when Edward Johnson sings; the one that paints song pictures in the middle tones and the one that soars into the unrivalled B Flat."

Edward Johnson seldom went to church on Sundays, but he was a deeply religious man and often stopped in at St. Patrick's Roman Catholic Cathedral, on his way down to the Metropolitan, for quiet meditation. Sitting in the Cathedral alone one morning early in March, his own words came to him: "When you are well fed, well clothed and have a big bankroll in your pocket, pleasure is very attractive; gaiety and frivolity seem to walk with you. But in hard times, men discover the truth of the grand old proverb 'Man shall not live by bread alone.' " As he looked up at the altar, a religious fervour swept over him; there was a prayer on his lips that he might live his life, as Christ had done, giving help and comfort to the needy. He prayed for confidence that some divine power would guide his steps and take care of his destiny. He began to feel relaxed and at peace.

As he got up to leave the Cathedral, an attractive young woman, with large soulful brown eyes and a mass of dark curls, entered the neighbouring pew. Eddie smiled at her, then immediately recognized by her attitude that she thought he was trying to make advances. At that, his smile became broader, and by the time he left the church, he found himself laughing aloud. Somehow, the girl's dark hair had reminded him of that time in *Carmen* when Maria Jeritza's wig had caught in his epaulet and he had come away with a long, black beard.

The mood was still with him as he walked his familiar route down Fifth Avenue, across 42nd Street to Broadway and down Broadway to 39th Street and the Metropolitan Opera House. The building still looked as much like a warehouse as it had the first time he had seen it back in 1899, but now it was rich for him with memories of personal relationships and operatic triumphs. How many more triumphs would he have, he wondered, but only for a moment. He was not in the mood for serious misgivings; he was in the hands of God.

He was, after all, Edward Johnson, leading tenor of the Metropolitan Opera Company, who had been selected by the composer Deems Taylor himself for the world premières of the two great American operas, *The King's Henchman* and *Peter Ibbetson,* and for the American première of Rimsky-Korsakov's *Sadko.*

"Good morning, Miss Berry," he said cheerily to the faithful telephone operator as he came in the 39th Street stage door of the Opera House. "And how are you this fine morning?"

"Oh! Eddie!" Having been there for many years, Miss Berry was almost part of the institution itself and was privileged to call the great and the near great by their first names when she felt like it. "I didn't feel so good this morning," she told him, "but I feel fine now. Here's some mail for you."

Mail. Messages. Rehearsals. Another day had begun. This time it was a special day: most of the stars of the Metropolitan were on hand for a rehearsal for Gatti's "Grand Operatic Surprise Party" on March 6, 1932. It would begin with "Ensembles from great operas" and go on to a "Surprise Party potpourri." Edward Johnson was to impersonate business manager Edward Ziegler in a skit to be called "A tryout at the Metropolitan before Giulio Gatti-Casazza and Edward Ziegler." The event had been conceived as a means of making money for the Musicians' Emergency Aid.

Artists, always the first ones to respond to a call for help for any worthy cause, were solidly back of the program. Even the seventy-year-old Ernestine Schumann-Heink, who would be making her farewell appearance as Erda in *Siegfried* on March 11, was there. Eddie couldn't resist speaking to her and wishing her well. He told her how breathtaking he had found her Erda, and how he felt she had captured the mystical embodiment of the character in her voice. He complimented young Göta Ljungberg on her début as Sieglinde and told her she had already given the Metropolitan a brighter look. He laughed with Elisabeth Rethberg and Maestro Wilfrid Pelletier about their days at Ravinia together. At the end of the rehearsal, Eddie and Ezio Pinza attracted a group of the men as they vied with each other telling stories. Everyone was relaxed; there was an overall holiday spirit.

The occasion itself netted $26,000 for the cause, with the list of participants a veritable Who's Who of the Metropolitan Opera, and the list of those who attended containing the names of all the leading figures of the musical world. Special guests had included Marcella Sembrich, a former star who had made her début the year the opera house opened in 1883 and who was currently on the vocal faculty of the Julliard School, and Walter Damrosch, who had conducted at the Metropolitan from 1884 to 1902, and under whose baton Eddie had made his first appearances with the New York Symphony and the Oratorio Society nearly thirty years before.

On March 9, 1932, Johnson received the following letter from Damrosch:

> My dear Johnson,
> I was almost going to begin, "My dear Ziegler," but whoever you are we owe you a tremendous debt of gratitude. I shall never forget your readiness to do anything, say anything, or sing anything

in aid of the good cause. I think that even Ned Ziegler should be grateful to you because of the very handsome counterfeit presentment of him that you made. If I had been the real Gatti, I would have offered you a life job immediately, and at your own figures. What a wonderful evening it was!

Very cordially yours,<br>
Walter Damrosch

After the March 10, 1932, revival of *Pelléas et Mélisande* at the Metropolitan, New York critic Pitts Sanborn expressed the opinion that although the original Opéra-Comique cast of 1902, with Jean Périer and Mary Garden, "had not been equalled and probably never will be," kudos were due Mr. Whitehill as Golaud, Mr. Rothier as Arkel, and "cordial praise" for Mr. Johnson and Miss Bori. Irving Weil wrote: "Miss Bori remained the figure of fable within the Debussy frame but, nonetheless, a figure that is alive, and her clearly enunciated singing is a joy. Edward Johnson, once more the Pelléas, has likewise contrived a properly dim picturesqueness in which to clothe the character, that admirably matches the quality of Miss Bori's Mélisande."

Eddie mused to himself as he read the reviews: "Not quite like 1925! It was 'memorable performance' then." He got out one of the original reviews: "It was a delight to hear the beautiful voice part, with its infinite varieties of nuance, so beautifully and so eloquently delivered." Then he searched the most recent reviews for some sort of personal reassurance. "Not bad," he concluded, "but not very good either."

Eddie tried hard to convince himself that all was well. In front of the public, and even his close friends, his smile was merrier than ever, his manner was more confident, his mood more carefree and cheerful and his step lighter and jauntier. But he was worried. He was nearly fifty-four years old, although he didn't look it and never admitted it to anyone except his doctors. A high C had become a hazardous challenge rather than the effortless pleasure of former years. He was in good physical trim, except for his arthritis. This was oftentimes so bad at night that he couldn't sleep, and usually so bad in the morning that he had to go through half an hour of painful, careful exercise before he was ready to present himself as the Eddie Johnson everybody knew and expected: gay, smiling and self-confident.

"How does he do it? What boundless energy!" was the general comment of disappointed hostesses when time after time his regrets, due to "previous engagements," kept him away from their private parties and pet projects. Actually, few of those engagements existed; Eddie went out very little. At the end of a long day of rehearsals, evening performances, arguments with his managers over his dwindling vocal powers and over Fiorenza's future, he would climb the stairs to his apartment at 687 Madison Avenue looking forward to a night of peace and quiet in his little haven.

At such times, he would not have been good company, and he had long since learned that even his closest friends, men and women alike, looked to him to lift their spirits. His cheerful manner and seemingly endless fund of stories for any and all occasions made it impossible to be sad in his presence. At social gatherings, he was the life of the party; it was an image he had to maintain. He often wondered whether he could have given as much happiness to others if he had gone into the ministry instead of music. "Probably not," he had to admit. Often he longed to talk things over with someone. But with whom? He had found it easy to talk freely with only one person—Bebe. People came to him with their problems, and went away feeling better. Eddie had no one.

In the back of Eddie's mind the ideas he had had concerning musical education for young people were beginning to fuse with his concern over the obvious scarcity of places for young artists to sing, once they were trained and ready to begin their careers. They still had to go to Europe, as he had had to do as a young man. Why not a short season of opera, perhaps in the spring, with casts made up of young singers? It would give them a chance, keep them at home, *and* put the price of tickets more within the reach of the public.

Eddie contacted Paul D. Cravath about his idea. (Cravath had succeeded to the chairmanship of the Board of Directors of the Metropolitan in 1929—the year Otto Kahn had resigned because he saw no hope of realizing his plans for a new Metropolitan Opera House.) "I believe that the future of the Metropolitan Opera lies in a Junior Metropolitan Company," he explained. "That way, you could develop young singers, and you could prepare and present new American operas which are too costly for production during the regular season. Besides, it is unfair to ask the public to pay seven or eight dollars a seat to see an untried opera. My Junior Company could use experienced personnel from the main company as a nucleus—chorus, orchestra, conductors and stage directors. The singers would be just as good only they wouldn't be as highly paid and people could afford to hear them."

Mr. Cravath was sympathetic to the idea and promised to think it over during the summer.

Much as Edward Johnson loved Europe and would have liked to spend the entire summer there every year, he had always looked forward to singing at Ravinia first. That year he had hoped the Park would open as usual. But on April 26, 1932, Louis Eckstein wrote, thanking

154

him for his "genuine personal feelings of concern," then going on to explain:

> It took a lot of courage to even begin the season last year, but I was bound to go through with it. I would have done so this year, regardless of existing conditions, had I not felt the people could not afford to come in numbers, which would make us all unhappy. I could see myself sitting there, night after night, with half houses, and this would have had its effect not only on me but on the artists. Many things come back to memory. I recall the evening when Bori fell out, and we brought Yvonne Gall over, and you studied *Louise* in short order, though it was not in your contract, and you did it cheerfully and willingly. I am definitely planning for next year, perhaps even a new stage will be built during the summer. It depends somewhat on the cost which we must reckon with nowadays.

There were many things on Eddie's mind as he set sail for Europe. New and younger tenors were coming along and the time was not far off when he would no longer be able to keep his place at the Metropolitan. What would he do? What *could* he do? What expenses would he have? What income? Should he think of teaching—voice? repertoire? where? His record was enviable: he had created the leading tenor roles in more world premières of new operas, he judged, than any other tenor in the world.

A sadness came over his face as he recalled the year of 1919 for it was that spring, on May 24, that Bee had died. He had come to America with a heavy heart, but with high hopes, to make his Chicago Opera début—that was before he had locked horns, as it were, with Mary Garden. A shadow again crossed his face as he thought of the stock market crash that had wiped out his "comfortable nest egg."

Looking out across the sparkling waters of the Atlantic one afternoon, he found himself answering the questions of an attractive, sympathetic and knowledgeable young passenger who had joined him on deck: "Yes, well, I must say this decade of work has flown by. I have been busy, too busy sometimes. The American operas were stimulating; *Sadko* gave me a long and attractive role; *Fra Gherardo* was not such a big success—I don't know whether it was the religious viewpoint or the new operatic idiom. Pizzetti is doing in Italian what Deems Taylor is doing in English—they both use the voice as an instrumental contribution to the opera, much as an instrument is part of the orchestra. It is really a more legitimate vocal operatic expression, but it doesn't get the applause. It is the new idiom, not the new bel canto. Whether we like it or not, the singer is judged much the same as a French horn player!"

155

There was a pause. "What about *Pelléas et Mélisande,* and some of the other operas?" his friend prompted.

"*Pelléas?* That's different. I really enjoy that because it gives me the opportunity to sing subtly beautiful music. But then I get a thrill when I sing *L'Amore dei tre re,* too, or *Pagliacci,* or *Tosca, Faust, Carmen*— Maria Jeritza and I revived that one at the Met, you know." He seemed proud of that fact. "And *The Girl of the Golden West*—I always get a kick out of singing the role of Dick Johnson, disguising myself in native togs and being greeted on stage with 'Hello, Johnson.' "

The time passed quickly that trip—a few turns around the deck each morning, some writing, reading, talking with his attractive young friend every afternoon, and dancing every night. They were soon landing in France. Edward Johnson bade his shipboard companion a reluctant adieu. Then he went on to meet Fiorenza in Paris. They had a glorious two weeks there, often being joined by Fifi Moulton, and the second weekend Harry and Aggie Higinbotham came from Brussels to be with them.

After Paris, the two Johnsons, father and daughter, journeyed to Munich, Salzburg, and Bayreuth for the festivals. They had so much fun together, Fiorenza told friends, that the hotels were surprised when they insisted on having separate bedrooms. Edward Johnson was still vital, handsome and young looking, but he knew the days were num-bered before his daughter would be marrying and going off to a life and home of her own.

Tata was waiting for them in Florence, and it was wonderful to be "home" again. They visited the familiar galleries, walked the cobbled streets, spent time with old friends and squeezed every moment of com-panionship and happiness out of that summer. There was a camaraderie between them that had never existed before. Fiorenza seemed to have found the social graces he had always been waiting for her to exhibit. They talked as friends and good companions. And when she said she had decided to stay on in Germany, to study in Munich with a teacher she had found there, and become familiar with the life, the people and the language, he was especially pleased at her development.

In later years, Fiorenza recalled that once while she was there she had seen Adolf Hitler, without thinking much of it at the time: "A group of us had gone to the Carleton Tearooms, a popular spot with the music students. Across the room from us sat some rather unpre-possessing people, two men and two women. A German fellow student pointed them out. 'That's Röhm,' he said, 'and the other one's Hitler. Hitler's going to lead Germany to greatness. Believe me.' . . . We were not as unaware of the undercurrents in Germany as the rest of the world, but we felt we must enjoy the present and let the future take care of itself." It was only a few months later, on January 30, 1933, that Hitler, the one Fiorenza spoke of as a "queer-looking little man," became chancellor of Germany.

Sailing home on the French liner *Trans-Atlantique* in September, Eddie literally "sang for his supper" and his passage, as he put it, by appearing in a concert one evening with baritone Désiré Defrère and soprano Hilda Burke.

Taking careful stock of his financial situation and the prospects for the year ahead, he decided to send a bank draft of 200 marks (approximately $50 at that time) to Fiorenza. "Buy yourself a birthday gift and a box of candy for Christmas," he wrote her. "It's very little, but it is unfortunately all I feel I can do for you at this time. All the world, and I no different from the rest, is passing through the most difficult economic crisis that history has ever known. If this fact has not yet sunk into your consciousness, it probably will in a very practical way during the next six months. For myself, I don't look to much more travelling for a while, but expect to be a fixture at 687 Madison Avenue."

WHEN THE BOAT docked in New York, Eddie went straight to his managers' office to see what his bookings were for the 1932/33 season. It wasn't too discouraging, he thought. At least they had two New York appearances for him: a Bagby Musicale at the Waldorf-Astoria Hotel, with Elisabeth Rethberg and violinist Mischa Elman; and a joint concert at the Waldorf for the benefit of the New York Diet Kitchen Association, with young Metropolitan soprano Helen Gleason.

Even while his schedule was being discussed, Eddie found himself bursting to tell Freddie Schang, his new manager, about his Junior Opera Company idea. It had expanded in Eddie's imagination since he had discussed it with Mr. Cravath, and now it included not only the Metropolitan, but the entire country. "Junior opera companies throughout the United States," he said. "Think of it. What a stimulus to our musical development. We could begin by starting music centres in the places where there are none; add more musical activities; and promote singing clubs, choruses, instrumental ensembles, small orchestras and music schools where there are none. We have to encourage young singers and give them practical experience—not in some third or fourth rate touring company, but in a regular standardized institution."

"Hold up a minute," Freddie interrupted him. "How is this supposed to work?"

"We act now. We start to develop a more operatic attitude in America, and we start people thinking and talking about Junior Opera Companies—for young people at the student stage. These companies could be established everywhere, no matter on how small a scale at first. Any beginning is good. It would mean an opera movement in every town and city. It's terrific."

Schang, swayed by Eddie's sparkling enthusiasm, agreed, but being practical-minded he wondered how long it would take to find the necessary money. He, like Cravath, was going to "think it over." Meanwhile, Cravath had some good news: "It looks as though we'll have the backing for it all right, Eddie, if you can find the time."

On October 22, 1932, Eddie made the final payment on his 1928 promise to give $5,000 a year for five years to promote a music program in the Guelph schools. He received the following letter on November 15 from Alfred E. Smith, secretary-treasurer of the Guelph Board of Education:

> Your favour of October 22, with enclosure of cheque for $5,000 is to hand, and I beg to extend to you our very grateful thanks for this, your fifth contribution towards the advancement of music in the public schools of Guelph. . . . No words of mine can express the Board's thanks to you for what you have done in promoting this advancement in our schools, nor do I think that any of us are in a position to judge the ultimate result of the seed sown in such a wide area. It will take years to demonstrate what has been and will be done in this respect—for it is unthinkable to imagine for one moment that we can let this good work cease because of the expiration of the period of the five-year experiment agreed upon. . . .

That letter meant more to Edward Johnson than it might have meant to almost anyone else, for, always the optimist, he had become an open crusader not only for the Metropolitan Opera, but for the cause of music education in general and of opportunities for young talent on the North American continent.

In fact, on February 19, 1933, he wrote Fiorenza:

> I've made so many speeches my head swims. But the Met season is drawing to a close, and, unless we can raise a guarantee of $300,000, there is every danger that the doors of the institution will not open next year. In the endeavour to raise this amount, a committee from the real estate company and from the operating committee, plus three artists—Miss Bori, Lawrence Tibbett, and myself—have been appointed to make a drive. We are appealing by means of radio, not only to New York but throughout the United States and Canada, to all those who listen in on our broadcast. The results of this will not be known until the middle or end

of March. Nor will we artists know until that time whether or not we will have contracts, such as they are, for next year.

Mr. Eckstein is holding off, still undecided whether or not to brave the disastrous conditions which exist in Chicago. The assassin's bullet which missed President Roosevelt, but reached Mayor Cermac, has left Chicago without its political leader, causing the next thing to panic. With these conditions, you may imagine that I have no plans beyond the next few weeks. However, as soon as something happens to help me decide, you will be informed.

More convinced than ever that something had to be done, Eddie came out publicly that spring with a plea for Junior Opera Companies. As he told reporters: "Truly the most needful thing to encourage young singers and to make their work joyful and entertaining, and also to make them meticulous and fundamental, is more opportunity for actual experience. Practical experience, however little, is worth much more than actual technical study. . . . Experience is the salvation of the rapid growth in music as in anything else. Our country needs it more than any other. . . .

"I have not had the opportunity of discussing the plan with Mr. Gatti-Casazza, and I do not know what he thinks about my idea. His direction at the Metropolitan these many years has been truly magnificent. I know, because I have seen things that the general public does not see, and I recognize how he has overcome difficulties of great size and also the unending trifles that antagonize, but he has been big enough to see beyond them for the benefit of the welfare of the whole. *Now* is a propitious time for everyone to act on my Junior Opera Company idea. . . . Companies should be established all over the country, no matter on what small scale. . . . Think of the impetus, the serious and systematic study they would provide."

Edward Johnson was ahead of his time for opera on the grand scale he visualized. But eventually his ideas would catch on. Under the aegis of the Metropolitan, in the 1940's, the Katharine Turney Long Studio for the training of young artists was developed; in the sixties a company of young opera singers was formed and, as the Metropolitan Opera National Company, toured for two years; later, a junior company known as the Mini-Met was tried. By that time, opera companies had sprung up in communities large and small all over the United States, and were beginning to appear in Johnson's native Canada as well.

During the summer of 1932, Eddie had often expressed doubts as to whether he would be able to afford further travels for a while. Nevertheless, on June 21, 1933, he found himself heading for Europe, reasoning that he was "understandably dead tired" and needed a long rest. As usual, the Metropolitan Opera season had left him completely exhausted. He was glad that there had been no spring tour which would have entailed, as it had in the past, "singing four or more times a week, sometimes two performances a day."

He joined Fiorenza in Munich where the two of them planned to work on German lieder together that summer. Staying in the charming little house owned by Fiorenza's teacher, they were always surrounded by young students. The years rolled back for Eddie. His exuberant spirit, enthusiasm and spontaneous gaiety won him acceptance as one of the group. "We never thought of father as old," Fiorenza wrote later in *Chatelaine*. "During the day he would study and work, as did the rest of us. At night we would all get together around the piano and sing all the operas we loved most. Father, the only professional among us, would sing all the duets, and suddenly our singing was greater than we could believe. We got drunk on music."

Fiorenza was nearly twenty-three and had had many beaux, but had never been serious about any of them. She casually mentioned to her father, almost too casually he thought, that she heard from George Drew often enough to believe she was not forgotten.

From Munich Eddie and Fiorenza went to Cologne from where, as he wrote his parents, they were to take a small boat and would be "going up the famous river Rhine where all the good wine is made, to Heidelberg where all the students sing about it, and I am told drink a lot of it. We're going to help them." They had "six glorious weeks" together before Eddie had to go back to his engagements in America.

Betweentimes, George Drew's unusual courtship of Fiorenza developed: a cable that summer told her he was in Berlin. He sent duplicates to Rome, Paris, Florence and Venice, just in case! "Where are you?" the cable read. "Let me know and I will join you."

They finally met in Venice and spent long hours in gondolas, and wandering along the historic streets and canals, not talking about what they were seeing, nor about themselves. George wanted Fiorenza's advice as to whether he should go into provincial politics!

Nevertheless, she did manage to show him many of the beauties and wonders of Venice. It was his first visit to Italy and he had purchased an expensive new camera in Berlin in preparation for the trip. At one point his picture-taking almost proved disastrous. It was when they were taking pictures of a charming old well. As Fiorenza told the story later: "George set the camera, then rushed over to be beside me in the photograph. He intended to hoist himself up on the edge of the well, but the surface was as smooth as glass—it had been polished for four hundred years by millions of hands—and he slid right on past me and would have fallen into the well, except for the protective grating that had been placed over it." The local *carabinieri*, witnessing the incident, asked for, and later received, copies of the picture in which the future representative to the Court of St. James looked anything but dignified.

Eddie had seen how things were with Fiorenza and George and had surprised his daughter one day by saying, "*Cara mia,* I really believe that George Drew is the man for you, and you could help him greatly in his career. But I don't want you to be hurt. I don't think you have a chance; he has too many girls chasing him." She had turned away, saying nothing. Even now, in spite of George's attentions, she, too, still believed the situation was hopeless.

When Fiorenza arrived back in Munich, there was already a letter from her father waiting for her. He had been in Guelph to see his parents for two days and had found them "pretty well under the circumstances. Dad has had another slight stroke. This time in his elbow, affecting two fingers of his right hand. Grandmother gets around the house with difficulty, and after the least exertion has great difficulty in breathing."

Jimmie Johnson made a remarkable recovery, but in October Eddie notified Fiorenza: "Grandad was knocked down as he was taking the young bull to the field, and had his shoulder dislocated and his wrist broken. He's in the hospital. Hard luck at his age. Mother looked fine when I was there." In the next sentence he told her: "I opened the new Massey Hall in Toronto and was the guest of Lady Eaton. It was a gala affair and I made a creditable showing." (Massey Hall, closed for renovations in June, 1933, was reopened on October 10.)

Late in October, Guelph was in a general state of excitement awaiting the unveiling of the portrait of Edward Johnson that had been commissioned by "his ain folk" as some Guelph residents liked to refer to themselves in connection with their "Eddie." It was by the painter Wyly Grier and was to hang in the Guelph Collegiate, Edward Johnson's old alma mater.

When a reporter went to Eddie's home for an interview on that occasion, he found the Johnsons in a reminiscent mood and ended up by mainly listening in as father and son talked together of the days when Eddie was a choir boy. What one couldn't remember, the other prompted. Once, looking off into space, Eddie started to hum. It was not something from the repertoire of a great operatic tenor, as the reporter might have expected, but from "Little Annie Rooney" that had been a favourite of Eddie's when he was growing up, singing and playing with the local band:

She's my Sweetheart, I'm her beau;
She's my Annie, I'm her Joe.

"That was the day you wore your first silk hat," Jimmie reminded him, at which they both burst out laughing. "And what a sight you were, too—it went right down over your eyes."

The stay in Guelph was all too short. Eddie had to return to New York. He had promised Lucrezia Bori to speak at another of the countless gatherings in connection with the drive to "Save the Metropolitan Opera." He had also donated his services for one of the American Academy of Teachers of Singing series of broadcasts called *Singing, the Wellspring of Music.*

Speaking on the subject of "The Singer and His Audience," he said he found *singer* an inadequate term and preferred to say *artist,* inasmuch as a singer, to be completely satisfactory, must sing as an artist. He compared "art" to "religion" as both being "manifestations by which man tries to capture and keep alive his shyest and most ethereal conceptions" and went on to point out that "music mirrors the emotions and quickens and enriches our feeling for life." He hearkened back to his operatic début in Italy when, although he had been so nervous, he said, there had arisen within him the profound emotion which brings sincerity and conviction, and through which is acquired assurance and authority —the kind of emotion that releases the artist from himself and gives him the power to translate the true meaning and feeling of the librettist and composer.

He spoke of *Green Pastures* on Broadway, with its all-black cast of singers who, by their sincerity and conviction, had projected a quality that was truly reverent. He also spoke of Toscanini and his conducting of Beethoven's *Eroica* symphony, as an example of the perfect artist: "The magnetic force of his miraculous personality was such that the audience was swept by an overwhelming emotion, seldom experienced, and carried by it into the limitless spaces of unrestrained exaltation. . . . The artist must use every resource—his nerves, his body, his every faculty—to give life to the characters he portrays on the stage. . . . There must be no evidence of technique, only feeling from within—the outpouring of his innermost emotions so that both he and his audience can escape into the magic world of the imagination where time has no place."

Eddie said, "Man is full of impulses, energetically demanding expression—urges, crying for relief. How can these forces better be directed than through the channels of music?"

He drove home his favourite theme: "The next generation will be luckier, for our public schools are taking care of that. Children of the tenderest years are being taught to appreciate and understand the beauties of this great art. The result will be twofold: to awaken and develop real talent on the one hand, and to make for a more intelligent and understanding audience on the other. Great music brings us together, irrespective of birth, position, culture or ability. Emotions translated into music assume heightened beauty and dignity—the only art worthy to reveal the Infinite."

Eddie frequently spent weekends with Florence and Schuyler Smith at *Smeaton,* their country place outside New York. (Mrs. Smith, as Florence Page Kimball, was on the faculty of the Juilliard School at the time.) He would usually play some golf and return feeling very fit. Often Edith Piper, the well-known voice teacher at the Juilliard School, was there, along with some of their other close friends, but generally speaking the weekends were quiet and private. Eddie could be himself, more or less. He confided to them, for example, that he was pleased with the plans Columbia Concerts had made for him for the 1933/34 season.

After the death of Wolfsohn in 1928, Eddie had gone over to the Metropolitan Musical Bureau for the 1929/30 and 1930/31 seasons. In December, 1930, CBS announced the formation of Columbia Concerts Corporation, which absorbed the Metropolitan Musical Bureau. It was with this organization, renamed (1948) Columbia Artists Management, that Eddie was affiliated until his retirement as a singer. Columbia Concerts had conceived the idea of the Metropolitan Opera Quartet as a touring vehicle for four of their artists: Edward Johnson, soprano Grace Moore, mezzo-soprano Rose Bampton and baritone Richard Bonelli. Johnson, for one, was grateful for the Quartet's twenty concerts that winter, in view of his light schedule at the Metropolitan. They would be singing a program of "duets, trios, quartets and solos drawn from the melodious operas presented at the Metropolitan Opera House, New York City." Of course Grace Moore, as the sensational new opera personality and film star (Jenny Lind in *A Lady's Morals,* with Lawrence Tibbett in *The New Moon*), was the big name at the box office, even though all members of the group had their own personal following.

According to Bonelli: "I'd met Eddie many times, but we had never been close friends until the Metropolitan Opera Quartet tour that threw us together. He was a good traveller and was always telling stories. I remember he would laugh so hard at his own stories sometimes that he could hardly finish them. Grace Moore was the soprano and she was often quite temperamental, even then. She knew she was musically uncertain and she always resented any artist who worked with her, especially a tenor, if he was musically sure; it gave her a nervous tension."

163

Eddie had been thinking over the situation at the Metropolitan for some time and was worried. It was common knowledge that Gatti-Casazza had made up his mind to retire, probably within a year or so. His leaving would pose many new questions. First of all, Gatti *was* the Metropolitan, and vice versa; it was impossible to imagine the Opera without him. Not only had he been the general manager since 1908, but he ran a tight ship with a capable and experienced hand. Well-educated and very knowledgeable, he fraternized with no one, but had the admiration, respect, esteem and trust of everyone. People spoke of him as a strong man and a great leader. Eddie wondered whether it might not be a good idea for him to resign while Gatti was still there—the future was so problematic.

How could he tell who Gatti's successor would be, or what the new general manager's views would be about artists, such as himself, who had been on the roster for many years and whose voices were no longer as fresh as they once were? Why not try a new field? For some reason, perhaps recalling his La Scala début in *Parsifal,* Eddie turned his eyes toward Bayreuth. While so much of Eddie's time at the Met had always been taken up in learning new works and new roles—even now he was preparing to create the role of Sir Gower Lackland in Howard Hanson's *Merry Mount* for its world première in February, 1934—Giovanni Martinelli and other tenors, such as the young matinée idol Nino Martini, for example, had been singing the prestige-building repertoire. He wasn't complaining, but . . .

Amid the many rumours to be heard on all sides—some good, some disturbing—was the one that Gatti-Casazza was grooming Edward Johnson to become the next general manager of the Metropolitan.

"Ridiculous," was Eddie's reaction. "What do I know about running a company? Besides, Gatti has never mentioned the subject to me, nor has he ever taken me into his confidence as to the problems of a general manager."

It was one thing, Eddie knew, for people to criticize what was being done, but quite another thing to try to do better. "Gatti is an experienced genius," he muttered to himself. "I'm not."

The daily rehearsals for *Merry Mount* usually lasted until late in the evening. Eddie wrote to Fiorenza in Munich: "Have rehearsed the new opera *Merry Mount* for the last two weeks almost every day, and am pretty well fed up with it. All the more so because my role is simply lousy! Am spending an evening with the DeLucas next week and will meet the Crookses and Lewises. *Pelléas* is announced for the 23rd, so that will ease my feelings a little. *Merry Mount* is a very pretentious, ineffective work with one principal role (Tibbett) plus much chorus and orchestra and a dozen minor parts of which I am the lover and hero, supposedly. Too long and large a ballet, but it is well organized by Rosina Galli, especially the Morris dancers and the second one of the Gay Nineties variety, less effective though inclined to nudity."

The *Merry Mount* première attracted a large expectant audience on Saturday afternoon, February 10. Reviewers pointed out that it was something new in more ways than one. Not only was it composed by an American to a libretto by an American, but the story was based on an American theme: the brief invasion of quiet Massachusetts shores by a mad Maypole-dashing group of celebrants. The composer was praised for the choral portions of the score, although one critic felt they "often suggested Mussorgsky rather than Massachusetts." The writing for the solo voices was considered "awkward." In addition, as Edward Johnson himself had said, it was almost a one-part opera, for a baritone, which was entrusted to Tibbett. Eddie's role of Sir Gower Lackland failed to give him the dramatic opportunities he would have liked. As he confided to his friends, the Schuyler Smiths: "If my career depended on *Merry Mount,* it would be over right now. Give me *Peter Ibbetson* any day, or *Pelléas.* Certainly nobody will ask to paint a portrait of me [in this]."

It was a relief for Eddie to be able to tell Fiorenza how he felt about it: "All our hard work and time and money are all gone for nothing. The critics tried to boost it, being American, but had to admit that as an opera it failed. Tomorrow we begin rehearsals for *Pelléas* and that will compensate a little for my outraged artistic and aesthetic sense. The season is half over and we've gone dreadfully behind. No one knows what will happen for next year. The world is in a difficult mess and we are having our share over here—but don't let us get to politics. It does no good and it isn't safe."

And then, in a surprise ending to this letter, Eddie, who had never been in the habit of having guests since Bee's death, admitted that he'd been constantly entertaining that winter—the Lewises, the Zieglers, Fifi Moulton when she was in New York, Stark Young and his boyfriend, Florence and Schuyler Smith and, inevitably, Edith Piper.

Three days after the première of *Merry Mount,* and while Eddie was hard at rehearsals for *Pelléas,* he received word of his mother's death. It was not unexpected, and she had had a long, full life—not like his beloved Bee who had left him when she was still young—but there had always been a special bond of sympathy between Edward Johnson and his mother. She and Bebe were the only two people with whom he had ever been completely relaxed—never acting, never playing any games, never calculating the effects, never weighing the pros and cons, nor

165

wondering whether what he had done was right or wrong. In that moment, he realized for the first time that with them, and only them, he had never worn a mask. He still missed Bebe, and now his mother was gone.

"Why couldn't I have been there with her to hold her dear hands, like I did Bee's," he cried, as the tears rolled down his cheeks. He wanted to rebel against life, against fate, against the confining routine of his career that had cost him so much, kept him away from his dear ones so often and made it impossible for him to comfort them when they needed him most.

The cable to Fiorenza on February 13, 1934, was brief: "Grandmother left us today quietly. Cable Grandad. Please acknowledge my birthday and Christmas cheques. All love. Daddy."

While he was in Guelph for his mother's funeral, he noticed that his father, who had always been so devil-may-care and, even after his strokes, had continued to have a ready quip for any and all occasions, needed several stiff drinks to give him courage that night. Jimmie had given his wife many a heartache in their long life together, he knew, but there was never any question that his whole life centred around her.

"Take care of yourself, Dad," Eddie said as he boarded the train for New York.

"He looks very frail," Eddie thought to himself. "He won't last long."

A few weeks later, Eddie received word from Fiorenza that she had made her début in Munich, singing some arias and songs. Everything had gone well, but she said that she was "sick with nerves."

A letter of fatherly advice was his reply:

> Nerves can spoil your life and your career. It has happened before and often. Nerves are the result of physical weakness or insecurity in your work, and communicate themselves to your hearers, spoiling their pleasure and listening. Your climate may be bad, but so is ours here in New York, so is London, so is everywhere in the bad season, and we always have to sing in the winter. Colds have little or nothing to do with the weather. For instance, how do the people in the North ever live? Colds come from a lowering of one's vitality —fatigue, the most common of reasons. Fatigue can come from legitimate overwork, but it can come from exhausting your reserve forces from too much "play," and again from faulty elimination— liver and kidneys that do not function properly when they are tired and overcharged.
>
> These are "truths" and took me thirty years to learn—some artists, I mean singers, never learn and go to their graves, artistically speaking, cursing the clamour of some other equally innocent offender. Look to your health if you want to be a successful singer.
>
> My season is over, that is I've exhausted my performances, but

next week we do a week in Boston and I am to sing *Pelléas*, then go to Toronto for a broadcast, and then to Rochester for a twelfth *Merry Mount*, the last in my life, I hope, then back home. This will close the season completely and perhaps—great secret—my operatic career. I am working on a scheme for next year that will require more of my time and give me new outlets, so I think the moment has come to say adieu to the Met.

In another letter to Fiorenza, on March 25, 1934, he said: "Thirteen seasons is a long time and the longest I've ever been anywhere. My opinion is that our public has turned back to German music and Wagner in particular. When Gatti goes, we shall be at the end of next season. I am sure the new director will be German or American. In any case, I feel you are on the right track and I want you to get all the experience you can, and be prepared to meet well the changed situation in this country. There will be Mozart and other revivals and I am sure Wagner will carry the brunt of the season. So work, don't talk or dream, just work."

Johnson was encouraged by the response of the several business friends with whom he had talked about backing his Junior Opera Company project, and by his managers who reported that the Metropolitan Opera Quartet was in great demand everywhere and was certain to give him about all the concert work he'd want to handle for the next few years. So, on April 7, 1934, he finally took the plunge and sent the following letter of resignation to Gatti-Casazza:

Dear Mr. Gatti:

A project on which I have been working for the past year has now reached the point where it requires my personal attention and much more of my time than it did formerly. It is therefore with the deepest regret and keenest sorrow that I tender you my resignation as a member of the Metropolitan Opera Company. In so doing, I wish to express to you my sincere appreciation and gratitude for all the kindness and consideration which I have received at your hands during the past twelve years. No artist could have had greater opportunity or greater satisfaction than was mine under your able direction—nor could I ever truly estimate what the association with the Metropolitan Opera Company has meant in my operatic career. May I ask you to kindly extend to Mr. Ziegler, to the staff, to the maestri and the personnel in general my thanks and appreciation for the assistance and thought which they have always so devotedly given to me and to my work. Let me again thank you for all that you have done for me, and though the years carry us in different directions, I shall always look upon you as my friend.

Very sincerely yours,

Edward Johnson

It was a big step, resigning from the Metropolitan, and Eddie couldn't help feeling gratified when Gatti asked him to stay on for the following season—it would be Gatti's last—to sing *Pelléas, Peter Ibbetson,* and, as an added inducement, a *Pagliacci.* Eddie accepted. There would still be time after the Metropolitan Opera Quartet tour—and during it, perhaps—to start work on his Junior Opera Company project. He hoped he had made a wise decision in both instances. If only he could talk it over with someone! His mother would have listened, and have given him the courage of his own convictions; Bee could have given him wise advice.

As it was, he held his counsel, even when Harry Higinbotham and his wife stopped in New York for a few days before sailing to Egypt. Eddie took them and Fifi Moulton, then in New York, to his favourite little Italian restaurant, Passy's. There, as he related to Fiorenza, "We ran into Schuyler, Florence and Ben . . . so we all dined together . . . very gay." He talked with his friends that evening about the Metropolitan Opera Quartet and his Junior Opera Company, of course, and was particularly full of cheer and confidence, everyone thought. His spirits rose and he himself became aware of the fact that he wasn't putting on a front—he had taken a step into an unknown future and was bubbling with real enthusiasm, ideas and inspiration.

"The Metropolitan situation still remains an enigma," he wrote Fiorenza. "No one knows what is going to happen, though we have already signed a kind of contract for next season. Mr. Gatti is still here and has not yet made his public announcement. Opera is taking a hold in other cities. Cleveland, for example, wants me for *Pelléas* in January. San Francisco wants me in October, and Detroit wants me for *Peter Ibbetson* and *La Rondine* next May. Moreover, my operatic quartet already has twenty bookings for next season. There is still hope."

He gave a Town Hall recital on October 7, 1934, for the benefit of Christadora House, a settlement school in a crowded part of the city. That concert brought him some of the most flattering praise he had enjoyed in recent years: "Edward Johnson can sing. That is a simple statement which should be emphasized by shoutings and underscorings in order to duly drive home how well he can sing . . . not only is he a master over his vocal resources, but his musicianship and scholarly attainment make it possible for him to round out a song of whatever style, and in whatever language, as a complete artistic entity. . . . None can surpass Johnson as a recitalist, and few can equal him." Another critic considered that the high point of the evening was an excerpt from Charpentier's *Louise,* in which "Mr. Johnson seemed to emerge from himself and reach Carusoan proportions in vibrancy and climactic grandeur."

# 7

ASIDE FROM OPERA and concerts, the New Year (1935) began for Eddie with his singing at President Roosevelt's huge Fifty-third Birthday Party on January 30. It was reportedly the largest birthday party in history, with four million guests, at various simultaneous parties, linked by radio to the grand ballroom of the Waldorf-Astoria in New York. It was to raise money for Infantile Paralysis Research. The soloists were Edward Johnson, Maria Jeritza and Giovanni Martinelli.

Not long after that, the public announcement was made of Giulio Gatti-Casazza's imminent retirement. New Yorkers immediately entered into a fury of speculation that constituted the Great Metropolitan Sweepstakes as to who would get the $50,000 a year post. Opera cognoscenti made up a list with their quoted odds. In part, it read:

> Edward Johnson, Canadian tenor 10:1
> Arthur Judson, Manager, New York Philharmonic 15:1
> Sir Thomas Beecham, English operatic conductor 15:1
> Cornelius Bliss, Board of Directors, Metropolitan 20:1
> F. C. Coppicus, concert manager 25:1
> John Erskine, Juilliard School 40:1
> Herbert Witherspoon, American bass 50:1
> Lucrezia Bori, Spanish soprano 25:1
> Edward Ziegler, Assistant Manager, Metropolitan 35:1

While Erskine and Ernest Hutcheson were mentioned as possible candidates, both were obviously satisfied with their Juilliard positions and not anxious to take on the onerous duties at the Met. Also Ziegler was said to have been asked previously whether he would accept the position of general manager when Gatti retired, and to have refused. It was considered unlikely he would have changed his mind. The name of conductor Artur Bodanzky was another that was mentioned. It was generally understood that there were fourteen names in all under consideration.

When the Board finally announced its decision, early in March, the winner was Herbert Witherspoon. Almost everyone was surprised. "Jolly!" Eddie grinned. "The dark horse came in!"

The announcement also included the information that Edward Ziegler was retained as assistant manager in charge of business administration, and that Edward Johnson was named assistant manager responsible for a supplementary popular spring season of opera. Eddie's appointment was an honour, but he confided to his close friend, baritone Emilio de Gogorza, that he had serious doubts about being able to work amicably under Witherspoon as general manager.

"Don't worry, Eddie," De Gogorza told him, "Herbert will die soon."

His only thought was to cheer his friend by reminding him that Witherspoon was a much older man. So even De Gogorza was greatly shaken, he confessed to soprano Leslie Frick, by the subsequent unexpected events of that spring.

Witherspoon and Johnson were to work under a program laid down by the Juilliard Musical Foundation in consideration of the Foundation's contribution of $150,000 to the guarantee fund (a further sum of $100,000 was to be raised by the Met's Board of Directors). The president of the Juilliard Foundation, Dr. John Erskine, was sympathetic to the wishes expressed in the will of wealthy woollen merchant Augustus Juilliard, on the strength of which the Juilliard School was organized in 1928: "To provide for the education of promising young musicians and to make such benefactions useful to the Metropolitan."

It was Dr. Erskine who had specified the Foundation's four-fold purpose in making its 1935 gift to the Metropolitan: 1) to provide educational opportunities, such as the privilege of attending rehearsals, for properly qualified students; 2) to enable the Metropolitan to serve a larger audience, by a supplementary opéra-comique season or by supplementary programs; 3) to make it possible to introduce modern stage methods; 4) to insure the production of American operas already commissioned.

Paul Cravath and Cornelius Bliss of the Metropolitan's Board of Directors were both "making a valiant effort to save the opera," according to Dr. Erskine. But Gatti-Casazza was still reporting such huge deficits that David Sarnoff, a new member of the Board, asked for an auditing sheet. There was none, and when an accounting was ordered Gatti was incensed at the implications. When the 1934 season ended, leaving a deficit of almost a million dollars, the Board considered closing the doors of the Met. The only alternative had been to ask for assistance from the Juilliard. Erskine's policies were accepted in principle by the boards of both the Juilliard and the Metropolitan. Under the new policy the orchestra, chorus, stage hands and ballet all had to agree to take a

170

cut in their weekly salaries on the understanding of a guaranteed longer season and slight increase in total yearly earnings. The Met was not in a bargaining position; only three weeks earlier Board Chairman Paul D. Cravath had announced: "It is not feasible to give opera at the Met next season on the basis of continuing to incur the large deficits of the last five seasons."

A longer season of opera would make it possible to spread out the overhead expenses, in addition to offering the personnel longer employment. There were the added stipulations that the best-selling operas of the last ten years be presented, the Sunday night opera concerts be abandoned, the number of popular-priced Saturday night performances be curtailed, and an expert salesman be engaged for a campaign aimed at reaching all potential opera subscribers. It was not an ideal situation in anyone's eyes, but it was a welcome collaboration in view of its life-saving aspects.

Witherspoon made it clear that he expected his assistant manager to devote his time to administration in the future. As though spurred on by the challenge, Eddie did some of his best singing that spring: March 10, an hour concert on the ABC radio, with an orchestra under Victor Kolar, included an aria from *La Bohème*, one from *I Vespri Siciliani* and many of his favourite English and Irish songs. The announcer for the program, Truman Bradley, was extremely enthusiastic about Johnson's singing, as was the *New York Sun* critic W. J. Henderson when he summed up the Met's 1934/35 season: "Mr. Johnson's Pelléas remains unsurpassed. The writer of these lines prefers it to that of the original, M. Périer."

On March 19, 1935, twenty-seven singers and three conductors appeared in acts and scenes from six operas in honour of Gatti-Casazza, who was concluding his twenty-seventh season as general manager of the Met. Eddie had been asked to address the capacity audience "on behalf of the staff, the artists and the entire personnel of the Metropolitan Opera Association." He told them in part: "It is our desire to honour publicly, before this representative audience, the man who for twenty-five years has so expertly guided the destiny of this theatre; to honour him who by his skill, his wise counsel, his far-sightedness and unerring judgment has brought the Metropolitan to the foremost place among the great lyric theatres of the world. It is also our desire to offer him our homage, our loyalty and our deep affection, for his untiring efforts, for his integrity and sincerity, and for his spirit of justice in whatsoever situation."

Eddie was all but carried away by his own enthusiasm. No petty argument, problem or situation marred his memory in that moment, as

171

he spoke "to honour this man, so justly recognized as the world's most able operatic administrator, our director and friend, Mr. Giulio Gatti-Casazza."

Eddie recalled Gatti's record of having presented a hundred and seventy different productions, fourteen of which were of American origin, and the fact that he had introduced to the United States the most famous European conductors and singers and had engaged and encouraged the many able American artists who then constituted a large part of the company. "In a word," Johnson said, "he has made the Metropolitan an international institution . . . of which not only New Yorkers, but every American citizen may well be proud."

The *New York Herald Tribune* of March 19 reported: "Mr. Gatti-Casazza, true to his custom of keeping himself in the background, made no public appearance. Earlier in the day, the general manager received an engraved scroll from the conductors of the Metropolitan, and a gold plaque with a testimonial message from the orchestra."

The Third Annual Metropolitan Surprise Party (March 31) was full of the kind of pranks and skits that did Eddie's heart good: the Niebelungen Ringling Brothers-Barnum Bailey and Götterdämmerung, in which the *Ring* was presented as a four-ring circus with an opera in each ring, all playing at the same time, "to satisfy the businessman who had only ten minutes to devote to it during his busy year." Eddie would have loved to be part of a skit like the hilarious "Allez-Oop," one that presented diminutive Lily Pons and Heldentenor Lauritz Melchior lifting each other off the stage, by means of invisible wires, in strong-man fashion. Instead, Edward Johnson and mezzo-soprano Gladys Swarthout danced in a number called "Music Without Words" to the tune of *A Waltz Dream* that had launched Eddie to Broadway fame back in 1908.

For Gatti's Farewell Luncheon (April 22), Toscanini and many leading artists, past and present, including Geraldine Farrar, Antonio Scotti, Pasquale Amato, Flagstad, Ponselle, Bori, Johnson, Martinelli, Richard Crooks, Charles Hackett and Herbert Witherspoon, were there. Miss Farrar proposed a toast, to which the great man replied, simply: "Long live the Metropolitan." Then she played some popular music on the piano while Edward Johnson and Lucrezia Bori danced. It was a carefree and happy occasion, though tinged with sadness. Gatti-Casazza's successor had already been announced: Herbert Witherspoon, with tenor Edward Johnson as assistant in charge of the new post-season schedule featuring mainly young American artists.

There were several meetings that spring between Johnson and Herbert Witherspoon before Eddie left for Boston and what Fate decreed to be his last singing engagement with the Metropolitan: *Peter Ibbetson,* April

4, 1935, with Lawrence Tibbett, Queena Mario and Gladys Swarthout. His final opera in the Metropolitan Opera House itself was *Pelléas et Mélisande,* with Bori, March 20.

As soon as the early auditions for the Spring Season began, it was obvious to Eddie that Witherspoon had no intention of allowing him to act as much more than an assistant. Inasmuch as he had felt this could be the first step toward his idea of Junior Opera Companies, he was disturbed. Already unsure of his future as a singer, he was also unsure of the chances Witherspoon was going to give him as an executive.

There were moments when he almost wished he were that other Johnson, Jack Johnson, the prize fighter he had envied so much as a young man. If Eddie's voice hadn't blossomed, after it changed in his teens, into a clear high tenor, he might very well have become a pugilist instead of a grand opera star. After all, he'd been able to lick every kid in Guelph and had always been proud of the way he could "handle his dukes"! But he was a great believer in Destiny. Time, he felt, would give him the answers, and he was confident they would be the right ones.

They came, in a most dramatic and unexpected way, before the summer began. In what proved to be his final season as a Metropolitan Opera artist, Edward Johnson was reviewed as favourably as ever. He particularly treasured critic Leonard Liebling's comment: "Edward Johnson, making his first appearance since his appointment to an executive post at the Metropolitan, delineates and vocalizes a Pelléas whom any tenor would find it difficult to surpass." And Olin Downes, in the *New York Times,* wrote: "Mr. Johnson, the future member of the Metropolitan Executive Triumvirate, who had earlier been refreshingly modest and discreet when asked questions about an operatic future which did not pertain to his task in hand last night, was in exceptional voice. His fine diction and stage presence completed the illusion he gave his part."

On May 7, 1935, nearly six thousand operagoers crowded into Detroit's Masonic Auditorium to hear the local prèmiere of Puccini's *The Swallow (La Rondine),* sung in English by the Detroit Civic Opera Company, with Edward Johnson as Ruggero. According to the *New York Times*: "Edward Johnson, making one of his last appearances anywhere in opera before he retires to become assistant general manager of the Metropolitan Opera Association, playing the role of the young lover opposite Lucrezia Bori, shared many curtain calls with her after the performance." The next day rehearsals began for *Peter Ibbetson.* At that time, no one suspected the imminent dramatic events that were to change the entire course of Edward Johnson's life.

On May 10, Herbert Witherspoon returned to his office at the Metropolitan Opera House after a long day of signing contracts. He was tired after the strenuous two-month schedule of speechmaking, union negotiations and general exhortations on behalf of public support for the Metropolitan. He and his wife were planning to leave for Europe the following day, in search of new singers and to study recent developments in foreign operatic production methods. He was in an exuberant mood, with the strain of the past few months over, and looking forward to the trip.

Mrs. Witherspoon was waiting for him in the outer office while he and Ziegler concluded some last-minute discussions. At one point, Witherspoon got up, having made a jocose remark, and stepped toward the doorway, chuckling, to tell his wife he would soon be with her. Suddenly his knees doubled under him, and without a sound he slumped to the floor. It was a coronary thrombosis and death was instantaneous. Speaking of those moments, in later years, Mrs. Witherspoon recalled: "That night Herbert died in my arms at the Metropolitan." The funeral was to take place on Monday, May 13, at 10 A.M. at St. George's Protestant Episcopal Church, Stuyvesant Square and East 16th Street.

Eddie would have left immediately for New York but there was no one else who could sing the dress rehearsal of *Peter Ibbetson* on the twelfth. He went as soon as that was over, but did not arrive in time to take his place among the twelve honorary pallbearers at the funeral. He was on hand, however, for several private discussions about the future, and able to make it known that he would consider the position of general manager himself only on the condition that both Edward Ziegler and Earle Lewis, treasurer of the Metropolitan Opera box office, were retained. After a visit with Mrs. Witherspoon, he boarded the train for his return to Detroit to sing *Peter Ibbetson* the following evening (May 14).

It was somewhat of a tour de force: thirty-six hours of travel and a day of constant meetings and conferences prior to what was to be his final performance as a tenor on the opera stage. The *Musical Courier* reported that "much of the success of the opera was due to the outstanding performances of Miss Bori and Mr. Johnson. Mr. Johnson's diction in English was magnificent. Both were in exceptionally fine voice . . . the huge audience thundered its applause and composer Deems Taylor, as well as Pelletier, Johnson and Bori received curtain calls too numerous to count."

Shortly before Edward Johnson left for the theatre that evening, he received the following telegram from Paul Cravath, on behalf of the Met Board: "Hope you will accept appointment as general manager Metropolitan. We are all agreed upon you and you will have loyal backing,

Ziegler not only satisfied but pleased." Eddie's reply, sent with a combination of excitement and misgiving, was:

> The appointment to the Directorship of the Metropolitan Opera Association moves me profoundly and leaves me deeply sensible of the confidence which the board of the opera association and that of the Juilliard Institute have reposed in me. Recognizing the obligation to carry on Mr. Witherspoon's design already so auspiciously conceived, and with the invaluable counsel of Mr. Edward Ziegler and the cooperation of Mr. Earle Lewis, I pledge my zealous devotion to its fulfillment and to the maintenance of the uninterrupted prestige of the Metropolitan Opera.

On May 15, 1935, following the receipt of this telegram, the Board of Directors of the Metropolitan met in David Sarnoff's office, 30 Rockefeller Plaza, and announced to the press that Edward Johnson had been appointed as Herbert Witherspoon's successor. Headlines immediately proclaimed: "Edward Johnson Appointed Metropolitan Opera Director" and "Johnson Made Opera Head."

AT SEVEN O'CLOCK that evening, with his *Rondine* and *Ibbetson* costumes carefully packed away, the new general manager of the Met boarded the *Wolverine* in Detroit, and by 9:20 the following morning he was back in New York. Reporters caught him as he came off the train. His first press conference took place, the *New York Sun* reported, "as the new director-general of the Metropolitan Opera Company sat on an empty baggage truck on the underground platform of the Grand Central Terminal."

Johnson talked enthusiastically about the future of the Company. "America's become opera conscious, thanks to the radio and concerts," he said. "We're going to make the Metropolitan Opera the clearing house for all the young artists who will go out to sing in the other cities of the country. . . . We can't accomplish what we wish overnight, but if faith in a cause and enthusiasm mean anything, I'm sure we'll succeed eventually."

The *New York Herald Tribune* published some of Eddie's remarks on his appointment: "I made every effort to avoid this thing. I didn't feel that I should really take on such a responsibility and, after all, the reasons for which I was not appointed before were still in force. I'm a romantic tenor, you know, and I've always been behind the footlights. But now that I am manager I shall bring to it all that I have, all my love and enthusiasm for my art, all my health and strength. . . . Of course, I'm so full of optimism and hope for the future there are no bounds to what I've planned. Being an artist and doing romantic roles all these years has kept me young. I'm still a romantic, and I expect a lot from the world."

Oddly enough, none of the newspapers commented when, some weeks later, the brown-haired romantic tenor became the white-haired manager. He had made the decision: no more tinting. Privately, Eddie told friends it was a great relief not to have to worry about the colour of his hair any longer!

When the news reached Italy, May 18, of the appointment of the new general manager, Giulio Gatti-Casazza said, "I am very glad at the appointment of Signor Johnson who is my dear friend. I am sure he will succeed, as he possesses excellent qualities."

Regarding the specific events that preceded his becoming general manager of the Metropolitan Opera, Johnson always said simply that while he was singing in Detroit he was notified of Witherspoon's death and invited to carry on. But many of the details were remembered by Eddie's friend and colleague Richard Bonelli and by Maestro Fausto Cleva.

According to Bonelli, years later:

> Johnson told me himself one day that Gatti had him in mind to succeed him. I don't know. But Witherspoon was chosen, and I'll always think that if he had been permitted to live, he might have made a very fine general manager. He could be ruthless, but he believed in right and wrong. I think he would have had the courage of his convictions and wouldn't have cared too much whether he was pleasing people or not. Right away he went in and told several of the mainstays, one of them was Martinelli, he didn't want them any more. Even Eddie used to say, on tour, 'Witherspoon will be just marvellous. He wants to get a bunch of young people and start to build up a really fine opera company. That's exactly what I want to do.' He didn't seem to mind that the idea of the Spring Season was Witherspoon's—Witherspoon had spoken quite openly and frankly about it; he felt the little Italian coterie had run things long enough.
>
> Most of the artists had to take salary cuts. I guess I was an exception, for Witherspoon called me into the office one day and said, "You've never been paid what you're worth. I'm going to raise you. It won't be a big raise—just a token raise—but you're going to get a lot more work." I expected this was the way it was going to be with Eddie, but. . .
>
> We were in Detroit and my wife and I were having an early dinner—it was May 10 and I was singing *Faust* with Martinelli that night—when the wife of Carlos Edwards, an assistant conductor and part-time photographer at the Met, came to the table and

showed me a telegram from Carlos: "Witherspoon dropped dead in his office today." It went on to say there would be a meeting of the Board of Directors two days later to decide on a successor. Eddie hadn't been told yet, so I went and found him and told him. As the assistant manager, he was in line for the job and I knew he was interested. I told him I thought he ought to be in New York for the Board meeting.

"Oh, they'll never take me," he said. "They'll take Ziegler or somebody like that. Besides, I can't get down to New York and back in time. I have to sing."

We told him, "Of course you can. Take the train in the afternoon, get there in the morning and go to the meeting. Take a train back—you're not singing until Wednesday—and nobody will know you've been gone."

It took some persuasion and argument, but finally he agreed he should go, if the manager in Detroit agreed. As I recall, he got the train the afternoon of the twelfth, and came back on the fourteenth, with the thing more or less confirmed. "At last we're going to have an opera company run by singers—people who understand," he told me, "and I want all my friends to rally round and help me." If Eddie had stayed as an artist, and retired as an artist, he'd always have been just the wonderful warm guy he was earlier. But he did change.

Eddie had always been a good sport, and a good colleague, and I was very keen about his taking over the Met. As a matter of fact, I can almost claim some credit for it, the way things happened. I can remember so well going to his room that day and showing him the telegram, and how my wife and I helped him pack his suitcase after the *Ibbetson* rehearsal and get out of there in a big hurry, because there wasn't so very much time—the New York train left at five o'clock. Anyway, if he hadn't been there, he mightn't have got the job, I don't know. But my wife and I felt that if we had not been there to put pressure on him to go down, things might have been different.

Italian conductor Fausto Cleva, another close associate of Johnson's during the years before and after 1935, recalled the events this way:

I remember we were in Detroit and he had had a telegram asking him to accept the position of manager of the Metropolitan—it was during the second intermission of *Peter Ibbetson*. "Fausto," he said to me backstage, "I'm not sure I should accept this position."

I said, "Why? Listen, we have another act to go; we'll talk it over later."

So after the opera we walked until two, three or four o'clock in the morning, on the sidewalk, back and forth. I talked, trying to convince this man to take the position. He was afraid, he said, but finally we came into the hotel and he wrote a telegram. But he just crumpled it up and threw it on the desk there in the lobby.

"Maybe you're right," I told him. "Why don't you take a good night's sleep and I'll see you in the morning."

He said, "I think that's very wise." Then he stepped over to read something on the board, and I picked up the telegram and went to the phone and read the telegram and sent it off. "By the way," he said when I came back to the desk, "I don't see that telegram I threw here."

"It doesn't matter," I told him, "because in half an hour it will be in New York."

Eddie couldn't believe me. "In the name of God, what have you done?"

"I sent the telegram. What's wrong?" I said. "While you were over there, I sent it. It was meant to be sent, no? Stop! Don't say anything. I sent it for you!"

On announcing Edward Johnson's appointment as general manager, the board of the Metropolitan also released the names of the nine artists who had already signed contracts with Mr. Witherspoon for the season ahead: sopranos Josephine Antoine, Charlotte Symons, Thelma Votipka; baritones Eduard Habich, Julius Huehn, Carlo Morelli; bassos Chase Baromeo, Dudley Marwick, Hubert Raidich; with Fausto Cleva and Konrad Neuger as chorusmasters. Questions immediately arose about such stars as Lawrence Tibbett, Rosa Ponselle, Lotte Lehmann, Lily Pons, Maria Olszewska, Nino Martini, Tito Schipa and Gladys Swarthout. Would they be back? Johnson quickly let it be known he was negotiating with them.

Johnson's first day as manager was a day of preparation as he settled into the new office. Bubbling with enthusiasm and optimism, he called a press conference for his first day of business, May 17. Richard Crooks came to the office with him that day, promising to back him up. "I'll do anything you want," Crooks assured him.

The new executive began by asking the press for "tolerance in my first days in office. I've just been through two of the hardest weeks in my life." His father had died on April 30 and immediately after attending the funeral, in Guelph, Eddie had had to go to Detroit. Then came Witherspoon's death, the unexpected trip to New York and Eddie's appointment as general manager. "The only things I bring to this post," he told reporters, "are experience behind the footlights, a love of music and personal enthusiasm. The cause of opera and of music in the United States is worth fighting for. That is what this job represents to me." He promised high standards of performance and economy in expenditures

178

for administration and production, and proclaimed that the whole organization was going to be "just one big happy family." There would be a slight shortening of the list of singers for the following season, in the interest of economy, but otherwise, he said, everything would be the same.

Eddie wasted no time. He entered into negotiations, happily kept the press informed of his every move and announced plans for extending both the spring and fall tours, to the southeast, to Mexico City and to Canada.

One of the quarrels of the Metropolitan Opera artists with the previous policy concerned outside engagements. Lawrence Tibbett said he could have made almost as much in two radio engagements during the winter of 1934-35 as he did the whole Met season, but had had to turn them down. Johnson promised to be lenient, although he had some reservations. "If you catch a cold on a pullman, coming back from an engagement, you might be unavailable even then."

Things had changed rapidly for Edward Johnson in the few short days since the telegram reached him in Detroit, notifying him of his appointment as the new general manager of the Metropolitan. He had presented a deceptively youthful appearance as he stepped from the Detroit train, neatly dressed in his dark double-breasted suit with white pin stripes and wearing a black tie, but he was apprehensive about the enormity of his new assignment. His confidence increased, even during his first day back, buoyed by conferences with his colleagues and Paul Cravath. Then, after spending an evening with Juilliard's John Erskine, he felt ready to outline to the press some of the basic plans he had in mind for the Metropolitan under his régime:

1) The establishment of a fund, with government or foundation assistance, to be used for productions and programs of artistic significance: e.g., certain spectaculars and works by promising young composers.
2) A popular Spring Season, to follow the international one, in which young artists could attain normal artistic growth rather than being obliged to step immediately alongside the world's great artists.
3) Comedies to be sung in English; standard works such as *Aida* and *Faust* to retain their original language.
4) The employment of artists, preferably Americans, whose first consideration was their art, with money of secondary importance.
5) No special consideration for artists of the Juilliard School, regardless of the fact that the Juilliard Foundation had guaranteed the opera season.

179

Rosa Ponselle had phoned him at the office and expressed her willingness to cooperate in every way. She asked him what was going to happen to his singing career. "That," he told her, "is over. *Pauvre Pelléas, hélas!*"

From the moment Edward Johnson took over as general manager of the Metropolitan, he had been as optimistic about the future as a young bridegroom. He admitted it. He also admitted, as he thought about the year ahead, to being "scared stiff." Still, the more he thought about it, the more he was excited over the prospect of being able to put into effect his new ideas; he couldn't wait to be about it.

Edward Ziegler and Earle Lewis were staunchly back of him as he went through union negotiations, contract disputes, casting and scheduling problems, to say nothing of the thousand and one production details attendant to getting the new season under way. As he told them later, "Without the two of you, it would have been impossible."

Of general concern that summer of 1935 had been the possibility of war in Europe. "There's no point in talking too much about that," Eddie wrote Fiorenza. "Personally, I feel that since the war did not break out last week, the moment has passed and there will be no war. I am convinced that all the fighting has been done in the newspapers and it breaks my heart to think that any such bellicose crisis between Italy and England could ever come to pass. The political aspect will pass quickly when things are adjusted. The hate and suspicion sown in the minds of men will take years and years to correct. The world has gone far askew."

Edward Johnson didn't change, but he noticed a difference in the attitude of many of his associates—a deference that neither Edoardo di Giovanni nor the tenor Edward Johnson had ever experienced. He was general manager of the Met; head of the whole house. It was exhilarating. It was exciting.

RUMOURS FROM CANADA were that Edward Johnson might be knighted. His first tangible intimation about it, however, had come via a telegram, April 17, 1935, from a family friend and prominent Guelph surgeon, H. O. Howitt: "Important to know citizenship of boy who sang 'Annie Rooney' years ago. This is King George's Jubilee year. Mum's the word. Wire me at once." The reply was immediate: "Always loved 'Annie Rooney' and 'Maple Leaf.' Have never changed colours."

Actually, Eddie had taken steps toward United States citizenship on May 19, 1921, giving his address at the time as Bay City, Michigan, the home of his brother Fred. For some reason, nothing further happened until September 19, 1927, when he filed a "Preliminary Form for Petition for Naturalization." Again the permanent address given was Bay City, Michigan.

On April 3, 1928, Fred sent the following letter to the Director of Naturalization, Detroit, Michigan:

Dear Sir,

Enclosed please find Declaration of Intention and also Petition for Naturalization, in the name of Edward Johnson, which Mr. Johnson misplaced for a long time and they have now just come to light, a short time before the Declaration of Intention becomes obsolete, as I understand the time limit is up May 19th, 1928.

Mr. Edward Johnson is my brother and is at the present time engaged in some work in New York, so that I am trying to help him in the matter of getting his final citizenship papers. Will you please acknowledge these papers to me and advise what the necessary steps required of him are so that I can telegraph these instructions to him and he can make his plans to come to Detroit whenever you say it is necessary.

Thanking you for this courtesy, and assuring you of my prompt attention, I am,

Yours very truly,
F. D. Johnson

The papers were returned on May 7 from the United States Department of Labor (Naturalization Service), following which there was no further activity until November 21, 1932, when a letter to Edward Johnson from the Department of Labor stated: "It has come to the attention of this office that your application for citizenship as filed with the Naturalization authorities at Detroit, Michigan, cannot be favourably acted upon as no record of your claim to legal admission to the United States through the Port of Boston, Massachusetts, on November 12, 1919, on the SS *Canopic* can be found . . ." He was told he would have to fill out designated forms "to have such a record created of your claimed entry . . ." Presumably the said forms were filled out and sent, for a subsequent telegram from the District Director of Immigration in Boston read: "Edward Johnson forty born Guelph Canada arrived Boston ex steamship *Canopic* October twelve nineteen nineteen admitted to proceed in transit to home Guelph Ontario."

From then on, Eddie took no further steps toward citizenship but simply carried an immigrant identification card or border crossing card with him. Later, when he received Dr. Howitt's telegram of April, 1935, he pencilled a note on the bottom of it: "re C.B.E." The point was, as he well knew, that had he ever become a citizen of the United States he would not have been eligible for the British honours list.

181

At the time he boarded the *Bremen,* May 28, 1935, for Europe, he had heard nothing further, and in the midst of his new responsibilities he had all but forgotten about it. He was bombarded with questions. Would Tibbett, Ponselle, Lehmann and Pons be back at the Met the coming season? The new general manager gave affirmative assurance. What would happen while he was away? He felt things would be in good hands, with Juilliard president John Erskine as chairman of the new Opera Management Committee, created as part of the Juilliard Foundation agreement.

On June 3 it was announced that the Canadian Edward Johnson had been made a Commander of the Order of the British Empire, Civil Division, in the birthday honours list of King George V. At the same time, Eddie noted with a twinge of envy, Ernest C. MacMillan, dean of the Faculty of Music, University of Toronto, also known as a composer, conductor and organist, had been given the award of Knight Bachelor, henceforth to be known as Sir Ernest. Eddie accepted his own honour with pleasure and pride, however. His two months in Europe were busy ones, and he was pleased, among other things, to have signed a contract with Belgian coloratura soprano Vina Bovy to début at the Metropolitan as Lakmé, December 30, 1935. (As it happened, Bovy didn't make her Met début until December 24, 1936, in *La Traviata.*) He managed to save three days, at the end of his trip, to go to Florence before boarding the liner *Rex* at Genoa on July 25 for the return to New York.

That trip passed more quickly than usual. At first, he spent most of the time in the company of Maestro Bernardino Molinari, who was on his way to conduct concerts in the Hollywood Bowl. Later, he managed to forget completely the problems of opera as he whiled away the hours on shipboard with fellow passenger Walt Disney discussing how Disney had created the popular Mickey Mouse cartoon character and what sort of system he had devised for running his studio in Hollywood.

It was Disney's opinion that going over the hundreds of applications and drawings submitted by graphic artists hopeful of joining the Disney Studios wasn't so different, after all, from auditioning hundreds of singers, of varying degrees of accomplishment, for the Metropolitan. He was intrigued and extremely interested in Johnson's conviction about the future of opera. "We are on the brink of a new epoch in the operatic field. Some day Europe may be sending its young singers over to us to learn their trade instead of the other way round," Eddie prophesied. "The Met is setting a good example to other opera houses by doing operas in their original languages."

Disney wasn't sure he agreed with that. After all, his whole premise was communication. "How can you communicate," he asked, "using a language the audience doesn't understand?"

Eddie, in his enthusiasm, ignored the question. "Why, the Metropolitan is a more prestigious place to make an important début than La Scala! Big names are hard to get, you know, but the Met is so strong that artists are willing to make a financial sacrifice to sing there." What Walt Disney recognized, but Edward Johnson did not realize for some time, was that the Met's new general manager had already identified himself with the Opera House in a personal way.

When the ship docked in New York, reporters were on hand for Johnson's latest news and predictions. "We shall proceed along lines of evolution rather than revolution," he told them. "There will be no costly experiments with doubtful outcome—better to produce standard works with great casts than to experiment at great cost. We're going to concentrate on performances and not on star performers, and give more emphasis to the composer than to the interpreter." Then he left them with a subject for speculation: "I have several new scores that will be submitted to the entire music staff for consideration and if there's something worthwhile among them, we will have a new production."

That was on August 2, 1935. Five days later he surprised the musical world by announcing the engagement of The American Ballet for the season ahead, with George Balanchine as artistic director and balletmaster. It was an innovation that would mean the return of independent ballet productions, absent for nine years.

With the Met having suffered acute financial difficulties in the early thirties, it had become obvious to most of the directors and their close associates that if the company were to survive something would have to be done to provide more revenue and to broaden the basis of responsibility. Meetings were held in the managers' offices, in the Opera Club, in Mrs. Belmont's home and elsewhere, over a period of many months, before a skeleton plan was finally agreed upon: form an organization that will bring its members into contact with the stars of the company, make it possible for them to attend selected rehearsals—a privilege enjoyed only by stockholders and directors until that time—and provide them with a special avenue for buying tickets to performances. Earle Lewis and Edward Johnson both felt strongly that the entire country should be involved, if possible, and that arrangements should be made so that school children and students could attend the operas.

Mrs. Belmont presented the plan to Executive Committee Chairman Anthony Bliss early in 1935, and in April the committee gave her the green light for forming an opera guild. As a result, with a distinguished group of political and social leaders from across the country heading the list of original members, the Metropolitan Opera Guild came into being. President Franklin Delano Roosevelt was the first on the list that included the names of governors of nine states and New York's

Mayor La Guardia. Mrs. Belmont was chairman. After the sudden death on May 10 of the Met's new general manager, Herbert Witherspoon, his widow, Blanche Witherspoon, was invited to become the Guild's first secretary, a position she was to hold for many years.

Eddie was enthusiastic about the new organization and was also among its first members. "It will bring the public and management of the opera into close cooperation," he said, "and I'm sure it will develop a 5,000, maybe 10,000 national membership. At last, radio listeners will have an opportunity, through membership in the Guild, to share in support of the opera." Sustaining memberships were $10, contributing memberships $30, and for patrons, $100. By the time of the first Guild "At Home" on December 8, 1935, the organization already had close to 2,000 members, a large percentage of whom were on hand to meet and greet Edward Johnson and his artists.

Within a year's time, the Metropolitan Opera Guild had provided a much-needed new cyclorama for the Met's stage and put out a trial issue of the *Guild Bulletin* that turned into *Opera News*. Before a second year had passed, the Guild had introduced the popular student matinées at the Opera.

At the end of that summer of 1935, Edward Johnson spent a few days in Guelph, returning to New York September 13 to be met as usual by an insatiable press. What about a new American opera? "Between forty and fifty American operas have been submitted to me," he replied, "but no decision will be made until all the first-line conductors are back." They asked him about the persistent rumour that Vittorio Giannini's *Lucedia* was being scheduled. Johnson refuted this rumour.

With the season scheduled to open December 16, Johnson was busy. Whereas Witherspoon had intended to discontinue the Met's regular Tuesday evening performances at the Brooklyn Academy of Music, Johnson said that four would be given during his first season, and announced that he was going forward with plans for a subsidiary spring season—just a new name for his old idea of a junior opera. Feeling that the new season should be sponsored by a new Board of Directors "drawn from the younger set," he called on the newly-formed Guild for support, stressing that such a development was "really necessary for the future of opera in America."

In his letter to Fiorenza in Florence, September 25, 1935, Eddie wrote: "As for me, you are quite right, I am in the throes of intensive and exhausting work at the Met. It is much more tiring than I could ever have imagined. I come home at night so fatigued that I am not fit for anything. Perhaps it will not be so difficult later on, and I will have become more accustomed by then. This explains why you have not heard from me. Besides, I have only theatrical stuff to talk about, and so much of it is in embryo or uncertain that I hesitate to put it on paper. Mr. Ziegler has been wonderful in his assistance and cooperation, and I don't know what I ever would have done without him. . . . As for Luigi [Luigi Villa, the secretarial assistant], he is simply a miracle man. Bori is likewise most helpful. . . . We had a meeting this afternoon . . . and when the meeting eventually broke up, Neddie Ziegler and I made for the Netherlands Bar for a good stiff cocktail to revive our fainting and exhausted spirits."

When Fiorenza came to New York that fall, Eddie told her that she would have to be his official hostess for social occasions and responsible at all times for guests in the manager's box at the opera. Her eyes lighted up at the prospect, but he quickly warned her that it would be no picnic, that the box was never to be empty, nor was it to be filled irresponsibly. Invitations were to be given for good reasons. Fiorenza thought it would be a lark. But it proved to be the most difficult challenge she had ever faced. There were times when she wondered whether she could carry on. Before the season was over, however, she was to learn that she had acquitted herself to her father's satisfaction. The old camaraderie they had enjoyed in Europe in the summer of 1933 had returned.

On December 15, the day before the opening, Johnson let it be known that the forthcoming fifth season of Metropolitan Opera broadcasts was not to be sponsored commercially. "We will pay for them ourselves," he announced, "because radio broadcasting makes the Metropolitan no longer a local affair; radio nationalizes whatever it touches and that makes the Met the central operatic theatre of the United States. The operatic situation is nationalized, with the Met as the hub." Plans for the 1935/36 broadcasts included the United States, Canada and Europe, he said.

Opening night of the 1935/36 season at the Metropolitan Opera was an especially gala occasion, at least for Edward Johnson, as he proudly presented Bori, Tibbett and his good friend Richard Crooks in *La Traviata,* conducted by Ettore Panizza. Eddie's smile was brighter than ever, his eyes alight with a new kind of pride, as he went backstage to wish everyone well before the opera, and later as he walked down the corridors sartorially striking in his white tie and tails and carrying his top hat and white gloves. The house was packed; the evening was a triumph. It had featured an American tenor and an American baritone, and marked the début, as Flora, of Thelma Votipka who was to become a mainstay for the next thirty years in supporting soprano roles— "Tippie's bits" they came to be called.

Speaking to the press while the audience in the house was still applauding *Traviata,* Johnson was obviously immensely delighted with everything. "There is a grand new spirit in the audience, among the cast and backstage," he beamed. "Telegrams of congratulations are pouring in from my friends in Canada, the United States and around the world, and there are a few of my Canadian intimates in that glorious audience." He proudly showed friends the beautiful green bronze desk set given him by the ninety-odd members of the opera's technical staff with the accompanying note: "We boys backstage hope you will accept this little token of our good wishes and esteem on the great day." Then Johnson remarked on the fact that it was almost exactly thirteen years since he had made his début (November 16, 1922) at the Metropolitan. "Things were different then," he said. "There was a good house, but not like tonight. Did you know that every seat in this massive building was sold out days ago? I've even heard that a few audacious speculators wormed their way through the crowd before the performance tonight offering $10 seats for $100. And hundreds stood in line for hours to buy standing room, and many had to be turned away."

Edward Johnson took a small group—with Fiorenza and the Higin-bothams—to Sherry's for supper after the opera. It had been an exciting evening, possibly the most exciting in his long career.

"Did you miss being on the stage yourself, Eddie?" someone asked.

He was surprised to be able to say, quite honestly, "No, I didn't. This new challenge is the greatest I've ever had, and Dick [Crooks] was great."

From opening night on, there was never a day without its crises and surprises. His first surprise came when Bori asked him to lunch with her, the day after the opening, and announced that she was planning to retire from the lyric stage at the end of that season. "I had thought I would retire at forty-five and I have stayed on for three years more in the cause of saving the Metropolitan from the financial disaster it was facing. But you are here now, and the new season is off to a successful start, and I think I can be more helpful on the outside." At her insistence, the announcement was given to the press.

"Last night," Bori told them, "we could see and feel that opera is not dying. It was clear that it is going to live. The time has come when I can carry out my resolution. I want to stop while people are saying, 'The voice is better than ever.'" She said she wanted to help the Met in every way and that she would remain with the Metropolitan as a member of the Board of Directors and the Management Committee.

"The loss of Miss Bori," Johnson added, "will be terrific. She typifies completely her generation of singers. I do not see how the Met will ever

186

replace her. Besides her great force as an artist, her work for the Met in distress has been without parallel. She kept up her work on the stage while labouring outside to keep the institution alive. A great part of the credit for the existence today of the Met belongs to Miss Bori."

Alone in his office for a brief second after the press conference, Johnson found himself fighting off a feeling of fatigue and depression. Then came a knock at his door, and there stood Lauritz Melchior. "Hello, Eddie," he said, in his typically hearty way. "Congratulations. That was a wonderful night last night and we are going to make it a great *Walküre* for you tomorrow. I like this new soprano Marjorie Lawrence. We can joke together . . . and she will be a good Brünnhilde."

Two evenings later, on December 18, *Die Walküre* proved to be the second success in the new régime of Edward Johnson. Melchior, as Siegmund, was in excellent form, and critic Olin Downes, in the *New York Times,* saw Miss Lawrence as one who was "tremendously in earnest, intelligent and of a consumingly dramatic temperament, who seems to have everything before her."

Rosa Ponselle's much-publicized Carmen, premièred a few days later, found Mr. Downes in a less generous mood: "We have never heard Miss Ponselle sing so badly and we have seldom seen the part enacted in such an artificial and generally unconvincing manner." Although Ponselle had heroically reduced in order to become a visually personable gypsy, the voice of the magnificent Norma, Leonora, La Vestale and La Juive, according to the review, "seemed to have lost some of its opulence."

Despite such a deprecating comment, *Carmen* drew full houses at the Met. Much later, as Ponselle talked about those experiences and her popularity in that role, she said:

> Olin Downes had a personal grudge with my manager and he took it out on me. It hurt him, poor darling, more than it hurt me, because he was always one of my most ardent admirers. The end result was that we became terrific box office. Everybody came to see if Ponselle could really be as bad as he said. It was Witherspoon, you know, who had asked me would I please do Carmen. I had never had to decide about my roles; Gatti just handed things to me, mainly all the Verdi, and I was so busy learning new roles I had no opportunity to think of anything or ask. If I'd thought, and had the time, I would have asked for Tosca or something. Anyway, I took the Carmen and it was such box office that I sang nothing but Carmens for two years.
>
> But when the time came for my contract to be renewed, I was married and my husband wanted me to cut down on my opera. So I said to Johnson, "Now listen. If I'm coming back I want to do a new opera, *Adriana Lecouvreur.* It's just been revised and is a

great success in Italy. I'll stay on if you'll give me that." It was the first time in my life I had ever asked to do a particular role. Johnson seemed to be in sympathy, being an artist himself—and he personally was a love—but he didn't have all the power. He had talked it over with Ziegler and Earle Lewis and they said it wouldn't sell and the answer was no. I think if Johnson had had all the say, when I offered all these performances for gratis, he would have agreed. He smiled that big smile—I always thought of Theodore Roosevelt when Edward smiled—and was charming, but the answer was still no. So I didn't go back.

The next year they begged me to come back on my own terms—said I could sing anything I wanted. If it were to do over again, I think I'd go back and have my career, but I was still mad and hurt and I didn't go. So the rumour went out that I had lost my voice. It took two recordings, a private one at a Christmas party and an RCA album in 1954, to convince people that I hadn't retired because of an impaired voice.

Bing once asked me at a dinner party in his honour here in Baltimore, "Tell me, madam, what was the real reason why you left the Metropolitan?"

And I said, "You want to know the truth? Because they wouldn't revive *Adriana*."

He told me, "I don't blame them. I loathe it; I wouldn't give it if I had to close the opera house."

And would you believe it? The following year it was announced that Tebaldi was doing it in Chicago and would come to the Metropolitan in *Adriana*. I never saw Bing after that to remind him of what he'd said. Anyway, I'm sure Eddie would have done *Adriana* for me, but Ziegler was against it, so he couldn't.

Kirsten Flagstad's first *Fidelio* brought a capacity audience to the March 7th matinée. The *New York Herald Tribune's* Lawrence Gilman wrote: "Her singing of the music was at all times nobly beautiful, thrilling in its sweep of line and fervor in such heroic outbursts as the concluding allegro section of the great aria where (despite a momentary lapse of memory) she took us to the heights of Leonore's fortitude and faith."

At the beginning of the season, the claqueurs had been summarily banished from the Metropolitan and were disgruntled about this. An estimate of the weekly earnings of the claque master, for example, was set conservatively at $100, with a larger take if the singers were "cooperative." Standard rates, officially, went something like this: $25 for a guarantee of two curtain calls, and an additional $5 for every additional bow. The lesser members of the claque got free entrée to the house, $5 for a curtain call, plus $5 for a bravo and $10 for a bravo followed by the name of the artist. Then, too, since leading singers had insisted in the past on receiving a small allotment of complimentary general admissions, good for standing room at any performance, the leader of the claque sometimes had as many as fifty admissions on hand. Thus the bill to an artist who was fond of curtain calls and bravos, and who sang several times a week, could run into money. Johnson's first step, therefore, was the forbidding of the giving of free tickets to the artists. If the artists were so desperate that they wished to purchase tickets themselves for the "gentlemen with the calloused palms," there would be little that he could do, he said. But he hoped that moral persuasion would be effective.

THE BIG TOPIC of conversation in opera circles during the holidays that winter was the Met's possible inauguration of a "supplementary season" of popular-priced opera in the spring. With money scarce and ticket prices soaring, many customers were thinking of waiting until then to attend the opera. The whole thing threatened to boomerang. At his January 7th directors' meeting, Johnson asked for a committee to deal with rumours and to plan details. He wanted neither all the work nor all the responsibility. His suggestions were that they announce a "Spring Season" rather than a "supplementary" or "popular-priced" one; that they feature young American singers; that the opera house be airconditioned; and that a separate corporation be formed, with "Metropolitan" appearing in the title, to handle the innovative season. A week later the announcement was made that a Metropolitan Spring Season Board had been formed with Edward Johnson pro tem president and Lucrezia Bori honorary president.

Meanwhile, everyone was insisting that Eddie sing *Pelléas* one more time. It would be big box office as well as Lucrezia Bori's final performance in the opera, they argued, inasmuch as she had announced her retirement for the end of the season. Eddie was torn, so he "sneaked away" into the country for a weekend "to think it over and brush up on the role." He still hadn't made up his mind when he returned to the city. Rumours had leaked out, however, that he might appear and Bori was begging him: "Just this one more time we will sing it together." Finally he gave in and the announcement was made that the performance would take place on March 19. How he was going to find time to rehearse and the energy to sing, in view of his heavy responsibilities and busy schedule as general manager of the Metropolitan, neither he nor the public could imagine. But the die was cast and from a combination of morbid curiosity and nostalgia the house was quickly sold out.

The *New York Times* (February 23) reported that Edward Johnson

189

had agreed to sing once that season, with Lucrezia Bori, in *Pelléas et Mélisande*. "It will be something of a farewell for Mr. Johnson as a singer." Bori's personal farewell, the report stated, would take place on Sunday evening March 29. Another paragraph called attention to the schedule: "Thus far there have been twenty-six different operas presented, not counting ballets or 'scènes intimes' at the Sunday night concerts. The season's total, in all likelihood, will be thirty, with four more operas due. They are *Norma, Fidelio, Pelléas et Mélisande* and *Parsifal*." As a matter of interest it was noted that Gatti-Casazza had presented thirty-seven operas in his final season the year before, and that that had also been a fourteen-week period. "It might be added," the article concluded, "that his was in the nature of an exhibition of the achievements of the twenty-seven-year Gatti régime. Like the racing charts of past performances."

The Dante Alighieri Society gave a big musicale and reception in Johnson's honour on March 15 as part of the inauguration ceremonies for a new auditorium in the Palazzo d'Italia in Rockefeller Center. Eddie was beaming as he spoke in his fluent Italian. On the seventeenth of March, following a board meeting in Johnson's office, Edward Wardell, treasurer, announced a Spring Season, to begin May 17, with the Juilliard Musical Foundation contributing $150,000 to the guarantee fund if the Met directors would raise a like amount. That same evening, following the Company's final performance at the Brooklyn Academy of Music, Johnson was on hand to thank the Academy's directors for their sponsorship and wish them well.

With many details demanding his attention, it was hard for the Metropolitan's new general manager to find as much as five minutes in any one day to think about Pelléas. Yet the thought of the scheduled March 19th performance was always in the back of his mind. What his inner thoughts were as the time drew near, no one knew, nor was anyone told what went on behind the scenes. The fact remains, nevertheless, that on March 16 Johnson "reluctantly" announced that Miss Bori was ill and that the *Pelléas et Mélisande* performance was cancelled. There would be a refund for ticket holders not wishing to attend the substituted performance of *Il Trovatore*. Miss Bori, recovered from the flu, sang *La Rondine* in the last subscription performance of the season on March 21, receiving a tremendous ovation. The *New York Sun* reported that after the second act she had dragged Johnson and Ziegler onto the stage—Johnson laughing and Ziegler "fussed"—and that at the end of the performance she had made a speech.

"I suppose it can't be helped," Eddie told Fiorenza, "but they're already criticising me for omitting major operas, even though they admit the financial handicap I'm under, and that I hired twenty new orchestra players in face of union opposition to changes in personnel. Mum's the word, but I think the union is going to agree to some cuts for the spring season."

"That's super, Babbo. Now don't worry," she consoled. "The audiences are with you and you've reduced the deficit."

Winthrop Sergeant, in the *Brooklyn Daily Eagle* of March 22, made the critical comment that the Italian and French repertoire continued to lag; and that the Met remained a "museum of antiquities" in that respect.

When interviewed by the *Musical Courier,* Johnson contradicted such a view: "The Metropolitan is more full of life than at any time in the thirteen years I've been here. . . . You can't break away from a $250,000 deficit in fourteen weeks, but we already know that we've run a season inside our budget and that receipts have been far beyond our wildest dreams."

Bori's farewell appearance at the Metropolitan in New York, on March 29, was in a concert for the benefit of the Metropolitan Opera Fund. She was assisted by her many colleagues over the years—Lawrence Tibbett, Rosa Ponselle, Elisabeth Rethberg, Ezio Pinza, Kirsten Flagstad and Lauritz Melchior—in a program of excerpts from various operas. Edward Johnson's personal tribute, printed on the last page of the evening's program, was: "To Lucrezia Bori: As a friend, most understanding; As a woman, adorable; As a colleague, ideal; As an artist, irreplaceable." W. J. Henderson wrote in the *New York Sun* that the audience "filled every inch of standing room in the Metropolitan Opera House. . . . Miss Bori ended a brilliant career of twenty-six years' association with the opera company as a soprano surrounded by her friends in the company and with a warm air of sentiment and affection pervading the ceremonies." It was a historic evening, and one long to be remembered. Afterward, Johnson invited Bori and Mr. and Mrs. Crooks to a small private supper at Sherry's.

Although the Metropolitan was having its problems, Eddie's prediction to Fiorenza, that the union would agree to cuts that would make the spring season possible, came true on April 8. The Theatrical Protective Union No. 1 agreed to a reduction in backstage staff and a modification of union scale. Therefore, at his first personnel luncheon, Johnson was able to announce: "The reduction in staff, plus other economies, will bring backstage costs from a normal $8,000 weekly to $4,000 weekly for the special season. Now we'll be able to give the people opera at truly popular prices: from 25¢ to a $3 top."

By this time, Eddie was used to the feeling of power that went with being general manager of the Metropolitan Opera. He had even come to expect the deference shown him wherever he went. An episode in Boston, during the Metropolitan Spring Tour of 1935, seemed to him as though it must have happened to someone else: he had been miserable with a cold; he was concerned about his voice; and Witherspoon had made it clear to him that his services as a singer would no longer be required at the Metropolitan—also that as assistant manager he would be expected to concentrate on being an executive. In a way, he was relieved about the singing. It had become a problem for him to be always in good voice—the high notes sometimes eluded him completely and forced him at other times to employ every bit of technique and know-how he had acquired over the years. More and more frequently it was necessary to call on the doctor to give him a vitamin injection to control his nerves before a performance. Even so, no one, especially a tenor, likes to be discarded without some face-saving impression that it would be hard to get along without him. But Witherspoon had been blunt.

Weighed down by such thoughts, Eddie had been strolling along the railroad platform in Boston waiting for the Met's special touring train to leave for the next engagement. He had never indulged in self-pity, and yet, that day, tears were rolling down his cheeks.

"Hello, I see you walking here by yourself— Heh! What's the matter with you? Something wrong?" It was the voice of the Met's new young Italian tenor, Nino Martini.

Eddie had no time to collect himself in front of this sympathetic young man who was as thoroughly self-confident as he himself had been in Italy in his own first years in opera. He admitted he was worried. "Witherspoon is going to throw me out. I don't have any money. I'm old, and the stock market catastrophe wiped me out. No one wants me any more as a singer. I don't know what's going to happen."

The young tenor was touched and sorry; also a bit surprised and perplexed. "Why you worrying? They're never going to throw you out. You're this man Witherspoon's assistant, yes?"

"What does that mean? He won't let me do what I want to do, I know that. I don't know how long I can take it."

Nino saw his chance to get the older tenor's mind onto something else. "What you *want* to do?" he asked. And it worked. Almost immediately Edward Johnson began outlining his ideas and warming to the subject of what he thought could be done. He spoke of his dream for a Junior Opera Company and of how young Americans of the future would have the same opportunities that young Italians, like Martini, had in their native country. Witherspoon was forgotten as he, Edward

192

Johnson, spoke of building a strong company of fresh young American voices that would be the nucleus for a stronger Metropolitan Opera.

"Heh!" Martini exclaimed. "You got something good there."

By the time the two boarded the train, they were both enthusiastic over Eddie's dream. Once on the train, however, they went their separate ways with their own friends, but Nino felt he had a friend—he had seen inside the man and, somehow, he had understood.

The next time they talked, it was different, however. Witherspoon had died and Johnson was the new general manager. Young Martini's managers had told him that Johnson insisted on his singing *Don Pasquale* for his first appearance of the season. "What the hell!" Nino said. "I won't do it. I'll talk to Johnson."

So he walked into Eddie's office, certain he could settle the matter quite easily. When Johnson, in spite of his big smile, still insisted on *Don Pasquale,* Nino asked him, "Why you want to give me that first? Give me a *Bohème* or a *Rigoletto,* and then I'll sing your *Pasquale* for you. But sing *Pasquale* first? No. What the hell!" Nino had a big following from radio and films and he felt he should appear at the Met in his best light for his first opera of the season.

"Just who do you think you are, talking to me like that?" Johnson retorted angrily. "You're nothing but a young fellow who had a lot of luck and it's gone to your head. You've made a few movies and you've sung on the radio. Well, I had straight legs and a good voice too, when I started out, but there wasn't any radio then. You're lucky to be here at the Metropolitan and lucky for what I'm offering you."

As Martini recalled it years later, "I know I got pretty mad, too, because I grabbed him by his coat and I called him a dirty old man and said I was going to push his face in. I was pretty young, you know, and I was proud too! 'Don't forget,' I told him, 'I knew you when you were afraid and crying there in Boston. You thought they were going to throw you out—that you wouldn't sing anymore. You were afraid, and I was sorry for you.' "

Johnson said nothing for a long minute, but his face was red, Nino saw. Then, surprisingly, he gave in: *Pasquale* would stay out of the repertoire and Martini would open in *Bohème.* But Johnson never forgave him this outburst, Nino said, and probably would not have had him sing at the Metropolitan again had he not been both a popular film star and radio idol and, therefore, good box office.

As it turned out, Nino Martini remained on the Metropolitan roster until 1946, but it was never again a happy relationship. There were always  contract disputes as to roles and fees. Once, after a particularly pinch-penny contractual argument, Nino, never one to pull his punches, passed the Met's famed Triumvirate—Edward Johnson, Earle Lewis and Edward Ziegler—on the carpeted stairs leading up to Sherry's restaurant. Before any of the three could say hello, Nino greeted them with, *Ahhh! I tre ladroni* ("Ah! The three big thieves").

"What did they expect?" Nino asked, as he recalled the incident. "Did they think I would bow to them?"

Long after such moments had been dimmed by the passage of time, Edward Johnson had retired as general manager, and Nino Martini had retired from opera and was living in his native Verona, Italy, Nino and his beautiful American wife, Nancy, had invited Frank Chapman and Gladys Swarthout to their home for dinner one evening. The Chapmans phoned and asked whether they knew Edward Johnson was in town. They didn't, but Nino instantly suggested, "Well, bring him along."

"Mr. Johnson appeared, bringing a distinguished-looking American woman of about fifty with him," Nino recalled, "and at dinner one of the first things he said was, 'I discovered this boy, you know.' And I shut up; I didn't say a word. I could see he really believed it. The past was past. What did it matter?"

Edward Johnson was proud of the record for his first season as general manager of the Metropolitan. With the spring season yet to come, they had given 109 performances of opera in New York, fourteen Sunday night concerts, Bori's gala farewell in New York, and performances in Brooklyn, Philadelphia, Hartford, Newark, Boston, Baltimore and Rochester. The total of 148 performances was nine more than in Gatti's final year. With affairs in New York well in hand, Johnson planned to sail for Europe early in June, at the end of the new spring season.

The popular-priced operas began on May 11, 1936, with *Carmen,* and featured a production of *The Bartered Bride,* starring Britain's Muriel Dickson, the toast of New York after her appearances as leading soprano of the visiting D'Oyly Carte Opera Company. Unfortunately, Miss Dickson's voice, ideal for a Broadway theatre, was light when required to cope with the large Opera House orchestra and the vastness of the Met's auditorium. She carried it off well, however, relying on her charm as a personality and an actress.

The announced spring repertoire included productions of the new American opera *Caponsacchi* (subsequently postponed due to "practical difficulties") and a revival of Gluck's *Orfeo.* Then Johnson looked forward to the three débuts scheduled for the closing week: radio audition winners Arthur Carron (tenor), and Anna Kaskas (mezzo soprano), and soprano Ruby Mercer whom he himself had discovered at the Juilliard.

194

But suddenly Eddie moved his sailing date ahead to May 26. "I have to confer with Marjorie Lawrence in Paris before she leaves for South America," he told newsmen, "and there are some new 'imperative arrangements' to be made that require my personal attention." For once he was vague in speaking with the press. Why? they wondered. Why this unwonted secretiveness?

One day that spring Fiorenza had taken her father completely by surprise when she told him she and George Drew were getting married.

"Well!" Eddie exclaimed. "When was all this decided?"

"It just happened, while I was in Guelph," she explained. "I was in the house helping get it ready for the painters, you know, and George dropped by after one of his political speeches to say hello. The house was in complete chaos, and the only place we could sit down was at the kitchen table. It's funny, but it just happened. He asked me when I was sailing for Europe, and, after that, how soon I was coming back. I said I wasn't sure—that I might be staying in Europe. He didn't say anything at all for a minute. Then he said, 'Will you marry me?' and I said, 'Yes. When?' before he could change his mind.

"So he's coming here to New York the first of the week to talk with you about it. We thought we'd get married in September; I'd like to buy my trousseau in Paris and London this summer."

So Edward Johnson *did* have some unexpected and "imperative arrangements" on his mind, other than his search for talent for the Metropolitan Opera, when he set sail for Europe several days earlier than originally planned. There were wedding invitations to be printed and sent out and many details to be looked after.

There was a record crowd of 10,000 on hand to visit the *Normandie* as it departed for Europe on May 26. Among the passengers were Mrs. Feodor Chaliapin and her daughter, manager Sol Hurok and the Met's general manager Edward Johnson. At the parting press conference, Eddie gave assurance that Lily Pons would be back at the Metropolitan the coming season and remarked that his only time off in over a year had consisted of one weekend.

No sooner had the boat sailed than there were rumours about a mysterious "Mrs. Johnson" travelling with Eddie. How had she escaped everyone's attention? Word of a secret marriage stopped just short of the printed page.

Travelling on the same liner, with her friend Margaret Eaton, eldest daughter of R. Y. Eaton, Fiorenza quickly sought out her father. "Daddy, there's been a mistake. You and I are booked as 'Mr. and Mrs. Johnson' and Margaret's alone in her stateroom. Everybody's saying you're married." Instead of being disturbed, as she thought he might be, her father threw back his head and laughed as she had not heard him laugh for a very long time.

"That will give them something to chew on for awhile," he said. There had been a strained relationship between father and daughter at times; he had been severely critical of her for what he considered throwing her time away, wasting her life and being extravagant. But the past year had evidently changed all that.

There was a quick meeting in Paris with Marjorie Lawrence who signed a contract for the coming season at the Metropolitan, and then Eddie went to London. An announcement, released from England the day after his arrival there, received top billing on the social pages in New York and Toronto: Edward Johnson's daughter, Fiorenza, was to become the wife of a rising young political figure in Canada, George Drew. The date of the wedding was set for September 12.

Juggling his responsibilities as father of the bride with those as general manager of the world famous Metropolitan Opera House would have been quite enough for Eddie. But he also sandwiched in a few other interests, like honouring a promise to his old friend W. J. Barry to get the Metropolitan Opera Quartet for him for the opening Presto Club concert in Guelph that fall. All in all, the summer of 1936 was quite a summer.

$\mathcal{8}$ "I WAS HAVING my morning coffee at the Hotel de l'Europe in Salzburg one morning," Edward Johnson told reporters when he returned from Europe, "when King Edward VIII came in, travelling incognito as the Duke of Lancaster, and obviously not wishing to be recognized. Everyone respected his wish except one brash photographer who snapped a picture of him, and he was promptly led away by two guards. I saw the photographer later and he told me his camera had been destroyed!" The men of the press shifted uneasily. "But I can see, gentlemen, that that is not the kind of thing you came to hear!" The tension was broken; everyone laughed.

Then Eddie told them that he had engaged Polish dramatic soprano Gertrud Ruenger for Wagner roles, signed Franca Somigli (an American soprano named Marion Clark in private life) and made a contract with mezzo soprano Kerstin Thorborg. He was most enthusiastic over his engagement of stage director Dr. Herbert Graf, having been greatly impressed by Graf's staging of *Falstaff* and *Meistersinger,* both conducted by Toscanini, in Salzburg. He was bubbling with enthusiasm: "No country today has such a wonderful opportunity to foster and develop its native talent," he told them. "We're going to lengthen our Met season—take more engagements in other large cities, and continue with the six-week spring season for our 'minor league' of young artists."

Life wasn't all work those days, for he took time off from the constant meetings and decision-making chores at the Metropolitan, and from overseeing preparations for Fiorenza's wedding, to go to see his colleagues "kick up their heels," as he described it, at the seventh annual Buck Hill Follies. Directed by Earle Lewis, they took the form of "Old Doc Lewis's Almanac," with an entertainment for each month of the year, together with appropriate comment. The outstanding item was a shortened hour-and-fifteen-minute version of *The Bartered Bride,* with radio conductor Robert Armbruster in charge and Eddie's good friend Mario Chamlee as the hero. Many members of the Met's techni-

197

cal staff had been imported for the opera, as well as for other portions of the program. No one took himself seriously. It was a true frolic. And no one enjoyed it more than Edward Johnson.

Fiorenza had favoured a small private wedding, but both her father and George wanted a big one. Consequently some four hundred guests from Europe, the United States and Canada assembled in St. George's Anglican Church in Guelph on September 12, 1936, to see Edward Johnson proudly escort his daughter down the same aisle he had often trod as a choir boy. The flowers in the church, the dresses of the attendants and Fiorenza's white silk velvet gown were designed to give "an Italian Renaissance painting effect." Although newspaper reports disagreed as to whether or not Fiorenza had been a frequent visitor to the Johnson home in Guelph, they concurred that she was a "beautiful and charming" bride and that the groom, Lt. Col. George Drew, was "tall, erect and handsome." Dr. Harvey Robb played the organ for the ceremony and Archdeacon G. F. Scovil officiated.

"It was a happy day," Fiorenza recalled some years later. "I remember we were held up getting to the church by a horse-drawn cart piled high with furniture, topped by the head and foot board of an enormous brass bed, and people along the road shouting, with cheers and laughter, 'Look, folks, there goes their furniture.' And when Archdeacon Scovil met us at the door of the church, he looked terribly anxious because, as he told us, he was just breaking in a new denture and was worried about the pronunciation of the Fiorenza d'Arneiro part of my name. We rehearsed it several times before he went to take his place at the altar and I prepared for my grand entrance to the tune of the *Lohengrin* Wedding March. I was terribly nervous, I'll never forget, but my father was having a wonderful time, bowing and smiling right and left and keeping up a running commentary to me to take my mind off myself: 'Well, well . . . how nice! There's Mrs. Curley, up from New York; and Auntie Jo [Josephine Casali] all the way from Florence.' And 'I wonder who that blond girl is over there—my word but she's good-looking!!' For him it was theatre and he was in his element. Never have I seen a father enjoy a wedding more."

Hundreds of guests crowded into Johnson's Elora Road home for the wedding reception, after which Fiorenza soon got her first taste of what life with her husband was going to be like. Their honeymoon was spent at the Seigniory Club in the hills above Ottawa. It was exclusive, but proved to be anything but a private romantic retreat. "We tried to dine unobtrusively at a little table behind a pillar for our first dinner," Fiorenza told her father later, "but we were discovered by sixty or more women on hand for the Senior Ladies Golf Championship. All of them seemed to know George and insisted on drinking toasts to us from across the dining room. Then Billy Bishop, the famous World War I flying ace, who was to have been best man at our wedding but whose mother had died two days before, showed up with his wife Margaret 'to assist us into married life,' as they explained it. And, well, here we are! George is back in business and I've already attended my first political rally. Oh, Babbo, I feel so ill-equipped to help George. Why, when a kind old lady came up to me and said I must be the Toriest of the Tories, I almost asked her what a Tory was!"

Then Fiorenza recounted a story that was to become a family joke for many years. "I was so proud of George, looking so handsome and speaking so well, and one of the young girls evidently agreed with me and, knowing that I was with him, said to me, 'Gee, you must be proud. Your Dad spoke just swell.' I'm never going to let George forget that one!"

Fortunately for all concerned, a close relationship gradually developed between Edward Johnson and his politically ambitious son-in-law, which proved to be very rewarding as well as a source of pleasure to both men in the years ahead. During his political career, whether unsuccessful or victorious, George Drew could always count on Eddie being there, an excellent counsellor, with his intimate understanding of human nature and his innate common sense. But at the same time the politician, never one to be concerned about opera, became intensely interested in everything concerning the Metropolitan. It became a way of life for Edward Johnson and the Drews to be together whenever possible whether in New York, Toronto, Ottawa or Guelph. It also became a sort of unwritten understanding that at nine o'clock on a Sunday morning they would talk together on the telephone, no matter how few or how many miles separated them. Before the Second World War broke out, they travelled in Europe together; later, when that was impossible, they met often in Canada.

Feeling very fit after a game of golf together, Eddie and George used to delight in walking down Wyndham Street in their native Guelph, visiting and chatting with everyone—they knew everybody in town and everybody knew them—then going back to the house to vie with each other in telling Fiorenza bits of history about the people they'd met.

The shy and austere-mannered politician had much to learn from the gregarious, warm-hearted and diplomatic general manager, while it was a comfort for the Metropolitan's new director to have such a legally-knowledgeable sounding board when knotty problems arose. That first winter, for example, Eddie asked George what he thought about his idea for an opera house to be included in New York's proposed new municipal arts centre. According to tentative plans, drawn up by architect

Benjamin W. Morris at Eddie's request the previous December, the new opera house would have adequate parking facilities, a capacity of 4,500 —900 more than the old Met—and, in order to popularize opera, at least 1,000 of the seats at a price "not to exceed one dollar." There would be a single tier of boxes, thirty-five in all, with vestibules, but no seats behind them; the stage would be of ample size and equipped with modern facilities. Furthermore, provision was to be made in the house for the storage of all scenery, properties and costumes required for a normal full season.

"The stage equipment," Eddie explained, "is to include new scenery, properties and costumes for thirty operas chosen by the management of the Metropolitan Opera Association from its standard repertoire. During the period of the present arrangement, the city will augment this equipment each year by scenery, costumes and properties for ten additional operas chosen by the management. All such scenery, costumes and properties shall be a part of the permanent equipment of the opera house and as such shall belong to the city."

The city would be expected to make every effort to complete the new opera house and have it ready for operation by October 1, 1937. All repairs and physical maintenance and insurance for the building itself, as well as workmen's compensation insurance for employees, would be taken care of by the city which would, in addition, provide an annual subsidy of $150,000 toward expenses of opera production.

"What do you think?" Eddie was so carried away with enthusiasm that the opera house, in his mind, had become almost a reality.

It sounded good to George but, being practical-minded, he asked, "Where is this Municipal Arts Centre to be located? And has any money been appropriated for it?"

"These are the flies in the ointment," Eddie had to admit. "We haven't been able to agree on a location yet and they won't talk money until we do."

George shot him a glance, and the subject was dropped.

Meanwhile, preparations for Eddie's second season as general manager of the Metropolitan were taking most of his time. He could easily have forgotten all about the Presto Club concert in Guelph. But Mr. Barry received a reassuring letter from Columbia Concerts: "The Metropolitan Opera Quartet, consisting of soprano Rosa Tentoni, mezzo Anna Kaskas, tenor Nicholas Massue and bass John Gurney will arrive in Guelph at noon, October 9, for the evening's concert."

Mr. Johnson and more than two thousand members and guests attended the Metropolitan Opera Guild's second "At Home" in the Metropolitan Opera House that season, on December 13. Eddie spoke, briefly.

200

Then Mrs. Belmont announced the acquisition of five hundred new Guild members and praised the success of Johnson's first season as general manager of the Met. She also spoke of his dream of having a ten-month opera season by the time the New York World's Fair opened in 1939. After the speeches, there was a program called "Opera as you like it in the year 2000 A.D."—spoofs on Wagner, Verdi and Donizetti.

Such activities were enjoyable, Eddie found, but very time- and energy-consuming. He still tried to visit a gym whenever possible, to keep in trim, but it had become increasingly difficult. He had developed a routine, however, from which he seldom deviated during the fifteen years he was to remain general manager: walk to the Met in the morning (from 67th Street and Madison Avenue to 39th Street and Broadway), go home for a rest in the afternoon (2-4 P.M., if possible), then back to the Metropolitan and a taxi home after the opera at night.

THE 1936/37 SEASON at the Metropolitan opened with *Die Walküre* on December 21. The house was sold out well in advance; the first standee lined up before 10 A.M. for one of the three hundred admissions that would go on sale half an hour before the performance started. Prospects were good for the fourteen-week season ahead: encouraging advance sales; a $250,000 underwriting by the Juilliard Musical Foundation; two novelties—Richard Hageman's *Caponsacchi*, with Lawrence Tibbett as Guido, and Cimarosa's *Il Matrimonio segreto* in English; an eminent new conductor and stage director; an enlarged tour; and an overhauled orchestra and chorus. *Musical America* summed up the prevailing spirit: "A new era of good feeling, inaugurated by the most engaging of general managers, the smilingly genial Edward Johnson."

The December 26 revival of *Samson et Dalila* brought two important Metropolitan Opera débuts: conductor Maurice de Abravanel and stage director Herbert Graf. Graf was quite new to the North American scene, having made his first appearance with the Philadelphia Orchestra Association's production of *Falstaff* in the fall of 1934, with Juilliard baritone Julius Huehn in the title role and soprano Ruby Mercer as Nanetta. Fritz Reiner was the conductor. Dr. Graf recalled in subsequent years:

> I practically offered myself to Johnson [in 1935] when he was talking about a spring season, but he considered me too modern. . . . Also, he loved Defrère. But Johnson was in Europe the next summer and it just happened I had *Fidelio* in Paris, with Lotte Lehmann and Bruno Walter; *Meistersinger* in Salzburg, with Toscanini; and *Tannhäuser* in Vienna under Furtwängler, with Thorborg as Venus. He visited all three and decided I was important and not modern, after all. Besides, I offered to work for very little money.

So I started with *Samson,* then jumped into the entire French repertoire, which was all new to me. I knew Johnson at the Met from 1936 to 1950 and was in contact with him almost until he died. He always kept his word about things. I was resident stage director for fourteen years. He wasn't much interested in details about productions, but very much interested in conductors. When Bruno Walter came, for example, Edward Johnson was practically trembling before their first meeting.

We had a real clash in Milan—Toscanini was to open La Scala with *Otello* and wanted me as stage director. I had to get permission from Johnson as I was under contract, and he flatly refused. He insisted I had to watch every performance at the Metropolitan, whether it was the first or the eightieth—not like today, when an assistant does that. Of course this may have had something to do with the fact that when I first came to the Met Edward Johnson asked me to go to Toscanini and tell him he could have anything he wanted—any cast, rehearsals and other conditions. But Toscanini refused to return. [During his days at the Metropolitan (1908-15), Toscanini had been the Company's leading and most popular conductor. But by the time he left, in the spring of 1915, he was so enraged over money-saving policies at the expense of art, among other things, that he vowed he would never return. And he never did. As Howard Taubman wrote: "He was fed up."]

We had another clash—that was over *Parsifal* in Philadelphia. I had expected to have our new Met scenery, but he had agreed, without telling me, that they could take the old *Parsifal* scenery. When he came on stage and asked, "How's the performance?" I told him the only "holey" thing was the scenery, and he refused to speak to me for weeks!

My father [noted Viennese music critic Max Graf] wrote an article once called "What's An Opening at the Met Like?" in which he spoke badly about Jeritza. So she said I should be dismissed. I didn't know what to expect from Edward Johnson, so I went to his office. He surprised me by meeting me with, "Thank you, my boy, for what your father has done for the Met. Now all the critics are writing about it—coming to our rescue."

As I say, I was with Edward Johnson at the Metropolitan for fourteen years—and two more under Bing—but after fourteen years we were never close. We knew each other well, and still he would often surprise me. For instance, I had done a Met *Orpheus* and he seemed pleased enough and gave me several compliments. But one time I did it in Central City [Colorado] and he was there, and when he came backstage after the performance he was in tears. And I felt, now there's an artist—simple and humble. But then he was away from the Met.

Everyone knew Edward Johnson could be dangerous when he or

the House was criticized. Once, at a big Opera Guild tea, Beecham was called on to speak. He got up and said, "Ladies and gentlemen, you expect me now to tell you what I think about the Met. I won't!" and sat down. Edward Johnson got red in the face, but didn't say anything—but he never hired Beecham again!

I often heard it said that Edward Johnson, Earle Lewis and Edward Ziegler were known as "The Triumvirate," but backstage Mr. Johnson, Désiré Defrère and Frank St. Leger were known as "The Three Musketeers"—the real inner circle. Still, if you wanted to get anywhere with Edward Johnson, you had to go to Ziegler.

One of Johnson's few sorties outside the Metropolitan that winter was to attend the world première of the new opera *Garrick,* with libretto by *New Yorker* critic Robert Simon and music by conductor Albert Stoessel, at the Juilliard School of Music in New York. The opera had had much advance publicity, with word that the Juilliard was going to go "all out" for the production. Eddie wanted to hear certain of the young singers involved and to see whether the work was of sufficient interest to be considered for the Met. It proved to have moments of interest, and was performed subsequently at Chautauqua and at Worcester, Massachusetts, but it never reached the Metropolitan.

In March, 1937, Edward Johnson was informed that he had been elected to membership in the exclusive Metropolitan Opera Club. As guest of honour at a dinner, he told the august gathering: "I have been unable to compose an expression of appreciation adequate to the occasion. . . . The Opera Club has interested and intrigued me ever since I first joined the company in 1922. Time after time, as I stood in the wings nervously waiting my entrance on stage, I would glance up at that row of shirt fronts, and with longing and envy wish I were rich enough to be one of such a distinguished group who could sit in ease and comfort while someone else did the singing. Even later, I approached these sacred precincts with a certain diffidence, not knowing whether or not the manager might be considered an intruder."

The Club's cordial reception cleared away any of Eddie's latent doubts and fears, just as their friendly gesture gave him assurance of their sympathetic attitude toward what his management was trying to do. "If our efforts fall far short of perfection and at times they are inferior to what has been done in the past," he entreated, "please remember that our Wagner performances are probably unparallelled in the world today. Moreover, there is no public today where enthusiasm and appreciation run so high. Only the other evening I inquired of our German artists if the audiences abroad gave them such loud acclaim. They assured me that nowhere did they find such a genuine response."

Almost every day brought a new pronouncement as to what could be expected the following season: ticket prices would remain at $7 top for orchestra seats; longer contracts for artists and stage crew would be awarded. Johnson was the man of the hour; board chairman Paul Cravath recognized this in his letter to the general manager in connection with his reengagement: "We realize fully to how great an extent the satisfactory artistic results of the current season are due to the efforts of yourself and the heads of your organization . . ."

*Musical America*, always a strong Johnson supporter, said: "It has been and remains a personality to inspire confidence, to engender cheerfulness, to cause all concerned to look on the brighter side of the operatic situation and to expect better things, rather than to go about wondering whether the prophets of gloom were right in assuming the opera never again could be what it had been, irrespective of any brightening of the economic skies."

There had been a number of important débuts during the season. Also, five years after its world première, in Freiburg, Germany, Richard Hageman's *Caponsacchi* had been presented in North America for the first time, at the Metropolitan, on February 4, 1937, with the composer conducting. It was sung in English, but even so it was given a very mild reception.

Olin Downes, one of the most reluctant to accept anything until it was proved true, gave an assessment, March 28, 1937, in the *New York Times*, of Johnson's 1936/37 season, listing his successes, admitting that the Met had advanced "a considerable distance out of the red," pointing out that Johnson had energetically sought out new singers( including Thorborg, Gina Cigna, Vina Bovy, Bidú Sayão) and presented novelties and revivals (*Caponsacchi, Der fliegende Holländer, Samson et Dalila, The Bartered Bride, Les Contes d'Hoffman, Il Matrimonio segreto* and *Le Coq d'Or*). He called attention to the list of 106 performances of 32 operas, of which *Tristan und Isolde, Die Walküre* and *Aida* were performed most often.

Eddie was as proud of the repertoire for the second spring season as he had been of that for the first. It opened May 3, 1937, with *Faust,* and included a revival of *Marouf, the Cobbler of Cairo* (in English) by Henri Rabaud and the world première (May 12, 1937) of *The Man Without a Country* by Walter Damrosch. The man in charge of the season was Lee Pattison, and two radio audition winners made their débuts.

*The Man Without a Country* was a big feather in Edward Johnson's cap, because it was the first American opera to be presented under his management. After the première, Lawrence Gilman reported in the *New*

*York Herald Tribune*: "The occasion assumed the aspects of a Damroschian apotheosis, with an audience of almost winter size and modishness. . . . It is impossible to doubt that Mr. Damrosch enjoyed enormously the fun of writing it [the opera]—almost as much as he quite obviously enjoyed the fun of conducting it last night." As for the work itself, Gilman said: "Mr. Damrosch has dealt simply and unpretentiously with a simple and unpretentious tale. . . . His music moves fluently, with apt and appropriate relation to what is happening on the stage and in the hearts of his characters. . . . Sometimes the music is richly flavored with tinctures of the past, sometimes it is straight Damrosch." Helen Traubel was "the embodiment of the heroine [Mary Rutledge]." *The Man Without a Country* found its way into the regular-season repertoire in 1937/ 38, with Wilfrid Pelletier conducting, and then was heard no more.

Even though it was imperative that Eddie be in Europe early again that year—he left aboard the *Rex* on April 10, 1937—his heart and thoughts continued to be very much with the second spring season. In spite of his activities in connection with his talent search for the Met, he kept in close touch with the opera house.

His first letter to "Neddie" Ziegler, dated April 29, 1937, told how he had arrived in Naples, gone straight to Rome and to the opera house, and been refused admittance to the Teatro Reale because he was not in evening clothes! "*Lucia* was the opera, so I did not cry," he wrote. He said he'd met Molinari—"quite attractive"—in Rome, and also many old friends such as Montemezzi, Gilda Dalla Rizza, Nicolo d'Atri (critic), Serafin, and Lauri-Volpi, and had heard Gigli, Giacomo Vaghi, Mario Basiola and Maria Caniglia.

Of the artists he heard in six operas at La Scala, he made these capsule comments:

Tagliabue:  Good timber and quality, very short role. Will want to hear him in something else.
Schipa:  Just made it.
De Luca:  With the same fine qualities but less voice.
Baccaloni:  Excellent. Voice fair, diction first class.
Caniglia:  Sang well and moved with understanding. Fine quality of voice.
Lauri-Volpi:  Sang with ardour and got big applause, but most uneven and ordinary. Ovation after his aria. He wants to return to New York, I'm told.

He mentioned that he had lunched with Gatti in Milan, and that Caniglia was free in February and March and "disposed to come to us for six weeks only. Rome and Milan are watching my every move very jealously."

He didn't bother telling Neddie that he had stolen a few days in April to go to Florence to see Jo Casali and other friends, but in subsequent letters he did mention that he had to meet Artur Bodanzky in St. Moritz for a day of auditions and that he would be going to Paris, before returning home, for a reunion with Fiorenza and George Drew.

He was looking forward especially to hearing George tell about his experiences in Russia that summer. But his second morning in Paris he was too ill to get out of bed and by noon was burning with fever. Rheumatism again, was his first thought. He knew the symptoms well. When Fiorenza came in, she immediately summoned the hotel doctor who diagnosed it as rheumatic fever. A room was requested at the American Hospital in Neuilly, outside Paris, and a nurse was sent in to look after the patient until a room became available.

"You know, Madame," the nurse told Fiorenza, "this can be very serious for an old gentleman like your father."

Old? Her father? But when she and George slipped into Eddie's room later and saw him dozing, they were shocked to find him looking very pale and, they thought, about twenty years older.

The following day a French ambulance arrived to take him to the hospital. He was in pain, but with his family, the doctor, a nurse and attendants as audience he managed to make everyone laugh. As they prepared to help him onto the stretcher, he suddenly demanded his smart navy blue and white polka dot dressing gown and his hat! Then off he went—crocheted blanket, dressing gown and black fedora at its customary rakish angle on his head. Just before the ambulance door closed behind him, he lifted his head, waved cheerily to the crowd that had gathered, and said to George, with a wink, "I'm sure they think I'm just another poor American suffering from the D.T.'s."

EDWARD JOHNSON was in the hospital for six weeks and in misery most of that time. Both knees were inflamed and swollen and extremely painful. Even so, his sense of humour never deserted him. Doctors and nurses alike found excuses to look in on him to ask about "Pete" and "Repeat," as he called his knees, and to hear him tell one of his ever-ready stories. In front of people he was always the performer, the entertainer, dedicated in spite of himself, it seemed, to making other people laugh. Sometimes they would scarcely be out of the room before he would close his eyes wearily. But soon all sorts of private thoughts would be racing through his mind: the miracles of the past two years, for example. With his singing days nearly over, he had succeeded to the top operatic post in the world. It was almost as though his long career as a tenor—in Italy, Chicago and even at the Metropolitan—had happened to someone else and his job as general manager was the thing toward which his life had been pointing. At last he would be able to implement his dreams: to make the Metropolitan an American opera house, filled with American singers; to make America an opera-conscious country through the Metropolitan Opera broadcasts and his Metropolitan Opera Auditions of the Air that had really caught on; and to get things going toward making Canada a singing nation, with Guelph as its musical centre. "Have to get well and get out of here," he would think drowsily, as he dropped off to sleep.

George's affairs called him back to Canada, but Fiorenza stayed on in Paris a couple of weeks until she was sure her father was well on the road to recovery. Then, with Fifi Moulton's promise to keep him from getting lonely, she left for Toronto to prepare for her first baby, due to arrive in January.

Meanwhile, Edward Ziegler came to Paris to see for himself how Eddie was doing and to go over with him the many questions that might have to be answered immediately at the Metropolitan. Johnson's recovery was quite rapid, as it happened, and he and Ziegler returned to New York together aboard the *Bremen* on September 21, 1937. To the barrage of questions from the New York press, on hand to greet him when he landed, Eddie replied: "Gentlemen, I had an attack of rheumatism, but I feel fine now. Everything's hunky dory and the program for the new season at the Metropolitan will be interesting and exciting." He reminded them that the season would begin on November 29 and run for sixteen weeks and that the Metropolitan Auditions of the Air, with himself as Master of Ceremonies, would be broadcast on NBC for the third consecutive season.

A personal note full of encouragement came from critic Lawrence Gilman that fall: "Permit me to offer felicitations upon all that you have accomplished since you took charge of the destinies of our Opera, and to thank you personally for the many hours of inspiring happiness and fulfillment which I have had on those unforgettable occasions when great music and great performances have coalesced. But I hope you will conserve your strength."

Johnson called the press in for cocktails on November 6 to announce, among other things, that Erich Leinsdorf had been engaged as an assistant conductor and that the season would include a new opera, *Amelia Goes to the Ball,* by the twenty-five-year-old Gian-Carlo Menotti.

At home, with the Drews expecting their first baby, Eddie was apprehensive as he recalled the dramatic and difficult night of Fiorenza's birth. "But I feel fine; I'm perfectly healthy, Babbo. Don't worry," Fiorenza kept telling him. She was all he had. If anything happened to her— His concern was needless, as it turned out, for right on schedule and with surprising ease she gave birth to a healthy little boy on January 6, 1938. At George's suggestion, he was named Edward—Edward Johnson Drew.

"I always wanted an older brother," Fiorenza told her father, "and I didn't have one. But it is all arranged now for my daughter to have what I missed."

"What daughter?" Eddie asked.

"My daughter to be."

And two years later, on the momentous May 10, 1940, when the Germans invaded the Lowlands and bombed Rotterdam, Edward's baby sister, Alexandra Beatrice Drew, arrived. "Sandra" he called her, as he struggled with "Alexandra," and the nickname stuck.

One of the events of the 1937/38 season that Edward Johnson never forgot was the Gala Program of Excerpts on March 20, in celebration of Martinelli's 25th year at the Metropolitan. It was a star-studded evening, attended by everyone of operatic and social prominence who could get a ticket. Johnson read a telegram from President Roosevelt, and Martinelli himself made a very amusing speech.

All hope for a 1938 spring season disappeared. Try as he would, Eddie could not get around the fact that there was a shortage of trained young singers to step onto the Metropolitan Opera stage in leading roles of the standard repertoire. He was also faced with the high cost of mounting new productions, especially new operas, that made it impossible to offer them to the public at the established popular prices. Besides, the Metropolitan had agreed to put on an expensive all-Wagner series the following spring on the occasion of the 1939 World's Fair and Johnson had agreed to sponsor an advance sale of cut-rate tickets to members of the musical profession.

The best part of the summer was spent in preparations for the 1938/39 season: productions, directors, casts, sets and costumes, orchestra, union negotiations and the everyday running of the Big House. The repertoire was more or less set, although Eddie didn't announce until October that it would contain revivals of *Boris Godunov, Louise, Falstaff, Orfeo, Thaïs* and *Fidelio*, and that two young Americans, baritone Leonard Warren and tenor John Carter, would be making their débuts. He managed to steal away for only two weekends before he sailed for Europe on August 3. At that point he was so tired that for once he definitely requested that his name be left off the passenger list. He was looking forward to a quiet and restful trip. He needed to recover from the months of constant work in order to be in shape for the schedule ahead: the opening of the opera season in Stockholm and six weeks of opera and contract negotiations in Paris and Milan. He left with at least one heartening

The Triumvirate that ran the Met from 1935 until 1947. Left to right, Edward Ziegler, Earle Lewis, Edward Johnson

...ward Johnson, photo-
...phed in front of the Met
...he late 1940's

Edward Johnson and staff members of the Royal Conservatory of Music of Toronto, in 1951. Left to right, Edward Johnson, Nicholas Goldschmidt, Herman Geiger-Torel, Dr. Ettore Mazzoleni and Dr. Arnold Walter

Edward Johnson under the big Met clock, waiting to give the signal for a performance to begin

*Below* Johnson on opening night, November 24, 1941, with members of *Le Nozze di Figaro* cast

*Opposite, bottom* Following his Gala Testimonial and Opera Pageant, February 28, 1950, Johnson receives a kiss from Lucrezia Bori.

*For names of members of the Metropolitan Opera in the photographs on this page and the opposite page, see photo credits page.*

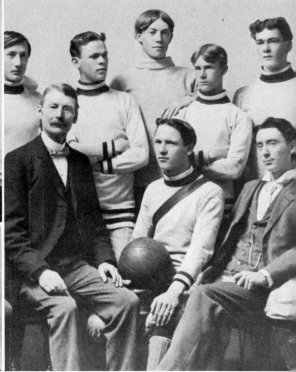

Edward at five, with brother Fred, and, *below,* at twelve

Captain Johnson and principal James Davison with the Guelph Collegiate champion soccer team of 1898

PANORAMA OF GUELPH, CANADA

Johnson family portrait taken during
dward's visit to Canada in the summer of
913. Left to right, Margaret (Mrs. James),
Edward, Fiorenza, Caroline (Mrs. Frederick
D.), Frederick, Beatrice (Mrs. Edward) and
James Johnson

*elow*   Guelph, Ontario, in the early 1900's

*Top left*   Maria del Moro Tazzi (Tata) with Fiorenza, soon after their arrival in Guelph, 1919

*Top right*   Edward Johnson was the proud father when Fiorenza and George Drew were married in Guelph, September 12, 1936.

*Bottom*   The Drews spent Christmas, 1958, in Guelph. Left to right, Sandra Drew, Edward Johnson, and George, Edward and Fiorenza Drew thought, however: subscriptions at the Metropolitan had increased again, making them by far the highest since he had taken office. "A further token of public confidence in Mr. Johnson's policies," the press noted.

Before the summer of 1938 was over, Eddie had signed contracts with Gigli, Jussi Björling, ballet master Boris Romanoff, soprano Maria Caniglia and Risë Stevens. "Why all the foreign names?" was one question. "We thought this was going to be an American company."

"As I have often told the Guild," was his reply, "a repertory is made from the artists available; it cannot be a cast-iron mould from which available artists will emerge. My first obligation is to secure the right people in the right places and after three years I am only just beginning to demonstrate a well-balanced company. And as for Miss Stevens, she *is* American. She just happens to be coming to us from Prague."

Commenting on these things during an interview in her New York apartment in the early 1970's, Miss Stevens said:

> The first time I met Edward Johnson was after he had heard me in a performance at the Juilliard School of Music in New York. He was not general manager then, Witherspoon was. But Johnson came back and seemed very excited. "I'm Edward Johnson," he said. And I said, "Look, you don't have to tell me who you are. I know exactly who you are."
>
> He was a very handsome and extremely attractive man, aside from being a man of great renown. He said he was going to keep his eye on what I did in the future and to keep up the good work. Then Witherspoon died, you remember; then came the Auditions of the Air, sponsored by the Sherwin-Williams paint company. Johnson asked me to try out and I got through to the semi-finals and won; but Anna Kaskas won the finals.
>
> I was disappointed, but they offered me a contract anyway, to sing in the pit for some dumb ballet. The whole thing didn't sound right to me and I said, "Look, this is no way to go into the Metropolitan Opera. If I wasn't prepared enough to win those auditions, then I'm not ready for the Metropolitan."
>
> My teacher, Schön-René, was marvellous. "All right! We will arrange for you to go abroad; you'll study in Salzburg with Marie Gutheil-Schöder." And she loaned me the money to go that summer with the clear understanding that I was to pay it back, with bank interest.
>
> After the decision was already made, Johnson said, "Risë, that was the best decision you could have made. Now let's see what we can do." But I didn't want him to intervene in any way; I wanted to do it by myself. I was beginning to get panicky, though, when the summer was almost over and I hadn't succeeded in getting a con-

tract any place. I auditioned for Artur Bodanzky in Vienna—it was arranged by Eric Semon, who was my agent, through Mme Schön-René—and he wanted to know where I was engaged! He was interested, but there was nothing immediate. So I went to Paris, had a little pension studio with a couch and used Semon's piano to practise.

I was working on the *Walküre* Fricka one day and who walks in but George Szell. I didn't know who he was, except that he seemed to be a good friend of the Semons. "We're looking for a mezzo-soprano in Prague," he said. "Would you be willing to fly to Prague and sing for the director?" Sure enough, by the end of the week I was in Prague, and as I walked on the stage of the opera house—I remember it very well—I was frightened because I knew my money was running out and if I didn't get this I'd have to go back to America.

I sang and I heard the familiar "Thank you very much, Miss Stevens." So I picked up my music and was starting to leave when I heard from the audience, "Where are you going?"

"Back to America, I guess," I replied.

"But no," said a voice with a heavy accent, "you are going to be our Mignon. Do you speak German?" I did not. "Well, don't worry about a thing," the voice assured me. "We'll teach you."

I was in Prague for two years. During the first year, I had a letter from Edward Johnson saying he was coming over to hear singers and he was coming to Prague to hear me. I sang Octavian in *Rosenkavalier* when he heard me, and he seemed very excited, but nothing happened until the early part of the winter when Bodanzky arrived in Prague looking for Wagnerian singers. Johnson had evidently asked him to look me up. He heard me in Hugo Wolf's [*Der*] *Corregidor,* I think it was, and after the performance he invited me to dinner. "I want to talk to you." He wanted to hear me in *Rosenkavalier,* it seemed, but I wasn't doing it for some time.

So he went off to Norway to hear Flagstad, then came back, heard me in *Rosenkavalier,* congratulated me, and that was that. Nothing was said. Then, all of a sudden, during my second year, I received a letter from Edward Johnson and a note from Bodanzky informing me that I was engaged for the following year at the Metropolitan Opera.

Rumour persistently linked the names of Risë Stevens and Edward Johnson in spite of the disparity in their ages. And gossip had them spending much time together during the two years after he had heard her in Prague. When reminded of this Miss Stevens laughed:

I know, but it wasn't true. He knew about Walter [Walter Surovy, who later became her husband] and so did Bodanzky. Walter was at my début; we had been married just prior to it. No, I think basically Johnson really looked on me as a daughter. And I never was able to get over a kind of awe for the man, as general manager and as a great artist. He was interested and very friendly, but there was always that certain distance between us—and he always kept it that way.

On our Met tours he always had a warm personality and a friendly smile for everybody, and he would celebrate with us in the cars on the train, and joke and cavort and tell all kinds of stories he knew. Even then, I think I would have to say, strange as it is, his whole manner, his bearing and everything, never let you forget that he was always a "first singer." He was very particular that all of us should make a good impression on the tours, insisting that we attend certain luncheons and functions, and associate with the influential people who brought the Company to town. He had a great manner in terms of warming people at a reception where he'd get up and talk about his company and his singers. If it was after a performance, he always introduced the artists who had sung and he always had something fantastic to say about them. He made them feel that there was not anyone else in the world who could have done a better performance in a better town for better people. And this is a great art. It gave heart to the opera. That's how the Americans in the company, like Eleanor Steber, Leonard Warren and I, came to be called "Johnson babies."

Delighted not only with the "Johnson babies" but with Edward Johnson's initiative and determination that had seen the Metropolitan through three and a half difficult years, the Board of Directors of the Metropolitan Opera Association notified Johnson on November 16, 1938, that he, Ziegler and Lewis had been reengaged for two more seasons (1939-1941).

DURING THE SUMMER new lights had been installed in the 39th Street lobby of the opera house to facilitate the taking of motion pictures. At the opening, November 21, 1938, a host of newsmen and photographers were there to take advantage of the notable occasion—the first standing room customer had arrived that morning at 6:55 A.M. Johnson let it be known that ten new players had joined the orchestra, in keeping with his goal of having two solo players for each major instrument. He himself, resplendent in white tie and tails as usual, entertained his daughter and her husband, George Drew, the newly-elected leader of the Conservative party in Ontario, at dinner before the performance.

The opera, *Otello,* won general praise for Johnson's policies, and proved that the Metropolitan's high standards extended past the Wagner repertoire. According to the *New York Times*: "Johnson chose not to cater to the more superficial aspects of the occasion, but rather to hold up to his patrons the highest ideal of musical drama and its worthy interpretation. The response of the audience said more than any words could have done as to the public approval. The cast included Martinelli, Tibbett and the much-touted Maria Caniglia making her début." *Musical America* carried congratulations, while the *Musical Courier* praised Johnson's policies and commented that even on opening night the standard was high and he was living up to his promise in seeing to it that there was no backsliding allowed under his direction.

"He was steel underneath that charming exterior," according to veteran Metropolitan Opera baritone Clifford Harvuot, whose career began in the Johnson era, continued through the Bing years, and on into the Schuyler Chapin regime. "I've seen him come to the orchestra rail at times when the orchestra wasn't paying attention to the conductor, plant his hands there and just stand. He wouldn't say a word, but the look on his face was enough. Everyone in that orchestra suddenly sat up and stopped fooling around. I saw that—many times."

Inevitably the Johnson management attracted its share of criticism along with the kudos. One of the first detractors, oddly enough, was Lawrence Tibbett who wrote an article for *The Rotarian* supporting opera in English—to which Johnson gave a rebuttal. Then Gigli, after returning to Rome in February (1939), made many disparaging remarks, publicly, about the general state of affairs in America and about the future prospects of the Metropolitan in particular. His comments were responsible for so much bad publicity that Johnson appeared on the Metropolitan stage during an intermission in *Boris Godunov* to refute the allegations and implications. The season ended with a favourable, though not large, financial balance and with the press commenting on "the public impression of new life and energy where artistic policies are concerned."

A particularly bright spot for Johnson, during the days of managerial responsibilities and political tension, had been a banquet he attended in Guelph, January 6, 1939, to celebrate George Drew's election as leader of the Ontario Conservative Party. The Guelph school orchestra and glee club were featured, and the announcement was made that both organizations were the result of Edward Johnson's "munificent gift to the city which made possible the teaching of music in the schools of Guelph." Eddie received such a tumultuous ovation that it was almost embarrassing, considering the raison d'être of the occasion.

The Wagner operas, presented from May 2 through May 23, and billed as the "New York World's Fair Metropolitan Opera" season, were a tremendous success, and Wagner continued to be favoured in plans for the regular 1939/40 season in New York. The Met's Philadelphia season was to be extended from five to ten performances to include *Der Ring*.

An early report had Johnson leaving for Europe on May 9, 1939, but he wanted to be on hand for the end of the Wagner Festival. Also, he was supposed to receive a Doctor of Music degree from New York University the first week in June, and he was needed for some last-minute conferences with writer H. Napier Moore in connection with the series of articles "Edward Johnson of Guelph" to be featured in *Maclean's* magazine. One of Moore's subheadings read: "Artist, skilled executive, showman, a man of deep human understanding—such is the ruler of the 'Met.' " The series appeared in the June 15, July 1 and July 15 (1939) issues and covered Johnson's life from the early days in Guelph through his singing career and his tenure as general manager of the Metropolitan. It recounted how, after his appointment as general manager, he had gone into the old Met office, hung up his coat and grey fedora and then, looking at the big chair Gatti had occupied for so many years and in which Witherspoon had sat for a short time, called for the house man and told him, "I think you can move that chair out; it's too big for me."

It was Mr. Moore's impression that Johnson's office was open to any and all of the artists, whatever their questions or problems. Few artists would have disagreed for there were few who were ever refused admittance. There was a general feeling of camaraderie—the backstage crew, for example, called Johnson "Eddie," which always pleased him. It was Napier Moore's prediction that Johnson, for all his honours, long international career and world fame, would someday "return to Guelph to live in the lovely old family home he has maintained there for many years. . . . He will, in short, continue to be what he is and always has been—Edward Johnson, of Guelph."

In view of the war panic, Johnson debated whether he should risk going to Europe at all that summer of 1939. The time passed and he had gone no further away than the Pocono Mountains, with Richard and Mildred Crooks, and Guelph, where he had spent a week. The latter trip led to the report that he was "vacationing in Guelph" and would not be making his annual pilgrimage to Europe. But a letter which came from Gatti in Milan, saying how much he was looking forward to seeing his old friend again, moved him so profoundly that when the *Ile de France* pulled out of New York harbour at 11:30 A.M., August 24, 1939, Edward Johnson was aboard. In a brief note to Fiorenza in Toronto, he confessed that "the European situation doesn't look so good today. However, I am an optimist and hope for the best."

As Johnson and Gatti-Casazza met again in Italy, there was a new and unspoken feeling of sympathy between the two men whose destinies the

213

Metropolitan Opera had so intimately entwined. The Metropolitan had become for Edward Johnson, as it had been for Gatti-Casazza, as much a part of him as breathing. He could understand, having been in office for four years, the proprietary feeling Gatti had had about the House. Now the Metropolitan *was* Edward Johnson; it was part of his very being; it was filled with *his* artists—of whom the dearest to his heart were "the Johnson babies"—his conductors, his directors, his people backstage, his staff. In short, it was *his* opera and *his* opera house and anything concerning it was something he took personally. Consequently, he was by turns delighted or annoyed, elated or infuriated, depending on the nature of what was being said or written about it.

Eddie had felt a great personal need to visit Italy—Florence, in particular—if only for a few days. In addition, he wanted to hear some new singers in Europe and to see M. Romanoff's ballets at the Trocadero in Orléans and also at the Opéra in Paris. The ballets were choreographed to new scores by Honegger, Milhaud and Ibert, and Johnson was considering them as possible material for the Met. The war interrupted the plans at the Opéra, however, and nullified Eddie's ideas about introducing the novelties in New York. He returned before September was over, while some members of the press were still reporting that the war had prevented him from going abroad!

THE MUSICAL DIGEST "rather liked Edward Johnson's straight-forward manner in presenting the new season's plans at his October, 1939, press conference. There was no effort at evasion or false promises but a sincere statement of what was going to be done and hints at what probably could be done." The repertoire would be enlarged, he said, in order to cope with sudden changes, and over 66 per cent of the company would be American. He went on to point out that, although he was not opposed to opera in English, he was convinced that the public preferred it in the original language as a rule. Recognizing the fact that few people were familiar with the Czech language of Smetana's *The Bartered Bride*, Johnson announced that the Met was returning to the usual German for the revival of that opera.

His reaction to the rumour that the Opera House was being sold by a real estate company was decisive: "I wish I were going to stay as long as *it* is." The Metropolitan's subscriptions were running slightly behind the previous year, he admitted, but added: "I believe that New York holds out to the artistic world what has been closed off in all the rest of the world; artists, composers and creative musicians are flocking here. The war hysteria affects everyone and we should not allow ourselves to become too emotional." Many Italian and German singers were detained in

Europe and were not expected to show up for the season, but Eddie said: "I am thoroughly convinced that we will go on with our season as planned: . . . We feel that at the Metropolitan we have a duty and obligation. I sincerely believe that the best way to serve, not only artistically but patriotically, is to do the job and do it well."

Sometimes Eddie wondered how people expected him to run an opera when there were so many demands on his time outside. On the other hand, he had to admit he enjoyed some of the social aspects of his job—sitting at a Musicians' Emergency Fund luncheon, for example, between Gertrude Lawrence and Mrs. Vincent Astor was something he would be happy to repeat anytime. Both women were interesting, stimulating and charming. Then there was the dinner with Lady Eaton, a party of four, before the November 27 opening of the Met's 55th season. The opera was *Simon Boccanegra*, with Tibbett, Rethberg, Martinelli, Pinza and Warren, Panizza conducting. Next day, the headlines read: "New 'Crisis' Fails to Daunt Enthusiasm" and "Traditional Glamour Surrounds Metropolitan Opening." Another time, *Musical America* carried a picture of Johnson and Richard Crooks with a newsboy they had brought across the country to New York. Johnson had supplied the tickets and Crooks the travel fare to fulfill the boy's dream of going to the Metropolitan Opera.

The statement in the *Musical Courier* that he was "brilliantly able to coordinate the artistic with the practical activities of the Metropolitan" was encouraging to Eddie. But he knew, as one of the critics pointed out, that it was going to take a miracle to bring the Italian and French repertoire up to scratch, and that it might require an even bigger miracle to keep the doors of the Metropolitan open.

On November 28, 1939, a letter came to the general manager's desk from the Metropolitan Opera Committee for the Orchestra, expressing their "sincere and profound regret at the passing of Maestro Bodanzky" and saying it was the orchestra's "greatest wish to cooperate" with the maestri and with Johnson in every way. Nevertheless, they wanted it known that they had "felt somewhat hurt when asked if they were tired the other evening, after first playing a four-and-a-half-hour *Boris* rehearsal and then three more of *Rosenkavalier*. . . . One tires after several hours of strenuous rehearsing, and it is not possible to give one's best at the latter part of a monumental day's work. We all love to make fine music and it is our wish to give the maestri what they desire." They asked for Mr. Johnson's cooperation in order that a happy atmosphere of mutual understanding might be established.

Such expressions of discontent from the orchestra were coupled with serious problems elsewhere in the organization. According to *Time* magazine of February 5, 1940, Johnson was "faced with mutiny" at the Metropolitan just as he was launching a $1,000,000 drive for public funds to refit the old house. It had all broken out after the death of the highly respected conductor Artur Bodanzky on November 23, 1939, when Johnson appointed the twenty-seven-year-old Erich Leinsdorf to succeed him in the Wagner repertoire. Both Melchior and Flagstad complained so openly about the inexperience of Leinsdorf that Johnson was nettled: "There are some old goats in the company who, because they have exalted egos since they have no competition for their roles, would like to be dictators of the Metropolitan. The operatic art and this institution are greater than these and will be here, along with Mr. Leinsdorf, long after they are gone. He will be so acclaimed in a few years that they won't want to remember that they opposed him." Unfortunately for Melchior, when he appeared in *Die Götterdämmerung* a few weeks later, one critic reported that he was "so nervous that he got his eagle-winged Norse warrior's helmet on backwards . . . the audience applauded him coldly and gave Leinsdorf an ovation."

Through such trying times of constant crisis, Eddie observed a daily routine that found him at the office at ten o'clock each morning. By that time, his secretary, the quiet, sympathetic and efficient Luigi Villa, had sorted out the mail—letters, press clippings and things needing attention that day—and had it ready for him. (Luigi's brother, Marino Villa, almost as sympathetic, was the advertising manager of the Metropolitan.)

At eleven o'clock, without fail, Eddie would switch on the loudspeaker system in his office so he could listen to whatever opera was in rehearsal. Even while busy reading his mail, looking over box office receipts and checking proofs for the next week's programs, he didn't miss a note. He kept tabs on his "family" of 35 leading sopranos, 13 mezzo-sopranos and contraltos, 25 tenors, 18 baritones, 11 bassos, 6 conductors, and 12 assistant conductors, not to mention the personnel of the chorus and orchestra.

In a little book in his desk drawer he filed away neatly the answers to every question or emergency that might arise—which artists could substitute on short notice in which roles, for instance. Every morning there were interviews and personal requests for favours. Although interviews seldom lasted longer than five minutes, Johnson had the happy faculty of making a person feel that he had all the time in the world to devote to their particular problem. Soprano Irene Jessner once said: "He was a marvellous manager because he was very diplomatic, you know. When you wanted something from him—let's say you wanted a certain part or you were dissatisfied about something—you would go and talk and he was very sweet. 'Well, Irene, what do you want?' And when you left you

216

were still guessing: 'Now do I get it or don't I get it?' I was fourteen years under Mr. Johnson . . . and in the fourteen years I think I went in to see him only once or twice because I wanted something . . . and even then I didn't know what was the result of the conversation!"

By noon, Eddie liked to be out in the auditorium with Ziegler and the stage directors, chief electricians and scenic directors watching the rehearsal. He might make a few quiet suggestions to the director as to the staging, or comment on some detail of costuming, before going across the street to the Opera Café for a hasty lunch. That was when he and Ziegler would discuss details such as those involved in taking the company to Brooklyn or Philadelphia, possibly that same evening.

Interviews and discussions on current business or the next season's repertoire would continue to take Johnson's time until he would leave for his apartment for a rest and a bite. But he was back at the opera house before eight, to check with Lewis about the boxholders of the Diamond Horseshoe, and greet any distinguished visitors who might be in his own Grand Tier box that evening. Then he would go backstage to wish the artists well before taking his stand, under the clock, to be sure the performance started on time, at eight o'clock sharp. Oftentimes he would listen to part of the opera over the loudspeakers while dictating correspondence, studying contracts or listening to the demands of truckers for moving the Metropolitan Opera scenery to and from its distant off-the-premises storehouse.

When the opera was over, Edward Johnson would be backstage again to congratulate and encourage the artists. Then, unless some special function demanded his presence, he would take a taxi and be home by one o'clock. Tuesdays were exceptional, requiring a dash to Pennsylvania Station at 4 P.M. to catch the special train for the Metropolitan's performance in Philadelphia that night. Even then, Edward Johnson was back in his apartment by 2 A.M., and on the job again by ten o'clock in the morning.

He was proud of his student matinées and of the enthusiasm expressed by the youthful audiences. At *Faust* (December 15, 1939), under the auspices of the Guild, he had to inform the children that there were receptacles for gum disposal—that it wasn't *de rigueur* to use the bottoms of the seats in the Metropolitan Opera House for such a purpose!

As the 1939/40 season progressed, the operas of Richard Wagner again led the repertoire in popularity, in spite of the unavailability of foreign artists. Italy's siding with Germany in the war made the situation "very muddled," Eddie said, insofar as Italian singers were concerned. However, the new American soprano Helen Traubel was making an "excellent impression." Olin Downes commented that the lack of novelties in the repertoire was understandable under the circumstances: *Coq d'Or* was cancelled; also the scheduled performances of *The Bartered Bride* in German, because of political difficulties (the Czech nationals wanted no German). But *Pelléas* was revived, and the production of *Le Nozze di Figaro* was a "tremendous success."

John Erskine, representing the Juilliard interest, congratulated Eddie at the end of the season on his "happy solution to all the problems." He remarked on the high calibre of the productions and told him, "The young Americans in the casts did you proud."

There was praise also from George Sloan, Chairman of the Metropolitan Opera Fund, for Eddie's having been a tower of strength during the campaign. "You already have your crown as a great artist and a great impresario—now let me crown you as a great fund raiser." Contributions to the Metropolitan Opera Fund netted $1,063,195. It was not unexpected that Johnson should lead a successful appeal for funds in New York but, according to statistics, 74 per cent of contributors to the Fund lived out of New York and gave 38 per cent of the total money. More than $325,000 was donated by radio listeners who had come to look on the Metropolitan as *their* House.

WITH EXPENSES WHAT they were and the world situation bound to make money even scarcer than in the past, the board made the historic decision to exercise its option to buy the Metropolitan Opera House. Edward Johnson, appointed the Met's general manager for another two years, joyously attached his signature to a money order, June 27, 1940, from the Metropolitan Opera Association to the Metropolitan Opera and Real Estate Company, for $500,000. It was "payment on account of purchase price of Opera House and 209/211 West 40th Street per agreement dated April 1, 1940." *Musical America*'s editorial comment referred to the Met now as the "people's opera instead of society's opera."

It was a momentous change; the Metropolitan had become a public enterprise. New York's Mayor Fiorello La Guardia telephoned his congratulations, and Mr. Bliss, Chairman of the Board, immediately announced other plans to "enhance the comfort of patrons at the Metropolitan and develop this institution further as a national asset." The House was to be closed for renovations (to cost $225,000 and to be completed by November 1) until the opening of the 1940/41 season on December 2. The seating capacity was to be increased by replacing the ground-level boxes with rows of seats; there would be a new gold curtain, new productions and new artists. The singers, Johnson added, would include more Americans than ever, partly because war was keeping Europeans away, and partly because better American talent had been discovered among the more than six hundred singers who had auditioned during the year.

Eddie and new board president George Sloan concurred that despite the talent situation there would be no curtailment of either the German or Italian repertoire. Bruno Walter was engaged as guest conductor for *Fidelio, Don Giovanni* and *The Bartered Bride*; Italo Montemezzi would conduct his own *L'Amore dei tre re*; *Ballo in maschera* and *La Fille du Régiment* with Lily Pons were to be revived; *Alceste* would be presented for the first time at the Met; and four Americans (including radio's Eleanor Steber) were among the ten new singers who would appear. In other words, the Metropolitan announced its intention to "go on as if there were no war. Opera has nothing to do with nationalism." And, according to box office treasurer Earle Lewis, the public responded with a "red hot interest in opera."

In the final analysis, all brave words to the contrary, Johnson did the only thing possible, as Olin Downes pointed out, and "turned to the difficult task of making a smaller but well-balanced repertory with the means at his disposal."

Eddie often felt he was being buffeted from one side to the other with a regularity and senselessness that was almost beyond human endurance. If he could have talked freely with even a few of his close associates, it might have helped. But only with Jo Casali and Hammie—a disparate duo as he thought of them—did he ever find he could simply be himself. With everyone else there was a shell, paper-thin in some cases but present, nevertheless. Men found him charming but remote, while his more intimate women friends would complain to acquaintances: "You probably know him just as well as I do."

Eddie's friend Gerald Reynolds wrote him at the time: "In the last analysis a man must live with himself, in his own spiritual sanctum, and in those forbidding night watches that will have their way with us, however our outer life seems protected from them. I imagine you have faced your Golgotha too well not to meet it now whatever form it takes, and that is the highest tribute one can pay to another—the deep respect inspired by the measure sensed spiritually in another human. I believe you possess a philosophy that gives you tranquility in any situation—not just an easily won tranquility but a knowledge that in serenity is both solution and comfort from any crisis. Such wisdom is the greatest benediction one can have and I felicitate you on its possession."

"Not quite, old friend, not quite," Eddie commented as he read, for he was thinking of a most unfortunate experience, and possibly the most unpleasant he was to have during his entire régime as general manager of the Met. It was one of the very few times he had completely lost his temper since the evening of his début in Padova, Italy, back in 1912. It started simply enough—he had been extremely annoyed by the steady criticism of the Metropolitan, week after week, by the *New York Herald Tribune*'s Robert Lawrence. It had seemed to Eddie like a veritable destructive campaign, culminated by what Lawrence had written about the Metropolitan's production of Gluck's *Alceste*. The evening of the day that review appeared, Mr. Lawrence and Mr. Johnson happened to come face to face as the critic entered the 39th Street stage door, which was also the anteroom to the Met's offices, to attend the season's final performance of *Die Götterdämmerung*. Suddenly, Eddie could no longer contain the anger that had been mounting within him during the season over what he considered to be unjustified attacks. With no warning, he launched into a verbal lashing of the surprised critic. Mr. Lawrence staunchly defended himself as a musician and critic who was dissatisfied, he admitted, with anything less than perfection at the Metropolitan. "I'm fighting to keep the curtain up, and you're undermining me," Eddie accused him, hotly. Tempers flared and voices were raised. Finally, after he had delivered a particularly impassioned diatribe, during which he found himself shouting, Eddie realized he would not be able to restrain himself longer if he stayed. He wanted to throttle the man. So, with an exasperated exclamation, he abruptly left the anteroom, went down the corridor to his office and slammed the door. It was going to take him some time, he knew, to cool off.

Two weeks had gone by when Eddie received the following letter from the *Tribune* publisher Mrs. Helen Rogers Reid:

Dear Mr. Johnson:

You and I have always had such friendly relations that I regret writing you about a matter that has given me considerable concern. It seems fairer, however, to take it up with you direct than to write to Mr. Sloan or anyone else connected with the Metropolitan.

Ever since your attack in the presence of other people on a member of our music staff, Mr. Robert Lawrence, during the evening of March 6th, I have fully expected that you would make some apology to him. Inasmuch, however, as none has appeared, and considerable time has gone by, I wish to tell you that the paper cannot let an occurrence like this pass unnoticed.

That there have been and always may be points of disagreement between the Metropolitan and our music critics is something that we both recognize and presumably accept as part of healthy criticism, but when the manager of the Metropolitan Opera Company makes statements reflecting on the integrity of a member of our staff in a public scene, we cannot ignore the event. I greatly hope

220

that you will see fit to send Mr. Lawrence a prompt and full apology and I feel sure that you will wish to do so.

Sincerely yours,

Helen Rogers Reid

The requested apology was forthcoming—Eddie even invited Mr. Lawrence to lunch, but there never seemed to be a day when both men were free at the same time. So the luncheon never took place. The critic continued his written attacks and Eddie did his best to ignore them.

That, fortunately, was a one-time-only incident. Generally speaking, Eddie enjoyed excellent relations with the press throughout his régime. Author and music critic Louis Biancolli spoke of Edward Johnson as "a man of enormous dynamism, love of music and people, quick to action in a crisis—he saw through all the critics. He was a man of great poise and dignity; an aristocrat without arrogance and condescension."

Toronto journalist George Kidd, who spent many hours with Johnson in preparation for a Toronto *Telegram* article, enjoyed the stories Eddie told. One was about the young soprano to whom he'd given a Metropolitan Opera contract, but when she showed up she was so much bigger than he remembered her that he was speechless. "Don't worry," she told him, "I'll have my baby soon and then everything will be all right." Another story was about Grace Moore, threatening not to go on in *Bohème* if Jan Kiepura didn't stop moving a certain chair in the first act of the opera. Persuasion failed, so Johnson had the chair nailed to the floor next time and enjoyed a good chuckle when he saw Kiepura try to move it.

Actually, Edward Johnson occupied a very unique position in his relations with others, according to conductor Edwin McArthur:

> Johnson had the respect and the affection of those who liked him and the admiration of those who didn't, which was quite a unique thing. Part of it was due to his spontaneous enthusiasm for things, I'm sure. For example, when Flagstad had her twentieth anniversary as a singer [December 12, 1938], she gave one of the most memorable parties in the history of the Metropolitan. It was a party for the entire personnel: office staff, make-up department, management, artists, orchestra, ushers, wardrobe, cleaning people, porters, electricians—everybody. Johnson was amazed. "I never saw anything like this any place," he told her. "The Met has made history tonight." Then he surprised Kirsten by embracing her.

Flagstad had mentioned several times the possibility of having Edwin McArthur, her coach and accompanist, conduct at the Metropolitan. Johnson was adamant against it because of McArthur's lack of conducting experience. But during contract negotiations, after the death of Artur Bodanzky, she became insistent. When he was recalling these events in 1972, McArthur said:

> I can tell you about this thing which was raging about me and my conducting for her. Johnson took Kirsten out to a four-and-a-half-hour lunch at some French restaurant. Obviously it was an endeavour to smooth things over. She repeated the conversation to me word for word.
>
> He told her he was facing great difficulty in coming to a decision, and she said, "There is no difficulty at all if you say, as general manager, I'm giving Mr. McArthur two performances or eight performances." Bodanzky had died and Johnson was giving things to Mr. Leinsdorf. Now I didn't claim to be a Leinsdorf myself, as they both knew.
>
> So Eddie told her, "It has to come before the board and the board is going to have a meeting on Wednesday." The meeting came and went, but she had no answer. So the whole thing went on for weeks, until everyone got in a real hassle about it.
>
> Unfortunately, the Met let the day slip by on which they should have taken up an option in her contract—it would have extended her appearances through March 18-24, 1940—and the Met had already scheduled two performances of *Parsifal* and one of *Tristan* for that period, as well as expecting that Flagstad would do some performances on tour in Cleveland and Boston. So Johnson called me in, and after still further hassling, because he wanted Martinelli for *Tristan* and Flagstad wanted Melchior, things were finally settled for me to make my début with the Company in Boston [April 1, 1940] with Flagstad, Thorborg and Melchior. Fortunately, the performance went well and the press was good.

It was only a few days later (April 8) that the Germans invaded Norway (Flagstad's homeland), and Flagstad's already complicated problems were doubled by concern for the safety of her husband, businessman Henry Johansen. Flagstad was willing to sign a contract with the Metropolitan for 1940/41 only if McArthur was engaged to conduct, and, according to McArthur, Johnson had several stormy sessions with her representative and negotiations went on for months.

Mr. McArthur told the rest of the story in his book *Flagstad*:

> Finally, the Metropolitan capitulated. They had to. Only a week before the crucial date, January 20, 1941, when they absolutely had to have her for a performance of *Siegfried,* a contract was arranged for me. It called for three performances in New York and one each in Boston and Cleveland. Flagstad was happy. So was I. And it is to Mr. Johnson's credit that he arranged an auspicious début for me in

the opera house in New York. He chose a Monday evening, the most important night of the week. The occasion, February 17, 1941, was also the fifteenth anniversary of Lauritz Melchior's début at the Metropolitan. On that night, too, Flagstad sang her one hundredth performance of Isolde. Messrs. Johnson, Ziegler, Earle Lewis, Melchior and I sent Flagstad one hundred roses with a charming verse that Mr. Ziegler wrote. . . .

McArthur admitted that the *New York Times,* the following day, was cautious in its appraisal of his reading of the score, although it did not question his talent for conducting and for opera.

Flagstad's last performance in the Metropolitan Opera House, prior to her going back to Norway, was *Tristan* on Saturday afternoon, April 12, 1941. A month after that Henry Johansen wrote McArthur that he and Flagstad were safe and happy together again, and that she was going to remain at home until the end of the war. Inasmuch as she had signed contracts with neither the Metropolitan nor NBC, both organizations could only accept Johansen's statement.

Unsubstantiated rumours that Flagstad sang for the occupation authorities precipitated violent reaction in the United States. Six years passed before she was to return to North America. By that time, the anti-Flagstad agitation was so strong that her Carnegie Hall concert, April 20, 1947, was solidly picketed by people who believed the allegations against her. Reportedly, Flagstad had to be spirited into the Hall via neighbouring rooftops. Nevertheless, a capacity audience gave her a twenty-minute ovation at the beginning of the concert that brought tears to her eyes and caused her to quaver in her singing of the first few phrases. From then on, however, the famous voice filled the hall as no other could do. Her return to opera in the United States (September 29, 1949) was as Isolde, not at the Metropolitan but with the San Francisco Opera. Critic Alfred Frankenstein wrote: "No *Tristan* in local history seemed so intense, so totally absorbing, so completely overwhelming in its impact." The conductor on that occasion was William Steinberg.

Just why Edward Johnson did not bring Flagstad back to the Metropolitan was never clear. Some people said he lacked the courage of his convictions; others, that he was forced to bow to social pressures. There was nothing as blatant as the ban put on Flagstad in July, 1949, by the trustees of the War Memorial Opera House in San Francisco (which was lifted after the directors of the San Francisco Opera said such a ban would mean cancelling their entire operatic season), but, nevertheless, Flagstad's first appearance at the Metropolitan after the Second World War was not until January 22, 1951, during Rudolf Bing's first season as general manager.

223

THE CONCERN ABOUT the effect of the war on the German and Italian repertoire for the 1940/41 season was premature, by all accounts, for Wagner continued to lead at the box office as attendance shot up more than 8,000 over the previous season's figures, and Mozart joined the list of favourites. The Metropolitan was said to be in good financial condition, with a comfortable bank balance left over from the 1940 Fund. At a Plaza Hotel luncheon he attended with Bori and Bruno Walter, Johnson did not hesitate to expand his chest a bit as he made the statement: "The Metropolitan Opera is today not only a repository of operatic masterpieces, but an active cultural and educational institution."

When he addressed the annual dinner of the prestigious Metropolitan Opera Club on March 12, he diplomatically told them: "The function of this Club is to preserve and develop the social dignity of Metropolitan Opera performances. Grand opera is and must remain a social event." It brought applause from some of the older members who had been most vocal in their criticism of changes such as fewer boxes, the installation of a broadcasting booth and the general democratization of opera.

It was natural, therefore, when the board wanted to expand the Met's touring operation and try to sell the Met to the Chicago crowd, that they should send Edward Johnson to Chicago to negotiate.

The Metropolitan's 1941 spring tour included Cleveland, where the company was, as always, a tremendous social success, and Atlanta, where Johnson did his bit by speaking at a Kiwanis Club luncheon. He described singing as "a sustained talking on a tune" and said: "When given a fairly keen sense of pitch and of rhythm, plus the capacity for hard work, singing becomes a mere matter of practical development under the guidance of linguistic and imaginative thought. Breath, pitch, vowel—the singer's trinity. . . . A great voice alone does not make a great singer. . . . Speech is man's greatest invention and upon it he has built up his entire civilization."

Because of the war, Eddie had to forego a trip to Europe that summer, so he travelled to Chicago, and westward, instead. From Central City, on July 20, he wrote the Drews that he had had "an exciting and stimulating trip. The opera, under Frank [conductor Frank St. Leger], most successful."

Another letter, from San Francisco (July 25): "In a few moments I will be off to the Bohemian Grove [near San Francisco] as guest of the celebrated 'Dog-House' camp. What happens there I've no idea, but the stories are 'grossi'. . . . It would take more than the minute at my disposal to tell you about my trip, but it is incredible how much I have crowded into seven days—New York, Chicago, Denver, Los Angeles and San Francisco. It seems more like seven weeks! . . . It has been constructive and instructive, but somewhat strenuous. Yesterday (Thursday) I spent the late morning and lunch hour with Risë Stevens at the Studio of MGM watching her make her picture with Nelson Eddy. She is strikingly beautiful and has made a big hit with everyone in the picture. They all say *The Chocolate Soldier* will 'click' and Risë is made. I am so happy for her. Mario Chamlee came over here with me. Earle Lewis is already in Camp."

On July 31, he wrote from the Bohemian Grove: "This has been an unusual experience and I'm delighted to have made it. Nearly a thousand men from all walks of life gathered in a wondrous primeval forest, living in tents and shacks and eating and drinking like two-fisted men under thirty years of age. It is a revelation and must be seen to be believed or appreciated. Music and alcohol are the bases of all entertainment and I really wouldn't know which comes first. The guests of whom I am one are names to be reckoned with—[Herbert] Hoover, [Wendell] Willkie, Sir Gerald Campbell, three or four army generals and a couple of admirals. The members are painters, musicians, writers, lawyers, doctors and businessmen all in search of fun and relaxation. . . . Earle Lewis, John Charles Thomas, Mario Chamlee and myself are in the same camp. The Dog-House! Melchior is in The Cuckoo's Nest. John Brownlee and Dick Bonelli, together with Alec Templeton, at The Land of Happiness. The fun, the music, the concerts and the plays I'll tell you about later." He added that he'd be returning to San Francisco from there "to conclude opera business."

Back in New York, at the annual press conference on October 8, Johnson announced that nine new singers would be heard; that Sir Thomas Beecham and Bruno Walter would be guest conductors; that conductor Paul Breisach, stage director Lothar Wallerstein and choreographer Laurent Novikoff would be joining the staff for another sixteen-week season; and that the traditional Sunday night concerts would continue.

Eddie was amused by a letter he received from the famed writer Hendrik Willem van Loon (November 24, 1941): "Have you a sufficiently elephantine memory to reach back to the days when you used to sing for your supper? One evening you did so at Cornell University and believe it or not I was concertmaster at that time of the Cornell University Orchestra. Afterward, I think we took you to the Savage Club and fed you beer and *Heringsalat*. The last time I saw you was in the Opera Cellar in Stockholm after a performance of Mozart and again you were eating *Heringsalat*. Which is a nice way to approach the subject I would like to discuss with you—that of Maria Markan, an Icelandic singer." Van Loon proposed a luncheon meeting to introduce the young soprano. It so happened that Miss Markan, one of the new singers Eddie had already engaged, was scheduled to make her début as the Countess in *The Marriage of Figaro* on January 7.

Hoping to offset the tragedy of war, the Metropolitan had chosen to open the 1941/42 season, November 24, with a comedy, Mozart's *Le Nozze di Figaro,* and had rolled out a stellar cast for the event: Ezio Pinza in the title role, Bidú Sayão (Susanna), Elisabeth Rethberg (Countess), Risë Stevens (Cherubino), John Brownlee (Count), Salvatore Baccaloni (Bartolo), Irra Petina (Marcellina), staged by Lothar Wallerstein, with Panizza conducting. That evening in Box No. 23, jointly shared by Johnson and Ziegler, there were the Zieglers, the Schuyler Smiths (Florence Page Kimball), the actress Ina Claire and Mr. and Mrs. Charles L. Gleaves (the former Miss Ziegler). By order of the Musicians' Union, "The Star-Spangled Banner" was to precede every performance of the opera that season. "But once the performance begins the tension evaporates and we proceed to do our job," Eddie explained.

*Collier's* magazine of December 6, 1941, carried a feature article by Howard Taubman titled "Boss of the Opera," with a long subhead: "The man who manages the Metropolitan Opera has to be adept at handling everything from high finance to artistic temperament. If in addition he's something of an international lawyer as well as a star singer, he's likely to make good. Meet Edward Johnson." Taubman began by telling how a friend had taken Johnson aside after he was appointed general manager and said: "Listen, Eddie, you have to step out. Get a decent apartment, live in style. You can't be a big shot and live in a joint like that!" But Eddie continued to live in his three-room walkup apartment, Taubman affirmed. He gave in to pressure only once and hired a chauffeur and limousine. That was in 1936. He was driven to the opera house in the morning and home at night, but the driver just sat most of the time. So Johnson got rid of both him and the limousine and "felt free again," walking to and from the opera house. "But by faith, conviction and works he is a democrat, and being at the head of the opera has only reinforced his ideas."

Taubman told how hard feeling against Germany and Italy at the time made Johnson skeptical about putting on *Aida.* He anticipated trouble when the chorus hails their hero with *Ritorna vincitor* ("Return a conqueror"). "Somebody might yell, 'Down with Mussolini!' Somebody, *Evviva Mussolini!* The first thing you'd know, the Metropolitan would have a riot on its hands." Later in the article Mr. Taubman wrote: "Eddie loves the opera. Having the missionary's impulse, he wants to communicate that affection to others. Since the world is at war, he wants to make the Metropolitan a place of good cheer."

At year's end, expressing the belief that the war difficulties were not

226

insurmountable, Johnson announced: "The time has come for us to put American music where it belongs and create an idiom of our own. If only we could develop music as a national sport, with all that implies, with professional standards and integrity—if only musicians and spectators alike were convinced that though doing it seriously it was, nevertheless, for their own pleasure." With the broadcast of *La Traviata* on November 29, he said, the Opera began its eleventh consecutive season on the air. It now had a listening audience of 14 million, and the intermission features "Music in America," "Guild At-home" and "Opera Forum Quiz" had been added. Eddie enthusiastically predicted "a highly promising and stimulating season."

It might have been expected that the members of the reactionary Metropolitan Opera Club would be, en masse, the most ardent supporters of the general manager, but such was not the case. There were the inevitable individual jealousies and personality clashes, and disagreements on policies. But one of the members, Major J. W. Rafferty, sent a heartening letter, on January 16, 1942, with a photograph of himself and three young officers: "My dear Eddy: I am off to my third war, but before I go I want to tell you that as manager of the Opera you have been a good soldier. You have shown those qualities that kept the army of the Opera together and have won over all enemies—lack of money, depression, war, etc. As an officer of the army and a West Pointer, I salute you for all you have done for this country. . . . As a member of the Opera Club I will be back, and may you have many years with us."

ONE AFTERNOON in February, 1942, Eddie complained to Ziegler that he was "not feeling so hot," but he ignored his friend's advice that he should take the evening off. At curtain time, he was standing under the clock, as usual, in his top hat, white tie and tails, ready to give the signal for the evening's performance to begin.

But once things were off to a good start, he admitted that he felt "rotten," and was going to "grab a cab and go home." His legs would hardly carry him up the flight of stairs to his apartment and the next morning he found it difficult to get out of bed. Harking back to the rheumatic fever attack he had had in Paris, he wasted no time in phoning the doctor, who ordered him to bed but reassured him: "I don't think this is anything we can't clear up in a few days with some medicine and rest. Stay away from the office and don't worry."

Eddie stayed away from the office, but the office came to him: Ziegler and Lewis were in every day, and he was on the phone to Luigi Villa. As for not worrying? How could he help it? After Pearl Harbor, December 7, 1941, the United States had joined the Allies and escalated the war into a world-wide conflagration. Business generally was suffering, and Eddie foresaw a large deficit for the Met. "The tour will help some," he thought, "but not enough." He knew there were rumblings among the board members that the 1942/43 season might have to be cancelled. "There's no way that's going to happen," he muttered through clenched teeth. "They're not going to close down *my* House."

Finally, after his weekly broadcast of February 22, 1942, in which he exuded his usual optimism and cheer, he wrote Fiorenza: "The doctor gave me a clear slate yesterday and sent me into circulation again. It was not serious but it could have been had I not taken it in time. . . . Tomorrow I'll take up my office work as usual. . . . The R. Y. Eatons were here just when I was ill, but they went to a couple of performances and I'm having them and the Smiths for dinner at Passy's. . . . We are on our last three weeks and it is nothing but miraculous how we have achieved this season."

The 1941/42 season closed, March 14, with *Faust* the final afternoon broadcast from the stage of the Metropolitan, and *Lohengrin* in the evening. Speaking on the air during an intermission that afternoon, Johnson reported that the season had gone well, under the circumstances, and he thanked the Guild and radio sponsors for their support. "I feel confident that, with your loyalty, and with the conviction that the Metropolitan stands alone in the world as a bulwark of grand opera as we know it—and that grand opera must be saved, I feel confident, I repeat, that we will be able to carry on."

*The New York Times* was less optimistic: "Whether there will be a season next winter has not been decided." The fact was that no old contracts had been renewed nor new ones signed. Such things as rationing of tires and, since Pearl Harbor, the constant fear of an air attack, even on New York City itself, combined to keep the crowds home. Furthermore, with no Flagstad, Schipa or Björling, some of the Met's "big guns" were missing. Then Pinza was detained on Ellis Island for a week as an "enemy alien."

Of necessity, there had been numerous changes of repertoire and casts during the season, but the audience reaction had been good on the whole. Olin Downes cited Bruno Walter and Sir Thomas Beecham as part of the reason, calling the German repertoire good in spite of the fact there had been no *Tristan* (Johnson had thought it unfair to ask someone else to sing Flagstad's role right away) and no *Meistersinger*. He also labelled *The Magic Flute*, in English, conducted by Walter, as a success.

Downes considered Traubel and Varnay good substitutes in the Wagner repertoire, adding: "It bears testimony, also, to the admirable flexibility and progressiveness of Mr. Johnson's policies, in the light of present and swift and significant changes in the world situation, and the necessity, as well as the eminent advisability, of seizing the moment to advance American singers." Maxine Stellman, for example, replaced Varnay in the middle of a *Lohengrin* in Boston, showing Johnson's well-placed faith in young singers.

There were conflicting views constantly being expressed about everything at the Met. Some people thought that ticket prices should come down but that orchestra players should get a raise. Some said there should be a shorter season, others that New Yorkers were "crazy for opera" and the season should, therefore, be longer! The chair of the general manager was not an easy one.

About this time, the Met's chorusmaster, Fausto Cleva, was becoming restless. Having conducted many of the Sunday Evening Concerts at the Met since the 1938/39 season and one *Barber of Seville* (February 14, 1942) with good reception, and failing to find his name listed on the tentative schedule for the 1942/43 season to conduct either concerts or an opera, he went to see Johnson. Cleva told about that meeting in later years:

"Listen," I said, "I have some good reviews and I deserve to conduct more. I make you a proposition. I will be chorusmaster and supervisor, providing you give me even one *Cavalleria* to conduct, to excuse my staying here. Otherwise, I must resign."

At the moment Johnson said "Yes," but the next day he called me to say some difficulty had arisen. So I resigned. A week later he wrote me—I still have the letter—saying the Board wanted him to ask me to reconsider my decision. I said "No."

One day, some time later, he called me in and said, "Would you accept the position of general manager in Chicago? We want to make an exchange [productions, artists, directors]— New York, Chicago, San Francisco."

I said, "What is the condition?"

He said, "Go up to Chicago and speak with them; they'll tell you. Then come back and report to me."

I went up there. I got the picture. They said, "We don't have opera. We will pay $12,000 and expect from you the best. You'll have here for eight weeks a budget of $600,000." That was a lot for 1942. So I accepted and promised to do my best for them.

The next spring, in Chicago, Johnson asked to see my contract. I showed him my contract and he saw the word *sole*—that I had power for the whole thing in Chicago. "I don't have that word in my contract," he said.

"This is what they offered me," I told him, "and I accepted."

He never forgave me that *sole*, I think, and he never forgave me the salary either!

As an artist I had always known Eddie as a good friend, but he was a man we never comprehended. When he was being coached by me, he used to be very humble. Other artists might say, "I'd like that," but not Eddie. He'd say, "What do you think?" I never knew whether he was really sincere or whether he was playing a game. He would search around for your opinion. He was impenetrable. He would never come out openly and express himself, like a Latin—what we have on our chest we have on our tongues. Sometimes I think the Anglo-Saxon is more smart.

On April 12, 1942, while Johnson was on tour with the Metropolitan in Bloomington, Indiana, Fiorenza was scheduled to speak on the radio. Eddie wrote that he was "mortified" to have missed her but that "the tenor was having trouble vocally and I got disturbed about tonight. He got through and he's okay now."

A bust of Edward Johnson by Guitou Knoop was unveiled on April 29, 1942, at a preview of the sculptor's exhibition at the Wildenstein Galleries in New York City. The show included busts of dancer Valentina, Boston Symphony conductor Dr. Serge Koussevitzky, Dr. Howard Hanson, and others. On Johnson's invitation to attend, the sculptor had scrawled: "Don't forget you are the prima donna of the show! Bring the town in!! Guitou."

Johnson was in demand as a speaker at various clubs and universities, for graduation ceremonies, Guild functions and special luncheons and dinners. Tiring though they were, these occasions provided momentary release from the burdening details of the Met office. His ready fund of anecdotes and amusing stories never failed. If he could make people laugh at such a tragic moment in history, and at the same time win a few supporters for his Metropolitan Opera, he knew he would always find the time and energy to oblige.

Speaking seriously to graduates of the Cincinnati Conservatory of Music (June 4, 1942), he told them: "We know that if we are to win the war physically, we must gird ourselves spiritually . . . the extent of American influence everywhere in the world is frightening. It is frightening because it measures the burden of responsibility which we have assumed. It is frightening because of the great expectations we have aroused—not only to win the war, but to solve the great problems of peace. . . . I believe that the day will come when we will have a well-defined scheme of general musical education on the same basis as other compulsory academic subjects—producing eventually a musically cultured people, with understanding, appreciation and discernment."

230

Receiving an Honorary Doctorate of Music on that same occasion, he stated: "This is a war of ideas—spiritual elements must not be condemned as a luxury, but upheld as a necessity to our freedom. In a war that is pitting nation against nation, we in America must strive to keep alive the arts that are international. Music is the universal language through which the Infinite is revealed."

*9*

THE TENSIONS, QUESTIONS, doubts, fears and crises faced by the Metropolitan's general manager and his staff and Board of Directors that summer of 1942 were trying, but Eddie was finally able to announce that his Opera House would have a season, as usual. "It is no secret," he said at the Brooklyn Academy of Music, November 10, "that only a few months ago there was every possibility that there would be no 1942/43 opera season. Financial problems, artistic complications, availability of artists, questionable public interest and wartime difficulties made things look very gloomy. However, thanks to a coordinated effort among artists, musicians, stage hands and staff, all of whom accepted voluntary reductions, a lower operating cost was obtained, and consequently a reduced ticket price has been possible without lowering the standards of the opera. Half the stories they tell you about prima donnas are not true."

Johnson also announced that the Metropolitan's Philadelphia season would include seven operas instead of the previous ten. Subscriptions in New York were encouraging, he reported, and the Sherwin-Williams paint company would again sponsor the Metropolitan Opera's Auditions of the Air.

"Opera is a good show," he said, "and should be thought of in those terms; opera is big business and particularly so at the Metropolitan." Then he made the pitch that became so familiar in most of his wartime speeches: "Axis Powers' radio has been announcing that the Met is not functioning in wartime, to slander American morale. Unless we are to succumb, we must win the war. Therefore, buy bonds, pay taxes, accept restrictions—take all the difficulties we have to meet with a smile, but don't forget that we are fighting for our culture and our way of life. And don't forget the opera!"

An intermission feature of the January 2, 1943, Metropolitan Opera broadcast celebrated the first anniversary of the signing (January 1,

1942) of a declaration by twenty-six nations affirming their union against the Axis Powers. Edward Johnson introduced the speakers. A week later he participated in the Victory Rally broadcast in which President C. J. Hambro of the Norwegian Parliament-in-Exile, Crown Prince Olaf and Norwegian Ambassador to the United States Wilhelm Morgenstierne spoke. The Metropolitan's popular mezzo-soprano Gladys Swarthout was chairman of the Rally. Meanwhile, Johnson was more than busy as chairman of the entertainment division of the Greater New York Fund for which a campaign for $4.5-million was launched.

On February 19 he journeyed to Chicago to attend a Chicago Opera Board of Governors luncheon and to make final arrangements for a two-week Chicago engagement for the Met that spring, beginning March 22. The Metropolitan had not been in Chicago since 1910. It was like a successful conclusion to the overture he had made, not too hopefully, on April 2, 1941.

A newspaper clipping, cherished by Johnson fan Estelle Maxwell, gave a report of an Illinois Opera Guild party that spring. Edward Johnson was described as the favourite tenor with the old Chicago Opera Association, and at Ravinia when opera was in its heyday there. He "stood next to Mrs. William E. Ragland, known better to opera lovers as (soprano) Edith Mason, who headed the receiving line. Mr. Johnson's unusual attire of stiff-bosomed, blue-striped shirt, wing collar, blue bow tie and dark suit, and his shining close-cropped white hair made him stand out in whatever little group he joined during the rest of the afternoon!"

The Opera that winter had opened on November 23, 1942, with *La Fille du Régiment*, with Lily Pons, Salvatore Baccaloni and Raoul Jobin, conducted by St. Leger. It continued to March 20, and saw Helen Traubel's first Isolde, the début of conductor George Szell with *Salome* and the farewell performance of the noted German bass Friedrich Schorr as The Wanderer in *Siegfried*, as well as the first appearance of Russian-born basso Alexander Kipnis in the title role of *Boris Godunov*. The regular season was followed, after the Spring Tour, by a Post Season in New York, April 16-24. Another year; another miracle.

Shortly after the Metropolitan tour ended, Erich Leinsdorf was inducted into the army. "Before leaving town," he wrote Johnson, "I must tell you that I am leaving full of gratitude and affection toward you, who have been such a great friend to me."

On April 24, 1943, at the final Metropolitan broadcast of the season, the Women's National Radio Committee presented the Metropolitan with an award for the musical program that had served the war effort the best. "All in all," the general manager stated, in accepting the award, "this has been an unusually successful season." According to *Time* magazine, 450,000 opera goers had paid $899,000 in New York (even with subscription prices reduced to a $5 top); two weeks in Chicago had grossed $166,000; one week in Cleveland, $185,000.

With the death (May 20, 1943) of Eric Semon, the Metropolitan's European representative, it was going to be extremely difficult to negotiate for the services of such artists as Flagstad, Pons, Lehmann and Melchior. Not only had the Metropolitan lost a fair and sympathetic representative, but Eddie had lost a colleague on whose judgment and honesty he could rely. George Sloan sent a memo to Johnson: "This afternoon I told Mr. Bliss of my suggestion that you should proceed to Europe at your earliest convenience to canvass the possibilities of new artists, and so on, for next season. He is heartily in sympathy with the plan. Let me know if I can be of any assistance to you in clearing through the State Department."

At the Opera Guild's meeting at Louis Sherry's in May, Bori presented the Metropolitan with the Guild's annual $15,000 contribution. Expressing thanks, Johnson warned that, in spite of the tax relief promised by Governor Dewey (which would not take effect until 1944), and recent generous donations, the Metropolitan continued to lead a precarious existence.

Eddie knew that although the Metropolitan's annual $200,000 deficit was considerably cut down, some directors were talking about moving the Met permanently to the Chicago Civic Opera House where they would not have an annual real estate tax of $150,000 to pay. Much as he was attached to Chicago, the idea of the Metropolitan Opera, *his* Metropolitan Opera, being any place but in its own house in New York City was anathema to Edward Johnson. Something would have to be done.

While the familiar wartime rumour circulated that the Opera would not be able to open its doors in the fall, Cornelius Bliss worked on tax exemption possibilities for the Metropolitan, and Johnson, admitting to "the bare minimum" of resources on hand, kept sturdily assuring the public that there would be a season in the Old House as usual. He announced a twenty-week season for 1943/44, November 22-April 18, and a reduced price scale, but was tight-lipped when it came to further details. Pointing to the shocking news of August 18, 1943, that the famed La Scala of Milan had been destroyed in a bombing raid, he stressed the comparative good fortune of the Metropolitan, no matter what the hardships.

The difficulties at the Met that summer were lightened for Eddie by

234

the good news from Ontario that the Conservatives had come to power in the August 4th election and that George Drew, the party leader, was the province's new premier.

Further news from Canada indicated that, even though Eddie's contract at the Metropolitan would run until 1945, his was one of the names being mentioned as possible successor to Dr. J. S. Thomson, general manager of the Canadian Broadcasting Corporation. Dr. Thomson was resigning, as of November, 1943, to return to the University of Saskatchewan. "I haven't heard anything about it," Eddie told reporters. "If I do, you fellows will be the first to know." One thing he did not tell them, however, was that repeated overtures had been coming his way asking that he become involved in the musical destinies of the Toronto Conservatory of Music. Thus far he had successfully fielded all queries and postponed committing himself in any way. His hands were more than full at the Metropolitan and, in spite of criticisms, he was the captain at the helm of the ship and was determined it should not go aground.

The opening of the 1943/44 season, on November 22, saw Edward Johnson wearing black tie and dinner jacket, instead of the silk hat, white tie and tails in which he had become such a familiar figure over the years of his management. The work was *Boris Godunov* with Pinza as Boris. Casually elegant, Johnson was backstage before the performance, as usual, to give reassuring words to the singers and director, maintaining a uniquely warm and friendly relationship with staff and employees. He liked to think of himself as having an "open door policy," and as being a goodwill ambassador for the Metropolitan to its millions of radio listeners over the Blue Network's 174-station hookup. In spite of the war, in spite of financial and artistic crises, they had kept going and growing, and the 1943/44 season would be the longest yet: twenty weeks in New York and four weeks on tour, for a total of 144 performances.

The *New York Herald Tribune* carried a Metropolitan Opera Jubilee article (November 27, 1943), subtitled "Metropolitan goes American and may become democratic," which mentioned that Johnson had been receiving approximately twenty letters a week asking him to cast Paul Robeson as Otello at the Met. Was he supposed to rewrite Verdi and make Iago a tenor? Eddie wondered. To all suggestions and requests Eddie was polite but noncommittal. Everyone knew the truth of the words of writer Douglas Gilbert: "The future of American opera is in Mr. Johnson's hands." And Edward Johnson knew it, too.

Meanwhile there were daily knotty problems, such as that of the temperamental former diva Mme Frances Alda who was incensed because Johnson had not shown favour to her pupil Lillian Raymondi. Alda was demanding that Raymondi be given better roles. Then there was the patron Helen Caputi who believed that the singers who patronized dressmaker Paul Engel were receiving preferential treatment in the newspaper reviews by critic Jerome Bohm. It all required the tact of a master diplomat.

THROUGHOUT JOHNSON'S time as a tenor at the Metropolitan, the role of Pelléas was recognized as more or less his personal property, with Lucrezia Bori as Mélisande. The opera was returned to the repertoire in the 1939/40 season, with French singer Georges Cathelat and America's Helen Jepson heading the cast. It fell short of the success Eddie had hoped for it. Inevitably there were those who maintained that he was secretly pleased, but the fact remains that he tried it again the following season with Canadian tenor Raoul Jobin as Pelléas. Again it failed to capture the public imagination. Then came French baritone Martial Singher who made his début as Dapertutto in *Les Contes d'Hoffmann*, and appeared as Pelléas on January 26, 1944, opposite the already-popular Brazilian soprano Bidú Sayão. "Martial Singher," wrote Virgil Thomson in the *New York Herald Tribune*, "as Pelléas, was the glory of the evening. Vocally impeccable and dramatically superb, he animated the opera personally and gave it the authority of his perfect French declamation."

As for Edward Johnson, he immediately began to regard Singher as someone who could step into other roles he himself had sung successfully. In Singher's words: "He came to me one day and asked me whether I thought it would be wise for him to schedule me for Hamlet—a role in which I had made a tremendous success in Paris and Buenos Aires. At the same time he told me there was a part of *his* that he wanted me very much to do, and that was Peter Ibbetson. He wanted me to look at the score. I did, but it was not possible for me—it was much higher than Pelléas."

Johnson, like the critics, was apparently undecided whether to class Mr. Singher as a baritone or tenor, but Virgil Thomson's evaluation coincided with the artist's own: "His voice is a light, high baritone."

Actually, Johnson had first offered Martial Singher a Metropolitan Opera contract in 1935, but said he could not guarantee leading roles. After thinking it over, the singer had thanked him very much but refused, saying he might be interested later. Speaking from his home in California in the 1970's, Singher recalled that subsequent events in Europe had caused him to change his mind.

Then the war came and we were caught by the invasion. We were under the Occupation for eighteen months and finally managed to escape and come to America in 1941, just before Pearl Harbor. I had been extremely sick, a kind of paralytic infection like Marjorie Lawrence's. She did not recover as well as I did; I was lucky. We arrived in New York as refugees and of course I contacted Mr. Johnson.

"Well, my boy," he told me, "it's very different this time. When you were in France, you were an established singer. Now you are a refugee and I don't know what I can do. See Pelletier. He's in charge of the Metropolitan auditions; maybe we can arrange something that way."

So they put me on the Auditions of the Air program in the RCA studios in Rockefeller Center. I sang two duets with the coloratura soprano Virginia MacWatters, and Figaro in *Il Barbiere* and the *Hamlet* drinking song. The next day Mr. Johnson called me and said, "Well, that's the way to have an audition for you. This way Ziegler heard you; we heard you; and the conductors heard you; and now we are all in agreement. I offer you a contract."

One of the conditions he made was that I sing the part of Pelléas. It was a severe condition for me, because I had never sung the part anywhere. But he was very wise; he made me sing some minor parts first. I had some bad reviews, but he stuck with me and never interfered with my study of Pelléas. He asked me once in a while how it was going. "You can make it," he would say. "I know you are going to be all right."

Then when we were getting ready for the performance the tailor came to me and said, "Johnson has just given you his costumes." We had the same measurements; they didn't have to be touched. I wore his costumes very proudly and it was a good omen, for *Pelléas* launched me completely. I remember that he and Bori came backstage before the performance—there's a picture that was taken of Bidú Sayão, Bori, Johnson and myself.

My original contract had been for eight weeks; after *Pelléas* I ended up with a contract for twenty-five weeks. I had come to sing *Pelléas* but he gave me *Tannhäuser* and *Parsifal* that same season! I fear that was my fault; I was never clever enough about watching what was put in front of me. I just took it!

Singher always abided by Johnson's decisions insofar as his roles at the Metropolitan were concerned, and looked on Eddie as someone who was genuinely interested in the welfare of each and every artist.

Edward Johnson was the kind of person who would take you by the arm and talk with you for four or five minutes if he thought something was bothering you or if he had something to say, unless it was about a contract or something serious. I was worried about my mother whom I had left behind in my apartment in Paris. After the invasion and then the liberation I had not heard from her. As I was walking down the corridor at the Metropolitan one day, Mr. Johnson took my arm and said, "So, Mr. Singher, I understand you are concerned about your mother. We have a Canadian Mission in Paris and I think I can help you." Well, through his son-in-law, Mr. George Drew, Johnson had a contact with General Vanier, who was the head of the Mission in Paris, and one day I received, through the Canadian Mission, the word: "Your mother is alive and well and is very delighted to know of your successes."

Another day, as I was walking down a corridor, he took my arm and said, "I have the impression you would like to bring your parents to this country."

"Of course I would," I said, "but it is not possible." But he arranged it so that my mother and my godfather came to America on board a Canadian troop transport with five thousand Canadian soldiers. They arrived when nobody was travelling. I will never forget him for that.

As general manager, Mr. Johnson gave the whole Metropolitan Opera House a certain cozy feeling. But he could be tough. I remember one time when I was very sick. I was living at the Ansonia Hotel at the time and the Metropolitan sent me a doctor. He said I was on the verge of pneumonia and that it was out of the question for me to sing *Pelléas* in Philadelphia that night [March 21, 1944]. When I phoned Johnson and told him I would not be going to Philadelphia, he was upset. "You are working against yourself. If you don't sing in Philadelphia tonight, you won't sing at the Metropolitan at all." But after he had talked with the doctor, he understood and Raoul Jobin sang that performance.

For some reason or other, maybe lack of funds, Johnson didn't seem to be very much interested in the stage sets. Singers were his main concern. In my case he proved himself to be a real friend. And I know he could be resourceful in meeting emergencies. There was the evening in Atlanta when the costumes had not arrived for *Carmen*, and rather than disappoint the audience completely he had us start the opera in our street clothes. And I remember the time we gave *Tannhäuser* in Chicago without lights, when a boat drifting on the Chicago River had knocked down a bridge, and all the electrical connections between it and the opera house were out, and besides there was a strike! I arrived in Chicago and was told I would not play that night because there was no electricity. But

Johnson was not so easily defeated: we gave a performance at the Chicago Civic Opera House with spotlights on the stage which were activated by a barge on the Chicago River which provided just enough light for the stage, leaving the house completely dark. Johnson was there and managed to turn the whole experience into a kind of lark for everybody.

Edward Johnson never had time to worry about any one problem for long—his path was constantly strewn with them. At the end of the 1940/41 season, for example, tragedy had entered the life of one of his leading artists, the Australian soprano Marjorie Lawrence. Some time before that, the onus of helping Lauritz Melchior maintain the box office popularity of the Wagner repertoire had fallen on the able Miss Lawrence and her American colleague Helen Traubel. Both of them were winning a following for themselves. A week after Miss Lawrence's Brünnhilde in *Götterdämmerung* on March 22, 1941, she married Tom King and left for Mexico City where she was to sing. But, during a performance of *Die Walküre*, she was suddenly stricken with poliomyelitis. Although she pulled through, it seemed that she would never walk again! It was only through a remarkable combination of faith, determination and slow steady work that she was able to fight her way back to the opera stage.

There was a concert at the Metropolitan in tribute to Marjorie Lawrence on December 27, 1942, in which Miss Lawrence, seated throughout, sang the Venusberg Scene from *Tannhäuser* opposite Lauritz Melchior. Then, in the spring of 1943, singing Isolde with resounding success in the Montreal Music Festival, she proved that many of the traditional stage movements and gestures were not necessary. Finally, on March 14, 1944, Marjorie Lawrence, despite physical limitations, achieved her long-cherished dream to sing Isolde at the Metropolitan in a highly acclaimed performance.

The season for 1944/45 was announced for eighteen weeks, November 27-March 31, two less than the previous season. Subscriptions were up by 10 per cent which was a good sign. Erich Leinsdorf, having received an "honorable discharge" from the American army, was returning as guest conductor; there would be nine new members in the company, including Regina Resnik, Mimi Benzell, Blanche Thebom, Florence Kirk and Martha Lipton. Many service people were expected back from Italy, where they had experienced opera for the first time, to add to the new widely diversified audience. There were to be revivals of *Die Meistersinger*, *La Gioconda*, a new English *Le Coq d'Or* (as *The Golden Cockerel*), *Fidelio*, *Don Giovanni* and *Lohengrin*. The conducting staff would include Paul Breisach, Emil Cooper, Erich Leinsdorf,

Wilfrid Pelletier, Pietro Cimara, Bruno Walter, Karl Riedel, Frank St. Leger, Cesare Sodero and George Szell.

Again the season was not without its problems: on October 9, 1944, Johnson received a letter from Lily Pons in San Francisco apologizing because, although plans for the 1944/45 season had been set, she would not be able to appear at all. "I am going abroad to entertain the troops" was her simple statement. It was an excuse against which there was no argument.

Pons or no Pons, the Metropolitan Opera was a reality for another year, beginning with *Faust* on November 27 (Jobin, Pinza, Singher and Albanese; Pelletier conducting) and ending April 4 with *La Traviata* (Albanese, Kullmann and Leonard Warren). Mimi Benzell stepped into the coloratura roles of Philine in *Mignon* and the Queen of the Night in *The Magic Flute*; Jennie Tourel turned Rosina back to its original mezzo key; Josephine Antoine took over as Gilda in *Rigoletto*; Patrice Munsel starred in *Lucia* and then proceeded to make a hit in *Le Coq d'Or*.

A few artists were causing trouble because Eddie insisted that they confine their performances to the Metropolitan Opera House. Lawrence Tibbett and others were interested in radio and film offers that at times could have interfered with their assignments at the Metropolitan.

In the midst of the constant problems, Eddie really appreciated little notes like the one of March 21, 1945, from Fortune Gallo, the energetic little impresario of the San Carlo Opera Company:

> My appreciation for your offer of cooperation on the projected Pittsburgh Opera season. The engagement has been postponed until October next. It appears pressure was brought to bear on the local committee, and this factor together with only a short time available for promotion was the reason for the postponement. Congratulations on the marvellous season in New York, and I am sure it will be duplicated at all stops on your tour. Every Easter I have a slight indulgence in neckties and when I bought myself one I thought of one for you and hope it will serve to embellish your new Easter suit if you were lucky enough to get one.

TOWARD THE END of February, 1945, Eddie received a surprise phone call from Colonel R. Y. Eaton, cousin of the late Sir John Eaton and past president of the T. Eaton Company in Toronto. Colonel Eaton was a long-time supporter of the Toronto Conservatory of Music and a former member of the board. "Things at the Conservatory are coming to a head," he said. "We need some strong leadership—the kind that you could give better than anyone else. I think you might be interested. In

240

any case, I'd like to make an appointment for Herbert Bishop and Floyd Chalmers to come down to New York and discuss the situation with you. Can it be arranged?"

Eddie knew both men well—H. H. Bishop, chairman of the Conservatory's Board of Governors and vice-president of the Robert Simpson Company (Eaton's leading competitor in the department store business), and Floyd S. Chalmers, vice-chairman of the board of the Conservatory and executive vice-president of Maclean-Hunter Publishing Company Limited. He also knew they were both extremely interested in the cultural welfare of Canada.

With his Metropolitan Opera contract coming up for renewal, but with no definite decisions made, Eddie told Colonel Eaton: "It would be a new kind of challenge—a chance to open up the opportunities for young people, and a chance to create greater public interest in music in Canada. Yes, I would be interested in talking with them. Send them down."

So the appointment was made, and the momentous meeting took place two days later. Bishop and Chalmers filled Johnson in on the background of the situation, much of which he already knew, although somewhat superficially. He knew, for example, that the Conservatory in Toronto was the most important national school of music in Canada and the largest in the Commonwealth. Founded in 1886 and operated under the direction of the University since 1921, the Conservatory had been not only self-supporting, but able, until 1937, to contribute tidy surpluses as well, mainly through its national examinations system.

He knew also that Sir Ernest MacMillan had been principal of the Conservatory from 1926 until his resignation in 1942, and was still dean of the Faculty of Music of the University of Toronto, a post he had held since 1927. Sir Ernest had organized a student chorus his first year at the Conservatory and had made several attempts to introduce opera productions there. Norman Wilks had succeeded Sir Ernest as principal in September, 1942, and had held the position until he died two years later (November 20, 1944). Since that time the highly esteemed organist and teacher Dr. Charles Peaker had been acting as director of the Conservatory.

"What about the Hutcheson plan?" Eddie asked his visitors. "What has been done about that?"

Chalmers handed Johnson the lengthy 1944 report on the history and future plans of the Conservatory. It incorporated most of the suggestions made in 1937 by Dr. Ernest Hutcheson, distinguished pianist and president of the Juillard School of Music, and had been approved by the board for presentation to the University's Board of Governors. The original report from Dr. Hutcheson had been the result of the Conservatory's request for an independent study of the Conservatory situation by the Carnegie Foundation. The 1944 Chalmers-Hutcheson report suggested:

(1) the establishment of a senior professional school to be integrated, in time, with the University's Faculty of Music;

(2) a new building, toward which the Massey Foundation had pledged $1-million; and

(3) a regular annual grant from the University which, in turn, would be reimbursed by the province.

Eddie could see the future possibilities for making a major contribution to music and music education in Canada. He was interested. But he explained that as long as he was at the Metropolitan he would not be able to involve himself in the day-to-day problems of the Conservatory. They understood, and returned to Toronto with the feeling that their mission had been successful.

When advised of these overtures on the part of the Conservatory, the board of the Metropolitan seemed reluctant to endorse any such outside appointment that might encroach on the time of their general manager. They gave their approval only after Eddie, in negotiating a new two-year contract in May, 1945, assured them that the Opera House would come first. The stipulation was made that he would be on the Conservatory Board "by courtesy of the Metropolitan Opera Association, Inc."

On the political scene, there was more cause for optimism than there had been for some time. The V-E Day celebrations of May 8, 1945, marked victory in Europe, and everyone was predicting that the war would be over before the end of the year. So it was with a light heart that Eddie faced contract negotiations, union discussions, casting problems and the finalizing of plans for the 1945/46 season at the Metropolitan.

But Eddie kept his eye on matters other than the opera, particularly in Canada. On June 6, 1945, he wrote to George McCullagh, publisher of Toronto's *Globe and Mail*: "Now that the smoke of battle has cleared away, but before the din and aftermath subsides, let me express my unbounded admiration for the uncompromising attitude taken by you and your estimable newspaper in the recent political campaign." He could heartily applaud the editorials, he said, and was certain that McCullagh's "stirring radio address had an immediate and decisive effect on the listening public, and was in no small measure responsible for the overwhelming victory for the Drew government." He suggested that Mc-

242

Cullagh should enter politics where they needed men of his calibre, who would "not be dissuaded by the fear of being exposed to the vicious and malignant attacks of hoodlums and gangsters. As a Canadian citizen—long absent but always loyal—I salute you, Defender of Right and Decency."

On reading about George Drew's success in the Ontario provincial elections, Eddie immediately sent congratulations. The reply, June 23, 1945, gave him much cause for joy:

> . . . Now so many of the things we have discussed and in which we believe so strongly are possible of achievement for the first time. Fiorenza has been wonderful. She emerged as an important public figure in this election and I wish you could have heard the applause she received at the great meeting at Massey Hall the Friday after the provincial election. When she was asked by the chairman to stand, she received an ovation which left no doubt about the extent to which she has left her impression on the minds of our people. Now she is doing splendid work on the committee which is conducting the campaign for $6-million to build a new Hospital for Sick Children, and I find that she is being sought and consulted for so many important tasks that I must try to prevent her doing too much.
>
> We have never been so happy as we are now and it seems that we are beginning a period of real achievement in a partnership that has been strengthened not only by our experience but to an extent you may not realize by your understanding and encouragement. I just want to thank you from the bottom of my heart for what you said and to try to convey a little of what it means to have your constant support and advice.
>
> Affectionately,<br>George

In July, Edward Johnson's new two-year contract as general manager of the Metropolitan was announced. He was happy in spite of the great strains connected with the office: constant problems, dissentions, compromises, hostilities, lack of understanding and vision where he most needed encouragement and backing. On the other hand, he realized these were some of the penalties for being at the top where he enjoyed a wealth of deep friendships, opportunities for accomplishment and much appreciation. Among the many letters of thanks for fine evenings at the opera was one from Mrs. Harry Truman and her daughter Margaret. And after reading the Metropolitan's June report on operations, Edgar Kobak, president of the Mutual Broadcasting System, sent Eddie con-

243

gratulations, July 27, 1945, on the fine showing for his ten years as general manager. Kobak hoped to have the opportunity of working closely with him again in the interest of broadcasting the Opera. He said he could "look out of his window on the twentieth floor of 1440 Broadway with longing eyes toward the Opera House."

Although there had been optimism in the spring that all hostilities would soon end, war clouds still darkened the Pacific skies. The climax came on August 6 when the United States dropped the first atomic bomb, on Hiroshima. The world was shocked and horrified. During subsequent weeks there was a prevailing fear of the awesome power of the bomb. No one could predict what was going to happen. Opera was about the last thing on anyone's mind. But the job of the general manager was to keep the Metropolitan going.

Preparations for launching the new season took all of Eddie's time and energy. Only at the end of August was he able to join the Drews for a holiday at their country home in Caledon, Ontario. Writing to Fiorenza after he returned to New York, he said:

> *Carissima amore—*
> It has been a lovely holiday and I've enjoyed it no end. We did so many interesting and exciting things that the time passed all too quickly. Not long enough in Guelph—nevertheless so delightful— and the children so very amusing and entertaining. George has been so thoughtful and devoted so much of his time even in his busy life and Tata has been so sweet and attentive as she has through all these many years. You have been your own sweet self and what more can I say. Thank you, my darling, and bless you all!
> Babbo
> P.S. Here is a little gift to get yourself something.

Such moments were oases in the desert.

By this time, the skies were beginning to brighten. Japan had admitted defeat on August 14. On September 2, 1945, came the signing of the unconditional surrender.

THE WAR WAS OVER. Foundations for a world community of united nations had been laid. But there was mounting tension between the countries that had emerged as the two leading powers—the U.S. and the U.S.S.R.—that would delay world peace for some time. On the periphery of things, Eddie had a rapid on-again off-again kind of exchange with New York City officials. On October 1 there was a Western Union telegram from Grover A. Whalen, Chairman of the Mayor's Committee: "Mayor F. H. La Guardia will give an official luncheon in honor of Marshal Georgi K. Zhukov, Marshal of the Soviet Union, on Friday,

October fifth at one fifteen P.M. at the Waldorf-Astoria. You are cordially invited to be the mayor's guest on this occasion. Telegraphic replies must be received not later than Tuesday October second."

A second telegram from Grover Whalen, on October 2, read: "Marshal Zhukov's illness will prevent his arrival in New York on October fifth. The President has extended an invitation to Marshal Zhukov to visit the United States later in October. Accordingly, all official plans are cancelled for October fifth." And that ended that.

Eddie was relieved. He hadn't looked forward to such a large official function. He was still upset over the death of his close friend and colleague, John McCormack, on September 16. James McCormack, of Ardmore, Pennsylvania, wrote him early in October: "Dear Eddie: I saw you at John's Requiem Mass at St. Patrick's and I was very deeply touched by this evidence of your affection for him. His death came as a great shock to me as only a few weeks ago I had a happy cheerful letter from him telling me he never felt better in his life. . . . John had a genuine affection for you and the highest respect and esteem as a fellow artist. Thanks for remembering dear John by paying this tribute to his memory."

On October 25, 1945, Edward Johnson was appointed to the Board of Governors of the University of Toronto, "to meet a need long recognized for a man on the Board with experience and knowledge in the field of music," as President Sidney Smith said in his announcement. He added, "It is expected that the University, with the direct benefit of Mr. Johnson's leadership, will play an even greater role in musical education."

The following month, at the annual Board of Governors meeting of the Toronto Conservatory of Music, November 29, 1945, Edward Johnson was appointed chairman of that Board. "I am very happy and very complimented," he said in his official statement from New York. "Toronto is one of the most musical cities in the Western Hemisphere and I have great hopes for the development of musical talent there."

The Toronto *Globe and Mail* called it the first major step in a program intended to bring about a closer integration of the Conservatory and the University.

Johnson had missed the annual meeting at the University in November when Colonel Eric Phillips, the new chairman of the University's Board of Governors, had expressed the opinion that the Conservatory had no need for a large board. Several of the long-term members of the Conservatory Board had then been ruthlessly dropped and there were many ruffled feelings.

When Eddie arrived in Toronto to preside over his first Conservatory

Board meeting, on December 17, 1945, he found himself in hot water. It was up to him to devise a way of easing the situation for the people whose names had been unceremoniously deleted. Always the diplomat and reconciler, he proposed the creation of a National Advisory Committee, to consist of all the people who had been dropped from the Conservatory Board, along with all personalities of importance in music in Canada. (It was a face-saving device that worked, even though the prestigious committee members—Lady Eaton, Jean Beaudet, Leslie Bell and Vincent Massey, among others—never once met, and the Committee was never mentioned again!)

The following day, December 18, addressing a special Christmas luncheon of the Canadian Club at the Royal York Hotel, Eddie announced his long-term plan for making Toronto a musical centre, pointing up the overall need for the teaching of music and for cooperation between the University's Faculty of Music and the Conservatory. "The plan is really a three-way street," he explained. "We want music taught, per se, as culture; we want to develop an understanding and sympathetic public; and we want to provide the best teaching and opportunities for our talent."

During the fall of 1945, Dr. Ettore Mazzoleni, who had come to Canada from England in 1929 and was on the teaching staff of both Upper Canada College and the Conservatory, was appointed principal of the Toronto Conservatory of Music. At the same time, Dr. Arnold Walter, Head of the Music Department at Upper Canada College, was appointed vice-principal, responsible for organizing and directing the new Senior School which he, himself, had suggested in 1944.

Whenever he was in Toronto that winter of 1945/46, Eddie found himself talking mainly with Walter and Mazzoleni and seldom, if ever, with Charles Peaker, Conservatory Director. So when Peaker retired in 1946, there was little change insofar as Eddie was concerned. Mazzoleni became chief administrative officer, with the continuing title of principal, and Walter, as vice-principal, was assigned the task of introducing new ideas and working out a plan of cooperation between the Conservatory and the University. "Johnson had to approve of everything I did," Walter explained years later, "and he had to help work things out and to understand what I was trying to do. He had to get his prestige back of things, too, you know."

There was a continuing rivalry, of a kind, between Mazzoleni and Walter, with Johnson seeing more of Walter, primarily because of his interest in the development of high-level professional courses. One of Walter's first moves was to take four of the best teachers from the

246

Conservatory's one hundred and eighty for his new Senior School. It was becoming integrated, gradually, with the Faculty of Music which, in turn, could offer a music degree. "I think the other one hundred and seventy-six started hating me immediately," Walter admitted, "but I wanted to get this whole sprawling enterprise organized. The fact that I was able to build up the Faculty as it is—if you look around the Edward Johnson Building—was an absolute miracle, because they always resisted me. They thought I was out to take the bread out of their mouths. The second thing I did, and Johnson was with me every step of the way on both things, was to establish, in 1946, the Opera School. We were both looking for outlets for the kids."

The cooperation between these two men took Dr. Walter to New York on many occasions. It was his task, he always said, to act as go-between and help iron out any difficulties occasioned by the fact that Johnson was in New York, as general manager of the Metropolitan, and therefore not in daily contact with the complex problems at the Conservatory in Toronto.

I usually went to New York to see him whenever something of importance had to be discussed. If Johnson agreed with my proposal, and generally he did, he would then go to the president of the University and say what he thought of it. Some of our meetings were very funny. We would go into his office and I would sit myself down and he would be very affable, and then, just as we would be about to start on the subject I'd come to talk about, somebody like Mr. Björling would come in and take his time and Johnson would have to charm him because he was complaining about this or that very bitterly. Then, after Johnson got him out, we would talk for maybe ten minutes and Frank St. Leger would come in. And by the time he was out, or there had been one or two other interruptions, it would be time for the performance and Johnson would say "Come with me and we'll sit in the box," and maybe it was something he had to watch. Then maybe Frank would turn up again with some backstage emergency, and we would go back to the office. I would try again to tell him what was so terribly important. Then we would go back for the second act of the opera—and finally the day was over and the great man went home!

That happened so often that finally he said, "Look, Walter, why don't we start at lunchtime?" So we would meet at his flat on Madison Avenue at noon and go to the Coffee Club. It was good and inexpensive and nobody bothered us—and that is where and how we finally managed to meet and talk things out. Of course he would usually suggest we continue at the Met because, after all, that was his first job and I knew I had to be sandwiched in. And that is the way it went until he retired from the Met and took up residence in Guelph.

The truth must be told, though, that he was very skeptical about the Conservatory as it was set up. He felt that the progress and development was all on the side of the Faculty, which was true.

"Arnold," he told me one day, "I want to divide the Conservatory and the Faculty completely. Let the Conservatory continue what it is doing—every child in Toronto, or for that matter in Canada, must have an opportunity for the day-to-day teaching, the lower part of the teaching."

I pointed out that conservatories in Germany, France, Russia, England (there they call them academies) don't bother about the lower part of teaching. They take students who need only four or five years of finishing.

But Eddie said, "It's too late to change things here. The Faculty can serve that need, and that is what I am going to propose."

I had to smile to myself for that was my idea exactly, but I knew it couldn't be accomplished overnight.

AN ARGUMENT between AGMA (American Guild of Musical Artists) and the members of the Metropolitan chorus threatened to jeopardize the 1945/46 season of opera. It developed when AGMA suspended a chorister and the rest of the chorus served notice they would attend no more rehearsals until that particular member was reinstated. A lockout followed. Eddie's diplomacy and powers of persuasion proved effective and an amicable agreement was finally reached.

A Special Preview Performance of *Roméo et Juliette* took place on November 23, 1945, with Raoul Jobin and Patrice Munsel in the title roles. It was sponsored by the Metropolitan Opera Guild as a "Benefit for the Production Fund." *Lohengrin*, which officially opened the season three nights later, had Helen Traubel as Elsa, with tenor Torsten Ralf and conductor Fritz Busch both making their Met débuts. "We have two winners," Eddie proudly proclaimed, after the papers had lavished praise on the two newcomers. "The Metropolitan has acquired, in Swedish tenor Torsten Ralf, a tenor better suited to the lyric Wagner roles than any singer heard here in a score of years," wrote one reviewer, while another stated, "[Mr. Busch's] personal immersion in the proceedings was felt from the very beginning of the prelude and lent the performance a sense of life and intensity it could not otherwise attain. . . ."

That was also the season that Canadian soprano Pierrette Alarie was heard at the Metropolitan Opera for the first time, making her début, December 8, 1945, as Oscar in *Un ballo in maschera*. Miss Alarie had warm recollections of her days at the Metropolitan and of Edward Johnson.

My teacher, Elisabeth Schumann, arranged an audition with Mr. Johnson at the Met for those Sunday afternoon Metropolitan Opera Auditions of the Air. I was scared, but he gave me a marvellous smile—he had such a warm smile and such warm eyes, and he was such a good-looking man. Oh, he was fantastic. That's about all I remember. I was too excited to observe everything. But I can remember very well when I made my début at the Met. I signed the contract in his office and he told me I was the first French Canadian woman to get into the Met in his regime and that he was pleased about that. They took a picture then, and Robert Merrill was there —he came to the Met that same year—and Johnson insisted that I stand on a chair. He told them, "That's my first French Canadian and she's so tiny we must bring her up somehow."

I made my début under the direction of Bruno Walter, with Zinka Milanov, Leonard Warren, Jan Peerce—you know, all those big ones—and I really felt small and tiny. But Johnson supervised the rehearsals. He was always there with good words and he told me he wanted me to make my début in *Ballo*, that I was just the type to sing Oscar. He was such a professional person and he was so artistic and so considerate. It was very inspiring for all the artists to have such a director.

There was not one single performance that he wouldn't come backstage to every dressing room beforehand and give us a kiss and a *bocca al lupo*. It was such a good feeling. He really wanted you to do your best.

Once, in his office, he said to me, "You know, Pierrette, you are very young and you are beginning, and the roles I will give you will suit you, but you will have to learn properly how to move on the stage. A singer can only move so much, so it has to mean much. How would you like to go to a dramatic coach?"

I was proud and excited, and he said, "I'll send you there, to Grace Christy [who specialized in mime]. You won't have to pay; this is our business and I want all the youngsters to do such things." And he sent many of us there for posture.

I was coaching all the big roles—Lucia, Lakmé—and he insisted that I work those specific parts with the mime so cadenzas would express something, not be just vocalizing. Then he had all of us beginners go over our roles with the same stage directors who were working with the big stars.

He came to one of my coaching lessons for Lucia one time. I was working on the big aria, the Mad Scene, and I was very nervous. But he listened all through. Then he said, just very nicely,

"Well, it's coming, it's coming quite well, but Pierrette, you are not ready." I felt a bit surprised because I had worked a lot on the part and I thought, as we all do when we begin, that I was more ready than that.

When I went back home, I remembered that he had given an explanation to what he had said: "Vocally, you are not ready to attempt such a big part yet. Because you are not ready vocally, you cannot express yourself stagewise; you're not relaxed enough to express everything you should, especially in this Mad Scene." But he kept on giving me lessons. I had coaching on the whole of Rosina, Lucia, Gilda and Lakmé, because I was then the understudy for Pons since we were the same size. It was a big opportunity for me, because she never came to rehearsals.

He gave me few roles, but he gave me the ones I could do: Olympia in *Les Contes d'Hoffmann*, Blonda in the Met's first production, in English, of the *Abduction from the Seraglio*, and the part of Xenia with Pinza in *Boris*.

He was such a perfect gentleman in every sense—his look, his way of dressing, his way of addressing his words. Everything was so clean. And on the stage, for him it had to be the same thing. He had a noblesse; he could not stand anything on the stage looking sloppy.

He liked it when some of the singers would give imitations— Nicola Moscona, for example, imitated St. Leger and Toscanini and all the big artists—and Johnson would laugh like mad—that was the kind of thing he really enjoyed.

The last time I saw him in New York was in 1947 when I went to tell him I was going to the Paris Opéra where I would have a chance to work with [Louis] Fourestier, the French conductor. He was awfully pleased and said, "That's the thing for you to do."

I just saw him one other time after that. It was at a Met performance in Toronto in 1958 and someone told me he was backstage, and I said I must see him. So I ran backstage and I saw him. He was exactly the same except that he was walking with a cane, and I just threw my arms around his neck and he just grabbed me and said, "Well, you're still a tiny little cabbage." It was a very short meeting because there were a lot of people there, so I really couldn't talk with him much. And that was the last time I saw him.

Eddie was used to facing problems at the Metropolitan, but once that winter of 1945/46, when the Company was presenting *Tannhäuser* in Philadelphia, there was a triple crisis: tenor Lauritz Melchior, bass-baritone Herbert Janssen and soprano Helen Traubel were all ill at once, and Torsten Ralf, Alexander Sved and Astrid Varnay had to be located and called in at the last minute to take over.

It sometimes seemed to Eddie as though he was leading two lives, with one foot in New York, or wherever the Met happened to be performing, and one in Toronto. He managed to attend five of the eight 1946 meetings of the Board of Directors of the Conservatory. "Not a bad record, if I do say so myself," he thought. Meanwhile, he was lucky in that Floyd Chalmers, whose business took him to New York several times a year, could act as a sort of liaison officer between Johnson at the Met and the Board of the Conservatory in Toronto. Chalmers later recalled:

> Johnson would set aside an hour for me in the morning and provide seats in his private box every evening. . . . He was particularly proud of his young Americans, and he was happy too about the Metropolitan's contribution to the training of the other young singers, waiting, so to speak, in the wings. "And many of them are Canadian," he would remind me.
>
> During many an intermission that winter, he took me up to the second and third balconies where the advanced students—the ones "waiting in the wings"—could sit on high stools and make notes in their scores during performances. He knew them all. "Here is a young man I want you to watch," Johnson would say. "He is going to be one of our great singers." I didn't make note of all the names, but I remember one young man whose personality I particularly liked. That was Jerome Hines, who amply fulfilled Johnson's prediction.

Long after Jerome Hines had become a world-renowned artist, he was reminiscing one time about his early years at the Met:

> My most vivid memories of Edward Johnson are backstage where, during a performance, he would come up to us, always with a helpful suggestion either artistic or vocal. "Why did you open that D Natural on an *a* vowel?" he asked me once. "Never mind that Pinza does it that way. For him it's all right but *you* should cover it." This sort of gentle but positive suggestion was most valuable. It was a rare experience to have a successful retired opera star as manager.
>
> He would often begin an address with "Making speeches is like having babies. They are easy to conceive and hard to deliver." He had a rare sense of humour at all times. Once when I was in his office, he told me they had just received an audition record from an up-and-coming tenor, and he said he'd like to play it for me and get my opinion of it. I listened and said, "It's a very good voice, but wouldn't it be best to hear him in this house first before giving him a contract?" He burst out laughing and handed me the record. The name was Edoardo di Giovanni—Edward Johnson's stage

251

name in Italy! Fortunately, I had not put my foot in it. By the way, he always introduced me as his "baby"—and I was six feet six, but I was, at the time, the Met's youngest member.

Johnson's thoughtfulness towards RCA head David Sarnoff brought a warm reply, on February 27, 1946: "Dear Ed, Many, many thanks for your kind telegram and good wishes which I deeply appreciate. . . . I went without sleep for seventy-two hours but I didn't break my previous record—in 1912—when the *Titanic* sank. I was a wireless operator then and I'd rather be at the key now than handle tugboat and transit strikes. But all's well that ends well. Thank you again, my friend. Sincerely, Dave." It was to the long-range vision of David Sarnoff that Edward Johnson largely attributed the success of the Metropolitan's radio broadcasts.

Springtime meant another spring tour, and Eddie, writing to Fiorenza from Boston, April 8, sent her a list of his hotels, adding: "Three cities in a week made the time seem long! Tonight we sing *Magic Flute*, and tomorrow *Meistersinger*, and I hope the press will be a little less critical. I am somewhat resentful of the 100 per cent perfectionists who have no responsibility. So what!"

The 1946 tour took the company from Boston to Philadelphia, Rochester, Cleveland, Bloomington, Minneapolis, Milwaukee, Chicago, St. Louis, Dallas, Memphis and Chattanooga, and resulted, as usual, in many incidents that were sometimes nerve-wracking and sometimes humorous. To the older members, it was "just another tour." But to the younger ones it was a new and wonderful experience in which Edward Johnson featured prominently. One of those was soprano Dorothy Kirsten.

> The first thing I think of when I think of Edward Johnson now, looking back after all these years, is the difference between him and most general managers—he had a warmth, and imbued every artist with confidence. He was always at the opera early, and always came backstage. As young artists we needed that, when we were shaking all over with fright about going on that stage. He was the greatest friend to the young artist.
>
> I remember the first tour we went on—I was the bright shining new soprano at the Met, and the tour is always very exciting, as you know. Pinza was on that tour. My room was between Johnson's and Pinza's, and they kept putting notes under my door all night, trying to get me to let them come in. It was fun—a big joke. I would hear Pinza at the door, then Johnson's voice, and I remember I was scared to death. I whispered through the door and asked them what they thought they were doing, and Johnson said, "I'm

252

trying to protect you from this great hero on the train." That was quite a night and I had no sleep. Later, we had to change my room.

But Johnson was a great ladies' man and he thought I was just "it" that year. He certainly had the spark, and I mean spark, that gets absolutely the top performance out of an artist. If he had been younger and more my age, I would have fallen madly for him. People used to say that he never joked on stage, but he told me that one time in *Bohème* he filled a singer's cap with water just for the laughs when the man put it on. "Artists had a lot more fun then, playing tricks on each other all the time," he said.

One evening I came to the opera house, I remember, and I had a cold and didn't think I could sing. I did my vocalizing, and he came in and said, "Your voice sounds fantastic. I know you can do it." He always sent me flowers. He was wonderful, and in that atmosphere artists sing one hell of a lot better.

There was happiness in the House.

On May 15, while in St. Louis on tour with the Metropolitan, Eddie wrote exuberantly to Fiorenza: "Over 30,000 people in three shows and $105,000 box office. Incredible! Everybody happy including music critics. Today we are off to Dallas over the weekend, and next week this time we will be back in New York. Sorry not to be together with you on May 24th and tell Tata I'll be thinking of you all. I spoke to her on Sunday—she was so surprised she could hardly talk. Give my love to George and the kiddies—and to Tata." It was while the Company was in Dallas, performing *Roméo et Juliette*, that someone asked Johnson, "Why don't you sing anymore? Have you lost your voice?" Eddie's reply came fast: "Oh no, I haven't lost my voice! But I gave away my purple tights."

The words and sense of humour were typical of the man to whom a Memphis paper that spring gave the headline "Long Struggle of Impresario Has Made 'Met' Democratic," and for whom, the following December, *Time* magazine coined the phrase "the Johnson Era." The Met's general manager was quoted in the latter publication as saying: "Reaching the public has been a long, slow, painful, expensive process, but I believe we have done it."

That summer, Eddie visited Lucrezia Bori at her place, *Bori Isle*, on Blue Mountain Lake, Hamilton County, New York. It was quite an experience, as he recapped in a letter to Fiorenza on August 18: "Mr. Bliss and I left New York on Friday at 8:45 A.M. in a grey overcast sky and landed here at Blue Mountain Lake in a downpour. The showers were unimportant but by the time we reached the mountains it came down in torrents . . . but today is truly superb. The kind of weather one hopes for and seldom gets. . . . Bori is her own boatman, but has an excellent French couple and a housemaid. She unfortunately is on crutches, having broken a small bone in her left foot. In spite of this inconvenience she is active and gay as ever and is a charming and delightful hostess."

WHEN EDDIE RETURNED to New York after visiting Bori, he found a letter in his mail that was indicative of the kind of rapport he had with the chorus members, workmen and staff of the Metropolitan: "Dear Mr. Johnson—I sincerely regret that I will not be with the Metropolitan Opera Chorus this coming year as I have accepted a position with the Associated Concert Bureau. I am most thankful for the very fine association I have had with the management of the Metropolitan Opera, and it will serve me in good stead in my present position. Thanks again, Mr. Johnson, and with best wishes I am, Sincerely yours, Anton Schubel."

The chorister received an immediate reply: ". . . No one regrets more than the general manager that you will be absent from the Metropolitan Opera Chorus next season. Your leadership while you were the chorus representative, your sincerity and understanding did much to maintain a sense of discipline and to inspire a spirit of cooperation in the choral group. The management wishes to express its deep appreciation of your valuable services and to convey its deep regret that you will not be with the organization during the coming season."

Perhaps no place were Edward Johnson's aims and feelings better expressed than in the article that appeared in the *Guelph Daily Mercury* of September 7, 1946: "I love Canada and I love music. I want to bring the two together. I want to share my knowledge and experience with the people of my own country. I'm not interested in building up music in Canada as a nationalistic art. For me, music is universal. It is as important to good citizenship as reading, writing and arithmetic. In a world that must soon face a sharp reduction in working hours, with the consequent creation of much more leisure time, it seems to me that music, both in its cultural and economic aspects, can help us solve one of our most baffling problems, enrich our lives immeasurably, and make us better citizens—perhaps better world citizens."

Often accused of being stingy, Johnson nevertheless gave generously to what he considered worthy causes and was a sentimentalist when it came to remembering family anniversaries and birthdays. It was not unusual on September 11, 1946, for the Drews to receive an envelope marked "To be opened September 12th." The enclosed note read: "Dear George and Fiorenza—To celebrate your tenth anniversary, won't you add the enclosed as a small contribution towards your new home.

254

May the next decade be as happy and successful as the past one and *così in crescendo*. Thank you both and the children for all the care and affection you have bestowed on Gogo—and bless you all (which includes Tata). *Tante cose dal cuore*. Babbo."

Fiorenza's reply was heartwarming: "You have been our greatest comfort. To know that you are there with your wonderful warmth and understanding ear, your keen brain, your infallible intuition—to know that we could counsel with you in our moments of doubt, of disappointment and of joy of accomplishment—that has been the greatest gift of all. . . ." Then referring to her father's ever-present union problems: "You are on our minds, always, but most particularly with all the troubles you have on your hands. We are both most anxious to hear the outcome of your meetings and to know what will happen to the Met this winter."

One of Johnson's first activities on the Toronto scene that season, as chairman of the Board of Governors of the Conservatory and a member of the University's Board of Governors, was to address the students of the Conservatory on October 28, 1946. "The Toronto Conservatory of Music," he reminded everyone, "has a glorious tradition of which it may well be proud. It has a firm faith in its future and it has, in its successful present, an excellent faculty and a fine executive staff. I should like to publicly express my thanks and appreciation to the members of the Board who have so ably and faithfully sustained me in organizing the new era of the Conservatory, and without whose help I feel sure I could never have proceeded with the undertaking. . . ."

He spoke of "the great advantage" of having the counsel and advice of the dean of the Faculty of Music, Sir Ernest MacMillan, and of the good fortune of the Conservatory in having for its principal Dr. Ettore Mazzoleni, a man of splendid qualities as organizer and leader, well worthy of following in the footsteps of his great predecessors, Sir Ernest MacMillan and the late Norman Wilks. Then he commented on his own policy which he hoped would result in making the Conservatory "the cradle of the musical life of the province." He referred to Dr. Mazzoleni's associate, Dr. Arnold Walter, as "a man of wide experience and vision . . . founder of the Senior School, whose purpose it is to provide the necessary training for especially gifted students who wish to enter the musical profession."

No hint of the behind-the-scenes turbulence, already apparent, crept into his words as he addressed the young people who had come from all parts of the province. "You must come here believing in yourself," he warned them, "believing that you are going to be a great musician, a great singer, a great instrumentalist, a great artist. And I say 'great' advisedly, because if you do not have the faith that you will become great, then you had better pack your bag and go home."

While dealing with many other matters that fall, Edward Johnson was constantly involved in the preparations at the Met for the world première of the new opera *The Warrior* by Norman Corwin and Bernard Rogers, set for January 11. It was a treatment of the Samson and Delilah story, and Johnson had great hopes that it would be one of the hits of the 1946/47 season. But he was due for a disappointment. The words of one of the critics reflected the general reaction: "Fifteen minutes of this is absorbing; an hour of it, monotony."

In the contents of a letter from George Sloan that came shortly after this, Eddie found an effective antidote to the discouragement of the moment:

> Dear Eddie:
>
> There is something that I have wanted to say to you for some time past, and after last evening's performance and again this afternoon I am not going to wait any longer.
>
> I have always felt that the loyalty of the artists, including the members of the orchestra, is one of the more precious assets of the Metropolitan. That perhaps more than anything else is responsible for the position that the organization occupies today, and can be responsible for still greater success.
>
> This year I have been increasingly impressed with the wonderful way in which everyone on the stage and in the pit rallies to the support of the company when one or more leading artists are indisposed.
>
> Last evening Leonard Warren seemed to sense an added responsibility and lived up to it handsomely. Ditto this afternoon with John Brownlee, Miss Browning, Kullmann, De Paolis et al, in both singing and acting. And the members of the orchestra at both performances seemed to give us that extra something which makes one forget the disappointments over last moment replacements.
>
> To me such performances are the most thrilling—for they portray a spirit that makes the rest of us happy to be associated with you and your fine family. Well done!
>
> Ever sincerely,
> Geo. A. Sloan

Although he had the loyalty and support of the artists, Eddie still faced financial problems that made every season questionable. Howard Taubman, writing in the "Guide to Listening Pleasure" in the *New York Times Magazine*, February 23, 1947, said that music organizations generally were considering asking the federal government for aid, probably in the form of a repeal of the 20 per cent tax on admissions. The Metropolitan's deficit that season had been $220,000, but the Opera had given the federal government over $300,000 in admission taxes for New York performances and another $150,000 for tour performances. Relief from the tax burden would mean a new lease on life for the Opera that had had capacity audiences for almost every performance of the post-war seasons, at top ticket prices in New York of $7.50.

Mr. Taubman also gave what he called a "Prescription for a New Kind of Opera." "It is certain," he wrote, "that the Metropolitan will have two homes—one in New York and the other in Los Angeles. On the west coast $25,000,000 is being raised to build a new cultural development, with an opera house at its center. . . ." The Metropolitan tour was scheduled to include Los Angeles in the spring of 1948. At the same time, Mr. Taubman discussed the need for a new opera house in New York and made some personal recommendations for the future— without once mentioning Edward Johnson!

Eddie noticed the omission, but that was the least of his worries. In the early spring he wrote to Fiorenza from the Ritz Carlton in Boston: "Our troubles have lightened for the moment, the stage hands having discovered that they had gone too far. The showdown will come next week in New York. I may not be able to come to the Conservatory meeting on April 1st after all. The performances have gone well here and all sold out. Where the money comes from heaven alone knows! *Otello* tonight, the only one that 'hesitated' at the box office."

Union negotiations in New York were especially difficult and sometimes bitter early in the spring of 1947. When there was finally an agreement Eddie made a public statement: "Let me compliment the press for the very able way it handled our labour problems this summer —especially that of the chorus. It was a delicate situation. Our greatest problem was to make the unions realize that the Board of Directors meant what they said—that they would close the Met, if necessary, rather than yield to impossible conditions—and that the Association would really abandon the opera season, 'unless.' "

All things to all people? How is it possible, Eddie wondered, as he signed a new two-year contract that was "more or less" to his satisfaction, "from June 1, 1947, to May 31, 1949, at the annual salary of thirty-five thousand dollars ($35,000)." His services were to include all duties as in the past, "and such other and additional services as the Board of Directors may request." Acting in accordance with instructions by the Board, and with the Board's approval, he was to "have authority over the whole personnel and service, artistic, administrative, and technical, without distinction," and all appointments and contracts were to be

257

made by him. The agreement included a trip to Europe, when required, for which the Association would provide him with two first-class round trip passages.

The job of general manager provided many compensations, but there were times when Eddie would have been willing to resign. Above all, he felt the board was strangling him with its tight money policies. For years it had been necessary, but now the war was over and the country was getting back on its feet. With money around, people were buying opera tickets again.

In contract negotiations in 1945, Eddie had stipulated certain conditions and had threatened to resign if they were not met. A *Liberty* magazine article on Edward Johnson as the "Personality of the Week" now quoted him as saying that he had tried to retire in 1945, had agreed to stay on, but was going to retire at the end of the 1948/49 season. He was described as 5 feet 8 inches tall, weighing 150 pounds, and "ageless." According to the article, he liked to read himself to sleep at night, preferring biographies, had been reliable as a singer, and was strictly a "no tantrums" director whose usual tactic in handling prima donna crises was to burst into laughter.

A note at this time from former diva Marguerita Sylva in Van Nuys, California, recalled the happy times she and Eddie had shared when they were both concert artists.

> Dear Ed:
> I know it all comes from you—those roses and bouquets that are being thrown to me from the Temple of Opera, while I am still alive. Thank you. I have not forgotten our wonderful association singing together at the Bowl—I pass it every day and think of you, and poor Henri Scott now departed. "Those were the days."
> I am slowly entering pictures—starting on the 23rd April on my first "real break" at Columbia. It may be a start. It was well worth waiting for, although I am so situated that I can live in quiet and peace just looking at the gorgeous hills of California and listening to the opera on Saturday. How lovely! and how I enjoy it. And sometimes you speak and I say "Hello, Ed."
> Thank you again.
>
> Sylva

For several months Eddie had been worried about Fiorenza, who was fighting some sort of baffling illness. The disease was finally diagnosed as jaundice and a complete rest ordered. Following the doctor's prescription was impossible for Fiorenza whose responsibilities and mental energies always drove her on. Writing her from Chicago, April

258

24, Eddie said, "Sorry the progress is so slow and can understand how impatient you must feel. But be glad it is clearing up and that no bad effects will linger on." He hoped the adjournment of the House would be giving her some respite. (Fiorenza, as the premier's wife, was unavoidably involved in public life while the House was sitting.) "I'm sure the sessions have been strenuous for you."

Eddie had feared he would be forced to make a trip back to New York about tour problems, and said he was relieved that Marks Levine was coming to Chicago instead to discuss the 1948 tour "since the auditoriums in the various cities where we appear are already being booked. Any decisions must be made." He added: "Also, a big reception for the Metropolitan was given yesterday at the Casino Club, which didn't finish until nearly seven o'clock. My hand was shaken off by hundreds of old and new friends. I was exhausted. . . . The season is ahead of last year by about $15,000 which augurs well." He had scrawled across the top of the letter, "My new stationery, please!" The letterhead carried the crest of The Canadian Society of New York, with "Edward Johnson, President, 147 West 39th Street, New York 18."

Election to the presidency of The Canadian Society of New York that year had been a greater honour to Edward Johnson (who never quite escaped from the feeling he'd have to "show them") than were many of the other important distinctions constantly being showered upon him. He also took great pride in being photographed at a Maple Leaf dinner in New York with Canadian Consul General Hugh Scully, General Crerar and Canada's Under-Secretary of State for External Affairs, Lester B. Pearson.

That summer Eddie was again invited to the Grove in California for a "stimulating, interesting and amusing, and tiring" week. "Only the champagne air keeps one going," he wrote Fiorenza, July 28, 1947. "I've met many old friends and many important figures, political and financial. Mr. Hoover is here, Governor Stassen and Governor Green of Illinois (a possible future vice-president). Dewey is expected, but doubtful. Admirals, generals, railway tycoons—all out to have *fun*."

IT WAS A TERRIBLE blow to Johnson when Edward Ziegler died on October 24, 1947. "Neddie" had been his right arm for so many years at the Metropolitan, a man without whose backing and counsel Eddie never could have managed. He and Earle Lewis and Edward Johnson had been, in truth, "the triumvirate" at the head of the Metropolitan. A letter that December from Suzanne (Ziegler) Gleaves thanked Johnson for the kindness he had shown after her father's death, and for his consideration in seeing that an extra month's salary was sent to the family.

With Ziegler gone, decisions for the 1947/48 season were up to Johnson and Lewis. The *Musical Courier* of November 1 in a pre-season feature, "The Metropolitan Will Introduce. . . ," said that the Opera would open in a refurbished house on November 10, 1947, with *Un ballo in maschera*, conducted by Giuseppe Antonicelli and featuring a cast that included Daniza Ilitsch, Pierrette Alarie, Margaret Harshaw, Jan Peerce and Leonard Warren. A new production of the *Ring*, made possible by a $100,000 production fund, was announced, as well as a pre-season production fund benefit performance of *Don Giovanni*. The eighteen-week season, to run through March 13, would include revivals of many tried-and-true box office favourites; fourteen new singers (75 per cent of them American); a new assistant conductor, Renato Cellini; conductor Giuseppe Antonicelli and technical director Richard Rychtarik; and the Metropolitan Opera première of *Peter Grimes*, which had had its first American performance at Tanglewood in August, 1946. The article also mentioned that the Metropolitan staff was trying to solve the problems inherent in producing Prokofiev's *War and Peace*.

Still smarting over the previous season's failure of Jonel Jorgulesco's *Walküre* sets, which had been called unfortunate, Eddie determined to take a real plunge this time. He engaged Lee Simpson to design contemporary settings for the new Wagner *Ring* cycle, Mary Schenk to design the costumes, Herbert Graf to restage it and Fritz Stiedry to conduct.

Olin Downes doffed his hat, as it were, in his "Opera Outlook" article of November 9, 1947, to a season that promised to yield one of the biggest box office intakes in recent times although, he said, the program contained "no important additions to the stock company repertory and fewer exceptional singers than in any previous period of which we know in Metropolitan history." He noted that selling opera to the public was easier, because the public was more aware and interested than ever before. "This has been accomplished before and throughout a world war, with all its dislocations of artistic effort and disturbance of the public mind, within a sadly limited budget, by the hardest work on Mr. Johnson's part, and the plainest common sense of policy and organization. . . ."

The management was concerned over the lack of dignity surrounding opening nights at the Metropolitan. There had always been people who attended the openings primarily to see and be seen, but recently certain publicity-seeking individuals had all but turned pre-performance and intermission periods into excuses for burlesque antics. Newspaper photographs and stories of that year's opening prompted board chairman George Sloan to write Johnson:

Dear Eddie:

I suppose there is nothing we can do about it. And yet it does seem a pity that an institution which has come to mean so much in the educational and cultural life of our community and nation should be used as a background to feature indecency.

. . . But it is difficult to understand how a reputable newspaper will admit in its columns that, having seen an indecent exposure, it will ask for a repeat performance so that the incident may be photographed for its front page. . . . Many must get the impression that our opening nights are a drunken orgy.

. . . A picture of a so-called gentleman in tails standing on his head in a barroom makes front page news as does a tiara-bedecked so-called society matron whose idea of "that new look" is to drape her legs over the top of the table. But we might consider keeping photographers out of the Opera House with the exception of the entrance lobbies and bring in a sufficient number of private detectives on opening night to enforce such a rule. . . .

I don't know the answer to the problem. But I feel that unless we do something about it, we are going to see many of the real friends of the Metropolitan stay away from opening night.

Faithfully yours,
Geo. S.

P.S. I would not have known of this morning's unchoice bit but for my taxi driver who handed me the front page copy with the comment, "Here is the Met opening—Jesus, what women go to that place!"

Geo. S.

In spite of facts to the contrary, there were repeated rumours that opera was dying, to which Edward Johnson offered vehement rebuttal in *Variety* newspaper, January 7, 1948. His closing words left little room for argument: ". . . when audiences fail to shudder at the terrible doom of Don Giovanni, when they are unmoved by the final choked 'Mimi!' of *La Bohème*, when they sit placidly through the 'Liebestod' of *Tristan*, and when they no longer feel the primitive terror of Azucena's wild jeremiads in *Il Trovatore*, then opera will be old-fashioned indeed and ready to make way for a more advanced form."

Meanwhile, Johnson continued his dedicated work of making as many friends as possible for opera. At a Canadian Club meeting in Montreal, at which Wilfrid Pelletier and Mayor Houde were among the notable guests, he strongly backed Pelletier's fervent cry for a large auditorium for concert and opera. A few weeks later he was again in Montreal, thanking the McColl-Frontenac Oil Company as sponsors of the Metropolitan broadcasts in Canada for the eighth consecutive year.

He made such a strong impression in those days on one young lad, Henry Wrong of Toronto, that when Henry had finished his schooling he wanted no other career than one connected with the arts and opera. He eventually became associated with the Metropolitan as an assistant in the Bing regime, then went on to become director of programming for Canada's National Arts Centre in Ottawa. Finally, in 1970, Henry Wrong was appointed administrator of the Barbican Arts Centre in London, England.

In his position as general manager of the Opera, Edward Johnson found the weeks on tour the most relaxed and the happiest. They were free from the constant day-to-day pressures and endless appointments that were so enervating in New York.

On tour, he felt like the benevolent father of a large travelling family. Ever-recurring emergencies were, in themselves, part of the overall appeal and the excitement. On April 1, 1948, in Atlanta, for example, a performance of *Carmen* was delayed almost two hours. The two special Metropolitan trains, carrying all the costumes, had been side-tracked to the end of the regular runs of the *Peach Queen* and the *Piedmont* because of a coal-strike order prohibiting special trains. The *Peach Queen* had broken a drawhead and the *Piedmont* had run into a delaying landslide in Virginia; Southern Railway finally saved the situation by hauling twenty extra carloads. The president of the Atlanta Music Festival Association, Jackson P. Dick, told the audience the delay was "due to a pair of bushy eyebrows," whereupon everyone cheered his oblique reference to union chief John L. Lewis. Johnson, Bori and others made speeches and told stories while patrons waited for the costumes to arrive. One report said that Kurt Baum *did* sing Don José in a business suit. In any case, and in true theatrical tradition, the show finally did go on!

*Carmen*, two weeks later in Shrine Auditorium, Los Angeles, came off on time and without a hitch. Risë Stevens was the Metropolitan's Carmen that year, and in view of her motion picture exposure was big box office everywhere. But the Company's greatest success in Los Angeles, oddly enough, was the April 15 performance of *Peter Grimes*, with Frederick Jagel and Polyna Stoska. That particular engagement provided a bit of nostalgia for Eddie: Amelita Galli-Curci visited him backstage after one of the performances. They had started their careers together in Chicago—she in 1917 and he in 1919—and had last sung together as Roméo and Juliette at the Metropolitan on January 18, 1930, with Tibbett as Mercutio and Gladys Swarthout as Stephano.

262

In his curtain speech on April 24, at the end of the two-week run in Los Angeles, Johnson warmly thanked the citizens for their support in the Metropolitan's first trip to that city in more than forty years and said the Company hoped to be back to open the new Los Angles opera house when it was completed.

While the Metropolitan was in California, Johnson, Frank St. Leger and Earle Lewis met with a group known as the Greater Los Angeles Plans, Inc. (an organization of culturally minded civic leaders) and their team of architects and engineers to discuss with them ideas for the proposed new opera house in Los Angeles. Eddie's chief recommendation, with the inadequacies of the Metropolitan Opera House in mind, was that they carefully consider backstage facilities. He also suggested that they start making plans for a permanent opera company of their own. However, the fact that two members of the Metropolitan Opera board, Sloan and Spofford, made a point of going to Los Angeles at that time seemed to indicate that there was an interest on the part of the Metropolitan in having a second home on the west coast until such time as a Los Angeles opera company might become a reality. In the long run, an opera company failed to materialize in Los Angeles, although a magnificent home for opera, the Dorothy Chandler Pavilion, was eventually completed in 1967 as part of the handsome new Music Center for the Performing Arts.

Starting off on his annual talent search in Europe at the end of May, Eddie received a letter from Frank St. Leger: "All friendships are grand but some are perfectly wonderful, and yours belongs in this latter category. I shall miss you very much, but will try to carry on, believing in your nearness at all times. That will be a help. Bless you. Bon voyage and every success in your 'safari.' I believe talent will be almost as scarce as mountain lions!"

That was the spring George Drew, premier of Ontario, called his second provincial election (June 7, 1948). It was a hard-fought campaign which the Conservative Party won, but Drew himself suffered personal defeat in his High Park riding in Toronto. He and Fiorenza left almost immediately afterwards for England and Europe. Eddie was in London just before the Drews arrived there. He wrote: "As for plans, I am here at this hotel until Tuesday night when I leave for Zürich—arriving Wednesday 16th in Hotel Bauer au Lac—and remaining 17-18th. And then I can arrange things freely—Vienna possibly?—and Milan about the 22nd June on my way to Florence. My stay must be a short one since I am planning to fly to Stockholm for July 2nd or 3rd, which leaves only a few days to come back to Paris and London before sailing July 9th. The time is all too short! Could you pick me up in Zürich June 19th or Florence later? I hope Fiorenza is well and survived her disappointment. She felt worse than you did I'm sure."

When he departed, he left a note at Claridge's for Fiorenza: "*Amore mio*: Sorry to hear the bad news (or is it bad?) but hope George and you have recovered your good spirits and are ready for the fray. In the meantime, just forget it all and have a good time. I'm leaving a bottle of Scotch for you and a basket of something. I'm off to Paris this afternoon. See you very soon. Love to you both. Daddy."

As it happened, they all met in Venice on June 20. "Being sentimental," Fiorenza recalled later, "we came together there because that was the day on which, in 1935, George had come to Venice to meet me, had had his funny slide over the railing and had *not* proposed, you'll recall."

From Venice, Eddie went directly to Florence before proceeding to Copenhagen. The Drews returned to Canada where they discovered that the federal Conservative Party was preparing to choose a new leader; John Bracken had requested relief from his duties because of ill health. George Drew was invited to stand for election along with John Diefenbaker and Donald Fleming. It took a lot of soul-searching and long family conferences for George to make up his mind.

In the end he did accept the challenge, and on October 2, 1948, during the Ottawa convention of the national organization, George Drew was elected federal leader of the newly named Progressive Conservative Party of Canada. Then, in a by-election in Carlton riding on December 20, 1948, he won a seat in the House. In the national election of June 27, 1949, although the Progressive Conservative Party was defeated, George Drew retained his seat and continued as leader of the Opposition.

The first year in Ottawa, the Drews lived in an apartment and sent Sandra and Edward to boarding schools—Edward to Ashbury College and Sandra to Elmwood School—because the apartment was not large enough to house all of them for any length of time. Then *Stornaway* was purchased and completely modernized by the government to serve as the official residence in Ottawa for the leader of the Opposition. The Drews were the first "residents."

WHILE JOHNSON was in Europe in the summer of 1948, serious trouble prevailed back in New York, according to St. Leger's letter of July 30: "In view of the very disturbing situation due to the repeated delays and impasse caused by the Union's failure to consummate agreements with the Metropolitan, and further in view of the involved situation facing us regarding artists and repertory in the very limited time remaining before the scheduled opening on November 8th, it is impossible for me to accept the responsibility of arranging a program which at this late date could not possibly be consistent with Metropolitan standards nor with the objectives of the management—of which I feel myself a part. To attempt such a schedule would leave the management wide open to justified attack. Therefore, in all fairness and with a heavy heart, may I be released from contractual obligations as of August 30th—obligations which were entered into in good faith before existing conditions proved insurmountable. While this is intended to be a formal letter, I am impelled to add a personal note. Words cannot adequately express the great happiness I have known over the years in my association with you as general manager of this great institution. I thank you most humbly for the trust you have placed in me and beg of you not to lose faith in me. Please understand that I thought long and seriously before making this difficult decision." It was a letter of resignation which Johnson persuaded Frank St. Leger to withdraw, for it was he who Johnson hoped would succeed him.

There were times when Eddie would say to such close friends as Florence Kimball, Jean Tory, or Richard and Mildred Crooks that he was tired and thought he'd like to retire as general manager of the Metropolitan. St. Leger knew of his feelings, of course, better than any of the others. But when Eddie was rested he was happy in the routine that had become an integral part of his life: opening night—*Otello* in 1948, rescheduled in view of the union problems for November 29, with Ramon Vinay, Warren and Albanese; a series of débuts; one or two new productions; and closing night—*La Traviata* on March 19, 1949, with Dorothy Kirsten, Ferruccio Tagliavini and Giuseppe Valdengo. Then the annual spring tour, to be broken that year, April 12-16, by seven post-season performances in New York of *Lucia di Lammermoor, Parsifal, La Bohème, La Traviata* and *Madama Butterfly*. Eddie always looked over the completed schedule with a deep sense of personal satisfaction.

Eddie used to joke about the fact that the Met's Board of Directors made him a present, in November, 1948, of a luxurious leather couch for his office. "Thought I needed a rest," he would say. To the Board, however, he officially expressed "keen appreciation" for the magnificent couch and said "it brings a new atmosphere to the entire surroundings and makes me wonder how I have gotten along all these years without it. . . ."

At the annual membership meeting of the Guild, November 17, 1948, a silver cigarette box engraved with affectionate sentiments was also presented to him by Lucrezia Bori "for twenty-five years service to the organization."

Edward Johnson performed many good deeds, but in accordance with his wishes, they usually went unheralded. When friends, young or old, came to him for help, he seldom refused. American soprano Teresa Stich-Randall, for example, wrote him on January 6, 1949: "I was so terribly near a hysterical burst of tears when I left you this afternoon that I wouldn't have been able to thank you even if I could possibly have found the words. It is completely unnecessary for me to tell you what this money means to me at this time. My parents are modest working people and although they have worked terribly hard, God bless them, to give me a solid musical foundation, they could never even begin to finance the tremendous amount of work I now need. And I know you understand, more than any other person in the world, how much it must mean to me. I don't know how to begin to thank you, Mr. Johnson. I only pray God will give me the grace to show you results in my work. I am deeply and everlastingly grateful."

Then there was the letter from the mother of a rising young director, acknowledging Eddie's financial assistance to her and her son when the going was tough: "It is impossible for me to express our thanks for your aid in getting us 'out of hock' and the confidence your assurance gave us when we were despairing."

As the time approached for him to make a decision as to whether he would retire from the Metropolitan or continue with his work for another year or two, Johnson sounded out Earle Lewis to see whether that member of the original triumvirate of Johnson, Ziegler and Lewis was planning to remain with the administration. On January 24, 1949, he received a letter of resignation from Lewis, along with this note:

> Dear Mr. Johnson: My years of association with you have been one of the most enjoyable periods of my life. The wonderful memories of those years make it difficult to anticipate the next season, and so after serious consideration I have decided that I should send the enclosed letter to the Board of Directors. I have, and always will, cherish the confidence that you have placed in me, and certainly no one could ever wish for a more wonderful friend, counsellor and chief. Always I shall be
>
> Your devoted friend,
> Earle

Johnson himself had originally announced his intention of resigning at the end of the 1948/49 season. But the Board induced him to stay for one more year. On that basis, reminding him of the pact they had made in 1935, Eddie was able to persuade his friend to withdraw his resignation. "In signing the new contract," Lewis wrote him, "the only condition that I wish to stipulate in connection with it is that, should you decide to retire before the end of the season 1949/50, then I, too, might have that privilege, and thus keep to our first agreement that we start and quit the job together!"

As early as February 10, 1949, Marks Levine, director to the National Concert and Artists Corporation, had written Eddie: "I have been wanting to write you a few lines ever since I read in last week's *Tribune* the story of your accepting your present post for another season. But frankly, I did not know whether to congratulate you or to express my sympathy. Upon ten days' reflection, it seems to me that congratulations *are* in order—to your Board of Directors, to the Metropolitan as an institution, to the public as the recipient of the Metropolitan gifts, to the artists and finally to the artists' managers, me included. I can very well visualize, in line with what you told me at our last meeting on January 22nd, you did not feel you could abandon your post at this stage of developments. What baffles me is the question as to what promises of support and cooperation did you receive to make your task easier? What financial guarantees are you getting, and what assurance for prompt action to insure that your final season should be the crowning artistic achievement of your career?"

Levine had read Spofford's statement to the press that the Metropolitan had terminated its arrangements with concert managers and would book its own tours. He was disappointed, he said, that the concert managers had not been credited with undertaking the risk when the Met was afraid to do so. It was the managers, he pointed out, who had enlarged the spring tours from a shaky two weeks in 1945 to a solid five weeks in 1949 with many headaches in between.

For more than a year, Doubleday publishers had been asking Eddie to agree to cooperate on a book of his memoirs. At this point, they redoubled their requests and there were competitive offers from several other firms. But for some inexplicable reason, Johnson deferred giving an affirmative reply to any of them.

Having signed a contract to remain with the Metropolitan for the 1949/50 season, Eddie was hoping for a smooth and successful final year. The ink was scarcely dry on the contract before he was faced with a serious and unforeseen catastrophe. On June 22, 1949, a fire swept through the Opera House. It originated "in the Dress Circle in the second section of seats toward the 39th Street side from the east and west centre line of the auditorium," according to Walter S. Finlay, Jr. of the J. G. White Engineering Corporation. "The fire burned through to the same section of seats in the balcony level. The actual fire was confined to these two sections, but water and smoke damage occurred in other parts of the House." The estimate of costs and recommendations for repairs submitted to the Board prompted Eddie to write Fiorenza: "There goes my money for new productions and everything else I'd planned. I'm hoping Bing can be helpful in some way."

That last remark referred to the fact that Rudolf Bing, formerly of the Glyndebourne Festival and a founder of the Edinburgh Music Festival, had been appointed on June 1, 1949, to succeed Edward Johnson as general manager of the Metropolitan in the fall of 1950. He was to arrive in New York in October, 1949, to "familiarize himself with the Met." His appointment had been preceded by two years of rumours as to who Eddie's successor would be. Among the names mentioned were Lawrence Tibbett, Lauritz Melchior, Erich Leinsdorf, Charles Kullmann, Laszlo Halasz, John Brownlee and Broadway show-man Billy Rose. It was generally understood that Edward Johnson had a direct hand in the final selection.

As to just what happened, and when and how the appointment of Rudolf Bing was made, we have the words of conductor Max Rudolf, who was the Met's musical secretary in 1949:

> What actually happened about Bing was this: [Conductor Fritz] Stiedry called Mrs. Belmont and arranged meetings in the afternoon and he took Bing to Mrs. Belmont during those days [February-March, 1949]. I knew Bing from Europe—we had been in the same theatre for one year in Germany. After Stiedry called Mrs. Belmont, she called Sloan [Board chairman] and arranged the meeting. Edward Johnson never arranged a meeting with Sloan. After that, Bing went back and was waiting for word, but nothing came. So he sent a cable to Stiedry. Then they sent Mrs. Belmont to England to talk to Bing. I know this from Mrs. Belmont. In May they asked Bing to come to New York and sign a contract. I think what I tell you now is fairly authentic. Mae Carey [Johnson's secretary] and Johnson himself wanted St. Leger to succeed him. . . .
>
> Now Miss Carey told me, during the winter of 1948-49, that Johnson was terribly worried because St. Leger was not liked by the Board—and he was worried they wouldn't accept him as his successor. So Johnson sent Frank to Europe in '49 to listen to singers, to improve Frank's standing with the Board—this I know from Miss Carey—which was why Johnson didn't go himself that year. So Frank was in Europe and we went on tour, and Johnson and I picked him up in Los Angeles at the railroad station on May 2, 1949. I had rented a car—I always did in Los Angeles—and I drove Johnson to pick up Frank, and Johnson told him, "I must tell you it doesn't look good—the Board seems to be very much interested in Bing." Now this I heard.

So a week or so later, still in the same month, the news came that the Board had engaged Bing. But as early as May 2 the question was still open. Whether Johnson really wanted St. Leger to get the job, no one will ever know. But all rumours that Johnson suggested Bing to the Board are completely wrong. Johnson never went to London to see Bing. He stayed in America for the entire period from January to the end of the tour, 1949.

On June 30, 1949, Bing wrote to Johnson from London, saying that he had heard of a new Stravinsky opera to be "completed in February, 1950, or thereabouts," too late for the 1949/50 season at the Metropolitan, and wondering whether Johnson would make tentative approaches to the publishers for 1950/51. "Naturally I do not wish to enter into any kind of official correspondence with anybody before I actually take over," he said. In a postscript he added, "It now looks as if my October visit is out and that I shall be going to the Continent for a few weeks in October and November, arriving in New York to settle down early in December."

Receiving no reply, Bing wrote on July 11, saying he had read the libretto of the new Stravinsky opera, *The Rake's Progress*, by W. H. Auden, and thought it excellent, but knew nothing of the music. He understood that the score was "very nearly ready," and added: "I would very much like the world's first performance and am anxiously waiting to hear from you how you would advise me to proceed. I know that Boosey and Hawkes, who are publishing it, have already suggested the world's first performance to Covent Garden. I have asked Ernest Ansermet, who is an old friend of mine, to approach Stravinsky personally, but of course I am particularly anxious to have your advice."

In his reply, July 15, Johnson apologized for not having answered Bing's letter sooner, and explained that he was endeavouring to procure some facts in relation to the opera's present status. "Mr. Hawkes," he wrote, "is in Australia until the autumn, but his representative in New York, to whom I spoke recently, informs me that: (a) the work will not be ready for production, according to the composer himself, for another eighteen months; (b) that the musical score is Mozartian and is intended for small orchestra and stage; and (c) gossip has it that the City Center group here in New York has asked for the première. (This is not official.) My many years of close association with the Metropolitan have gone deep into my blood and will not permit me to disinterest myself in its future. May I take this occasion to thank you for your earlier letters and to assure you of my continued help in any way that I can be of assistance."

Bing wrote again on July 21 and thanked Johnson for the valuable information. "I am most gratified to hear that you do not intend to disinterest yourself in the Metropolitan's future, and that I may therefore rely on your continued help and assistance. I shall indeed need them!" He also asked that St. Leger "very kindly send me a list of artists of particular interest whom he heard during his recent European trip by way of saving time and expense." At no point, however, did Bing ask Johnson for any help or advice insofar as the Metropolitan was concerned.

Twenty-two years later, finding himself in much the same position, Sir Rudolf Bing would be as disappointed in his turn as Edward Johnson was then. "I am not being asked for my advice by my successor," Bing said at the time. "But why should I expect it? I didn't ask my predecessor for any advice either."

WHEN THE CURTAIN went up on November 21 for the first performance in Eddie's final season, Fritz Reiner was in the pit for what, by all accounts, was a memorable performance of *Der Rosenkavalier*. Standing under the clock, about to give the starting signal and to face his last opening as general manager, Edward Johnson was heard to remark: "I feel something like a football coach going into the big game."

The opening was televised, for the second year, with Johnson unanimously dubbed "glamorous." This prompted Fiorenza to begin her next letter to him with "My dearest 'videogenic' Babbo." She had a lump in her throat, she wrote, over the beauty of all she had seen and heard. She again tried to influence her father to tell the story of his life: "George agrees with me that you should write a book. . . . I can only say that my feeling goes well beyond a simple filial devotion, to the deepest admiration for what you are in yourself and what you have done with your life to this point, and I add to this my complete faith that you will stagger me again by some further achievement. I know how energetic you are, but let's stretch that energy and have a little fun as well in the future."

Most of Johnson's associates were still with him, having been persuaded to stay, out of loyalty, for his final year. His long-time secretary Miss Carey had written a letter in the early fall to "Dear Bossee," saying she planned to quit even though she loved working with him, a great boss, but that she couldn't take the pressure and work load any longer. In a subsequent letter, she had agreed to stay out the year until he retired.

The 1949/50 season began in an atmosphere of apparent goodwill and cooperation between Eddie and his successor. Attention soon centred on Bing, however, as some plans for his first year leaked out. It was a difficult situation at best: Eddie trying for a brilliant finale, and Bing intent on a rousing overture. Being neither a secretive nor a subtle man, Bing made Eddie's life miserable. It seemed to Eddie that whenever he turned around Bing was always there—even in the general manager's box—aloof, observant, non-committal. Before the season was over, an air of hostility had developed which made the spring tour, usually such a carefree and happy event for Eddie, the most miserable experience he had ever had. For him, it was a bitter and unhappy end to a régime in which he had successfully steered the Metropolitan through perilous times. Fiorenza even said at one point, "If the situation rolls along this way, your position as a Board member would be untenable. In the meantime, don't worry. Go on in your sweet inimitable way, and be canny as hell."

St. Leger wrote Johnson on December 9: "Nobody knows better than I how much your great optimism has meant to not only myself but to all who have had the privilege of being associated with you at the Metropolitan." That same day, St. Leger sent his resignation to Board Chairman Charles M. Spofford: ". . .It is now thirty-one years that I have been actively concerned with opera in America and Europe. The time came when the Chicago Opera Company (with which I was connected for fourteen years) went bankrupt; and then Covent Garden, London, (where I served for ten years) got into difficulties. These factors were most unhappy ones for me. My association with the Metropolitan (where I am commencing my eleventh year) has been a most happy one and, therefore, I am indeed loathe to interrupt or relinquish it. However, I think under the existing circumstances it would be only right for me to voluntarily withdraw from the picture in order that the Association and Mr. Bing may feel completely free to make whatever appointments may be desirable and without feeling the slightest embarrassment on my account. . . . If at any time I can be of help to the Metropolitan, to you, or to Mr. Bing, you will find that I shall be ready to do anything I can. . . ." His resignation was to be effective at the termination of the 1949/50 season.

The final months of that New York season passed all too quickly for Eddie. The idea of leaving the place where he had spent twenty-eight years of his life, first as an artist, then as general manager, was difficult to accept. Almost every time he walked down a corridor, opened a door, sat in the House, crossed the stage, mounted the stairs, took the rickety little backstage elevator or stepped into the too-small yet familiar office, a wave of nostalgia came over him.

He loved the Old House and everything about it, even while recognizing its inadequacies and the constant problems they imposed. Although some of his happiest moments had been spent there, it was he who had been pushing the hardest for a new Metropolitan Opera House. He recognized the fact that as long as the Opera stayed within those musty, though history-filled walls, that much longer the Company would be unable to grow and take its proper place in the fast-moving technological world. He had cleared the way: they owned the building and had been relieved of tax burdens. He could do no more. He had hoped for agreement on a new location and the construction of a new Metropolitan Opera House during his regime. That would have been the realization of one of his early dreams.

When interviewed by Herbert Kupferberg for the *New York Herald Tribune* on January 12, 1950, he said: "We've had some good shows. We don't hit it every time, of course; even Babe Ruth fanned. But we have our standards, our goals, and a season like this is the kind I'd like to go out on. I'm retiring, not resigning. They want me to write books. I'm afraid the singers who read them would throw firecrackers at me. What I want to do is to go to Europe and South America, where I sang as a youngster. I want to see how the other fellows do it—to applaud if they're good and walk out if they're not."

Among the facts and figures published in the newspapers were the salaries Eddie received during his last nine years as general manager: 1941/42, $30,000; 1942/43 through 1945, $27,000; 1945/46 through 1947, $30,000; 1947/48 through 1950, $35,000. Musical and cultural publications praised his work in continuing the Saturday afternoon Metropolitan Opera broadcasts, begun in 1931, and for initiating the Met's Auditions of the Air which ran from 1936 to 1948. An item that brought a somewhat wry smile to the face of the weary general manager was the one in *Who's Who in Canada* that listed his recreations as "walking, golf, tennis, swimming, handball, gymnasium work." He had had little time for any of them.

A big Gala Testimonial celebration took place at the Opera House in honour of Edward Johnson on February 28, 1950. It consisted of a performance of *Tosca* followed by an "Opera Pageant and Ceremony," broadcast to a nation-wide audience over the American Broadcasting Company network. There was a full house that night, and waves of enthusiastic applause and shouts of "bravo" were heard many times for the famous artists—all favourites. But the greatest ovation of the evening came after the opera when the master of ceremonies for the Pageant, John Brownlee, turned to the wings and called: "Eddie!" The applause was long and thunderous—a testimonial in itself to the kind of respect, love and esteem few people, particularly general managers, ever know.

When it was time for him to speak, Edward Johnson began: "What can one say? In a situation like this even Winston Churchill would be stymied. I am grateful to each and every member of the Metropolitan family for the loyalty and support given me through these years. These fifteen years have been fruitful and exciting and, in spite of everything, very happy years. . . ."

One newspaper reported: "A minor hitch to the Testimonial developed during the afternoon rehearsal for it. One of the foreign members of the chorus whispered worriedly to another, 'Do you know the words of "For he's a jolly good fellow?" ' 'The words?' the other replied. 'I don't even know the melody.' By evening they had learned both, and anyway the audience was singing it too."

The evening's proceeds, $46,000, went to the Edward Johnson Testimonial Fund that, by Eddie's request, was to be used to assist needy artists.

A note from the Metropolitan board's Lauder Greenway was one of the hundreds that came to Eddie during the final weeks and months, but it prompted such a warm thank-you from Johnson that Mr. Greenway wrote again:

Dear Eddie:

Really your note of January 12 has touched me deeply. The wretched little words I could say in no way convey my own feelings during this entire year. You so wonderfully represented the opera to me that I should have broken down entirely if I had attempted to be explicit the other night. I do hope that I will continue to see you during the coming years as I have since the war.

Always yours,
Lauder Greenway

From Lowell Wadmond, a past president of the Metropolitan Opera Club and past chairman of the Opera's Board of Directors, Johnson received tribute on March 4:

Dear Sir Edward:

Last Tuesday's evening for the benefit of the Edward Johnson Testimonial Fund was a magnificent occasion. I have never heard a *Tosca* performance so musically fine and dramatically perfect. But most of all, and best of all, the evening was a moving tribute to the great Sir Edward, beloved by all and esteemed by all for his magnificent career at the Met and for his own endearing qualities of heart and mind. I felt quite sad all through the evening, and still do, because I am unhappy about your retiring from the post as General Manager. In my opinion the Met needs you and I should like to have seen you stay on for years to come. All the things that were said about you Tuesday night I am sure were sincerely meant, and only voiced the sentiments that were seeking expression from all the audience. You handled yourself as a great trouper, standing there in the centre of the stage and then making that excellent little speech, the embodiment of all those qualities of grace, charm, sensitivity and integrity which make you the greatest General Manager ever.

With sentiments of esteem, I am

Faithfully yours,
Lowell

During a newspaper interview at the time of the Metropolitan's final visit that spring to Baltimore, Johnson described his career as general manager as "just a matter of getting the curtain up and bringing it down twenty-seven hundred times in fifteen years, with never a miss."

One of Eddie's major accomplishments was the discovery and introduction of new young talent by way of the Metropolitan Opera Auditions of the Air. The Auditions were his idea and he had inaugurated them himself in the spring of 1936. For the first time, talented singers were invited to audition publicly for contracts with the Company. When he thought of the many winners over the years, Eddie couldn't help being pleased and impressed by some of the names on the list: Risë Stevens, Leonard Warren, Eleanor Steber, Mona Paulee, Raoul Jobin, Clifford Harvuot, Martial Singher, Patrice Munsel, Regina Resnik, Richard Tucker, Robert Merrill, Frank Guarrera and more than threescore others. At the beginning the Auditions were sponsored by the Sherwin-Williams Company—a coup for Edward Johnson who had been able to arrange this. Then, after ten years, the Firestone Corporation took over for the final two years.

The conductor and musical director for the Auditions for the entire twelve years of their existence was Wilfrid Pelletier. In the 1970s he recalled: "Johnson's heart was in those Auditions of the Air; he was advising all the youngsters as to what they should do and he followed their progress and development. Later, when some of them were singing at the Met, he was there at every performance to encourage them. We always looked for him in his familiar full dress. He had worn that when he first became general manager and I am not criticizing but, as the years went by, it had become shinier and shinier and shinier and a little bit tight. I don't know whether he had grown a bit fatter or whether it had shrunk. But we would always laugh when we would see him coming— you could almost comb your hair looking at his back!"

Interviewed on May 31, as he was about to leave the Metropolitan Opera House for the last time as general manager, Edward Johnson said his first intention on retirement was "to get my brain purged of complicated Met problems, and to sail for Italy with the Drews on June 16." He expressed confidence in Rudolf Bing as his successor and promised that he himself would still be a devoted fan.

"I'd much rather leave here," he said, "with my full faculties, than hang on until I become dilapidated and old, or have to be taken out in a wheelchair—or a square box. Moving out now leaves me with a sense of accomplishment. . . . I had one big advantage, that of coming up through the ranks. My approach has been that of a colleague rather than a boss. When I took over, the organization was flat on its back, without artists and without money. Now there are fourteen United States cities on our touring list."

He was proud of his record.

In the spring of 1950, Olin Downes paid tribute in the *New York Times* article "Edward Johnson's Rich Career in Opera." In it, he quoted Johnson as saying: "If you ask me what I consider the Metropolitan's highest achievement in the period in which I have been associated with the organization, it is this: We have developed as never before . . . the American people's love and understanding of great music."

# 10

IT WAS A HAPPY GROUP that set sail for Italy on June 16: Eddie, Fiorenza, Edward and Sandra Drew—then aged twelve and ten —and Tata. George Drew would be joining them in Florence after the House of Commons closed. The villa they rented for the summer, *Bellosguardo*, had been built in 1462. Its huge rooms and twenty-foot ceilings gave it a special kind of atmosphere. Its position overlooking Florence afforded an inspiring panorama. Eddie was in his element, taking the children on long walks, showing them all the treasures of the city he knew so well and loved so much. When George arrived, he was duly impressed by all the children had absorbed.

Eddie still talked of the idea of investing in a little villa, and he had found one, he said, near Jo Casali's palazzo. But Fiorenza noticed that as her father began to relax his conversation included more and more references to the amount of time he would be spending in Canada and all he wanted to do there. "You know," he said to the family one evening, as they all sat on the terrace looking out over Florence, "Canada really can become the musical centre of the world. I'm going to go prospecting. I'll bet there's a whole gold mine of talent that nobody knows anything about. . . . And another thing: we've got to have better musical education for our children in Canada. I've got to get things straightened out at the Conservatory in Toronto—and I know just what needs to be done."

"Listen to you," Fiorenza chided. "I thought you were going to take it easy for a while!"

"Yes," George joined in, "this is your first free summer, and you're supposed to be on vacation."

"Look who's talking!" was Eddie's retort, recalling the many political discussions they'd been having. "I know what can be done in Canada musically, and it's up to me to do it." Eddie stayed on in Florence for another month, however, making motor trips here and there with

Jo Casali, and it was at her home, on August 22, that he celebrated his birthday that year.

When the Metropolitan opened in the fall of 1950, most of the faces so familiar through the years were gone. Even Edward Johnson, who had been like the Metropolitan itself for the past fifteen years, sat in his little apartment in New York and listened to the opening production, *Don Carlo*, on the radio! "You were so darn smart to let Bing have the rat race all to himself," his brother Fred wrote when he heard about this.

That winter, too, Edward Johnson began a new pattern of life, dividing his time between New York and Toronto, punctuating it with speech-making trips of a week or ten days to Guelph, Chicago, Montreal, and taking an annual trip abroad. Holidays were usually spent with Fiorenza and her family, and he followed closely the ups and downs of George's political career. Everyone in the family knew that, no matter what else happened, on Sunday morning they would all be together, on the telephone at least, if not in person.

Since 1945, one of Eddie's main concerns as chairman of the Board of Governors of the Royal Conservatory of Music of Toronto had been the lack of established professional opera companies in Canada where graduates of the Conservatory's Opera School could gain practical experience before live audiences or earn a livelihood in their chosen profession. Now he was putting the full weight of his prestige and position behind the Conservatory's fledgling opera company as the obvious organization from which a professional opera company might one day emerge. (The Conservatory had changed its name to the Royal Conservatory of Music of Toronto in May, 1947. In connection with the Conservatory's Diamond Jubilee, His Majesty King George VI had acted on a pre-war request and had issued a warrant for the use of the prefix "Royal.")

Mrs. Floyd S. Chalmers had been chosen in the late forties to head an Opera and Concert Committee to promote performances by students of the Toronto Conservatory of Music. They sponsored the first public performance by the Opera School of the Toronto Conservatory of Music: *The Bartered Bride* in Eaton Auditorium, April 28 and 29, 1947. A production of *Hansel and Gretel* followed that same year on December 18 and 19. A third production, Gluck's *Orpheus*, was presented in the auditorium on February 6, 1948, under the joint sponsorship of the Committee and the Women's Musical Club of Toronto.

Edward Johnson offered advice on the development of the opera company, based on his years of experience, and gave enthusiastic support. Arnold Walter and his staff—stage director Felix Brentano, conductor Nicholas Goldschmidt and assistant director Herman Geiger-Torel—

were ambitious to progress into a proper theatre. They organized the Royal Conservatory Opera and scheduled *Rosalinda* (the version of Johann Strauss's *Die Fledermaus* which Brentano had staged on Broadway) for a trial week in Toronto's Royal Alexandra Theatre during the first International Trade Fair of June, 1948.

At that point, however, President Sidney Smith stepped in. "It is not the function of the university to promote commercial productions, especially those involving a monetary gamble," he told the Conservatory board. He gave consent for the project to continue only if guarantees were provided by private citizens. Not one to give up easily, Arnold Walter managed to find time to get ten guarantees of $1,000 each—not actual cash, but agreements to share any losses. Lady Eaton and Edward Johnson were two of the first guarantors, but they, like the others, were never asked to make good their promise. *Rosalinda*, which cost $10,000, realized $7,000 at the box office for the week. With public interest running high, Walter and Mrs. Chalmers decided to gamble on running the show a second week. It paid off. The cost-income figures were reversed; the production closed with a $46 profit.

On December 9 and 11, 1948, the embryonic company was back in Eaton Auditorium: "The Royal Conservatory Opera presents *The Marriage of Figaro*." The production was in English, with Goldschmidt conducting and Geiger-Torel the stage director. But the following season it was the Royal Alexandra Theatre that housed the first "Opera Festival," February 3-11, 1950. The opera was *Rigoletto* as Director Arnold M. Walter officially presented for the first time "The Royal Conservatory Opera Company." Edward Johnson was jubilant. "What these young Canadians have done in a short period is phenomenal," he told the press.

By 1951, a more formal citizens' committee, under the chairmanship of R. H. Lorimer Massie, took over financial responsibility for an opera festival by the Royal Conservatory Opera Company. In 1955 the company became known as the Opera Festival Company of Toronto, and, finally, under Herman Geiger-Torel's direction, the fully professional Canadian Opera Company emerged.

The opera festival flourished even though there was trouble behind the scenes at the Conservatory. "I always thought three *p*'s [ *ppp*] meant very pianissimo," Eddie said to George Drew on the phone one Sunday late in 1951, "but here it stands for personalities, personnel and publicity, and it is developing into a veritable gabble of tongue-wagging."

In January, 1952, Sidney Smith, president of the University, presented a reorganizational plan for the Royal Conservatory of Music: it would be a college of the University of Toronto with two branches—the Faculty of Music (degree courses) and the School of Music (chiefly

278

diploma courses). The college was to have a "rector" with overall authority, a principal for the School of Music and a director for the Faculty of Music. With Mazzoleni as principal and Arnold Walter as director, the question was, Who should the rector be?

Sir Ernest MacMillan, meanwhile, was quietly attending to his responsibilities as Dean of the Faculty of Music at the University, and to his many conducting responsibilities with the Toronto Symphony Orchestra and the Mendelssohn Choir. Having heard rumours, however, of an imminent reorganization in the Conservatory that would affect his position, he wrote President Smith asking for an appointment.

"I waited for some time, hoping for a personal interview," Sir Ernest recorded in his notes, "but no invitation was forthcoming. So I had to write again. Finally, on March 29, I met with Johnson and the president in Smith's office. There they suggested to me that I take on the senior post of rector, and said they would match whatever salary the Toronto Symphony paid me. I naturally refused, pointing out that I had made this choice ten years before."

Sir Ernest learned that under the new organizational plan his present office of dean would cease to exist, and he sent advice of his retirement from the University to the members of the Faculty of Music saying: "The president has kindly invited me to take over supervision of post-graduate work, and has also expressed his wish to recommend my appointment as Dean Emeritus. These offers I have declined with thanks. I should like, in making this announcement, to express my warmest thanks to all members of the Faculty for their loyal support in past years."

Although the original plans for the reorganization called for a co-ordinating personality, or rector, over the heads of the two divisions in the new Conservatory setup, the University Board of Governors wondered whether that was necessary. In the end, Dr. Walter was promoted from vice-principal to head of the new first division, Mazzoleni was designated head of the second division, and nothing was done about a third appointment. According to the *Telegram* of Toronto, April 29, 1952: "Dr. Mazzoleni found himself in charge of a lesser division of the new Conservatory which would be confined to beginners and students who had earlier training without professional activity." So he resigned. The *Toronto Daily Star*, April 28, 1952, carried a picture of Johnson with the cutline: "Key Figure in the Dispute."

Something had to be done to save the situation. It was at that point that Edward Johnson, chairman of the Conservatory's Board of Governors, agreed to act as coordinator, without compensation, until a permanent appointment was made. This arrangement reassured Mazzoleni that the intentions of the University Board were in line with his own views as to the conditions essential to the future of the new organization. Accordingly, he was persuaded to rescind his resignation, and offered, in a letter to the Board of May 2, 1952, full cooperation and dedication toward the success of the enlarged Royal Conservatory of Music.

The University Board advertised widely in Canada, the United States and the United Kingdom to find the right man to fill the new position of dean. (Somewhere along the line the term "rector" had disappeared.) Carefully considering all possible candidates, the Board narrowed the choice down to three: 1) Sir Steuart Wilson, a senior administrative officer of the Royal Opera House, Covent Garden, was the most experienced and qualified of the three, but he was sixty-three years old; 2) Boyd Neel, forty-seven, had graduated as a medical doctor but was internationally known as the founder and director of the famed Boyd Neel Chamber Orchestra; and 3) Robert Ewing, forty-three, was conductor of the Sadler's Wells Ballet Orchestra.

Eventually it was Boyd Neel who was offered the position. It came about, as he recalled later, after some rather informal negotiations between Edward Johnson and himself:

> For me it all began when Arthur Judson heard me at the Edinburgh Festival and fixed a North American tour for the Boyd Neel Orchestra. "When you're in Toronto," he told me, "go see Edward Johnson—they're looking for someone like you at the Royal Conservatory." So when I was in Toronto, that was 1952, I phoned Johnson, and he said, "Oh, Arthur Judson told me about you. Come down." I did, and while I was there he asked me how I'd like to come to be dean. I said I wasn't interested, because I had two more years of contracts to fulfill with the Orchestra.
>
> Less than two weeks later, I had a phone call in London: "This is Edward Johnson, I'm at the Park Lane Hotel. Can you have dinner with me?" While we were at dinner, he said, "You're the one we want for dean," and suggested my coming over "with a key to the place" to look the situation over and get the feel of it.
>
> I came, in April, 1953, and was given a fine lunch at the Hunt Club. They offered me the job. I finally said the only way I could possibly manage it was to come for two years, eight months each, with four months off for my orchestra. So I came, and at the end of that time Sidney Smith asked me if I'd like to stay on, and I said I thought so, because I could see great possibilities developing. "Well, stay," he told me. And I stayed—for seventeen years. No contract or anything to start.

A difficult period followed. Neel had been brought in to assume responsibility for coordination of the Conservatory's affairs, but Edward

Johnson was still involved in the situation. As Arnold Walter later remembered, those first few weeks were not pleasant ones for Dr. Neel:

> He came to me one unforgettable day and said, "Obviously you don't need me here. You do this work; Mazzoleni does the other work; and I am not needed at all. What should I do? Why do they want me?" I told him quite frankly that it was a political exercise in order to keep Mazzoleni and myself apart. . . .
>
> For some time Neel looked around, not understanding. Then, at one of the Board meetings, he exploded: "If you treat me like this I will go back to England. I don't have a proper office; I don't have a desk . . . I sit in a little anteroom." It was where Sir Ernest's secretary used to sit. The president didn't know anything about this, so *he* blew up.
>
> But before all of these things were settled, President Smith became so tired of the constant personality battles and intrigues in the Conservatory controversy that he told Johnson, flatly, he "was not to interfere with the day-to-day management." Johnson was secretly relieved, but he was also frightfully angry that he should be asked to step out.

In retrospect, Floyd Chalmers summarized the events in this way:

> Neel arrived in Canada, signed a contract and met the members of the University of Toronto Board of Governors. Johnson had been very enthusiastic about Neel at the time of his appointment. But, for some reason his enthusiasm waned before Neel reached Canada. From the very start, Neel was doomed to carry on his duties, develop a program and implement it with a minimum of cooperation from Johnson. Mazzoleni and Walter were each jealous of their prerogatives in their own areas and, if not indifferent, at least not inclined to devote much thought to the other half of the Conservatory's functions. There was a dignified courtesy in the relations of the three men, but it is unlikely that at any time, and on any subject, was there enthusiastic cooperation. . . .
>
> Undoubtedly Neel must be given much of the credit for the subsequent rise in the Conservatory's and Faculty's fortunes—a magnificent new building with opera house and concert hall, and the refurbished McMaster University building for the School of Music. But it was Johnson's prestige and persuasive powers that had to carry the day at the University Board. . . .

Eddie hated to admit to himself, and never did admit to anyone but his secretary Hammie, that Smith's dictum asking him not to interfere in matters that concerned him so deeply had taken the heart and soul out of his enthusiasm for developments at the Conservatory. "Enthusiasm is like love, Hammie. It is easily killed. . . ." Then, at her questioning glance (she never dared voice an opinion at such times), he added, "Of course I will continue to do what I can, but it will never be quite the same. I think I'm going to spend more time in Guelph—organize the music education there. I'm going to see to it that those kids have a better chance." Hammie felt relieved; the old enthusiasm had begun to creep back into his voice.

Almost a year after the "Big Fracas of 1952," as it was called, Sidney Smith wrote Eddie on April 30, 1953, saying:

> The progress of the Conservatory under your captaincy has been phenomenal! By reason of your tact, your wisdom and your vision, compounded with your musical talent and your rich experience, the Conservatory has a fine record of attainment and a challenging opportunity. May you long be spared to guide its policies. Your work among us has been a boon not only to the Conservatory, the University and Toronto, but also a superb performance in nation-building.
>
> Yours with humility and with admiration,
> Sidney

While the many struggles at the Royal Conservatory were in progress, Fiorenza had constantly urged her father not to get overtired. Buoyed up by the excitement of it all, he thought that her concern was unnecessary. But once things were finally resolved, he had to admit to himself that he was very tired indeed.

As USUAL AT such moments, Eddie's thoughts turned to Europe and Italy. So, late in the summer of 1952, he embarked on what proved to be a lengthy and eventful trip. It started in Italy—to be among the familiar hills and to walk the familiar streets of Florence, Milan or Rome was always a balm to his soul. As he and Jo Casali took long trips together, the soothing countryside cast its warm, healing spell over these two old friends.

From Italy, Eddie went to Switzerland to visit Sandra and Edward Drew in their respective schools. Next he investigated the experimental opera school in Zürich, hoping to pick up some good ideas for the Conservatory. After that he joined a group, including his long-time friend Charlie Meehan then with the American Consulate in Hamburg, for a motor trip to the Matterhorn.

There were no mishaps on the trip except that near the summit of the mountain, when they were walking around on the ice, Eddie slipped and fell. He picked himself up fairly easily and thought little more about it. But the next morning he could hardly move because of the pain in his shoulder and hip. Hoping to stave off any rheumatic or arthritic complications, he visited the hot baths and a local osteopath, and felt much improved. "Fit as a fiddle," he told his friends at lunch, with a reassuring smile. It was many months, as it turned out, before the effects of that fall had completely disappeared.

Meanwhile, before Eddie set foot in North America again, he was to go through what he always spoke of as his "London dilemma" of January, 1953. Scheduled to leave England on a Tuesday for New York, he was held up when it was discovered he had no entry permit for the United States. He contacted his friends, Major J. S. P. Armstrong in London, and Lester B. Pearson, foreign minister in Mackenzie King's cabinet in Ottawa. After a week of uncertainty, the necessary word finally came through late on Monday afternoon.

Even then, as Eddie wrote to Dr. and Mrs. Hubert Dunn (Margaret Eaton) in London: "You will be amused to know that, after the re-entry difficulties and having been fog-bound, the plane on which I was supposed to leave Tuesday had to return to Heathrow after forty minutes in the air because of engine trouble. Following an hour of desperate expectation, we were told that the delay would be twenty-four hours, and a bus took us, bag and baggage, to Selsdon Hall, beyond Croydon, where we remained until late the next afternoon. Fortunately all was in order this time. . . ."

After a few days in Ottawa, Eddie motored to Guelph, taking the Drews with him for the weekend. Then, when they had gone, he invited Arnold Walter to visit him so he could catch up on what had been happening at the Conservatory. He learned that Boyd Neel was still happily ensconced in "the big office" and that Mazzoleni was running the Conservatory end of the operation. "The budget and control of the Faculty is my business," Arnold said. "It goes directly to the president's office—not through Neel."

They spoke of the success of the Opera Festival put on by the Conservatory Opera Company in the Royal Alexandra Theatre the previous winter. "I think the Company ought to develop and grow into a solid professional company," Eddie commented. Arnold replied that in his opinion it was well on its way to becoming just that. And what was being planned for the special series of concerts at the Conservatory, Eddie wanted to know, having pledged two thousand dollars toward them.

The whole visit was easy and relaxed, covering the past, the present, the future—and women. "We always talked about women," Dr. Walter admitted when he recalled those conversations. "I thought it was funny when he would say about some pretty girl, 'Arnold, I'd like to take her home with me, but I'm too old.' Now I say the same thing! But at that time—well, I was thirty years or so younger, you know, and I guess we talked about girls the way we shouldn't have, but we understood each other. He was always very discreet, of course, but he knew we were both caballeros."

Walter enjoyed visiting Johnson in his home in Guelph, especially in the forties and early fifties.

It was a smallish house, but it was charming. Downstairs it had two rooms which I remember particularly—one was a library and television room (Eddie used it in his last months as a bedroom), and the other housed a harpsichord—a rather large and valuable one which he had bought from a junk dealer in Italy ever so many years ago. I think his wife had bought it, although I am not sure. He had brought it over and still had it and I told him how to have it repaired. The sleeping quarters were in the upper part of the house which was very high like the upstairs of an English country house. The place wasn't elegantly furnished but very serviceable. It was lovely, particularly with the relatively large garden. Some of the trees he had planted himself years before. They were very tall and beautiful. He had an old gardener who looked after all this, living in.

It was almost a sort of country squire business, and Eddie liked the idea of having a small estate there. However, the surroundings got worse every day, and this bothered him because Guelph was moving in that direction, and suddenly there were filling stations in the area and a Loblaws across the road. But he loved that house and so did I.

He also loved Guelph and did his best for it—for musical education, starting a music festival. He wanted to start a foundation long before the Edward Johnson Music Foundation was contemplated, but he didn't want to *be* the foundation. He was never impractical; he was much too clever. He was a man who, I think, was between the devil and the deep blue sea. He wanted to do good—but he didn't want to have to pay for it all himself. He didn't think it unreasonable that other people should come and help. He would put say $10,000 into a foundation if another ten men would put in equal sums—but he didn't want to spend $100,000 himself.

I think that's one reason why he didn't leave any money to the foundation. The other was that I think he assumed that Fiorenza would continue to do the things he had done, at her discretion. I think he and Lady Eaton had somewhat the same idea about these things. One day she said to me that there were a lot of things she didn't do in her lifetime or in her will because she assumed that her heirs would carry on the tradition for the family and would do exactly as she would have done. I know Eddie wanted to give everything he had to the one person he loved, and that was his daughter.

Johnson was invited to talk to the Conservatory students and professors at the University of Toronto in February. Walter had expected he would just say a few words extemporaneously, requiring no preparation or worry of any kind. "But no. I found him sitting in front of a mirror and practising," Walter recalled, "to be sure he was going to get the vowels out, and the consonants in the right places! It was as if he were practising for a great role—as he probably had done all his life as a singer. He was performing again and going through the whole rigamarole. It was fantastic. He told me that he intended to give them his best, but that he was a little out of practice."

Insofar as Eddie was concerned, once he faced his audience it didn't matter that he was out of practice, for he spoke from the heart. He reminded the students how fortunate they were to have such golden opportunities, and he exhorted them to make the most of their good fortune. Then finally, speaking of himself, he told them: "When I was young, I wanted to be a missionary; now I want to share what music has given me of happiness and pleasure. You might say I'm a propagandist for beauty in life—for art in culture and art in living. I am glad I was an opera singer. It was not an easy career but it was exciting, and in spite of everything the years were fruitful and happy ones. Can you imagine, when I was in school in Guelph, Queen Victoria was still alive and Thomas Edison was trying to persuade people to buy little wax cylinders that recorded the voice. There was little music in our town, except what we made among ourselves—in church and with the local band. How in the world I ever took up the profession, I'll never know. But it was wonderful. . . ."

Shortly after that, Fiorenza was visiting with her father in Toronto when George phoned from Ottawa to say that Tata had had a stroke. It was impossible for Eddie to leave Toronto at the moment, but Fiorenza returned immediately. Tata was in a coma and died shortly after Fiorenza's arrival. "Terribly upset about news," Eddie wired. "It's a crushing blow. God bless you both. Love . . ." Thinking of Tata, he automatically signed the telegram "Edoardo." Newspapers stated simply that Maria del Moro Tazzi had died at the residence of the Drews, 541 Acacia Avenue, Ottawa, February 17, 1953, that services were held at the Church of Our Lady in Guelph and that she was buried in the Johnson family plot in Guelph on February 19. In two other corners of the plot were the graves of Eddie's father and mother. The fourth was reserved for Edward Johnson.

Tata had been like one of the family, having come to the Johnsons in Florence in July, 1910, when she was twenty years old. Over the years her life had been intimately interwoven with theirs—Eddie, Bebe, Fiorenza, the Drews—until she felt closer to them than to any of her own relatives. They *were* her family. After Eddie's career had taken him to America, he had often sent Tata back to Florence to look after his villa there, as long as he kept it. But as soon as she had been in Canada for five consecutive years, the time required to become a Canadian, she had made application for citizenship, and on April 26, 1950, with Fiorenza sitting in the back of the courtroom, Maria Tazzi had proudly taken the oath of allegiance to Canada.

ON APRIL 21, 1953, Edward Johnson was present at a gala banquet at the Waldorf-Astoria to receive the Canadian Club of New York Award and Gold Medal in commemoration of the fiftieth anniversary of the Club. He became the fourth man to be so honoured. The others had been Gerald Campbell, Cordell Hull and Mackenzie King. In accepting the award, Eddie said: "Of all the honours, national and international that have come to me in the course of my long professional career, no honour has moved me more deeply than this award." He had been a member of the Club since 1922.

That same month, Johnson met with Leopold Stokowski and a group of Canadians and Americans to implement a plan to bring some of the best works of Canadian composers into Carnegie Hall in the fall. The program was to be determined by a selection committee which included three Canadians, Claude Champagne, Sir Ernest MacMillan and Wilfrid Pelletier, and four Americans, Aaron Copland, William Schumann, Roy Harris and Henry Cowell.

Again in Canada, on April 25, Eddie gave his blessing to the young Canadian singers who had won scholarships on CBC Radio's "Singing Stars of Tomorrow" series, sponsored by Canadian Industries Ltd. On that occasion he was introduced as "a man who still lives in New York but flies to Toronto regularly for Conservatory duties."

In Fiorenza's letters to her father, she constantly expressed concern for his health. "Take care of yourself. Don't get overtired," she kept repeating. It was a relief for Eddie—who had no intention of heeding her advice—when she began writing him from London that spring. George Drew, as leader of the Opposition in Canada, had been invited to attend the Coronation of Queen Elizabeth II. Fiorenza's letters were filled with great excitement as June second, the date set for the royal event, approached. "We arrived yesterday afternoon," she wrote, "and are ensconced at the Dorchester in a suite on the seventh floor overlooking the route—what a pity no one will be at our windows." The children, she reported, could hardly wait to join them from Switzerland the following week. "We are deluged with invitations—three to Buckingham Palace. . . . George lunched with the Commonwealth representatives on Monday and we both dined with them on Wednesday. . . . Furthermore, there are invitations to garden parties for the Queen, at Blenheim House, from the Duke and Duchess of Marlborough, and Hatfield House, from the Salisburys, and Lambeth Palace, from the Archbishop of Canterbury, and dozens of other invitations to luncheons and cocktails."

In her account of the festivities, aside from the magnificence of the Coronation itself, Fiorenza was most impressed by the dinner party at Buckingham Palace—the breath-taking sight of women in priceless jewels and dresses, men in satin breeches, velvet sashes and decorations being ushered up the long curving stairway into what is known as "The Long Hall" hung with the most magnificent paintings, ranging from the early Italian primitives to Rembrandts, Tintorettos and Rubens. "But for a moment," she wrote, "all I could see was that the Sultana of Jahore and I were both dressed in exactly the same dress." Fiorenza's was a Norman Hartnell model "for which I had given my all for this splendid occasion," whereas the Sultana's (Fiorenza discovered later) had been made for her by Hartnell in England.

As Eddie read Fiorenza's bubbling account of the occasion, he was happy again that she should have the advantage of such experiences. "The Queen herself was a truly magnificent sight that evening," Fiorenza wrote, "for she wore the dress she had worn at the Coronation, the ivory satin embroidered with all the symbols of the nations of the Commonwealth. On her head was a fabulous tiara of diamonds, and between each gothic point hung a beautiful drop pearl."

It was a disappointment that the Drews couldn't remain in London long enough to savour every bit of the aftermath of the excitement. Also, they had planned to go from there to Switzerland for the children's school closings. But as soon as Prime Minister St. Laurent returned to Canada, he called an election, and George had to go back home immediately.

The front cover of the *Steinway News*, September, 1953, carried a picture of Edward Johnson selecting the ten young pianists to be featured in the Steinway Centenary Concert in Carnegie Hall, October 19. Josef Hofmann, who opened the program, was honourary chairman of the Steinway Artists Centenary Committee of which Johnson was executive chairman. The pianists were featured in several multi-piano arrangements and all ten joined the Philharmonic Symphony Orchestra of New York, under Dimitri Mitropoulos, in a special Morton Gould arrangement of "The Stars and Stripes Forever." The one hundredth anniversary was marked again, December 20, by a dinner "in honour of Steinway and Sons" given by the Bohemians (a theatrical club) at the Plaza Hotel. On that occasion, pianos were again the main feature, but Eddie made sure that opera was also represented: Metropolitan Opera soprano Victoria de Los Angeles sang a group of songs. Little did anyone suspect at the time that a Steinway son-in-law, Schuyler G. Chapin, would one day hold the position (from May, 1973, to July, 1975) that Edward Johnson relinquished to Rudolf Bing in 1950, and would be the last general manager of the Metropolitan Opera before the title was retired.

On January 26, 1954, Johnson presided at a special concert in Toronto where he proudly presented two outstanding Conservatory singers, soprano Irene Salemka and baritone James Milligan, as well as Conservatory teacher, Maestro Ernesto Barbini. Next, Eddie was in Montreal, along with conductors Emil Cooper and Wilfrid Pelletier and *New York Times* critic Olin Downes, to pay tribute to the turn-of-the-century diva Mme Pauline Donalda. A few weeks after that, he held a press conference in Toronto to announce that an audition board had been set up to award musical scholarships at the Conservatory and he invited parents of all talented children to bring them in.

That spring he spoke in Guelph at a concert in honour of local music teacher Jessie Hill, the close friend who had often been his accompanist through the years. The soloist that evening was young Guelph singer Anthony Kefalas, whom Eddie enthusiastically introduced as "a young man you're going to hear about some day." Again, at the opening ceremonies of the Conservatory Summer School in Toronto that year, Edward Johnson was the speaker. He stressed the importance of a broad musical education and his contention that it was up to the young people to make the future a good one. He liked to be with young people—it made him feel alive and useful.

Eddie had been trying for so many years to convince people that one of the greatest problems in the future would prove to be the handling of leisure time that he had begun to feel like a prophet in the wilderness. "The development of the spirit," he would say, "is the most important thing in the world today," and he had many clippings that proved his point. Meanwhile, whenever he himself was not on the move, the television screen became his window on the world, and he would often phone a friend or one of the young artists he had "discovered," after seeing them on television, to congratulate them.

It was disturbing for Eddie to realize how many of his old friends had already died. In Guelph, as he walked through the cemetery sometimes with Jim Barry or young Eva Howlett, he would comment, "More of my friends are here, now, than are walking the streets." It seemed to be a simple observation, rather than a remark in which there was any hint of loneliness or self-pity. The same could be said of his comment to Arnold Walter in June of 1954: "There are too many funerals these days—now I have to go to New York for the funeral of my old friend, Elsa Kutzbauer. She used to be the language instructor at the Met."

When he went to Europe that summer, Eddie took a villa in Florence for a month before going to meet the Drews in Paris. After a few days at Le Rosay, in Switzerland, for Edward's school closing, the Drews had motored through Spain and Portugal—because Fiorenza wanted the children "to know a bit about my mother's country"—and through Belgium, France and Germany because George wanted "to visit the battlefields where so many of my friends from both wars are buried." They all converged in Paris on August 22 for a family birthday party for Eddie. He was so enthralled by the enthusiastic stories of their travels through the picturesque towns and villages of Portugal and Spain that he decided to go there himself the next year.

By September, the children were back in their respective schools; George and Fiorenza had returned to Ottawa; and Eddie was about to resume his now familiar pattern of activities in New York, Toronto, Chicago and Guelph. He stopped first in New York. Rudolf Bing had invited him to participate in the Met's opening night festivities on November 8. Eddie was to act as Master of Ceremonies for the intermissions and he wanted to know just what was expected of him. It would be his first public appearance at the Metropolitan since his own testimonial there in 1950. "Everything considered," Fiorenza remarked, "it seems like the beginning of a wonderful winter for all of us."

But on November 10 Eddie received a phone call from Fiorenza. She sounded frightened. George had come home from a speaking engagement in London, Ontario, that evening, she said, looking terribly ill and with a high fever. Their doctor, Harry Whitley, a friend of George's since the First World War, thought George had meningitis. Eddie did his best to comfort her, and asked that she phone him again in the morning. Toronto diagnostician Ray Farquharson, who happened to be in Ottawa, confirmed the diagnosis. For more than two weeks it was not certain whether George was going to live. Then, once the danger period had passed, there was still the question as to what the aftereffects of the illness might be.

It was Christmastime before the doctors gave George permission to get up and move about. Even then, they advised him to take a long rest —at least six months. Instead, feeling that his party needed him, he was back in the political harness early in the year and carrying an even heavier work load than before: long and tiring debates, speeches, endless conferences. . . .

Reassured that George was all right again, Eddie turned his attention to a painful situation in New York—within a few months he would be forced to leave the apartment that had been his home for such a long time. The building was being torn down. Going through his things, he decided that certain scrapbooks, costumes and other items connected with his years at the Metropolitan Opera should remain in New York. He approached the Museum of the City of New York about making such a gift to them, and received a letter asking him when they might "have the opportunity of receiving your collection and of welcoming you as an important donor to our Museum." The items included a scrapbook from Eddie's years as general manager of the Metropolitan, a costume worn by Enrico Caruso as Samson and one of Johnson's Pelléas costumes. The Museum's official acceptance of the "valued gift," signed by director John Walden Myer, was dated September 27, 1955.

Prior to the visit of the Metropolitan to Toronto that spring, Eddie spoke before the Toronto Rotary Club, admitting to a bit of egotism when he read the list of operas finally chosen for presentation. "At one time or another in my career," he told the members, "I sang the leading tenor role in all seven operas to be presented—*Butterfly, Cav* and *Pag, Traviata, Tosca, Carmen* and *Andrea Chénier*—and the composers of five of the seven works were, in a way, friends of mine. That is, I knew them well, through working with them. Puccini, particularly, who chose me to create two of the leads in his *Trittico*; Mascagni, who conducted when I sang his opera *Isabeau*; Giordano, in whose *Andrea Chénier* I made my début in 1912." Verdi had died before Eddie reached Europe, he said, and Bizet died about the time Eddie was born. Eddie spoke with modesty of having been asked to participate in functions during the forthcoming Metropolitan appearance in Toronto. "It is like a 'return engagement' for me," he said, "and I am flattered."

At the party on May 23, following the Met's opening performance in Maple Leaf Gardens, Mayor Nathan Phillips introduced Edward Johnson to the three hundred invited guests, including members of the Metropolitan Opera Company, as "the man that made good music possible." Eddie then spoke for five minutes—"for five minutes by my watch," George W. Rayner wrote to Colonel Drew, "after which all the performers stood on chairs, on the piano, on tables, and everything else and gave Mr. Johnson such an ovation as I have never seen before. I thought you ought to know this because he was very touched by this tribute and it was then that my own eyes filled with tears of joy from the enthusiasm shown by those assembled guests. . . ."

That was in Toronto. But a few days later, in Guelph, the *Daily Mercury* carried the three-inch heading "Royal City On Musical Map After Symphonic Preview," with the sub-heading "Plaudits of 800 Assure Future." The story opened with the sentence, "Musical history was made in Guelph Sunday night." The occasion was the Guelph Civic Symphony and Chorale's Symphonic Preview Concert, conducted by Maestro Barbini, for which Eddie had been largely responsible. "I am proud this evening," he was quoted in the story as saying at the end of the concert, "proud of the music and of the audience." He reaffirmed his oft-repeated belief that there was "a surprising lot of talent in Guelph" and expressed the hope that he would live to see the day when the city would have its own musical festival.

"Much as I love Canada," he told George and Fiorenza when he phoned them in Ottawa that Sunday, "I am still counting the days until I can go to Italy; I feel different over there." They understood; especially Fiorenza, who felt somewhat the same way.

IN HIS ALMOST-DAILY letters to the Drews that summer, Eddie painted glowing word-pictures of his experiences, and revealed a renewed exuberance of spirit. The first letter came from Florence, June 25, 1955:

*Eccomi a Firenze!*

I arrived last evening amid the booming of the fireworks from Piazza Michelangelo. It was *la festa di San Giovanni* and everything that could move was on the streets. You can imagine what it was like along the Arno—both sides. All public buildings were illuminated and Piazza Signoria still held the sand and the tributes, evidence of the great football match in the afternoon. I slept in until nearly noon and recovered only in time to catch some lire at the American Express. . . .

In the hotel are Mr. and Mrs. Fredric March (he is making a picture), Mrs. Jean Tory and a friend from Toronto who are going to the Palio in Siena, and—as I came in just now—Frank Chapman and Gladys Swarthout. Spoke to Josephine by telephone and am seeing her tomorrow.

The trip over by T.W.A. was easy and pleasant. Stops at Gander —Paris—Geneva—and Rome. On board was Zinka Milanov and her brother en route to make records of *Aida* in Rome. Slept uncomfortably, ate little and drank less. Consequently my dinner at "Fagiano" was a *maraviglia—prosciutto coi fichi e mellone—sogliola al burro con fagiolini verdi, insalata piccolina con frutta fresca, pesche, e caffé espresso, senza contara tutto il pane e burro—poi a letto. Che vita. Vita bella!* . . . Today I lunched at Camillo's and was he glad to see me. He thanks you for all the clients you've sent him. He and Leland greeted me like a long lost brother. So it goes! This is Florence! The bells are ringing and so is my heart. Love to you all.

Babbo

From the San Domenico Palace Hotel in Taormina, Sicily, in July, Johnson wrote that he had run into an old friend from Pittsburgh, some ladies from Minneapolis, and Mr. Bing's right-hand man at the Met, John Gutman, and his wife. "From Taormina I go to Milan," he said, "and over to Verona for the opening on the 20th with *Otello*. I expect to find all the world and his brother there. The porter in this hotel gave me a surprise! He must have learned thru Gutman who I was and, being from Verona and an opera fan, says he remembers me in *Gianni Schicchi*. Anyway he keeps calling me Di Giovanni—strange sound after all these years. Does something to one's ego just the same! The period of deflation, after the retirement from the Metropolitan, was sometimes a bit depressing—and the lack of cooperation and the misunderstanding at the Conservatory was very often discouraging. It is refreshing to find someone who speaks your language and knows your *ambiente* and remembers! Blessed be the Italians!"

July 23, from Venice: "With the arrival [in Milan] of E. P. [Edith Piper] I fell into the rhythm of the Galleria in no time. . . . Bright and early the next day we got off to Verona where through the porter of the Grand Hotel I had reservations at Colombo d'Oro. Frank Chapman and Gladys were there and we were all the guests of Nino Martini and his pretty American wife for dinner. Then we all proceeded to the great Arena. What a sight! Twenty thousand people like half a house. The candle effect was delightful and the audience full of anticipation—*Otello* with [Mario] Del Monaco and Maestro [Antonino] Votto. Roberto Rossellini was to have directed the stage, but as he had quarrelled with the tenor the day before he had walked out on the show. The whole town was buzzing! Even Ingrid [Bergman] could not calm him.

"The first act was superb, and the opening phrase of the tenor 'Esultate!' magnificent. The chorus and orchestra were most effective. The stage business was confused—naturally R. R. had tried to Hollywood the scene! The wind carried the smoke from the fires (*Fuochi di gioia*) across the front of the stage, almost obscuring the set and choking the singers."

Returning to Florence, Eddie found in his accumulation of mail and messages a cable from a New York friend, Dr. Max Silbermann, with whom he had planned to attend the Salzburg Festival. Dr. Silbermann suggested they meet in Zürich. The next word the Drews received was a card from Zürich on July 30: "This is where Wagner wrote 2nd Act of

*Tristan*. Very lovely overlooking the lake—now a museum. Dr. Silbermann has a big car and drives very well. He met me at the airport. Am feeling fine."

After a day in Zürich, they went to "a charming place and luxurious hotel"—which was St. Moritz. "We made the Julia Pass (over 9,000 feet) and lunched at Trefencastel—a fresh *'fiorelle blau' mit salat*—and finally reached here in time for dinner. The last time I was here was to make auditions with Bodanzky. It was not a very happy occasion and ended me in the American Hospital in Paris, as you will well remember.

"Silbermann loves to motor—knows and loves intensely the territory over which we travel and is a most agreeable companion. With his German and my Italian we manage very well."

They left St. Moritz on August 8 and drove to Lucerne. "On Sunday, the 14th, we leave for Salzburg, and arrive Monday in time to hear the general rehearsal of the *Irish Legend* by Egk, conducted and prepared by George Szell. Later, *Ariadne* and *Magic Flute*. . . ."

There were numerous enthusiastic postcards from Salzburg. Then, on August 26, a letter from Munich. "This morning at 9 A.M. I said adieu to Dr. Silbermann. He was a delightful host and a good travelling companion. His contacts here and in Vienna made my visit very pleasant. Everyone was most cordial and friendly [in Salzburg] and gave me as much attention as if I were still the Gen. M. of the Metropolitan. Many of the artists of my time are in Salzburg—Szell, Schoeffler, Frantz, Gueden, to name a few. They were so glad to see me and spoke so nicely of our regime. . . . We motored to Wolfgangsee and Berchtesgaden (Whow!) and the mountainside, Reichenhall Bad [sic]—I heard four operas and two concerts plus *Jedermann*. Tonight I am hearing *Elektra* and tomorrow A.M. I fly to Paris (Grand Hotel, I hope!) and then London, September 3rd—no doubt I'll find letters there. Thanks again a thousand times for your cable and its loving message. It was deeply appreciated." Edward Johnson had just passed his seventy-seventh birthday on August 22.

When Eddie reached Paris on September 1, he found a card awaiting him from his travelling companions of recent weeks signed by all of them, wishing him good luck. "*Voilà Paris!*" he wrote Fiorenza. "It doesn't seem crowded, but confusion reigns on the streets because of a general strike of all auto buses. Poor France! Her troubles keep growing daily. . . . I took Edith Piper and Lydia Steinway and her husband Eric Cochrane to dinner at Coconnas. Tonight I've invited Annie Moulton to dinner—Lolotte is *en vacances* and Emilie in Dinard. No theatres going and no opera or music of any importance. Opéra-Comique with same old repertoire and no singers of repute. So on Saturday 3rd I am flying to London, where I hope to have my return ticket extended for another week. Hammie writes that the courts have given the merchants in my block until January 1st to move. So again I am safe from moving for another three months!!!"

The idyll over, Eddie said he could hardly get into his apartment in New York or his house in Guelph because of the "mounds of letters and papers." He took a room at the York Club in Toronto, had dinner and attended the Canadian Players' performance of *Macbeth* in Eaton Auditorium (October 7) with Lady Eaton; had a long lunch with Arnold Walter to bring himself up-to-date on what was happening at the Conservatory; spent an evening with Mrs. Tory; then flew to Los Angeles, where he spoke on October 26 as guest of honour at the Tenth Annual Luncheon given by the Opera Guild of Southern California.

Next, Fiorenza heard that her father was thinking of going to Vienna for the opening on November 5, 1955, of the newly-reconstructed Vienna Opera House. She was worried. "Gogo, don't you think you have done enough travelling for one year?" she questioned. "You will be exhausted." But the temptation was too strong for Edward Johnson to resist, and, besides, Lady Eaton was going and had urged him to go with her.

Everyone from the musical world was in Vienna, it seemed to Eddie, and he was glad he had gone. It was an interesting experience. The production of the opera *Fidelio* left something to be desired insofar as the cast was concerned, he reported to Fiorenza, and the staging was unfortunate. "But the house was surrounded by thousands of people listening to the performance over the specially installed loudspeakers— the opera was being broadcast on the radio—and many of them were following the opera from vocal scores they were carrying. Those were opera lovers!" All the members of the Staatsoper sat on the stage and listened as Ernst Marboe welcomed the honoured guests from all over the world—Edward Johnson, Lady Eaton, Bruno Walter and Lotte Lehmann among them. Dr. Karl Böhm was given the "Keys to the Opera" by the Government Minister, then conducted the "Blue Danube Waltz" and the Prelude to *Die Meistersinger*. Maria Jeritza had been invited, but did not attend. "She was *jung verheiratet* ['newly married']," Eddie explained, "and was incensed that the invitation had not included her husband."

It was exciting but tiring, and Eddie had more aches and pains than he cared to recognize: his back was bothering him—stiff and sore; and his feet were so puffed up he had trouble getting his shoes on—which happened too often to be excused by weather, altitude or fatigue. He was in trouble.

*11*

EDWARD JOHNSON was intensely proud of the fact that a fine, new modern public school in Guelph was to bear his name. Speaking at the opening on November 29, 1955, he said: "For me this is truly a memorable occasion. When time has taken its toll and I am no longer in this world, and should the events of my life ever be reviewed, the one thing that will remain to prove that I once lived will be the Edward Johnson School. Singers, you know, occupy an ambiguous position in the world. They are interpreters—conveyers—links in a chain. Once heard, they are forgotten. Today it is different, of course— we do have records and radio. . . . We hear a great deal about 'higher education' and 'equal opportunities' for all, but what we need is a much better grade of lower education for all, especially so in languages and speech—both of which are grossly and woefully neglected. Some people speak of education as if it were a substance to be distributed by coupon. The truth is that education is a voluntary process and doesn't come to anyone who doesn't want it. . . . The teaching profession is a noble calling and deserves our greatest respect. . . .

"In choosing one of your native sons for the distinction of giving his name to the newest and most modern of public schools you have added immeasurably to his prestige, and lent unbounded dignity to his name and fame. In so honouring him you have broken the long accepted rule that a man is not without honour save in his own country. You have placed him on an intellectual pedestal that no other singer, to my knowledge, has ever attained. You have perpetuated his memory for future generations and enhanced his reputation as a citizen of Guelph. With pride and joy, therefore, and in all humility, I accept the honour you have conferred upon me, and I will follow with interest the future progress and achievements of the Edward Johnson School."

The idea was beginning to hang heavily over Eddie's head that he would soon be forced to move from 687 Madison Avenue. The simple apartment he had called home for more than a quarter of a century, representing a great section of his life, was to be torn down. New York City had always meant two things to him: the Metropolitan Opera and 687 Madison Avenue. The curtain had already fallen on the part he had played in one of them, but even after 1950 there had always been his little apartment. Now that, too, was about to go. He was too old to change apartments; he would pack his things and send them back to Guelph. In the future, he would be a visitor in the great city.

Except for one week in Guelph, an I.O.D.E. dinner at the Royal York Hotel on February 13 and the Italian Immigrant Dinner and Ball at the King Edward the following evening, a dinner with Arnold Walter, and Jean Tory's birthday dinner in Toronto, Edward Johnson spent the first two months of 1956 in New York City. Mornings were occupied with going through and sorting the many things he had collected over the years. Each day he would fill his calendar with engagements. It was as though he was trying to crowd as much as possible of the spirit and way of life he had known in New York into those last few weeks. He had stubbornly refused to believe he would ever have to leave; had ignored the landlord's notices to tenants. Now even the merchants were gone, and he was alone in the building! There was a strange silence in the halls and an unfamiliar echo as he walked up the narrow stairs. Many times during the past year he had said he would never leave; let them tear the building down around him—this was his home and he was going to stay. Even then, although his words were filled with bravado, he knew he was only whistling into the wind.

Hammie had made arrangements for the movers to arrive at 687 Madison Avenue at 8:30 A.M. on Wednesday, February 29. Bulldozers were scheduled to begin demolition on March 1. Hammie helped pack and said nothing. That was her way. Eddie felt sorry for her, for he knew the big move meant the end of a great chapter in her life as well as in his.

They worked with the packers all day Monday, also Tuesday, after which Eddie mournfully wrote in his diary: "Just another day." Wednesday, after seeing the big moving van depart at 5 P.M., Guelph-bound, he went off to the nearby Ritz Hotel, at 14 East 60th Street, exhausted. He slept late the next morning.

Edward Johnson's fondness for that New York apartment was one of the things that Jean Tory remembered when asked about her old friend later.

> Edward lived in an apartment in New York—687 Madison Avenue —just a walk-up off Madison Avenue, and there was a store at the bottom. It had a funny little side-door entrance. The apartment was very dark and all of his over-sized old Italian furniture was

crowded into the very small space. He'd always lived there, though, and it was home to him—and it was economical and he was always very careful about spending money. I remember one time when we were going out to the Cloisters [Fort Tryon Park, at 190th Street in New York] he said, "Do you want to take a taxi?" and I said, "No, I love taking buses." So we went on a bus.

He was very gay and fun-loving; and a good companion. He was a great story-teller too—I especially liked to hear him tell about the famous musicians he'd known intimately. At the same time, he was a very hard-working and very conscientious man.

As to what he liked and didn't like: one of his *bêtes noires* was night clubs. He didn't like them at all—he said they were "just gyp joints" insofar as he was concerned.

Edward was a very self-sufficient man. I had just begun to live alone and he was a great inspiration to me by relating his own experiences and telling me how he found it much more fun to travel alone. "You meet many more interesting people that way," he would say.

He was a perfect ladies' man and he completely captivated me. I was in love with him—yes, very definitely!—for a time. It didn't last long—only until I realized that he was a very mercurial sort of person. You could never really depend on him, because he was always flitting here, flitting there. And he wouldn't hesitate to call you at the last minute when he was supposed to come to dinner, and excuse himself, if a very important invitation came along that interfered. But if you knew him, you understood. I enjoyed him always—we had such fun together. There was nobody like him.

Once back in Guelph, Eddie looked around and wondered how the little house at 673 Woolwich Street was going to be able to accommodate his New York belongings. It would take some time to arrange things, and he was glad not to have to face it by himself. Fiorenza had sent Maria and Rudi Russi down from Ottawa to help him, and Amy Grace Howitt stopped over several times to offer suggestions.

In the midst of it all, there was a brief interlude that offered a new kind of experience: Eddie went to California to appear in the "This Is Your Life" telecast of the life and career of famed soprano Marguerita Sylva, March 14, 1956. Eddie had sung with Mme Sylva years before. ("This Is Your Life" surprised featured guests by confronting them with family, friends and colleagues brought from all over the world for that one occasion.)

"On Tuesday, Ralph Edwards handed me the script I was to use next day, and I spent the evening looking it over," he reported to friends upon his return to Canada. "We left Los Angeles at noon on Wednesday

297

for Burbank for rehearsal and makeup. It was a whirlwind experience, with a supper party after the show, a luncheon party the next day and a flight back to Toronto that night."

A letter from Marguerita Sylva a few days later brought back some of the details of those crowded two days in California for the television show, as well as memories of their singing together on the stage:

Dear Eddy,

What a good angel you have been in my life, ever since 1922 and the never-to-be-forgotten performance at the Hollywood Bowl. And you were the greatest of all the directors of the Met—and I knew them all since 1896! How many wonderful reports have come to me, from time to time, of such wonderful things you said about me and my work. . . . How gorgeous of you to come all that long trip, to pay me such a tribute! Your presence, your statements were the greatest endorsement of anything I might have ever tried to achieve—thank you, thank you. Seeing unexpectedly my adored girls I thought deep in the snows of the East—the wonderful presents and—*le coup de grâce!!*—that gorgeous Mercury—a dream (the most extravagant of any present in my life)!! Now I drive a faithful but dilapidated '41 Ford convertible which has only one merit—it gets me there and brings me back. Let me repeat that your Don José was one of the three greatest ones I met during my several hundred performances of Carmen. The other two were [Edmond] Clement and [Thomas] Salignac, but neither had what you had—the glorious voice added to the great dramatic genius. *We* had 40 thousand in the audience, wish it had been the 40 million I am told saw us the 14th of March last. I sign with, and say, deep affection, gratitude, admiration and love!! and hum the song "Till we meet again." Hope soon—Sylva.

As to the Guelph house, Eddie was relieved when he returned to see that his books and pieces of furniture from New York seemed to fit comfortably in their new surroundings. "Couldn't have done better myself," he admitted with satisfaction.

Although Eddie didn't talk much about it, his arthritis had been bothering him more and more, and his visits to the osteopath had become more frequent. There were times when he had difficulty getting his shoes on over his swollen feet. Fiorenza was doubly concerned. Not only was her father's health giving way, but for months George had been constantly exhausted and overworked.

In May, 1956, when the trans-Canada pipeline controversy became the central subject of concern in Parliament, there was a period of extreme tension for all the MPs and their families. The public galleries were always crammed and long queues stretched outside the Parliament Buildings. It was one of the most dramatic spectacles the House had ever produced. The final weeks were a nightmare for Fiorenza because she could see how much the proceedings were taking out of George. When the debate was finally over, the doctors found that George was suffering from extreme exhaustion and ordered him to take a long and complete rest.

No one knew better than Edward Johnson how difficult it must have been for George to relinquish the helm of a ship he had guided for so long that it had become part of his very being. He also knew that there were times when one has no choice! In George's case, the doctors had said the least that could happen, if he continued to try to work, was that his health would be ruined forever. So he would have to make the only possible decision: resign and leave Ottawa. "We're looking for a house in Toronto," Fiorenza told her father, "and as soon as we find it, we're going to take a long trip—probably to the Middle East, where neither of us has ever been before."

THE EARLY SUMMER of 1956 included for Edward Johnson several visits to the young Stratford Shakespearean Festival in Stratford, Ontario—performances in the big tent were exciting—and a motor trip through the province of Quebec. He felt better than he had for months, and after a reassuring annual checkup he set off for Europe, on August 2, with a light heart.

His first letter to the Drews was written in Florence: "Last night the Countess Dandini sent her nice car for me and we had a tête-à-tête dinner at her beautiful villa. My! It was something to sit out on that terrace and look over Florence under a *quasi piena luna!*" Fiorenza's cable of good wishes for his birthday didn't reach him until the twenty-third, just as he was leaving San Remo for Nice and London on his way to Edinburgh to see *Henry V* performed by Canada's Stratford Festival Company, and the Hamburg Opera production there of *Die Zauberflöte*.

Lady Eaton, also in Edinburgh for the Festival, left on September 1. Two days later Eddie departed for Madrid which impressed him as much as it had the Drews. "What a beautiful city!" he wrote to them. "When I went to the Prado I sought out immediately the Velásquez, and then went downstairs to see the Goya murals. My but they are gorgeous! . . . Yesterday I ran into Val Pareira—husband of the late Grace Moore. What say you? No word from Bori—she must still be in Italy and I'm here ahead of time. No matter. I'm a born tourist. Tomorrow I'm off on a week's tour of Granada, Cordova, Malaga and Seville—returning to the hotel the 14th. If all goes well, Bori or no Bori, I will fly Air

France 19th to Paris (Grand Hotel) till 23rd when I am for Park Lane in London."

Another enthusiastic letter reached the Drews in Bermuda where they had gone for a holiday: "If you are enjoying your vacation in Bermuda half as much as I am mine in Spain, I know you are alright. My knowledge of this country has always been a bit vague, but now I'm informed —and how! The distances are enormous (one thousand miles by the time we get back to Madrid)—but side stops are frequent (this saves me!)—the countryside astonishing and the art side simply marvellous. History, art and religion all intertwined! Hot as Hades! But last evening it poured. . . . Extraordinary climate!! Just this line to let you know I'm fit and having a good time."

Good health seemed to accompany Eddie throughout his travels in Europe, but soon after he was home his back began bothering him again, also his legs—sometimes it was almost impossible for him to get up in the morning. Then a severe "bilious attack," as Eddie called it, caused Dr. Mutrie to send him to the hospital the last week of October. As he left the hospital on November 1, he noted in his diary: "Still feeling quite shaky." He went out to the Dunbars for dinner on the fourth of November, but two days later he had a relapse that put him back in the hospital for another week of tests and X-rays. He made Dr. Mutrie smile when he asked: "Why do they always speak of doctors as 'practising'?" As soon as Eddie was back at home, his former Toronto secretary, Madge Day, offered to help with his letters; Hammie came up for several days from New York; and his housekeeper, Mrs. Bassett, prepared his food. He was well looked after.

By November 26 he was much better, and again it was "life as usual." That day he took a train to Toronto to attend Lady Eaton's birthday party and didn't return home until midnight. Next day the entry in the diary read: "Very tired—slept late." But at noon of the second day he was on the train to Toronto again: "Dinner, York Club, Lady Eaton— Vienna Orchestra Concert. Excellent. Boskovsky party at Plaza." Eddie had lunch with Jean Tory at the York Club the next day, and he was once more in Guelph by evening for dinner at Phyllis Higinbotham's and a performance of *Così fan tutte* at the Presto Club that evening. Again a day of rest (Friday), and he "watched the Big Fight [Floyd Patterson-Archie Moore] on TV." On Saturday, he boarded the overnight train to New York and, once there, followed his usual round of activities: "Found Apt. 10B, Shoreham Hotel, ready for me at 9:30 Sunday morning. Lunch with Edith Piper; supper with F.P.K. [Florence Page Kimball]; Sullivan Foundation meeting on Monday." Then back to Canada on a sleeper: "Hamilton 7:30 A.M. Breakfast and bus to Guelph.

300

Attended a funeral with the Dunbars and the Drews at St. George's Church (Tues.) and saw the Drews off to Ottawa again."

Eddie was constantly on the go: Guelph, Toronto, New York, Buffalo, King—operas, auditions, board meetings, lunches and dinners with friends—it had all become a routine. Then Christmas with the Drews in Ottawa.

The *Ottawa Journal* carried a fine tribute to George Drew as he and Fiorenza took official leave of Ottawa on March 14, 1957, and flew to England on the first lap of a three-month trip to the Middle East. Eddie was pleased for George as he read the item: "Drew's eight years as leader of the Conservative party were not easy; fortune came and fortune fled, with disappointments and frustrations. But no leader of ill-fortune ever left his command with more compensating evidences of admiration and affection, and with compensation all the greater seeing that such evidences came alike from friend and foe, from those who fought him as well as those who followed him. It is the fate of strong and resolute character that it invites enmities as well as loyalties. George Drew, his sword never sleeping in his hand, invited both."

When the Drews returned to Ottawa on June 9, 1957, after their trip, Eddie was there waiting for them with Sandra, who had stayed in Ottawa while her parents were away. It was an exciting reunion, everyone talking at once about travels and friends. They were together for the election of June 10, 1957, that brought the Conservatives, under John G. Diefenbaker, the long-awaited victory. "Poor George! After all those years of tough fights and uphill battles," Eddie thought as he joined George and Fiorenza in offering congratulations to the new Prime Minister.

The following week, Eddie had a call from Fiorenza asking him to join them again in Ottawa for a family conference concerning an important decision. Mr. Diefenbaker had asked George whether he would accept an appointment in London. "You know George as well as I do," Fiorenza said to her father, "and you know how he would love to be back in harness again. But we want to think it over carefully." The family conference took place, and the decision was made to accept the appointment. On June 26, 1957, George Drew was named High Commissioner to the United Kingdom at the Court of St. James. So in August, instead of retiring to Toronto as planned, the Drews—George, Fiorenza and Sandra (Edward was already enrolled at McGill University in Montreal)—took up residence in London.

"George has a full 9:30 A.M. to 7:30 P.M. work day before him every day," Fiorenza wrote to her father soon after the move. "Besides his liaison work between Ottawa and the British Government, there are the

301

endless visitors, speeches to make and numberless dispatches. The fact that he can handle this, and then top it with the evening receptions, demonstrates how completely he has recovered from his illness."

When Fiorenza had discovered that the Russis did not wish to accompany her and George to London, but preferred to remain in Canada with their two small children, she had suggested their moving to Guelph to look after her father on a full-time basis. They liked the idea and, to Fiorenza's great relief, her father was delighted—he would be able to talk Italian to his heart's content. So Maria and Rudi had gone to Guelph to discuss the situation and, on July 22, had left Ottawa and moved into their spacious, well-equipped apartment above the garage at 673 Woolwich Street.

*12* It was obvious to Eddie and to his doctors that the time had come for him to cut down on some of his responsibilities and, particularly with Fiorenza in Europe, to be free to travel at will.

"I recall one of the Board of Governors meetings concerning the location of the proposed new building for the Faculty of Music," Arnold Walter said, shortly before his own death in 1973. "Johnson was not feeling well. He was in great pain—and he didn't say a word. Afterward, he asked me to come to see him in Guelph so we could spend a day together. I went, and he told me about the books he wanted me to have for the library of the new building, and how he was thinking of resigning as chairman of the Board of Governors of the Royal Conservatory so he could be free to travel and spend more time in Europe. . . . The only reference he made to his arthritis was that perhaps he should go to Mexico and take the baths there. He wasn't very serious; I think he believed he would wake up some morning and the pain would all be gone. I don't know. Anyway I don't think he thought too much about death as such and he didn't talk about it. But I think he was feeling lonely."

Eddie and his old Guelph fishing crony Martin J. Barry used to motor somewhere almost every other day. Barry reminisced, in 1972, about their trips:

> Mostly we didn't know where we'd go. "We'll just motor," Ed would say. But one time in 1957 we were going to New York because he had to attend his niece's birthday party there. Before we'd gone very far, I began to feel sick. We discovered the exhaust pipe was leaking and we never did get to New York. We spent two nights in Geneva. While we were there, we took advantage of the time to visit Cornell Agricultural College. Professor Leo Klein toured us around; it was very interesting. En route back home, we touched most of the towns in southern Ontario and landed in

303

Batavia for a Rotary luncheon. When we got to Guelph about 7 P.M. we were both tired but we stopped at the Cutten Club for a glass of his favourite drink, Tio Pepe. We didn't stay long because he had to visit the osteopath early the next morning.

Another time we motored to Kitchener, and I remember he bought a three-quarter violin there and gave it away as soon as he got home, to one of Jennie Lamb's violin pupils. He was like that.

He was an Anglican, you know, and one time we motored to Grimsby to see our old archdeacon, who was retired and living there. Edward Johnson took him a bottle of sherry, I remember. And I think that was the same trip when we had dinner in the Cottage Inn Motel in Smithsville, my old home, and they served us steak that filled our plates. He remarked as a joke that they served small steaks, but the woman seriously apologized because they hadn't been able to get any bigger plates!

In the fall of 1957 after attending a Board of Governors meeting in Toronto, Eddie "packed for New York and 10B at the Shoreham." He was there several weeks that trip: Lotus Club, Dutch Treat Club, Town Hall auditions, several lunches at the Coffee House, Juilliard and Sullivan Foundation meetings, a Bagby meeting and concert, lunches and dinner with Edith Piper, Mrs. Belmont, Bori and others, and the Queen's Ball with Florence Kimball. He had several letter-answering sessions with Hammie, attended a Canadian Society dinner and made a couple of visits to his bankers and stockbrokers. The Met opened early that year, on October 28—*Eugene Onegin*, with George London, Lucine Amara, Richard Tucker—and Eddie was on hand with the Guild's Mrs. Vera Gibbs. He looked drawn, people thought, but was flashing his familiar smile and giving no hint of the pain in the hip that plagued him. He would have been more comfortable using two canes instead of one that evening, but pride forbade it.

Florence Kimball was his companion for the season's second performance, *Don Giovanni*, on October 31, with Cesare Siepi, Eleanor Steber, Lisa Della Casa and Roberta Peters in the cast. After that, he took his usual sleeper to Hamilton and 9:50 A.M. bus to Guelph.

Four days later Edward Johnson was back in New York where he stayed until the middle of December. That time, however, except for an occasional play, concert or opera, he spent the evenings in his room, watching TV. The days of meetings, lunches, teas, and even the sessions with Hammie that sometimes culminated in an evening of scrabble, usually taxed his endurance to the limit. Nevertheless, when Eleanor Robson Belmont's book *The Fabric of Memory* came out the first week of November, Eddie was prominent among the guests at the reception in connection with its release. That day he was in greater pain than usual and it took constant effort for him to maintain a cheerful front.

It was during that visit that Eddie ran into the author Quaintance Eaton one day as he was making his way along 57th Street. Speaking of that encounter, Miss Eaton said: "We had quite a chat. He told me he wasn't feeling well at all and that even though he was busy, he was very lonely up in Guelph. I think that's why he liked to spend so much time in New York, where he had so many friends and where there was always something to go to or somebody to see."

As it happened, Eddie was on his way to have lunch that day with John Majesky, publisher of *Musical America*, at the Plaza Hotel. They talked about the times they had run across each other during the summers in Europe. Eddie was in a rather reminiscent mood, Majesky thought in retrospect, and they both enjoyed themselves. Majesky was rather surprised when Eddie told him how lonely it was for him in Guelph. "I like it better here in New York, but I've got a lot to do up there. We're getting music in the schools and training violinists and singers. You know, John, Guelph is going to lead the way in making Canada a singing nation."

For all his brave words, and for all of his love of New York, Eddie found it a comfort, when he returned to Guelph on December 18, to be able to give in to himself. There he could use both of his canes when he needed them. He could enjoy being spoiled by Maria and Rudi—being served his favourite Italian dishes for lunch and dinner and having his mail sorted and neatly stacked for him each morning.

For the first time in many years, the family did not celebrate Christmas together. Only Edward Drew spent the holidays with his grandfather. "The long distance calls between the parents in London and the two of us in Guelph must have run up quite a bill," Edward commented in the 1970's. "Grasping at straws to keep back the tears, we all spoke about the coming summer," he said, "and about the celebration we would have for Babbo's eightieth birthday. He thought he would like to spend the whole summer in Florence." But Fiorenza wanted him in London for the "first Royal occasion" in their new home when Princess Margaret would be dining with them before going to Canada.

George was in Canada in the spring of 1958 and returned to London with depressing stories about how Eddie's arthritis had become acute and how he often had trouble walking, even with two canes. Fiorenza was inclined to minimize George's dramatic account until she saw her father get off the plane in London one morning early in July. She was shocked at the change in him. There were no canes, his head was high and the familiar loving smile was on his face, but every time he took a step she could tell that he was in pain. As might have been expected, Edward Johnson took part in all the gatherings they had planned, and sitting beside Princess Margaret at the big dinner he seemed to enjoy himself thoroughly and to amuse the Princess as well. "We had a good long gossip together about all the people we both knew in the theatrical world," he reported. "She is a most attractive young woman; she should make a big hit in Canada."

Fiorenza had heard that the baths in Ischia—the small island that they all knew so well off the coast of Italy—could do wonders for arthritis. She kept mentioning them to her father. Finally, toward the end of July, Eddie agreed to "give them a try." So, leaving George and Sandra in London, Fiorenza and her father flew to Naples, missed the deluxe boat they intended to take to Ischia, and joined the hordes of men, women and children, with their bundles, cases and parcels, pushing their way up the gangplank of the general passenger boat that would take them across. The only seat Fiorenza could find for her father was one with a young husband and wife and their brood of squiggly children. But Eddie, once seated, had a wonderful time. They were soon friends, discussing their lives and hopes at such length that the people on the neighbouring benches joined in, contributing stories of their own. It was familiar Italy again, Fiorenza thought, and she marvelled at her father's obvious enjoyment of the situation.

The series of vigorous treatments lasted two weeks, after which Eddie and Fiorenza left, this time by the luxury boat, for Naples. Their train departure for Florence, thanks to Eddie's sense of humour, had its funny side. After he had climbed twenty-five steps to the track level and painfully made his way to their coach at the end of the long platform, Eddie discovered that they had the wrong train. As Fiorenza told the story in the April, 1963, *Chatelaine* article: "I was in tears. The temperature was in the nineties. I could see perspiration pouring down my father's face and the terrible strain of pain about his mouth. The baggage porter saw it, too, and said to me, 'Signora, if the gentleman doesn't mind sitting on my baggage cart and going down in the freight elevator. . .' My father agreed delightedly and off we went to the right train this time." When they were finally settled in their coach and the train began to move, Eddie started to laugh at the picture he must have presented, riding along in that little cart, perched on top of all the baggage.

They had several weeks in Florence seeing old friends and visiting familiar haunts in the little Fiat Fiorenza had rented. Eddie had even insisted on going off on his own in a taxi one afternoon, for tea with Josephine Casali.

That day stood out in the memory of Assunta Leita, Signora Casali's housekeeper since 1939: "I saw him coming and I told the Signora, and she was more excited than I'd ever seen her. That time neither one of them was feeling well but they went out for a while to take some flowers up to Mrs. Johnson's grave. This time it was very difficult for both of them, climbing up the slope to the grave in the Cimiterio degli Inglese [English Cemetery]. They were both very sad when they came back and I made them a nice espresso and then he left. I remember they were embracing each other a long time, and kissing, before he said good-bye. She stood there, watching him go, and there were tears streaming down her face. 'Assunta,' she said to me, 'love never dies; it's just as fresh when you're old as it is when you're young. I'm afraid I will never see Johnson again.' And she never did." Eddie was tired when he returned to the hotel; he said nothing, just went in for a rest. Fiorenza understood.

A few days later, before he was to leave by train for Rome, Eddie suggested to Fiorenza that they visit her mother's grave together "for one last time," not mentioning the visit he had made there with Josephine Casali. So, in the cool of the evening, they drove out to the Cimiterio and climbed the tree-lined terraces to Bebe's grave. Standing in front of the black marble monument, they silently read the inscription: "Beatrice d'Arneiro, beloved wife of Edward Johnson, Florence, May 24th, 1919," and the words of the poet Thomas Campbell, "And is he dead whose glorious mind/Lifts thine on high? /To live in hearts we leave behind /Is not to die."

Eddie squeezed Fiorenza's hand. "Your mother would have been proud of you," he told her. It was a nostalgic moment. They stood there a long time, lost in memories of the past, before they turned to leave.

The next day, on the train to Rome, Eddie had time to think about the future and how he was going to face it. For him who had always been so independent and proud the idea of being in a wheelchair, perhaps for the rest of his life, was intolerable. He intended to avoid that wheelchair if it was humanly possible. He had great faith in both his doctor and his osteopath at home, and even though this might prove to be his last visit to Italy he could hardly wait to get back to Guelph.

There was a delay of several hours at the Rome airport, and at that point Edward Johnson was more than grateful when he was offered a wheelchair. Besides being more comfortable, the chair brought him attention and privileges he would not otherwise have had. The role of invalid was a new one for Eddie, but, ever the actor, he made the most of it.

THE PLANE TRIP seemed interminable and Eddie was miserable in spite of all the attention and service. It cheered him to see Rudi waiting for him at the airport in Toronto. In an hour's time he was back in Guelph. Home. It was a good feeling.

He soon began to recover from the enervating effects of the over-strenuous "cure" in Ischia. "It was a mistake to allow myself to be talked into taking those treatments in Ischia," he told Arnold Walter when Arnold visited him a short time later, "—the biggest mistake I ever made in my life since the time I turned down a chance to buy the first Coca-Cola stock at ten cents a share! I didn't really think those treat-ments were going to help me. Still, I hoped they might. But they only aggravated the condition."

Eddie's arthritic hip joint was so painful that he had all but given up the idea of attending the opening of the Metropolitan Opera that season. But a letter from Mrs. Belmont gave him courage and inspiration:

> My dear E. J.—
>
> What has come over you? The last time we met you seemed in marvellous good health. True, it is quite some time ago—far too long, in fact. But now I hear that you have been ordered to take a complete rest. Have you caught a bug—or I should say, has a bug caught you? Please take care of yourself.
>
> Alas, it is difficult to even contemplate a Metropolitan Opera or a Guild Anniversary without you. If there is any chance of your coming, let me know. We long to have you. In fact everyone— Board, Management, Guild—all want you with us for the annual meeting, October 22nd.
>
> Particularly disconsolate and lonely will be your admiring friend, partner and associate,
>
> Eleanor Belmont

In the fall of 1958, Edward Johnson was not only in New York for the Guild Anniversary and subsequent Met opening, but also amazingly cheerful during all the festivities. Very few people suspected how hard it was for him at times to maintain a bright front. He stayed in town until after the Bagby Music Lover's Foundation Benefit performance of *Madama Butterfly* at the Metropolitan on November 8. Returning to Guelph, Eddie quickly came down to earth again when he received a letter from his New York stockbrokers with the uninspiring news that his account showed a balance of $10,695.50.

The Drews flew to Canada for Christmas in Guelph that year. Eddie had been observing "the doctor's ground rules," as George called them, for the use of pills and medicines, and seemed to be responding to the treatment. When the family left to spend New Year's with the Jack Eatons and other friends in Ste. Agathe, Quebec, Eddie was sad. But he realized almost immediately, much as he loved them all, how wonderful it was to have a quiet house again with just Maria and Rudi there to look after him.

From Ste. Agathe, on January 4, in the midst of "a true winter scene, masses of snow and mild weather," Fiorenza wrote her father a note of thanks: ". . . perfect and memorable Christmas . . . the magnificent gorgeous gifts—the colossal cheque and the really beautiful earrings—to say nothing of all the other countless and thoughtful things you did. . . . I only wish it had been a little more restful for you. . . ."

Letters from the children, Edward and Sandra, were stamped with their own individual personalities and signed with the pet names Eddie had given them: Eddo and Sandy Pooh.

During the first days of the New Year, a number of young people came to visit Dr. Johnson, asking for his opinion of their voices and for advice. It made Eddie feel younger just to have them around. "But he overdid it," Maria Russi said later on. "He didn't have to see and hear all those people who came—it was too much for him."

Eddie was especially happy when Fiorenza decided to return to Guelph for a few weeks with him after the Drews ended their holidays in Quebec. Sandra had gone to Ottawa; Edward was back at university in Montreal; and George had returned to London. Fiorenza told her father she just couldn't bring herself to leave, somehow, without seeing him again. They spent many delightful days and evenings together, and sometimes the Dunbars or the Higinbothams would stop in. "I am hoping to get him to write his memoirs," Fiorenza told them, "but he just won't settle down to it. I have even given him a tape recorder to make it easy, but he hasn't used it."

For Eddie, it was enough that Fiorenza was with him and that the children turned up for weekends. Only George was missing, but he kept telephoning from England. When Fiorenza finally left on February 13, she had a feeling that they would never see each other again. The picture was indelibly printed on her mind of her father standing at the top of the steps as she got into the taxi. With a jaunty lift of his right hand and a characteristic smile, he called out, *Addio, cara.* She caught her breath. Always before it had been *Au revoir,* or *Ciao,* when they had parted. This time he had said *Addio.*

Guelph architect E. J. "Manny" Birnbaum remembered one of the ruses Eddie used, to avoid having anyone see him in physical discomfort: "If he was having people in for dinner at a time when it was painful for him to get into his chair at the table, he would manage to disappear when no one was looking. Then, when we went into the dining room, there he was, smiling and cheerful, already in his place at the head of the table. And when we'd go to the other room after dinner, he'd stay behind, pretending to have something to discuss with Rudi. He was too proud to let anyone see him getting up and down from his chair."

"It was only in the last months," as Arnold Walter remembered it, "that he broke down. When he always had to walk with canes, very slowly and painfully, he felt badly about himself. Even then, when we talked about other things, some of the old enthusiasm would return. I asked him if he ever thought of writing his memoirs.

" 'See that thing down there?' he said, pointing toward a tape recorder under his bed. 'I am supposed to talk into it, but I haven't told it anything yet!' He gave me a sly wink. Then he spoke a little sadly. 'Arnold, I tell you I would sell my soul to the devil right here and now if I could sing just once as I sang forty years ago.' "

That winter, except for a few short drives and an occasional brief motor trip, as he called it, to Toronto, Eddie never left Guelph. When he went to the Dunbars' for dinner, as he often did, the conversation would generally centre around some of the experiences of the past. He never tired of hearing Mrs. Dunbar, for instance, tell stories about the summer when she was a teenager and spent several weeks with Fiorenza at Ravinia while he was singing there. Eddie seldom went to the parties after the operas in those days and thought the girls were silly because they wanted to go to all of them. "Once," Mrs. Dunbar recalled in the 1970's, "Fiorenza and I came home late at night expecting to find her father asleep, but there he was, sitting up in bed wearing his green eyeshade and studying."

Eddie was beginning to take a philosophic view of his condition and was determined to make the best of it. He got into the habit of "lazy mornings," but was up in the afternoon and early evening. Rudi and Maria insisted on helping him as much as possible, but he preferred not to be pampered any more than was necessary—wanted to do things on his own. His activities, nevertheless, were limited; his walks to town were very occasional. He spent many hours in his library with Eva Howlett, who was helping him put his books and records in order. "Once, when he was edgy," she said, "I told him it was too bad he didn't smoke. That was when he admitted that he had endorsed a certain cigarette, years before, and that the advertisement had read: 'These cigarettes never hurt my throat.' He laughed and laughed and then explained, 'That was because I never smoked them!'

"He'd sit and ask me to bring him this book or that book—usually from a very inaccessible far-away location. Then he'd ask me to read a particular section of it to him—and no sooner had I started than he would be reminded of something and start reminiscing, and that would be all I'd get done that day or evening. I often went in the evening

310

because I worked in the public library during the day. But on holidays, or on my days off, I'd sometimes go to Dr. Johnson's."

Another welcome diversion for Eddie in those days was a visit now and then from Maria and Rudi's two little girls. They had been strictly forbidden to disturb him, but one Sunday morning after mass they had escaped their parents' watchful eyes and were found sitting on the end of Eddie's bed. The three of them were all laughing merrily as they exchanged stories and jokes. "Why did the elephant sit on the marshmallow?" the children asked him. He gave up. "So he wouldn't fall in the hot chocolate," they triumphantly explained.

And Eddie told them about the little boy who visited the circus and didn't have enough money for a ticket. He was on his hands and knees, watching the show from underneath the canvas of the tent, when a guard came along and gave him a boot that sent him right into the middle of the ring. Eddie was laughing the hardest at that one when Maria came in with disapproving words because the children had disobeyed orders. But Eddie said, "Let them come in. I like it. We are having a good time." And from then on, every Sunday morning, Maria knew where to find her children: perched on either side of the foot of Dr. Johnson's bed. It became a routine for them and one to which he looked forward.

In March, 1959, Mrs. Belmont asked Johnson to join the board of the Metropolitan Opera Welfare Fund, but he regretfully declined. He had already found it necessary to resign all his positions, he informed her. "The only interest I've retained," he wrote, "is the local 'Crusade for Strings,' promoted and sustained by the Edward Johnson Music Foundation, for the encouragement of music in the community of Guelph and in the public schools in particular. . . ."

Easter was an especially pleasant period for Eddie that year, with Florence Kimball up from New York for a visit. He was his usual ebullient self and, at some cost, eschewed the use of one of his canes while she was there. Even with someone he had known so long and so well, the rule by which he had lived his life still prevailed: Let people see you only at your best. Guelph portrait painter Evan MacDonald once said of Edward Johnson, "He was a man who was always acting— and he didn't have to."

MARIA AND RUDI RUSSI probably knew Edward Johnson more intimately than anyone else during his last months. There was an understanding among them ever since the evening, soon after they arrived in July, 1957, when he had come out to the kitchen and suggested they all go to a movie together. They had gone—he, Maria and Rudi—to see

*Auntie Mame.* He felt comfortable with them, he used to say, and they had a sincere affection for him. "Mostly, at first, he was never home, except for a few days at a time," Rudi said, "and even then he'd be out for dinner. He'd come home around ten-thirty or eleven and he'd have a glass of juice and a cookie. He liked to watch hockey on TV. So twice a week we would sit and watch it together and Maria would make us *risotto alla Milanese*—that was his favourite."

"Or I might make a steak and kidney pie," Maria added. "That was one of his favourites, too, with vegetables, then pears and provolone cheese. He couldn't eat a really big meal at night. He liked a good luncheon though, about one o'clock; and for breakfast, about eight forty-five, it was always the same thing—apple sauce, cream of wheat, brown toast and jam and coffee. He liked to come in and sit at the countertop in front of the window and we'd talk. Same thing at lunch. He never ate in bed, until the last few months. . . . He'd eat applesauce three times a day if I'd give it to him—I made it fresh. We had a tiny little apple tree in the garden and in the summer we'd pick the apples from that."

"The last few months he was full of new ideas like we hadn't seen him for a long time," Rudi interjected. "He was going to go on the radio every week, with a young woman. 'I discovered her,' he told us, 'and brought her to the Metropolitan when I was general manager. Now she's married and living in Toronto.' It was to be an opera program ['Opera Time' with Ruby Mercer, on CBC]. He was really excited. And he was making plans to sing in a quartet of old-timers, too. 'When we get the thing together,' he said, 'and if it turns out, we'll put it into a record.' "

Around the middle of April, Eddie phoned his old friend Jessie Hill and said he wanted to give a luncheon party for her on April 21. "I would have phoned you earlier," he told her, "but my leg was all puffed up."

"It is impossible for a man of your temperate habits to have the gout," she joked, and they both had a good laugh.

"You know, Jessie," he told her, "as one grows older one's friends grow more endearing, in almost precise ratio with the years that pass." And she heartily agreed.

Eddie was feeling so bad the week of the luncheon that he wondered how he was going to manage. In addition, he had promised The National Ballet of Canada to attend their performance in the Guelph Memorial Gardens on April 20. On the afternoon of the twentieth he phoned Mrs. Stella Johnson, widow of his cousin Gordon, and asked whether she would go to the ballet with him. She agreed, and said her grandson, Brad Young, could drive them.

312

There had been some chance that Sandra might be coming to Guelph for the ballet, but she phoned from Ottawa to say she couldn't make it. "Crawley Films is working on a TV series and I'm sort of general factotum—costumes and everything—and I have to be there." Then she told Eddie about a book she'd been reading—*A Most Remarkable Father* by "Doodie" Dale-Harris—that she thought he would like. He was interested, and she said she'd send it to him the next day. She was puzzled when he told her, "Don't bother. It might not get here in time."

"Every time I tried to sign off that evening," Sandra told her mother a few days later, "he would stop me with another funny story. He just didn't seem to want me to hang up."

When it was time for Eddie to get dressed for the theatre, Rudi could see that he was procrastinating. "Don't go if you don't feel like going," he told him. "Don't go."

"Oh, no! They expect me there. I must go," Eddie protested.

Maria and Rudi helped Eddie dress, and they noticed that as he found himself in the familiar white tie and tails, a veritable uniform for him during his years as general manager of the Metropolitan, he again began to be excited over the prospect of going out. When they came to the shoes, there was a serious problem: they wouldn't go on. "Don't worry, Dr. Johnson," Maria said. "Wear your slippers."

"Oh, I can't do that. How would it look for me to appear, all dressed up like this, in my bedroom slippers?"

"Nobody's going to be looking at your feet," she assured him. "And everybody is looking forward to seeing you. I think you should go."

Eddie sat for a moment, with his eyes closed, gathering strength. Then, brightening, he said, "You are right! On with the slippers!"

"As he was leaving the house," Rudi recalled later, "he told us to be sure to keep the fire going in the library. Then Mrs. Johnson and I swung his feet into the car. He was all smiles again, and he said, 'Well, I'll see you later.' And then to Maria, 'I hope you enjoy it.' He had bought tickets for her and one of the girls."

Stella Johnson related the subsequent events of that evening:

> He looked so happy as we drove away. "Ed," I told him, "by spring you're going to be as good as new."
>
> We went right to the door of the Memorial Gardens so he wouldn't have to walk. He grabbed my arm, and we walked into the lobby of the Gardens for the National Ballet performance. We were given a program, and he said, "Just a minute—here's a dollar —buy another."
>
> "Why buy it?" I asked.
>
> "I helped sponsor it," was his reply.
>
> We started up the tiny ramp to go into the arena—he was ahead

of me in the crowd. He was just inside the rail when he hestitated and took a couple of steps back—wavered and gasped. Young Tom Colley caught him. I called out for a doctor. And Ed kept saying, "Air, air!"

A stretcher was brought up, and I went with Ed to the General Hospital where he was carried into the emergency room. I couldn't go in there, but the intern was with him, and Dr. Bolley—Ed's own doctor, Eric Mutrie, was away. I wondered what I could do—who to tell. I phoned Angus Dunbar and told him, "I'm at the hospital with Ed—I think he's dying."

Angus arrived just as Dr. Bolley came out of the room and said, "Sit down, Mrs. Johnson, sit down. I'm sorry to tell you, but Mr. Johnson just passed away."

Angus said to me, "Don't worry. I'll take over from here."

My grandson went along to tell Rudi. Rudi went all to pieces—he'd just helped Ed into the car half an hour before. Angus phoned Fiorenza, and she told us later, "As soon as the phone rang, I knew something had happened to my father."

The next morning banner headlines announced the death of Guelph's most famous son, Edward Johnson. He had died quietly in hospital on the night of April 20, 1959, it was reported, shortly after collapsing among the people he loved most—the people who appreciate music. As a patron of The National Ballet of Canada, which was opening its spring tour with a performance of *Les Sylphides* in the Guelph Memorial Gardens that night, Dr. Johnson was on his way to take his place in the capacity audience when he collapsed.

"Even if he had dictated the kind of death he would like," Arnold Walter commented later, "it couldn't have been more wonderful. Imagine a man like that, whose whole life had been in the theatre, and who was so intensely interested in the cultural growth of his hometown of Guelph, getting up and dressing in white tie and going to that performance, at eighty, and with no inkling of any kind having a heart attack and dying. There was nothing melancholy about him to the end."

PEOPLE CAME from all over the world to pay tribute to Edward Johnson. St. George's Anglican Church, in the heart of the city, where Eddie had sung as a choirboy and later as tenor soloist, was crowded for the funeral service. Famous opera stars and political dignitaries mingled with Johnson's colleagues, close friends and neighbours.

The Metropolitan Opera that had been Edward Johnson's life for twenty-seven years was on tour at the time, which made it impossible for members of the company to attend the funeral. Soprano Licia Albanese, for example, was represented by her husband, Joseph Gimma, who was also a close friend of Eddie's. Among the singers present, however, were Lucrezia Bori, with whom Eddie had sung so many times; Risë Stevens, one of "Johnson's babies" during his regime as general manager at the Met; soprano Irene Jessner, whom he had brought to the Met from Europe; and auditions-winner Emilia Cundari.

The active pallbearers were Francis Robinson, assistant manager of the Metroplitan Opera; John Steinway; Fred Johnson, a nephew from California; Dr. Eric Mutrie; Angus Dunbar; and Metropolitan Opera baritone John Brownlee. The honorary pallbearers were Prime Minister John Diefenbaker; Finance Minister Donald Fleming; *Globe and Mail* publisher Oakley Dalgleish; former Lieutenant-Governors Herbert A. Bruce and Ray Lawson; University of Toronto President Dr. Claude Bissell; former Canadian Consul-General in New York Hugh Scully; the National Research Council vice-president, Dr. Ray Farquharson; *Ottawa Journal* editor Grattan O'Leary; Ontario industrialist E. W. Bickle; Dr. Arnold Walter; the Juilliard School's Mark Schubart; Joseph Gimma; singer Hugh Guthrie; former Metropolitan Opera executive Earle Lewis; and Mr. Drew's brothers-in-law, A. M. German and David Lloyd.

The prelude and postlude music was by Bach and English composers, except for the note of opera introduced by organist David Ouchterlony, of the Royal Conservatory faculty, when he included a selection from Gluck's *Orfeo*. Choir boys, in red cassocks and white surplices, preceded the forty-five members of the adult choir as they slowly walked up the long aisle and passed the closed flower-laden casket. During the Church of England's simple Order for Burial service, conducted by Archdeacon Stanley A. Kirk, choirmaster Ralph Kidd directed the choir and congregation in the singing of Edward Johnson's two favourite hymns, "Abide with me," and "Praise my soul, the King of Heaven," and in the intoning of the twenty-third Psalm. Then at the end of the service, as the coffin was slowly borne down the aisle and out into the street, the choir sang Nunc Dimittus: "Lord, now lettest Thou Thy servant depart in peace."

The long funeral procession threaded its way up Woolwich Street and paused for a moment as it passed number 673, the Johnson family homestead. Eddie would surely have laughed and have made some witty remark about the pace at which the cortège moved past the Speed River on its way to the Woodlawn Cemetery.

After a brief committal service in the dimness of the crowded mausoleum, the immediate family—the Drews (Fiorenza, George, Sandra and Edward), Mrs. Gordon Johnson, young Fred Johnson—and other relatives, colleagues, close friends and notables, such as Prime Minister

315

Diefenbaker, Lieutenant-Governor and Mrs. J. Keiller Mackay, and Premier Leslie Frost, gathered at the Johnson home in final tribute.

On April 28, members of the Metropolitan Opera Association received an invitation to attend "Special services for Edward Johnson, former General Manager of the Association, at St. Bartholomew's Church, 109 East 50th Street, New York City, at 10 o'clock in the morning of Friday, May 1st, 1959."

"That particular day," former Metropolitan Opera board chairman Lowell Wadmond recalled, "I had to go to Atlanta to be Master of Ceremonies for a big Opera Guild luncheon at the Riding Club there. I told the guests, 'At this moment, a memorial service is being held for Edward Johnson in St. Bartholomew's Church in New York City. This program, with our four Metropolitan Opera artists to sing, is also a memorial among his many friends here in Atlanta.' Then I recited what I told them was Eddie's favourite poem: Tennyson's 'Crossing the Bar.' "

On the second anniversary of Edward Johnson's death, April 20, 1961, more than one thousand people, including students and faculty members of the Royal Conservatory of Music of Toronto, stood before a steel skeleton of the new Edward Johnson Building. They listened to a choir sing the national anthem, to trumpets heralding the important occasion—presided over by Henry Borden, vice-chairman of the university's Board of Governors—and to commemorative speeches by Dr. Claude Bissell, Dr. Boyd Neel and Dr. Arnold Walter. Then Mrs. George Drew took silver trowel in hand to lay the cornerstone of the building named for her father. "This building is in spirit," Fiorenza said, "the true receptacle of his heart, and so it will always remain."

Eddie would have approved of those words, for he himself had declared some twenty years earlier: "Of all the arts that serve mankind, none is more powerful nor more universal than music. . . . We hold to the pattern of the past while formulating a design for the future; we work with but a single purpose, to keep alive the torch that in due time we may pass it on to our successors, undiminished in beauty and in strength."

What better tribute could there be to the man whose entire life had been dedicated to music and the theatre than the building named for him—a building designed as a home for the Faculty of Music, University of Toronto, and containing two theatres and the Edward Johnson Music Library. It stands as a continuing source of knowledge and inspiration for all who walk and work within its walls.

# The recordings of Edward Johnson
*by J.B. McPherson and W.R. Moran*

The following chart contains essential details of all known recordings featuring Edward Johnson as a singer.

The recordings are divided into four categories:

1/
The mysterious Victory Kalliopes about which virtually nothing is known (at least, by the present writers) but one or two copies of which have turned up in recent years on dealers' lists.

2/
The Columbias, presumed by most authorities to have been made in Italy about 1914–15.

3/
The Victors, made in the U.S.A. between 1919 and 1928 and thus covering both the end of the "acoustic" period and the beginning of the "electric" period. In the matrix column, B indicates a 10″ acoustic recording, C a 12″ acoustic, BVE a 10″ electric, and CVE a 12″ electric.

4/
The three radio transcriptions of complete operas recorded "live" during actual Metropolitan Opera performances in 1934. These recordings are of the poorest technical quality. They were privately circulated for a limited time under the New York based Golden Age of Opera label, with catalogue numbers as shown in the last column of the discography.

A few guidelines to interpretation of the discography:

A/
Titles are listed alphabetically.

B/
In the Columbia section, the nine columns give details of, left to right:
1   Title and matrix (or master record) number
2   American single-face catalogue number
3   American double-face catalogue number
4   English single-face catalogue number
5   English double-face catalogue number
6   Italian double-face catalogue number

7    South American double-face catalogue number

8    Re-Issues (re-recordings of the original, issued on 78 rpm by the defunct International Record Collectors Club and Collectors Record Shop)

9    Correct playing speed of the original

C/

In the Victor section, the seven columns give details of, left to right:

1    Title and matrix (or master record) number

2    Exact date of recording (day, month, year)

3    American single-face catalogue number

4    American double-face catalogue number

5    English single-face catalogue number

6    English double-face catalogue number

7    Correct playing speed of the original

D/

An asterisk (*) indicates the Canadian catalogue number. (Certain Johnson records were issued only in Canada.)

E/

A catalogue number in parentheses—e.g. (66210)–indicates that the number was assigned but the record was not issued.

F/

The title line also gives the composer, the language in which the record is sung (English, French or Italian) and, where applicable, the conductor of the orchestra. For the Victors, the conductor is either Josef A. Pasternack (1881-1940) or Quebec-born Rosario Bourdon (1885-1961), both music directors of the Victor Talking Machine Company for the bulk of the period covered by the discography.

## VICTORY KALLIOPE, London(?), 1908(?)

1/AIDA: Celeste Aida (Act 1)
  (Verdi)
  1192 (6126)

2/ANDREA CHENIER: Un di
  all'azzurro spazio (Improvviso)
  (Act 1) (Giordano)
  1189

## COLUMBIA, Milan(?), 1914–15(?)

| Title and matrix number | USsf | USdf | UKdf | ITdf | SAdf | Re-Issue | Speed |
|---|---|---|---|---|---|---|---|
| 3/ANDREA CHENIER: Un di all'azzurro spazio (Improvviso) (Act 1) (Giordano) (I) (Or) 74743-1 | 74743 | ........ | ........ | D-17537 | S-50 | IRCC 3089 | 81.00 |
| 4/ANDREA CHENIER: Si, fui soldato (Act 3) (Giordano) (I) (Or) 74744-1, 2 | 74744 | ........ | ........ | D-17537 | S-50 | IRCC 3089 | 81.00 |
| 5/Garden Of Sleep (Isidore de Lara) (E) (Or) 74746-? | 74746 | ........ | 502 | ............ | ........ | ................ | 81.00 |
| 6/IN A PERSIAN GARDEN: Ah, fill the cup . . . Ah! Moon Of My Delight (Edward Fitzgerald-Liza Lehmann) (E) (Or) 74758-? | 74758 | ........ | 502 | ............ | ........ | ................ | 82.77 |
| 7/MANON LESCAUT: Ah! Manon, mi tradisce (Act 2) (Puccini) (I) (Or) 42153-? | 42153 | ........ | ........ | ............ | S-61 | CRS 22 | ........ |
| 8/Mother o' Mine (Rudyard Kipling-Frank E. Tours) (E) (Or) 42187-1 | 42187 | A1673 | 2537 | ............ | ........ | ................ | 81.00 |
| 9/O Come With Me In The Summer Night (Van der Stucken) (E) (Or) 42198-1, 2 | 42198 | A1673 | 2537 | ............ | ........ | ................ | 81.00 |
| 10/PAGLIACCI: Recitar . . . Vesti la giubba (Act 1) (Leoncavallo) (I) (Or) 42154-? | 42154 | ........ | ........ | ............ | S-61 | CRS 22 | ........ |

| Title and matrix number | | | | | | Speed |
|---|---|---|---|---|---|---|
| 11/PARSIFAL: Il santo Gral (Es starrt der Blick) (Act 2) (Wagner) (I) (Or) B-74741-2 | 74741 | A5630 | ....... | D17536 | ......... ................. | 81.00 |
| 12/PARSIFAL: Soltanto un'arma val (Nur eine Waffe taugt) (Act 3) (Wagner) (I) (Or) 74742-2 | 74742 | A5630 | ....... | D17536 | ......... ................. | 81.00 |

## VICTOR RED SEAL, U.S.A., 1919–28

| Title and matrix number | Date | USsf | USdf | UKsf | UKdf | Speed |
|---|---|---|---|---|---|---|
| 13/Because You're Here (Harold Robe-Gitz Rice) (E) (Or: Pasternack) B-23760-6 | 6/3/20 | 64970 | 690 | ............ | ............ | 75.00 |
| 14/LA BOHEME: Che gelida manina (Act 1) (Puccini) (I) (Or: Bourdon) CVE-45625-2 | 11/6/28 | ............ | *29002 | ............ | ............ | 76.60 |
| 15/CARMEN: La fleur que tu m'avais jetée (Flower Song) (Act 2) (Bizet) (F) (Or: Bourdon) CVE-45614-4 | 8/6/28 | ............ | 9293 *29003 | ............ | ............ | 76.60 |
| 16/Colleen o' Mine (Terence O'Shea-Lily Strickland) (E) (Or: Bourdon) B-29003-3 | 8/11/23 | (66210) | 978 | ............ | ............ | 76.00 |
| 17/Dear One (Fisher-Richardson-Burke) (E) (Or: Bourdon) BVE-32532-2 | 22/4/25 | ............ | 1087 | ............ | ............ | 75.00 |
| 18/ELIJAH: Ye people, rend your hearts . . . If with all your hearts (Mendelssohn) (E) (Or: Pasternack) C-24174-6 | 13/10/20 | 74654 | ............ | ............ | ............ | 76.00 |
| 19/LA FANCIULLA DEL WEST: Una parola sola . . . Or son sei mesi (Act 2) (Puccini) (I) (Or: Pasternack) C-23460-2 | 7/11/19 | ............ | ............ | ............ | ............ | 76.00 |
| 20/LA FANCIULLA DEL WEST: Ch'ella mi creda libero (Act 3) (Puccini) (I) (Or: Pasternack) B-23461-4 | 5/3/20 | 64886 | 689 | 7-52156 | DA 166 | 75.00 |

21/FEDORA: Amor ti vieta (Act 2) (Giordano) (I) (Or: Pasternack)

| Matrix | Date | | | | | Price |
|---|---|---|---|---|---|---|
| B-24171-4 | 18/6/20 | 64905 | 689 | 7-52158 | DA 166 | 75.00 |

22/Heart To Heart (Don Valentine-Frederick W. Vanderpool) (E) (Or: Pasternack)

| B-24172-2 | 17/6/20 | 64998 | 690 | ............ | ............ | 75.00 |

23/Her Bright Smile Haunts Me Still (W. T. Wrighton) (E) (Or: Pasternack)

| B-23459-2 | 6/11/19 | 64839 | ............ | 5-2147 | ............ | 76.00 |

24/I Had A Flower (Lawrence Kellie) (E) (Or: Pasternack)

| B-25368-6 | 24/6/21 | 66061 | 693 | ............ | ............ | 76.00 |

25/I'll See You In My Dreams (Kahn-Jones) (E) (Or: Bourdon)

| BVE-32533-4 | 22/4/25 | ............ | 1087 | ............ | | 75.00 |

26/I Love And The World Is Mine (Spross) (E) (Or: Pasternack)

| B-23462- | 7/11/19 | ............ | ............ | . ............ | ............ | ........ |

27/I Love You More (Eldred Edson-Dorothy Lee) (E) (Or: Bourdon)

| B-25369-3 | 23/6/21 | 66060 | 691 | ............ | ............ | 76.00 |

28/Just That One Hour (Avery Werner-Vernon Eville) (E) (Or: Pasternack)

| B-24170-4 | 18/6/20 | 64946 | 694 | ............ | ............ | 75.00 |

29/Land Of The Long Ago (Charles Knight-Lilian Ray) (E) (Or: Pasternack)

| B-23458-9 | 6/3/20 | 64895 | 694 | ............ | ............ | 75.00 |

30/Lassie o' Mine (Fred G. Bowles-Edward J. Walt) (E) (B Or: Pasternack) (BVE Or: Bourdon)

| B-24173-3 | 13/10/20 | 64930 | 692 | ............ | ............ | 76.00 |
| BVE-24173-9 | 7/6/28 | ............ | 4088 *24006 | ............ | ............ | 76.60 |

31/LOUISE: Depuis longtemps j'habitais cette chambre (Act 1) (Charpentier) (F) (Or: Bourdon)

| CVE-45615-4 | 8/6/28 | ............ | 9293 *29003 | ............ | ............ | 76.60 |

32/The Maple Leaf Forever (Alexander Muir) (with male quartet) (E) (Or: Bourdon)

| BVE-45613-3 | 7/6/28 | ............ | *24005 | ............ | ............ | 76.60 |

| | | | | | | |
|---|---|---|---|---|---|---|
| 33/MIGNON: Elle ne croyait pas (Act 3) (Thomas) (E) (Or: Bourdon) B-29001- | 8/11/23 | ............ | ............ | ............ | ............ | ........ |
| 34/O Canada (Robert S. Weir-Calixa Lavallée) (with male quartet) (E) (Or: Bourdon) BVE-45612-3 | 7/6/28 | ............ | *24005 | ............ | ............ | 76.60 |
| 35/PAGLIACCI: Recitar . . . Vesti la giubba (Act 1) (Leoncavallo) (I) (Or: Pasternack) B-23457-3 | 7/11/19 | 64840 | ............ | 7-52149 | ............ | 76.00 |
| 36/PAGLIACCI: Recitar . . . Vesti la giubba (Act 1) (Leoncavallo) (I) (Or: Bourdon) CVE-45266-3 | 11/6/28 | ............ | *29002 | ............ | ............ | 76.60 |
| 37/Run On Home (Lily Strickland) (E) (Or: Bourdon) B-29004- | 8/11/23 | ............ | ............ | ............ | ............ | ........ |
| 38/Someone Worth While (Johnstone-Ward-Stephens) (E) (Or: Bourdon) B-25366-3 | 23/6/21 | 66029 | 693 | ............ | | 76.00 |
| 39/Sunrise And You (Arthur A. Penn) (E) (Or: Pasternack) B-23759-5 BVE-23759-8 | 6/3/20 7/6/28 | 64864 ............ | 692 4088 *24006 | ............ ............ | ............ ............ | 76.60 76.60 |
| 40/Tho' Shadows Fall (Annelu Burns-James G. MacDermid) (E) (Or: Bourdon) B-29002-3 | 8/11/23 | (66211) | 978 | ............ | | 76.00 |
| 41/The Want Of You (Marian Gillespie-Frederick W. Vanderpool) (E) (Or: Bourdon) B-25367-7 | 24/6/21 | 64985 | 691 | ............ | ............ | 76.00 |

## METROPOLITAN OPERA BROADCAST TRANSCRIPTIONS,
### New York and Boston, 1934

| | | |
|---|---|---|
| 42/MERRY MOUNT: Complete Opera (as Sir Gower Lackland) (Hanson) (E) (Or: Serafin) | 10/2/34 | EJS 134 (2 LPs) |
| 43/PELLÉAS ET MÉLISANDE: Complete Opera (as Pelléas) (Debussy) (F) (Or: Hasselmans) | 7/4/34 | EJS 487 (3 LPs) |
| 44 /PETER IBBETSON: Complete Opera (as Peter) (Taylor) (E) (Or: Serafin) | 17/3/34 | EJS 187 (1 LP) UORC 143 (2 LPs) |

# Decorations, awards, degrees and honours

1914   Designated Cavaliere della Corona d'Italia by King Victor Emmanuel III

1917   Recipient of a Souvenir Gold Medal commemorating official visit of Prince of Wales to King of Italy

1919   Received the cross of an Ufficiale dell'Ordine della Corona d'Italia (Officer of the Order of the Crown of Italy) from King Victor Emmanuel III

1928   President of the Canadian Society of New York (Member, 1928–1959)

1929   Honorary Doctor of Laws, University of Western Ontario

1934   Honorary Doctor of Music, University of Toronto

1935   Named a Commander of the Order of the British Empire, Civil Division, in the birthday honours list of King George V

1939   Honorary Doctor of Music: New York University, University of Pennsylvania and University of Michigan

1940   Honorary Doctor of Music, Wesleyan University

1942   Honorary Doctor of Music, Cincinnati Conservatory of Music

1943   Honorary Doctor of Literature & Humane Letters, Union College, New York

1945   Honorary Doctor of Music, Chicago Musical College
Named Chairman of the Board of Governors, Toronto Conservatory of Music
Became member of the Board of Governors, University of Toronto
Citation from the Board of Directors of the Metropolitan Opera Association on Edward Johnson's tenth anniversary as general manager

1946   Received Kong Christian den Tiendes Frihedsmedaille (King Christian X's Medal of Liberation)

1947   Made a Chevalier in the order of La Légion d'honneur
Awarded the Gold Medal of the National Institute of Social Sciences in New York

1948   Made a Knight Commander of the Royal Order of Vasa by King Gustav of Sweden

1949   Awarded the degree of Officer of the National Order of the Southern Cross, Brazil's highest honour
Received the Stella della Solidarietà Italiana

1950   Honorary Doctor of Music, Oberlin College

1953   Appointed Chancellor of Chicago Musical College

1955   Official opening of the Edward Johnson School in Guelph

1962   Posthumous dedication of the Edward Johnson Building, University of Toronto

## Photo Credits

The author and publisher wish to thank Alexandra Drew Scholey and Edward Drew for permission to reproduce the photographs from the Edward Johnson family collection.

We would also like to thank the following individuals and organizations for the illustrations listed below.

Teatro Verdi, Padova: the management of Teatro Verdi

Edward Johnson in front of the Met: Edward Johnson family collection (*New York Herald Tribune* photo by Nat Fein)

The Met Triumvirate 1935–47; E. J. Gala Testimonial, 1950: E. J. family collection (Wide World photo, Canadian Press)

E. J. and staff members of the Toronto Conservatory: *Opera Canada* (National Film Board photo)

E. J. and members of *Le Nozze di Figaro* cast, November 24, 1941: E. J. family collection (Acme photo)

Lady Eaton: Archives, Eaton's of Canada, Limited

Lotte Lehmann: *Opera News*, published by The Metropolitan Opera Guild, Inc.

Lily Pons: E. J. family collection (Photo by Alfred Eisenstaedt, Time/Life Picture Agency © Time, Inc.)

Gladys Swarthout: E. J. family collection (Photo by Gene Lester)

Herbert Witherspoon: Canadian Press (Wide World photo)

The publisher welcomes any information which will enable him, in subsequent editions, to correct any errors made in giving credit lines.

In the group photographs, the members of the Metropolitan Opera are as follows:

On tour in 1948: Left to right, front, Dezso Ernster, Frank St. Leger, Edward Johnson, Jan Peerce, Gerhard Pechner, Giacomo Vaghi and Francis Robinson, and, rear, Martha Lipton, Désiré Defrère, Dorothy Kirsten, Frances Greer, Herta Glaz, Alessio de Paolis, Irene Jessner, Mario Berini, Mae Frohman and Marks Levine.

On opening night of the 1941/42 Metropolitan Opera season: Left to right, front, Bidú Sayão, Edward Johnson, Risë Stevens, and, rear, Marita Farell, Ezio Pinza, Elisabeth Rethberg, Irra Petina, Salvatore Baccaloni and John Brownlee.

# Index

328

329

334